talk with you like a woman

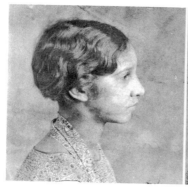

TALK WITH YOU LIKE A
WOMAN

AFRICAN AMERICAN WOMEN,

JUSTICE, AND REFORM IN NEW YORK,

1890–1935

Cheryl D. Hicks

The University of North Carolina Press   Chapel Hill

The paper in this book meets the guidelines for permanence and
durability of the Committee on Production Guidelines for Book Longevity of
the Council on Library Resources. The University of North Carolina Press
has been a member of the Green Press Initiative since 2003.

Library of Congress Cataloging-in-Publication Data
Hicks, Cheryl D., 1971–
Talk with you like a woman : African American women, justice,
and reform in New York, 1890–1935 / Cheryl D. Hicks.
p. cm. — (Gender and American culture)
Includes bibliographical references and index.
ISBN 978-0-8078-3424-4 (cloth : alk. paper) — ISBN 978-0-8078-7162-1 (pbk : alk. paper)
1. African American women—Employment—New York (State)—New York.
2. African American women—New York (State)—New York—Social conditions—History.
3. Sex role—New York (State)—New York—History—19th century.
4. Women's rights—New York (State)—New York—History—19th century.
5. Racism—New York (State)—New York—History—20th century. I. Title.
F128.9.N4H53 2010
305.48′8960730747—dc22
2010027107

cloth   14 13 12 11 10   5 4 3 2 1   paper   14 13 12 11 10   5 4 3 2 1

Portions of this work appeared previously in somewhat different form in
Cheryl D. Hicks, "'In Danger of Becoming Morally Depraved': Single Black
Women, Working-Class Black Families, and New York State's Wayward Minor Law,
1917–1928," *University of Pennsylvania Law Review* 151 U. PA. L. Rev. 2077 (2003)
(printed here with permission); and Cheryl D. Hicks, "'Bright and Good Looking
Colored Girl': Black Women's Sexuality and 'Harmful Intimacy' in Early Twentieth-
Century New York," *Journal of the History of Sexuality* 18, no. 3 (2009): 418–56
(© 2009 by the University of Texas Press. All rights reserved).

for my parents,

THEODORE W. HICKS

and

DELORIS J. HICKS

and my sister,

MICHELLE R. HICKS

contents

illustrations

acknowledgments

It gives me great pleasure to thank the many institutions, colleagues, friends, and family members who have supported and encouraged me during the research and writing of this book. Many of them are as happy as I am that I have arrived at this stage.

When I was a University of Virginia undergraduate, Reginald Butler and Patricia Sullivan were engaging mentors who helped me understand that I could turn my love for history into a career that I had not imagined possible. In graduate school at Princeton University, I benefited from both the African American studies and women and gender studies programs. I am grateful for the support of fellow graduate students Shalanda Dexter-Rodgers, Andrea Morris, Crystal Feimster, and Keith Mayes.

I learned what it meant to be a scholar-teacher in the history department at Williams College. I received significant support in many different ways from the college and my colleagues. I am particularly indebted to Kenda B. Mutongi, Craig S. Wilder, Shanti Singham, Regina Kunzel, and William Wagner.

In 2007, I joined the University of North Carolina at Charlotte's history department, which provided a wonderfully collegial environment for me as I completed manuscript revisions. Outside of the department, I am especially grateful for the supportive friendships of Julia Robinson-Harmon and Sonya R. Ramsey. Frank Bravo, from the technology support department, deserves special thanks for his assistance with many of the book's images.

I am indebted to the various institutions, organizations, and seminars that have supported this project. I began writing this book with a Chancellor's Minority Postdoctoral Fellowship at the University of Illinois at Urbana-Champaign. Working with Dianne Pinderhughes in the Department of African American Studies and James Barrett in the Department of History was instrumental in helping me think through the revision process. I had the pleasure of presenting my first set of ideas at the University of Houston's Black History Workshop with Linda Reed and Richard Blackett. When I joined the University of Maryland's "Meanings and Representations of Work in the Lives of Women of Color" Interdisciplinary Research Seminar, directed by Sharon Harley, I had a wonderful opportunity to present my work, receive feedback, and learn from an inspiring set of junior and senior scholars. As a resident scholar at the Schomburg Center for Research in Black Culture, I really began to understand the book through the incredible collections, support staff, and engaging fellow scholars. I thank Diana Lachatanere for her assistance with logistics and questions. I learned so much from Colin Palmer, who showed an impressive commitment to the program and scholars. As a postdoctoral fellow at the University of Virginia's Carter G. Woodson Institute for Afro-American and African Studies I benefited in numerous ways from working with Reginald Butler and Scot French, from the intellectual community of fellows, from Alderman Library's interlibrary loan service, and from Deborah McDowell's hospitality as well as penetrating, constructive criticism of my research. Joseph Miller also deserves special thanks for helping me to choose the appropriate book title. Presenting ideas at the University of Mississippi's Porter L. Fortune, Jr., History Symposium, the Center for Africanamerican Urban Studies and the Economy at Carnegie Mellon University, and Drexel University's Africana Studies also enriched my work. I am also grateful that the New York State Historical Association awarded *Talk with You Like a Woman* the 2007 Dixon Ryan Fox Manuscript Prize.

I have been extraordinarily lucky to have been inspired by the scholarship and the thoughtful responses and positive criticism of those scholars whose work has shaped so many disciplines. At various phases of writing and research, my thinking has been influenced by feedback from and conversations with Elsa Barkley Brown, Joy Damousi, Doreen Drury, Estelle Freedman, Kevin Gaines, Evelynn Hammonds, Nancy Hewitt, Robin D. G. Kelley, Regina Kunzel, Jacqui Malone, Nicole Hahn Rafter, Nayan Shah, Kimberly Springer, Craig S. Wilder, and Francille Wilson. I am particularly grateful to Tera Hunter, Patricia Schechter, Timothy Gilfoyle, and Gunja SenGupta, who read the entire manuscript and whose engaged comments and critical suggestions have improved the book immeasurably. I also received invaluable feedback on conference papers from Barbara Ransby, Kathy Peiss, and Marlon Ross.

I have benefited from the many people who graciously shared ideas and sources regarding the profession, research, and writing. They include Nichole Rustin-Paschal, Lisa Levenstein, Crystal Feimster, Mary Ting Yi Lui, Deborah Thomas, Ginetta Candelario, Sandy Alexandre, Judith Weisenfeld, Heather Williams, Jerma Jackson, and Dorothy Rice. Norlisha "Tish" Crawford helped me think through and clarify my ideas at earlier stages in the project. I also had the privilege of developing working/writing schedules with Sarita See and Robyn C. Spencer. At different moments, they both helped to keep me on track with research, writing, teaching, and life.

Librarians and archivists at the following institutions have been instrumental in helping navigate their manuscript collections: the New York State Library, the New York Public Library, the Haverford College Quaker and Special Collections, the Lesbian Herstory Archives, the Library of Congress, the Rockefeller Archives, the Fisk University Special Collections, and the Library of Virginia. I am particularly grateful for the assistance from the staff at the Schomburg Center for Research in Black Culture, Jim Folts at the New York State Archives, Kenneth Cobb at the New York City Municipal Archives, and Ben Doherty at the University of Virginia School of Law.

Sian Hunter, at the University of North Carolina Press, has been the best kind of editor. She supported this project from the beginning. Her patience, support, pep talks, and vision have made finishing the manuscript a much easier process than it otherwise would have been. I am also grateful for the UNC staff who have kindly answered my questions. Kim Bryant, who designed the beautiful book cover, and Mary Caviness, who guided me with enormous patience through the final editing process, deserve special thanks. I am extremely glad that I worked with Grey Osterud during the final stage of revisions. Her editorial expertise, important questions, and great insight helped me focus my ideas and articulate my arguments in ways that have improved the manuscript tremendously.

I have come to depend on a group of dear colleagues whose own scholarly work is groundbreaking, and they have become the best kinds of friends within and outside of the academy. Their research, suggestions, criticisms, and activism inspire me. Kali N. Gross's intelligence, scholarship, and activism have encouraged me to think more deeply about my own work and commitment to freedom struggles. Claudrena Harold is simply brilliant. She is an extraordinarily successful scholar-teacher who has taught me a lot about history and music. Luther Adams has taught me much about the value of friendship. He is smart, empathetic, and one of the funniest persons I know. Kathy Perkins sees each day as an opportunity to make a difference. She is the best kind of mentor in the sage advice she provides, but the example of her actions illustrates just how wonderful a person she truly is. Kenda Mutongi always knows the right thing to say, whether I want to hear it or not. Her friendship has sustained me through some difficult times. I am so glad that she and her family—Alan, Ada, and Stephan—became my family when I lived in the Berkshires.

I have some special friends who have encouraged the completion of this project and have enriched my life in countless ways. They have heard about the highs and lows, and I appreciate them more than I think they know. When I lived in New York, Catherine Bowles, Annette Johns, and Annette Burrus helped me see Manhattan and Brooklyn with new eyes and helped me understand the city in ways that I will never forget. Rose Judkins-Mayes is a remarkable friend who has shown me through example what it means to persevere and tackle life's challenges with dignity, humility, and beauty. Nyasha Junior has always been there to help me to see life and work from a clear and disciplined perspective. I treasure my long-standing friendship with Cheryl Warfield. With savvy, intelligence, and enthusiasm, she has created her own successful career and supported me at each and every stage of my postcollege life. Paul (Devon) Chineyemba probably does not have a sense for what a crucial role he has played in my life helping push me toward completing the book. Finally, my childhood friend Angela Meyers, whose love for life and pursuit of her dreams changed my life. Her passing in 2006 prompted me to make one of the most daring but satisfying decisions regarding my life and career.

Nell Irvin Painter has shaped my intellectual trajectory in ways that I am still discovering. I admire and appreciate her intellectual acuity, generosity of time, and enormous, unwavering support of my scholarly pursuits. She believed in my abilities when I stumbled and doubted myself.

My family provided steadfast support throughout the entire process. My parents—Theodore and Deloris Hicks—have always encouraged me to work hard in order to fulfill my dreams. They also taught me to value education, treat others with respect, and fight for the ideas and goals that are important to me. Words cannot adequately express the profound love and respect that I have for them. My sister, Michelle R. Hicks, is in a class all by herself. Her love, encouragement, and friendship have meant more to me than she knows. Other family members and friends—especially my grandmother Lucy J. Parham, Shirley Robinson, Chioma Onyekwere, and Mrs. Edna Scott—have been instrumental in helping me throughout this process as well. They will be delighted that they will no longer have to ask the dreaded question, "Are you finished writing the book?"

Acknowledgments

talk with you like a woman

introduction

TALK WITH YOU LIKE A WOMAN

The "other side" has not been represented by one who "lives there." And not many can more sensibly realize and more accurately tell the weight and the fret of the "long dull pain" than the open-eyed but hitherto voiceless Black Woman of America.

—Anna Julia Cooper, 1892

It afford me to write to you . . . This is business I want to talk with you like a woman.

—Lucy Cox, letter to superintendent of Bedford reformatory, 1924

Anna Julia Cooper and Lucy Cox both struggled to be understood as women of intelligence and vision, yet their differing positions shaped how they voiced their grievances regarding the treatment of black women in America. Cooper, born into slavery in 1858 in Raleigh, North Carolina, exemplified racial advancement after emancipation. Influenced by the Reconstruction era and the dictates of the dominant nineteenth-century gender ideology, she was one of a handful of black women to graduate from Oberlin with bachelor's and master's degrees. Eventually earning a Ph.D. in 1925 at the Sorbonne in Paris, she had a long career as an activist and educator in Washington, DC. Cooper consistently questioned the sexism and racism she encountered and is best known for her germinal 1892 black feminist text, *A Voice from the South*.[1] In contrast, Lucy Cox, born in Tarboro, North Carolina, in 1898, represented a segment of the black working class that, despite myriad obstacles, sought to improve their lives through education. Although both of her parents died by the time she was fifteen, they taught Cox the value of learning. Unlike most young women in her socioeconomic position, she completed the eighth grade. However, her studies at the Colored State Normal School in Elizabeth City, North Carolina, which trained black teachers for the segregated school system, ended after a year because of her inadequate finances. Subsequently, Cox attempted to further her education but supported herself primarily as a domestic.[2] Cox, a child of the Jim Crow era who embraced the less restrictive social and sexual norms of the 1920s, joined the stream of black southerners who migrated to New York City around World War I. Although her higher education had been cut short, she envisioned a career as a skilled worker and took a typing course at one of the city's business schools. Yet she soon found herself arrested for prostitution and imprisoned in the New York State Reformatory for Women at Bedford. Both Cooper and Cox faced enormous challenges in gaining a higher education, and the contrasting outcomes of their trajectories illuminate the varied struggles and strategies of black women in the early twentieth century.

Both Cooper and Cox insisted that their voices be heard and demanded black women be acknowledged as legitimate examples of respectable womanhood. In her 1892 collection of essays that addressed racism, sexism, and imperialism, Cooper wanted all Americans — black and white, men and women — to recognize the injustice suffered by the "mute and voiceless" black woman, while she simultaneously contended that elite and middle-class black women's moral superiority was imperative for racial advancement: "Only the Black Woman can say 'when and where I enter, in the quiet, undisputed, dignity of my womanhood, without violence, and without suing or special patronage, then and there the whole Negro race enters with me.'"[3] For Cooper and her contemporaries, an emphasis on black women's virtue reinforced their unique position as respectable women as well as their mission to improve the material and moral conditions of black communities by uplifting their working-class and poor black sisters.[4] We hear Cox's voice in the three letters of protest she wrote to the prison superintendent at Bedford. Her third letter of protest emphasized her individual concerns as a parolee who wanted prison administrators to recognize her perseverance, honesty, and ambition and admit that she could be law-abiding and respectable in spite of her prior mistakes and her working-class status. Her frustrations with those officials' dismissive attitude were crystallized at the beginning of her 1924 missive when she declared, "This is business I want to talk with you like a woman."[5] As a female offender, Cox might be taken to represent the perfect candidate for black female reformers' mantra, expressed in the National Association of Colored Women's motto, "Lifting As We Climb," yet her letters belie the assumption that she needed moral reform.

Comparing these two women's ideas about the challenges facing black womanhood redresses a serious imbalance in current understandings of early-twentieth-century black women's experiences and perspectives. Scholars and students know far more about the objectives and accomplishments of elite and middle-class black women than about the goals and strategies adopted by the masses. We hear more about how black activists like Cooper addressed the plight of working-class and poor black women than what those women thought about their own straightened circumstances.[6] On a broad level, this study embraces scholar Mary Helen Washington's concern with the "tone" in Cooper's work wherein the activist seemed to speak "for ordinary black women."[7] Women like Cox, however, were not "mute" or "voiceless" but could be quite open about the challenges they endured. Privileging Cox's voice and that of other working-class and poor black women in crisis, *Talk with You Like a Woman* charts the complexity and significance of their New York experiences by examining how the uplift ideology and reform programs of Cooper's generation affected their lives.

By examining African American urban life in early-twentieth-century New York through the experiences and perspectives of working-class black women, *Talk with You Like a Woman* places the hopes, difficulties, and decisions of women like Lucy Cox at the center of urban history. Regardless of the dominant society's negative evaluation and their own community's more mixed assessments of them, ordinary black women held their own distinct notions about feminine dignity. Cox's predicament as well as her articulation of her concerns represents the viewpoints of many black working women who struggled to be seen, heard, and understood as fully competent, moral, and respectable adults. Exploring how black women, in youth as well as adulthood, understood their lives as African Americans and wage laborers, this book illuminates the range of black women's ideas about respectability, domesticity, and sexual desire.

Most significantly, this study compares the viewpoints of white and black elite and middle-class reformers with those of black working-class women who were imprisoned in New York State's criminal justice system. Examining the lives of convicted female offenders does not equate black working-class women with criminality, but rather captures the complexity and contested character of class and gender relationships within black communities. While these women are not representatives of working-class black women as a whole, their predicaments illustrate the many ways that black women's behavior was regulated by their kin and by the state. Making unfortunate choices did not always result in incarceration, but when it did, black women were more vulnerable than white women to being seen as criminal. The overwhelming majority were charged with sexual offenses, especially prostitution and, later, vagrancy; smaller yet substantial numbers were arrested for property crimes, such as theft, as well as violent acts, such as assault, murder, or infanticide. Whether they admitted their wrongdoing or argued that they had been framed by law enforcement, female offenders were connected to communities that often provided them with much-needed support. In other instances, these women's relatives were as desperate for stability in housing, employment, and wages as the women who sought their help. Examining the situations of women in crisis through a set of amazingly detailed institutional records provides us with a unique perspective on the common problems that all black women and their communities faced.

Female offenders' lives in New York offer an illuminating window onto black working-class life in the urban North. The unbalanced pairing of Anna Julia Cooper's book and Lucy Cox's letters is typical of what is possible to uncover. Historians approach ordinary people's experiences by using a variety of sources, including the annual reports of state institutions, civil rights organizations, and charitable associations; periodicals and newspapers; and manuscript collections, but the black working class rarely left personal documents attesting to their lives and is often underrepresented in black organizations and the press. This study scrutinizes the records of women who were imprisoned in the New York State Reformatory for Women at Bedford (Bedford) and the New York State Prison for Women at Auburn (Auburn); it does not examine those in local reformatories (House of Good Shepherd or House of Mercy) and penitentiaries (Blackwell's Island, Randall Island, and the Tombs) unless they were later sent to Bedford or Auburn. This project profits from the fact that by the turn of the twentieth century the professionalization of social work led to the creation of a profusion of records—institutional case files, prison ledgers, court records, and parole board testimony—that document the lives of black women, providing precious information about their migrations, family and kin relationships, neighborhoods, employment and wages, leisure opportunities, and romantic and sexual attachments, as well as their experiences with police harassment.

New York State, which was a leader in the reform of penal institutions for men and women, offers a unique perspective on how the rehabilitation of female criminal behavior developed as a distinct reform enterprise. The state established two types of prisons for female offenders of all races. Auburn (1893), which housed female felons, and Bedford (1901), which housed juvenile offenders, were created to separate female from male felons and "wayward girls" from hardened female recidivists, respectively. Auburn's records contain vital statistics for 1,674 inmates, including 536 black women incarcerated between 1893 and 1933. The state prison's records also include annual reports; parole case files that might contain letters from the inmate, the district attorney, family members and/or administrative officers; and parole board transcripts. Bedford records contain over 400 extant case files in varying size and length, with 100 files taken between 1916 and 1928 documenting the experiences of black inmates.[8] The reformatory's focus on rehabilitation means that we can glean varied accounts of a young woman's life, including the girl's own statement; her verified history; letters from probation and parole officers, family members, and informants; and, in some cases, assessments by psychologists in the reformatory's Bureau of Social Hygiene. Records for both institutions provide a lens through which to examine the problems faced by black women in New York City as well as southern communities.

Rather than placing the criminal justice system at the center of this narrative of black New York, I interpret the long and troubled history of native-born black city-dwellers in relation to the demographic changes that stemmed from residents' attempts to improve their living conditions and contest racial discrimination and antiblack violence within the city, as well as the migration of black southerners and immigrants who changed these dynamics.[9] From Dutch colonial rule to the end of enslavement in 1827, black people labored to build the island of Manhattan and inhabited most of the various boroughs and counties of what became New York State. Principally urbanites, they lived in lower Manhattan among Irish and German immigrants with whom they increasingly competed for employment, housing, and social space. In the Draft Riots of July 1863, a mob of working-class whites, many of whom were Irish, brutally attacked black men, women, and children, lynching eleven black men, destroying blacks' homes, and decimating their social, business, and charitable institutions. In the wake of the riots, blacks felt compelled to leave lower Manhattan, migrating out of state, moving uptown, or crossing the river to Brooklyn.[10] With high mortality rates from disease, poverty, and violence, black citizens formed a small proportion of the state's population, declining from 2.3 percent in 1830 to 1.2 percent in 1890.[11]

At the turn of the twentieth century, with a massive influx of immigrants from southern and eastern Europe, black Manhattanites moved farther north as well as west and were joined by a growing number of southern migrants and black immigrants from the Caribbean. They settled in areas such as the Tenderloin (between Twentieth-forth and Fifty-fifth streets) and San Juan Hill (between Sixtieth and Sixty-sixth streets). Many blacks also moved to eastern Manhattan. In 1897, journalist and clubwoman Victoria

Earle Matthews, a Brooklyn resident, opened a black settlement, the White Rose Mission, on 234 East 97th Street. Her family's 1873 migration from Georgia placed her among the contingent of freedpeople who left the South after the Civil War. During her twenty-five-year residency she worked as a domestic and then as a professional journalist, garnering the middle-class status that authorized her to take on the task of uplifting the race. With perseverance and moxie, she accepted her calling and opened a small mission that began to address the needs of an estimated five to six thousand blacks concentrated on 97th Street east of Third Avenue. According to her, the influx of "Italians and Franco-Americans" who moved into West Third, Bleeker, Macdougal, Thompson, and Sullivan streets (present-day Greenwich Village) forced blacks to the Upper East Side between Fiftieth and 130th streets east of Park Avenue.[12] In a constant search for better living conditions, blacks continually moved within New York City. After the horrendous Tenderloin race riot of 1900 and the 1904 opening of the Interborough Regional Transit system, the uptown Harlem neighborhood in the West 100s became the center of concentrated black residency.

Between 1890 and 1935, the majority of black working women in this study lived in the Tenderloin or Harlem. Some were native New Yorkers, as were their parents. Others were born in New York City to southern migrants. The rest moved to the Empire State alone or with family members. From 1920 to 1930, the proportion of the city's population identified as black rose from 1.9 percent to 3.3 percent.[13] Although some black women traveled alone, most migrants had networks of relatives and friends who helped them navigate the urban terrain. Lucy Cox left two brothers and a sister behind in the South, but another sister and brother also migrated to New York, living near her on West 142nd Street. When she arrived in 1922, she encountered the postwar militant movement for full citizenship that became known as the New Negro, which influenced the black cultural revolution known as the Harlem Renaissance and fueled the civil rights activism of established organizations and the development of new groups, as well as the Jazz Age of uninhibited youth culture, commercial amusements, and music. Harlem had become the Mecca for black culture.

For many migrants, New York represented the possibility of social, economic, and political freedom in a society where black people's civil rights were increasingly violated. In contrast to the Reconstruction era, when black citizenship, the male vote, and the growth of black schools and colleges coupled with federal government support encouraged hope among freedmen and freedwomen, the late nineteenth and early twentieth centuries were marked by antiblack violence, the imposition of white supremacy in the form of Jim Crow, and the relegation of blacks to second-class citizenship. Nothing more powerfully illustrated this dynamic than the accommodationist strategy of promoting "self-improvement" through developing a compliant workforce of manual laborers and servants in the age of industrial capitalism epitomized by Tuskegee president Booker T. Washington's 1895 Atlanta Exposition speech. Subsequently, the nation dismissed black people's civil rights through the segregationist "separate but equal" doctrine of the 1896 Supreme Court decision in *Plessy v. Ferguson*. Finally, many blacks saw themselves mired in what scholar Rayford Logan called the nadir of race relations.[14]

The two generations represented by Anna Julia Cooper and Victoria Earle Matthews on the one hand and by Lucy Cox and her sisters on the other responded to this trajectory somewhat differently. A prominent educator and activist, Cooper attended St. Augustine's Normal School and Collegiate Institute before the end of Reconstruction. By the time Jim Crow was firmly ensconced, Cooper was a well-established scholar-activist in Washington, DC. Lucy Cox, born four months before the devastating Wilmington Riot of 1898, grew up in an environment shaped by the unchecked reemergence of white supremacist, antiblack violence and the suppression of black North Carolinians' political and economic power. In 1901, the final congressional speech of the last Reconstruction-era black congressman, George H. White of North Carolina, indicated the dire state of race relations and expressed blacks' immense sense of disappointment, yet it articulated black people's collective commitment to continuing their struggle for freedom. He explained: "These parting words are in behalf of an outraged, heart-broken, bruised, and bleeding, but God-fearing people, faithful, industrious loyal people—rising people, full of potential force."[15] Lucy Cox and other migrants of her generation envisioned a more viable future outside the South. Yet gender, generation, and socioeconomic status affected how migrants were received in the urban North. Single female migrants like Cox had long been met by moral panics that characterized these vulnerable southern women as dangerous as well as endangered and as immoral as well as unprepared to confront urban conditions.[16] Southern black women's migrations to New York caused just as much consternation in the 1920s as they had at the turn of the century. Cox joined a class of women who black and white reformers believed needed protection in the city.

Late-nineteenth- and early-twentieth-century ideas about black women's protection reflected the larger problems that black people faced as they struggled to enjoy their civic rights in a nation that still failed to accept and acknowledge that former slaves, especially black men, were now first-class citizens. Nineteenth-century politics shaped the vision and reality of white male freedom as American freedom. As scholar Gunja SenGupta notes, "With the inauguration of universal male suffrage . . . the idealization of democracy as an American norm unfolded in tandem with the construct of the color white as normative—all the more powerful for its 'structured invisibility,' defined against the aberration of slavery and its all-too-visible, equally aberrational, marker, blackness."[17] The Civil War and Reconstruction inaugurated universal black citizenship but, as SenGupta argues, "did little to check the hegemony of whiteness in defining the American nation after Reconstruction."[18] Black people's postemancipation struggles entailed seeking the enforcement of their new rights as well as redefining themselves in relation to the gendered language and behavior of the dominant society. As historian Michele Mitchell contends, "Gender assumed special significance for African Americans due to persistent arguments that blacks were 'feminine' compared to 'masculine' Anglo-Saxons, that slavery left black men emasculated and made black women into viragos." Black people also struggled against sexual stereotypes that defined black men as sexual predators and black women as naturally licentious and prone to prostitution. Emphasizing black women's protection addressed a pressing need for women vulnerable to rape, physical violence, and moral downfall while reinforcing black people's advancement through the enforcement of "respectable femininity" and "uncompromised manliness."[19] As a result, reforming working women's behavior became one of the central ways to enforce these gendered mandates and pursue racial advancement.

Community members focused on efforts to protect urban black women as an extension of their discussions regarding labor, the patriarchal black family, and race progress. Black female wage-earners' disproportionate numbers in relation to black men resulted from the combination of the increased availability of personal-service positions that white, native-born and immigrant women deserted as they headed for industrial factories and the insufficient number of stable jobs open to black men. As black leaders contemplated their achievements after nearly thirty years of freedom and considered the next phase of racial progress, urban working black women posed a social problem because their surplus numbers, especially of single, southern migrants, suggested to some observers an increased susceptibility to immorality.

The legacy of enslavement included conjoined notions of racial inferiority and immorality that prompted reformers—black and white—to embark on a "civilizing mission." The black elite and middle class imagined their task as "racial uplift." They regarded their own success as proof that black people were capable of civility and respectability, yet they understood that they had to make sure that the masses also had a chance. Focusing as much on the moral conduct of the black masses as on their economic circumstances, black reformers sought to advance the race by mutual improvement.[20] White reformers proceeded from different premises. Comparing black migrants from the rural South with new immigrants from Europe, most mainstream reformers were inclined to favor the recent arrivals over African Americans. Although some held nativist sentiments, they believed that European immigrants possessed the innate capacity to adapt to modern society and attain citizenship. Immigrant groups that were identified as white enjoyed economic and political opportunities that black citizens were denied. More liberal white reformers formed or joined interracial organizations that contended that blacks could be rehabilitated. These conversations and urban reform campaigns during the Progressive Era can be assessed through their focus on the behavior of black working women.[21]

Talk with You Like a Woman diverges from most histories of social welfare reform within black communities by reframing a discussion of racial uplift, respectability, and black women's protection to include black working-class activism. The emphasis in current scholarship on the black elite and middle class's definition of respectability stems from the effective ways in which they positioned themselves as spokespersons for the race and their near-monopoly of the available sources on urban reform.[22] Such sources reveal that in addition to their concerted efforts at racial uplift, members of the black middle class often encountered distinct challenges to their attempts to live as respectable, first-class citizens that were as equally demeaning as what the working class experienced.[23] Other types of sources show that black working-class notions of respectability, like those of other ethnic working-class groups, were not inculcated from above and did not entirely concur with those of their middle-class counterparts. Historian Victoria Wolcott argues that studies of Anglo-American society in Britain and the United States understand respectability in varied ways, distinguishing between the "rough" and "respectable" elements within the working class of the eighteenth and nineteenth centuries as well as the nineteenth-century bourgeois emphasis on "class status and privilege through dress, deportment, and organizational affiliation."[24] Wolcott also notes that African Americans had a distinct sense of respectability that was shaped by how they fought the stigma of enslavement and ordered their concept of everyday survival. This study shows how historian Evelyn Brooks Higginbotham's important term "the politics of respectability," which is usually associated with how the black middle class and elite used decorum to engage black

Introduction

civil and political rights and uplift the masses, was equally applicable to the black working poor.[25] The fact that ordinary working-class men and women embraced "values of hard work, thrift, piety, and sexual restraint" might be overlooked given that the black elite treated them as an undifferentiated mass mired in moral backwardness.[26] Indeed, respectability claimed just as important a place in the lives of working-class and poor blacks.[27] Black women believed "it was a foundation of" their "survival strategies and self-definition irrespective of class." There were many instances when the two groups—the respectable black working class and poor on the one hand and the black middle class and elites on the other—expressed common intra-racial interests in urban problems; the protection of black women was a shared goal.[28] This book explores problems within black families and reveals the extent to which the working class upheld its own ideas about black women's respectability and morality. It also illuminates black women's experiences of fundamental tensions and serious conflicts regarding appropriate female behavior with their family members, who sometimes handled disputes by aligning themselves directly with the state.[29]

When these rehabilitative programs and actions are examined from the point of view of black working women, social reform looks quite different. The oppressive, even coercive dimension of urban reform is visible in the influential and mutually reinforcing connection between preventive reform and criminal justice initiatives—that is, the state. Most scholars have focused on preventive efforts involving young women who were lodged in working-girls' homes or were sent to local or state reformatories.[30] Other scholars have emphasized the conditions of female felons who were incarcerated in local or state prisons.[31] This study examines both types of female offenders and illustrates the central dilemma they faced when racially segregated policies and institutions exacerbated their inability to deal with their mistakes, crimes, or frame-ups.[32] Black activists' attempts to address the crisis of black women's rising rates of incarceration reveal new insights and historicize the concerns of black social and civil rights organizations. Indeed, in the early twentieth century many protective organizations and settlement houses worked in tandem with official state institutions, including reformatories and prisons.

Black families' use of state resources to regulate the conduct of their female kin shows how powerful state ideologies shaped working-class behavior even as members of this group contested those state practices that denied them first-class citizenship.[33] Working people believed wholeheartedly in the Fourteenth Amendment's stipulation that no state should "deprive any person of life, liberty, or property, without due process of law;

Introduction

nor deny to any person within its jurisdiction the equal protection of the laws." Yet nationwide, states, whether directly or through benign neglect, imposed and supported discriminatory policies that became obstacles to civic equality. When southern migrants sought to escape de jure racial segregation by leaving the South, they entered a social order that discriminated in housing and employment opportunities, and even in social reform and criminal justice initiatives. A 1906 letter to the editor of the *New York Age*, titled "Afro-American Women—They, Not White Women, Really Need Protection," exemplifies the dilemma of urban communities and particularly that of black people's frustrations with state policies. Emphasizing the racial double standard, it sarcastically expressed the dilemma of black citizens: "The principles for the blacks, as interpreted by the whites, must read: 'Honor and obey the white man, to whom God, in His superior judgment, saw fit to entrust the destiny of the blacks. Never complain of what may seem to you His injustice: for verily, it is the very essence of equity.'" Yet consistent inequities also provoked a sustained critique of the contradictions that pervaded race relations, as black people remained deeply invested in the democratic principles of a repressive state. "How long will a powerful and Christian Nation like this one permit a part of its heretofore helpless but most loyal citizens to be sacrificed upon the alter of prejudice and hate by other citizens, whose loyalty to the Republic is, indeed, questionable? I have said 'heretofore helpless' because the Afro-American, as a citizen, has never lost faith in the willingness of the Nation as a whole to protect his rights, as it does those of all other citizens."[34]

Working-class black people often articulated the myriad ways in which their citizenship rights were ignored. Contradicting the stereotype of the slave as a deferential dependent, black people fought to enjoy their full citizenship rights. Yet they came to understand better than most how what seemed to be a southern race problem was really America's racial problem. When one southern migrant declared that New York allowed her and other migrants only the "theoretical equality of Northern life," she pointedly critiqued the difficulties black people of all socioeconomic backgrounds encountered with the dominant society as well as with one another.[35]

Looking at the interactions between the working class and the middle-class reformers within the black community sheds new light on intraracial and interracial relations. Discussions of black reformers' efforts highlight the class, gender, and color hierarchies within black communities. While these tensions receive careful attention here, this book also emphasizes the practical everyday work of racial uplift. Most reformers agreed about the ideological underpinnings of reform, but the routine of home visits, settlement house work, and encounters with ungrateful clients tested the stamina of even the most enthusiastic and dedicated of them. Alice Ruth Moore held deep racial and class prejudices regarding black people in general and the working poor in particular, but the light-skinned African American activist could not ignore the very real and deplorable poverty that so many of her clients faced. During a year of working among the impoverished, she thought she "ought to be hardened." Instead, she was profoundly affected by case after case: "I never see one that something doesn't rise and grip my throat."[36] Many black women activists found that white activists and black male reformers' refusal to treat them as equals compromised their ability to provide resources and services to black communities. White urban reformers advocated measures that did not always coincide with what black people felt was in their best interests. These activists' ideas usually stemmed from their previous work with immigrants, but their attitude toward black communities was influenced by ongoing discussions about the lasting effects of enslavement on black people's ability to be moral, respectable, first-class citizens. A number of white reformers understood the grave conditions that early-twentieth-century black city-dwellers faced as they struggled to maintain a sense of dignity and respectability, while others had an essentialized view of black New Yorkers as one of the many problems associated with urban life.

As an everyday reality and a political tool, respectability shaped black working-class and middle-class lives in similar but distinct ways. Historian Elsa Barkley Brown has reconstructed how, as black people strove to "establish their own behavioral norms and still exercise basic educational and political rights," the "struggle to present Black women and the Black community as 'respectable' eventually led to repression within the community."[37] This intraracial repression generated tensions among various groups, between the middle class and working class as well as within the working class between the "respectable" and "rough" contingents. Generally, studies of black working-class communities focus on struggles for survival that encompass political activism in relation to labor concerns and sometimes the informal economy's relationship to lack of employment and low wages. This book's focus on New York's criminal justice system reveals equally significant ideas about ordinary black people's attempts to reinforce their working-class respectability.[38] Black people understood the weaknesses of respectability as a strategy for equality but still emphasized its utility for activism, especially in relation to black women. As Barkley Brown notes, "It is instructive to realize the degree to which Black women's sexual and political history has been shaped by a widespread belief that while respectable behavior would not guarantee one protection from sexual assault, the absence of such was certain to reinforce racist notions of Black women's greater sexuality, availability, or immorality, as well as the racist notions of Black men's bestiality which were linked to that."[39] In this sense, working-class black women and their behavior were central to struggles for racial justice and ideas regarding black people's advancement in early-twentieth-century New York.

Talk with You Like a Woman addresses these critical issues in three sections with nine chapters that provide a more thematic rather than strictly chronological focus. Combining a discussion of the book's major themes and issues along with the story of eighteen-year-old New York native Ethel Boyd provides a revealing portrait of how black women's behavior became a central concern for their families, communities, and the nation. Like a number of working women during the early twentieth century, Boyd was arrested for prostitution. Her familial background and response to her predicament captures the complex ways that working-class black families negotiated everyday survival, their own concepts of respectability, various family members' differing responses to parental and familial instruction about decorum, and the integral changes in urban reform and criminal justice that affected Boyd's entire family and New York's black communities. The first section traces the dynamics of African American life in New York City and explores the multiple meanings of protection for black working-class communities and black women.

Chapter 1 discusses black women's search for economic, political, and social freedom. It examines their expectations, the options they believed were available to them, the unexpected constraints they discovered, and the various choices they made. Writings about urban working-class black women, today as well as in the past, usually define their presence and prominence as a problem for black families and the race. To some, their disproportionate numbers in relation to black men was the problem; to others, their independence of mind and action was most disturbing. In 1900, scholar-activist W. E. B. Du Bois defined "the excess of women" as one of the major "peculiarities in the colored population" of New York. Du Bois's arguments failed to encapsulate the dynamics of single black working women's experiences: he defined them as problems rather than considering the problems they faced. In Boyd's case, her mother migrated from Virginia with a husband who deserted the family and died shortly thereafter. His absence limited the family's financial base and profoundly altered the household. Boyd's mother depended on other migrant family members as she "made a comfortable living" doing day work and laundry.[40] Yet she struggled with overwork, exorbitant rent for inadequate housing, and the nagging fear that her constant labor and inability to monitor her two daughters' behavior would hinder their life chances. Her response to her predicaments is representative of many working women who sought to "live a fuller and freer life." She became a laundress, which would provide her with more independence as a worker, and she paid $18 a month to maintain an apartment and rented two rooms for $3 a week to three male lodgers whom she described as "decent respectable men."[41] Like other working poor parents, she also made the difficult yet practical decision to utilize public institutions for her own benefit: she sent eight-year-old Ethel and her sister to the Howard Colored Orphan Asylum because she believed she "could not give them proper care" while she worked and "was afraid they might run the streets."[42] While they recognized her work ethic, several neighbors and social workers still regarded Boyd's mother with special animus because she chose to pursue a romantic relationship that they deemed unsuitable.[43] No matter what choices they made, however, black working women were morally suspect. This chapter examines how working women negotiated the city on their own terms, which did not comport with the definition of them held by many reformers—black and white, women and men.

The next two chapters show how black communities' and reformers' response to working black women centered on the idea of protection in the city, which involved safeguarding the bodies and moral lives of women as well as the first-class citizenship rights of all black residents. Chapter 2 examines the 1900 race riot, raising new questions about black women's protection as well as black communities' collective attempts to protect themselves against racial violence. Boyd was only two years old when the riot occurred, but her mother and older relatives would have understood the tenuous character of race relations when an individual incident between a white police officer and a black couple precipitated a race riot. The devastation caused all black New Yorkers to reevaluate their ideas about the abuses of state power and their second-class citizenship. Dealing with rampant police brutality and other urban dangers, black women often found that they had to enforce self-protection and defense, not only in violent encounters with white and black men and with the city's police but also when dealing with black leaders who constantly questioned their domestic respectability. When Arthur Harris's attempt to protect May Enoch from police officer Robert Thorpe resulted in the officer's death, Harris's actions became a catalyst for discussions about the parameters of black women's protection and black working-class respectability in light of the volatile relations between black migrants and white immigrants. Black elites readily recognized and distinguished between the "respectable" and "rough" working class but seemed to define all working black women as morally suspect. When Enoch revealed that Harris was the "only one" who cared about her safety, she exposed the intraracial and gendered dynamics of protection that highlight how black women's defense of their own rights put them in conflict with the state, white society, and the black elite, as well as black working men.

Chapter 3 focuses on black clubwoman and journalist Victoria Earle Matthews and her settlement house, the White Rose Mission (1897), and white social scientist and reformer Frances Kellor and her organization, the National League for the Protection of Colored Women (1906). These women's organizations and institutions allow for a broader context from which to understand black women's protection at specific historical moments. Boyd's family may have heard of these reformers' efforts to protect black women, but these turn-of-the-century initiatives would have been more apt for the many single female migrants without relatives nearby. The careers of these two Progressive reformers illuminate how social reform played out in related but distinct ways for black and white activists. Matthews, a former slave, provides the best example of what scholar Michele Mitchell terms the "aspiring class": she struggled to improve her life through self-education and eventually became a well-respected journalist in the white and black press as well as a proponent of racial uplift.[44] Matthews's work shows the delicate balance between evangelical reform and social-scientific investigation of contemporary problems. As a black woman, she saw protecting black women as a practical issue for many urban migrant women and a duty to her race. In contrast, Kellor grew up poor but was able to attain an education at elite universities. She not only addressed social problems directly but advocated that the federal government take responsibility for resolving them. As a sociologist, she made significant discoveries in criminology as well as labor studies that influenced how she characterized and worked for black women. She represents the small contingent of white reformers who chose to work with rather than exclude black women. As white activists like Kellor worked to protect migrants from the moral dangers associated with inadequate wages, unscrupulous labor agents, and employment agencies, as well as prostitution, they retained ideas of black inferiority and immorality and questioned black women's moral capacity because of the legacy of enslavement. Attempting to assist black women in the city, both Matthews's and Kellor's efforts significantly influenced how New York's criminal justice system defined moral and, later, legal behavior for women.

The book's second section examines the connections between urban preventive reform and criminal justice initiatives. While the dominant society—and even some prison reformers—believed that they needed protection from black female felons, Chapter 4 illustrates the vulnerability of black women to poverty, domestic abuse, and police harassment. A careful look at black felons' response to their predicaments shows that they were intimately engaged in everyday struggles for domestic respectability. In many ways the unstable categories of respectability, marriage, and motherhood influenced their actions and prompted them to incorporate or dismiss the gendered conventions of womanhood. Some women found that they were charged with manslaughter when domestic disputes with their husbands turned deadly. Being unwed mothers without financial, social, or moral support prompted some women to commit infanticide. Other women tired of too much work with inadequate pay and succumbed to a life of crime. Members of Ethel Boyd's family made consistent efforts to define themselves as respectable through their work ethic and respect for the law, although one of Boyd's aunts, who worked as a domestic servant, was arrested and incarcerated for grand larceny. Decorum was contested within families, and the emphasis on respectability served as a buttress against the inevitable possibility of downward mobility.

Chapter 5 looks at the professional biographies of black probation and parole officer Grace Campbell and white municipal judge Jean Norris in order to address how race shaped the kinds of public services that black women received and the effects of discrimination on the numbers of black women who entered the criminal justice system. Campbell believed that young black women should receive full state services, while Norris believed that the black community should undertake more self-help initiatives. Influenced by an earlier generation of "race women," Campbell saw the need to address not only racial uplift but also the increasing problem of arrested and incarcerated black women. Working within the National League for the Protection of Colored Women and later the National Urban League, she disagreed with her colleagues regarding the need for criminal justice rather than preventive efforts. She also differed with the black women whom she chose to help. Ethel Boyd was one of the young women whom Campbell tried to help as superintendent of the Empire Friendly Shelter for delinquent women. Boyd's incorrigible behavior in the local facility caused Campbell to recommend her imprisonment in the New York State Reformatory for Women at Bedford. From 1911 to 1925, Campbell worked to improve the lives of troubled women and found that the discriminatory treatment within the local and state systems for which she was employed, as well as the simultaneous violation of black people's rights during and after World

War I, called for a more radical politics that embraced socialism and communism. Judge Jean Norris, who was white, worked within the system to help young women. She became representative of women's advancement, especially through female suffrage, as the first female magistrate in New York. Her views about young black women reinforced racial discrimination within the criminal justice system, which provided local rehabilitation and probation for native-born white and immigrant women but excluded black women from these services. Yet Norris's ideas about working women's morality failed to coincide with the equitable rulings that she was supposed to enforce, and she was removed from the bench. She became a victim of her own reform crusade.

Chapter 6 traces the connections between black working-class communities' grave concerns about protecting black women and the specific ways that black families tried to use the law to enact their ideas regarding moral conduct. A substantial segment of working-class blacks, like Boyd's family, adhered to strict notions of morality because they did not possess the conventional accoutrements of respectability, such as higher education, professional careers, or leadership positions in prestigious civic and social organizations. This chapter shows that, instead of being the successful products of middle-class reform, ordinary black people's standards of respectability were rooted in their socioeconomic status. When their rights or ideals were violated by antiblack violence or compromised by the actions of their female relatives, some black people appealed to the state to reinforce their positions. For instance, during the 1900 race riot, they expected that they would receive police protection when their citizenship rights were legally violated. In the mid-1910s and 1920s, they used New York's wayward minor law to regulate the behavior of female relatives who failed to live up to their moral code. Examining urban reform through the actions of black working-class parents and relatives, the chapter offers insights into how black communities interpreted the law and attempted to use the state for their own ends.

Chapter 7 provides a distinct perspective on how moral panics about working-class women's sexuality in the 1920s were defined initially as a social welfare problem and subsequently a criminal issue. It offers another lens from which to understand black women's sexuality in early-twentieth-century New York by illuminating the terrain of sexuality and the language that ordinary black women used to express heterosexual and same-sex desire. Living in the midst of the early-twentieth-century sexual revolution, which transformed young women's ideas about romance and sexual desire, Boyd was one of many young women who engaged in a new form of sexual barter known as treating. In particular, black working women made specific

Introduction

distinctions between immoral and promiscuous behavior. They understood and accepted the fact that their choice to engage in premarital sex would be defined as immoral according to the Victorian standards of their elders. Yet they rejected the prevailing idea that they were promiscuous because they deemed this connotation a sexual stereotype connected to their racial and socioeconomic status. In Harlem, young women also explored their desire for women in ways that had not previously been possible. The kinds of relationships they chose, the activities they participated in, and the sexual violence they experienced are revealed in what they chose to share with social workers. Yet the freedom that many associate with early-twentieth-century Harlem coincided with a pervasive surveillance and regulation of working women's and particularly black women's bodies that landed them in Bedford.

The third section discusses the influence of race and respectability on the rehabilitative process during parole in New York and in the South. Chapter 8 shows how parolees dealt with their families' and state administrators' expectations of appropriate female behavior. Although parole indicated prisoners' ability to regulate their own behavior and reintegrate themselves into society, prison officials, employers, and family members consistently reminded young women of their mistakes and the stigma of their imprisonment. In Boyd's case, parole did not offer much more freedom than her two years of imprisonment; prison officials initially questioned whether to allow Boyd to "come home to see" her mother, despite the thirty-seven-year-old woman's numerous pleas during what seemed to be a terminal illness brought on by overwork and unhealthy living conditions.[45] Sometimes women's attempts to follow the dictates of traditional respectability were obstructed by paperwork and discriminatory practices. Former inmates also dealt with wary family members who recalled their mistakes in order to temper their growing independence and, in some instances, used the state to mediate everyday conflicts over mundane and vital issues regarding family stability. Indeed, myriad expectations from different groups conflicted with what these women wanted for themselves; in other cases, working-class black communities expressed and enacted their own ideas and definitions of moral respectability.

Chapter 9 examines the complex dynamics of southern parole by addressing the motivations of prison administrators and the responses of black working-class women as well as their families and communities. In the wake of declining state funding and the nativist sentiments that led to the 1917 and 1924 immigration restriction statutes, black women who had relatives in the South were "deported" there even though they were incarcerated in New York. Boyd would have been an unlikely candidate for southern parole, as most of her known relatives had migrated from Virginia to New York or New Jersey. But those with kin who had stayed behind were sent back to them, as if the southern environment was itself a corrective. This unofficial process highlighted how administrators' doubts about black women's capacity for rehabilitation were disregarded as they shifted their responsibilities to reform to the South. Black women, some of whom were not southerners, faced a region that had perfected its control of black bodies through Jim Crow and antiblack violence. Just as imprisoned women were forced to learn their gendered place within the realm of domestic respectability, southern parole forced black women to stay in their racial and gendered place within the racial hierarchy of the southern United States. Yet the shared struggle to survive Jim Crow conditions did not always create cohesive familial relationships, and when a woman's independent behavior failed to coincide with her relatives' moral code, conflict ensued. Parolees also complained to prison officials when lack of employment or pitiful wages left them indigent—the very problem that propelled so many blacks out of the South.

Excavating the cohesive and divergent experiences of black New Yorkers, *Talk with You Like a Woman* offers a new vantage point on life in early-twentieth-century New York City by taking the voices and viewpoints of black working-class women seriously. Differing with both reformers' and relatives' gendered mandates, they expressed their own concerns about city life and perspectives on womanhood. Finally, this study shows that members of the black working class saw themselves as respectable and moral within their own communities and explains why they themselves took on efforts that were commensurate with those of better-known middle-class reformers.

I

AFRICAN AMERICAN URBAN LIFE AND THE MULTIPLE MEANINGS OF PROTECTION IN THE CITY

1

to live a fuller and freer life

BLACK WOMEN MIGRANTS' EXPECTATIONS AND
NEW YORK'S URBAN REALITIES, 1890–1927

I couldn't stand the treatment we got in the south, so I came north to
escape humiliation and to live a fuller and freer life. . . . And I'm happier
even though I'm finding it harder to make enough to live on.

—Black woman migrant, 1919

The will to improve their lives propelled African Americans from the South
to the urban North. Beginning with a steady trickle during Reconstruction
and increasing through the turn of the twentieth century, the Great Migration swelled to a flood during the years around World War I. Women migrants, whether on their own or aided by family members, moved in the
hope of enjoying freedoms denied them in the Jim Crow South. They found
that freedom was incomplete and came at a price. Some made occupational
or financial sacrifices. For example, the woman interviewed in 1919 was a
trained teacher who had left her professional position in the South to work
in New York City's garment industry. Still, she spoke for other black migrants as well as herself when she judged the move worthwhile.[1] Some migrants improved their economic as well as their social position. When she
was interviewed in 1917, twenty-nine-year-old Leslie Payne, a native of Virginia, remembered her comfortable home, her Baptist upbringing, and her
caring and supportive parents. When she was fifteen, her brother, who had
migrated to Yonkers, New York, had "sent for" her to come north in order to
earn more money. She had been working for three years on a Virginia plantation for only three dollars a month. In 1903, Payne moved to Yonkers near
her brother and began making twenty-two dollars a month as a domestic.
Throughout her time in Yonkers, White Plains, and Peekskill, she continued

23

to work as a domestic and laundress. By 1917 Payne was earning $6.00 a week doing laundry and $1.50 a day working two days a week as a domestic.[2]

Migrants' stories bear witness to their determination to escape the social and economic limitations they faced below the Mason-Dixon line, yet they also attest to the difficulties they encountered in New York City. The urban North had its own problems with race relations, especially in the housing and labor markets. The former teacher-turned-garment-worker was not alone in "finding it harder to make enough to live on." The struggle for economic survival shaped the trajectories of all African Americans in New York. Conversations with the city's native-born black residents would have clued them into the fact that working-class black urbanites, despite their diversity, were engaged in a constant and collective struggle to live a "fuller and freer life." Twenty-year-old Edith Smith, who grew up in Manhattan, remembered that she had been frustrated by having to leave school at thirteen in order to care for her "sick" and "helpless" mother and believed that getting married at fifteen would allow her to be "free from [her] parents." But, unlike her father who worked every day, her husband had "refused to work." Eventually, Smith, by then the mother of two children, left her husband on Long Island and returned to her Catholic parents' more stable home on East Ninety-eighth Street, where she toiled at dissatisfying, low-paying jobs in personal and domestic service.[3]

Difficult financial circumstances facing southern migrants and native-born women alike influenced the lives of women like Hazel Dixon, who was born in New York to a woman who had migrated there from Virginia. Dixon's mother, without a husband or helpful kin nearby, was unable to parent her. At the age of three, she was placed in the Riverdale Colored Orphanage. Although she was released after seven years, she was sent to the Howard Colored Orphan Asylum four years later. Dixon's mother struggled to raise her daughter but was unable to make a home for her, perhaps because of alcoholism. Her decision to place her child in a residential program was not unusual; many destitute black parents concerned about their inability to provide for their children proactively used the services of public institutions. Dixon experienced neither the humiliations of the Jim Crow South like her mother nor the benefits of a close-knit New York community; instead, her future was shaped by her early and prolonged institutionalization. Several years after her mother's death, orphanage administrators placed Dixon in a housework position in Delaware.[4] The relatives who had made several attempts to become her custodial guardians gave up because they feared that "their own reputations might suffer" as a result of her incorrigible behavior.[5] By twenty-three, she had two daughters and was separated from her husband; she worked as a domestic and lived on West 134th Street in Harlem. For Dixon, Smith, Payne, and the anonymous teacher-turned-garment-worker, New York City held as many trials as it did possibilities. Many black working women's attempts "to live a fuller and freer life" were thwarted by poverty.

Examining black working-class women's expectations and experiences in New York City during the early decades of the twentieth century requires us to embrace their multifaceted yet interlocking concerns and to explore what they wanted for themselves as well as for their community. The gap between what they aspired to and what they encountered set in motion a complex negotiation between their dreams and the obstacles they faced; black women maneuvered as best they could to find a measure of freedom and even pleasure amid straitened, sometimes dangerous circumstances. In considering this city of black women,[6] from the Tenderloin at the turn of the century to Harlem during the 1910s and 1920s, we must scrutinize the daily interplay between gendered urban life and the complex dynamics of migration, employment, housing, and the criminal justice system. Through this investigation, we come to appreciate the options that black working-class women believed were available to them and the choices they made.

African Americans in New York City

Blacks have always had a significant presence, both numerically and symbolically, in New York. Africans arrived as slaves in the Dutch colony just four years after they disembarked in British colonial Virginia. Black people's labor contributed to the growth of the region, and their consistent numbers and distinctive culture shaped its identity.[7] Yet by 1827, when New York State's gradual process of abolition was completed, African Americans made up a smaller proportion of the city's population than they had in the mid-eighteenth century as a result of high mortality rates. The black population in Brooklyn and Manhattan declined from 16,000 in 1830 to 14,804 in 1860.[8] Although blacks lived in all the neighborhoods that became New York's five boroughs, during the nineteenth century they were concentrated in lower Manhattan. The center of black residence shifted from the Five Points area of lower Manhattan slowly uptown as well as across the river to Brooklyn after the 1863 Draft Riots and from the Tenderloin and San Juan Hill in midtown Manhattan uptown to Harlem after the 1900 race riot. Competition from the rising tide of European immigrants and a search for better housing spurred many to move uptown. By then, New York's black neighborhoods were being swelled by new arrivals from the South and the Caribbean.

At the turn of the twentieth century, the resurgence in antiblack violence and the contravention of black civil rights that accompanied the institutionalization of white supremacy propelled many African Americans from the South to the North and West. Black people expressed their dissatisfaction with second-class citizenship with their feet and in new forms of collective action.[9] In 1894, addressing an interracial audience in New York City, antilynching crusader Ida B. Wells highlighted the unfulfilled promises of Reconstruction: "Although the United States guaranteed to the negro the rights of life, liberty and pursuit of happiness, freedom and citizenship, these rights have gradually been taken from him. The negro . . . believed that the government which had the power to make him a free man and a voter . . . also [had] the power to enforce protection of those rights."[10] Organizing through the black press, Wells promoted forms of protest ranging from armed self-defense to boycotts. She memorably remarked that "a Winchester rifle should have a place of honor in every black home, and it should be used for that protection which the law refuses to give."[11] When she was living in Memphis, Tennessee, blacks "denounced the lynching of three of their best citizens," and after the authorities failed to address the situation, "black men" at her urging "left the city by thousands, bringing about great stagnation in every brand of business."[12]

Southern migrants increased New York's population considerably. The acceleration was rapid: between 1880 and 1890 only 6,634 black southerners moved to New York State, but 20,361 arrived during the 1890s and another 16,557 came between 1900 and 1910.[13] In 1901, after making trips to Virginia and North Carolina to discourage prospective migrants, a black minister, Rev. Simon P. W. Drew, estimated that "twenty thousand colored people hope to leave the South and come North." Drew worried that black southerners had "fallen victim to advertisements offering flattering salaries to all who wish to desert the land of Dixie" when such a move was "against their own interests."[14] Between 1870 and 1920, almost 28,000 blacks came to New York State from Virginia alone; another 37,223 came from North Carolina, South Carolina, Georgia, and Florida.[15] Most settled in or near New York City.

Scholars attribute the Great Migration to a convergence of political, socioeconomic, and structural factors, including racist violence and terror, the imposition of Jim Crow, the exploitative sharecropping system, and environmental disasters such as boll weevil infestation.[16] But, in the end, most African Americans left the South to "live a fuller and freer life." A twenty-one-year-old migrant from Richmond, Virginia, stated that he based his "belief in the absolute equality of men on the Bible and the Declaration of Independence" and that he thought "the colored people of the South ha[d] been barbarically oppressed."[17] Vivid letters and firsthand accounts from family and friends in northern cities, labor agents promising better jobs and higher wages, and positive editorials and articles in the black press prompted many migrants. A black South Carolina woman commented, "People is leaving every day and going some where so they can make a living."[18] A 1913 study of Harlem residents illustrates the confluence of factors that motivated migrants. An investigation of thirty-five new arrivals noted that "nineteen came for work, eight came with either parents or relatives, six came to see the world, two came because of race friction."[19]

They were not welcomed with open arms, especially by the city's African American activists. Black leaders were concerned that the influx of working-class and poor southerners would impair their own social, political, and economic standing. In 1899, one southern black minister, speaking to New York's community leaders, called southern migrants "undesirable." Intraracial class and cultural prejudices shaped ideas regarding appropriate comportment: "You don't ever see the representative negro in New York. We get the nigger up here with a cigar in his mouth, with a gold-headed cane and a high silk hat, and it's doubtful if he's got enough money in his pocket to pay his room rent." In 1907, the prominent black newspaper the *New York Age* contended that most migrants were "loud of mouth, flashy of clothes, obtrusive," and the "uppish southern Negro."[20] Even the 1895 Atlanta Exposition speech by Booker T. Washington, Tuskegee Institute's black president, raised concerns about black people leaving the South. His speech is best remembered for its accommodation to segregation, epitomized in the declaration, "In all things purely social we can be as separate as the fingers, yet one as the hand in all things essential to mutual progress." But another admonition, "Cast down your bucket where you are," warned blacks not to fall into the delusion that they would be "bettering their condition" by moving to a "foreign land" (such as Liberia). He also worried about migration to southern, western, and northern U.S. cities.[21] In 1903, Washington deplored the problems that he believed resulted from black people "flocking into the great cities where temptations are more frequent and harder to resist, and where the Negro people too often become demoralized."[22] Indeed, prominent blacks worried that working-class and poor people were ill-prepared educationally, occupationally, and socially for northern urban life.

Ironically, some of the most vocal opponents of black migration were former migrants themselves. Although they had successfully negotiated the urban terrain, these more established migrants, along with black activists and native New Yorkers, were not convinced that recent arrivals could do the same.[23] At a time when all black people's capacity for civility was questioned, such concerns conflated cultural and regional differences with the perceived inability of working poor migrants to adjust appropriately to urban society. Successful Ohio migrant and well-known author and poet Paul Laurence Dunbar raised concerns that reinforced the unease of the black elite: "Until they show greater capabilities for contact with a hard and intricate civilization, I would have them stay upon the farm and learn to live in God's great kindergarten for his simple children."[24] Critics like Dunbar were especially concerned that the behavior of these newcomers would tarnish their own hard-won reputation. In their eyes, working poor migrants were less able to survive the urban North because their socioeconomic status made them more susceptible to immoral as well as criminal activity. Many protested that, as one black woman asserted in 1895, "we are not to be judged by the street loungers and drunkards of our race."[25] De facto segregation in the urban North, especially in housing, exacerbated this intraracial tension. George Haynes's report on his 1913 study of migrations to cities highlighted this dilemma: "Respectable Negroes often find it impossible to free themselves from disreputable and vicious neighbors of their own race, because the localities in which both may live are limited."[26] Recalling the sentiments of several black friends, white reformer Mary White Ovington remarked that the black middle class often saw working-class black southerners as "violators of the law" who were arrested for "pilfering, for street fighting, for razor slashing" and whose deviant behavior cast a negative "reflection on the whole race."[27] Indeed, established black residents worried that the sheer volume of migrants would change the composition and public image of New York's black urban dweller. Many activists, who understood that white New Yorkers would never recognize the socioeconomic differences within the black population, were anxious that the newcomers' presence would overshadow their own achievements and impede racial advancement.

Paul Laurence Dunbar stressed black southerners' inability to survive without harm in the North, even though he acknowledged that some migrants demonstrated their capacity to handle urban life. In 1897, he argued that black migrants had "the right to the joy of life. But they are selling their birthright for a mess of pottage. . . . They have given up the fields for the gutters. They have bartered the sweet-smelling earth of their freshly turned furrows for the stenches of metropolitan alleys."[28] Curiously, Dunbar failed to mention the rise in lynchings and disfranchisement, as well as the continuation of exploitative labor conditions. Instead of focusing on the crimes done to black southerners as he had in some of his other work, he emphasized the criminal element among well-established residents: "Is it not enough to say that there are intelligent, moral, and industrious Negroes in the city? Of course there are, and about them there would be no problem. But their influence for good and for respectability cannot be fully felt as long as so large a part of the race are operating in a different direction."[29]

Dunbar's description of "the better-class Negro" as "intelligent, moral, and industrious" reinforced the popular image of the black masses as a group in need of moral and social uplift. Dunbar never envisioned that a significant number of working people had acquired and displayed tenets of respectability without the educational background, wealth, status, and connections of the black elite. Indeed, the black middle class and portions of the black working class shared some of the same ideals regarding racial progress. These similarities among black people, however, were often obscured by ideas about class and character when reformers, like Dunbar, addressed urban dilemmas and especially problems related to black working women. Preconceived notions about the negative impact of black women's presence in the city, rather than their actual troubling experiences, dominated public discussions about racial advancement among the black middle class.

The Problems of "Excess" Black Women

Black women migrants found that urban life posed serious problems, specifically as it related to wage labor. Facing discrimination based on the potent combination of their race and sex, they were largely restricted to positions in personal service. A 1919 report on black women workers revealed that when domestics sought to "advance to more skilled work," they "soon found that race prejudice barred the way."[30] Domestic servants either did not make enough money or, as many of them complained, had to work too hard for the wages they received. Payne left several jobs because of overwork. Although she gave up one position because "she did not feel like working anymore,"[31] her primary concerns coincided with those of most black female domestics, who argued that they never received sufficient wages for their onerous workload. The same 1919 study found that 90 percent of 175 black women interviewed had "changed jobs in the effort to increase their wages."[32]

Discussions about urban black women often disregarded their concerns, addressing instead the problematic nature of their presence. Black scholar and reformer W. E. B. Du Bois, after completing the sociological study of Philadelphia's Seventh Ward that culminated in *The Philadelphia Negro* (1899), assessed what he saw as the negative impact of urbanization on African Americans and southern migrants' limited capacity to adjust to the demands of city life.[33] In his article "The Black North in 1901: New York," Du Bois acknowledged that migrants' diversity included the "competent and incompetent, industrious and lazy, the law abiding and the criminal."[34] Yet he saw the overall composition of the city's black population as particularly troubling. He compared New York with Philadelphia: "Let us now examine any peculiarities in the colored population of Greater New York. The first noticeable fact is the excess of women. In Philadelphia the women exceed the men six to five. In New York the excess is still larger—five to four—and this means that here even more than in Philadelphia the demand for negro housemaids is unbalanced by a corresponding demand for negro men. This disproportion acts disastrously to-day on the women and men."[35] Du Bois contended that the lack of commensurate job opportunities for black men undermined the formation of stable heterosexual relationships. In 1903, he reiterated that black women between the ages of twenty-five and thirty-five outnumbered black men and that "so large an excess is . . . quite abnormal." Indeed, the unbalanced sex ratio of New York's black population alarmed black leaders: "In 1890 there were 810 men for every thousand women; in 1900, 809 for each thousand; in 1910, 850."[36] Black women moved to cities like New York and Philadelphia in larger numbers than black men, primarily because of the employment opportunities in domestic service. In 1905, Howard University professor Kelly Miller defined them as "surplus negro women" and explained that they experienced greater scrutiny because of "the enormous preponderance" of black women in various cities.[37] In New York, census data shows that the numbers of black women exceeded those of black men by 5,996 in 1900 and 6,123 in 1910.[38]

While Du Bois understood that black women's disproportionate presence in New York was generated by economic demand, he concentrated on the moral predicament he believed that situation created: large numbers of single, independent black women in a city without a corresponding number of prospective husbands.[39] For Du Bois, "restricted economic opportunity for . . . men" constituted "a source of social disorder."[40] The dominant ideal of black family life, in which men should be primary breadwinners and their wives should be homemakers, was contradicted by the New York labor market, which offered domestic jobs to black women workers and failed to

AFRICAN AMERICAN URBAN LIFE

provide enough jobs that garnered sufficient wages for black husbands and fathers.

Du Bois concentrated on what he believed were the negative effects of black women's disproportionate presence on the stability of black families and the city's black community. His preoccupation with the numerical "excess" of women meant that he ignored the experiences and perspectives of the women themselves. Other African American reformers, such as Mrs. M. C. Lawton, president of the Empire State Federation of Women's Clubs, expressed a different perspective. Black clubwomen were devoting substantial time and energy to helping black women who had recently arrived in the city. In 1911, she wrote a letter to the editor of the *Standard Union* highlighting the social work that many "honest, hardworking women" were doing for African Americans, especially black women. Her sisters' work to "uplift . . . those less fortunate in life" revealed that the problems Du Bois had exposed a decade earlier were still significant issues for black communities. Yet, as someone who saw herself as a part of "a splendid force of women who are . . . not only talking but doing," Lawton highlighted the distinctions among working-class and poor black women. She argued that there was "a vast difference between poverty and immorality"; belonging to the working poor did not—or, should not—automatically constitute "disgrace and dishonor."[41] Her focus on the worthy poor and working class, distinguishing them from those Du Bois had characterized as "incompetent," "lazy," and "criminal,"[42] highlights a dimension that studies of black urban life often ignore: the complex interactions among working-class black people, particularly women, the elite, and the criminal element. Black communities were not monolithic masses but composed of a range of groups that charted their own destinies. Black activists' awareness of the various perspectives within the black working class is clear in their writings. Still, many leaders chose to focus on what they believed to be one of the most pressing issues regarding racial advancement: the problem of the unattached working woman who had migrated to the city.

Alice Ruth Moore and Leslie Payne

Victoria Earle Matthews, an African American writer and social reformer, urged black people to stay in the South and away from New York's urban slums. Matthews, who founded the White Rose Mission, a settlement house for migrant women, was concerned about the moral issues faced not only by the race but by black female migrants themselves:

Many of the dangers confronting our girls from the South in the great cities of the North are so perfectly planned, so overwhelming in their power to subjugate and destroy that no woman's daughter is safe away from home. . . . The sending of untrained youth into the jaws of moral death must be checked. . . . Unless a girl has friends whom she and her family know are to be trusted, unless she has money enough to pay her way until she can get work, she cannot expect to be independent or free from question among careful people.[43]

Matthews's vivid warning defined the preconditions for the success of a young black woman's adjustment to the city. Without direct and sustained familial support, independent young women might fall prey to the moral dangers of urban life, becoming "women adrift."[44] Her admonition that young women needed trustworthy friends and relatives, adequate finances, and solid moral training suggests what reformers like her believed most working-class black women lacked. These reform activists failed to consider that working-class and poor blacks left the South with many of the same aspirations as their more accomplished counterparts: they believed that the urban North offered them a better opportunity for freedom and first-class citizenship. Many were unprepared for the difficulties they encountered. But the gap between their expectations and experiences, not their own personal qualities, was the main source of their distress.

Comparing the stories of Alice Ruth Moore and Leslie Payne highlights the central importance of socioeconomic status to black migrants' experiences. These two women and their families had similar expectations about the promise of northern urban life, and both had family support before and after they arrived in New York. But Moore had an excellent education and had already made a name for herself as an author, while Payne was a poorly educated and low-paid plantation laborer. Both needed employment. Moore obtained a teaching position and continued a successful career as an educator, author, and activist. Payne became a domestic servant and was initially impressed by the wages she could earn, but ultimately she was unable to escape urban poverty. Their stories demonstrate that access to opportunity was just as important as moral training in shaping the choices young black women made in the city.

Alice Ruth Moore was born in New Orleans, Louisiana, in 1875. While little is known about her father, Moore, along with her sister, was raised by her mother in modest circumstances. After completing public school, Moore, in 1892, finished a two-year teacher's program at Straight College, one of the "premier institutions for African Americans in the South."[45] Embarking on one of the most respected and rewarding professions for black women, Moore taught elementary school for four years. She made a name for herself at the age of twenty when she published *Violets and Other Tales* (1895), a book of short stories and poems. She became a prominent participant in local and national social activist circles, especially by writing for the black clubwomen's journal, the *Woman's Era*. "Educated and cultured," Moore did "useful 'race' work."[46] Her appearance also contributed to her social standing and celebrity. She grew up influenced by the Creole society of New Orleans, which conjoined "wealth and education, light skin and mixed ancestry."[47] Her "long, thick auburn tresses and alabaster skin" placed her in the midst of elite black society before her northward migration.[48]

In 1896, another Louisiana native, Homer Plessy, lost his civil rights suit against segregation in intrastate transportation. The U.S. Supreme Court declared that "separate but equal" accommodations were constitutional, striking down the equal protections under the law to which black citizens had been entitled. The Citizens' Committee of New Orleans (Comité des Citoyens) had planned this test of the state's 1890 segregation law and recruited the light-skinned "colored" man to be arrested after he bought a ticket and boarded a first-class train car. The Moore family, along with the rest of the city's people of African descent, would have clearly understood the federal government's validation and reinforcement of their second-class citizenship.

That same year, Alice Moore moved with her mother, Patricia, sister, Leila, and brother-in-law, James Young, to West Medford, Massachusetts, where they "set up a prosperous catering business."[49] A year later, Moore moved to New York City. Like many other women in her set, Moore discovered that her financial circumstances did not correspond with her credentials and social status. After her New York arrival, she remembered, "I was *so* hard up," necessitating that she pawn a cherished watch for twenty-five dollars.[50] Fortunately, she boarded in Brooklyn with a friend, the social reformer Victoria Earle Matthews, and her husband, William Matthews.[51] After passing the New York State teacher's examination, she got a teaching position at Brooklyn's Public School 83 and taught evening classes at Matthews's settlement house.[52] Unlike most migrants, Moore had decent housing: "The house we are in now is as near ideal as a city-house can be. My room is a choice one, and filled with all my old time girlish things which I brought from home with me." She led an active social life and traveled in elite circles. In 1897, for instance, she wrote an admirer, "Thursday I am going to Poughkeepsie to stay over until Saturday for the Harvard-Yale boat race. I am going to wear the red of Harvard and shout its nine Rahs!"[53] As a

New York's Urban Realities

34

middle-class black woman, Alice Moore represented a successful migrant. She had moved north with her family, lived as a single woman in a middle-class household, obtained reliable employment, and had the best circumstances under which to maintain her own standards of respectability.

Leslie Payne's migration experience differed considerably. Born in 1888 in Farmville, Virginia, she was a middle child with two male siblings. Payne's parents "worked steadily," her mother as a domestic and her father on a plantation. While Payne remembered that her parents "earned enough to make a comfortable home," she and her older brother "went to work when they were very young and contributed their wages to the family income." Payne attended school sporadically and left for good at the age of nine when she had only completed the first grade. She could not remember "anything that she learned except how to read and write a little." Payne recalled that "very few colored children" in her community went to school.[54]

While poverty and racism limited the opportunities that were open to Payne, it did not prevent her parents from teaching her their moral standards. Like most Farmville residents, they were working people "with tendencies distinctly toward the better class rather than toward the worse."[55] Although some members of the black elite, like W. E. B. Du Bois, believed that black working-class people were not "generally very energetic or resourceful" and that their "moral standards have not yet acquired . . . fixed character,"[56] Payne described her parents as "very religious," "strict in their standards," and "good people [who] tried to do all they could for their children." She recalled that the young people had a curfew and "were not allowed to make friends their parents did not know." While her family's socioeconomic position curtailed her schooling and pushed her into the low-wage labor force, Payne's formative years were guided by moral principles.[57]

Payne's move to New York stemmed from her relatives' concerns for her welfare. When her older brother discovered that young women could earn much more money in New York, he invited the fifteen-year-old to join him in Yonkers. Her family's financial troubles more than likely persuaded her parents to agree. Payne's wages more than doubled when she left plantation labor in Virginia for domestic work in New York.[58] Her mother was a domestic in Farmville, but they averaged only "from $1 to $5" a month, the same amount Payne had received as a farm laborer. Farmville residents regarded domestic service as "a relic of slavery," saw it as "degrading," and only took it up "from sheer necessity." While Du Bois noted that live-in domestics in the county received "good board, fair lodging, much cast-off clothing, and not a little training in matters of household economy and taste," many black parents disagreed with this positive assessment. They were particularly concerned that domestic service in white households exposed their daughters to sexual harassment and the "ever-possible fate of concubinage."[59] In 1904, clubwoman Fannie Barrier Williams of Chicago observed: "It is . . . a significant and shameful fact that . . . I am constantly in receipt of letters from the still unprotected colored women of the South, begging me . . . to find employment for their daughters . . . to save them from going into the homes of the South as servants, as there is . . . nothing to save them from dishonor and degradation."[60]

In New York, Payne struggled to find a tolerable domestic position that paid enough money to live on. By working steadily as a domestic she averaged at least twenty dollars a month, yet she complained that the work was "too hard" and that she "wanted a change." In 1908, at the age of twenty, she returned briefly to her family in Farmville. Her father had died in 1907, so she probably came to help her mother, but her own personal problems also prompted her departure from New York. She had been arrested twice, in 1903 for fighting and in 1908 for disorderly conduct, though both charges were dismissed. She seems to have been pregnant or brought her infant with her, for when she left Farmville for New York in 1910 she left the child with her mother and stepfather. Later, when her brother moved back to Farmville, she asked that her son, now nine years old, be allowed to come live with her in New York. Her mother responded that her grandson was "now helping with the plowing" and the family could not "give him up."[61] To suggest that her mother's decision was solely about the family's need for labor would ignore the evidence of Payne's childhood moral teachings. Having seen the impact of her daughter's struggles in the urban North, Payne's mother most likely attempted to shield her grandson from Payne's troubling lifestyle. This choice may have been the best. When Payne returned to New York, she became caught up in an abusive romantic relationship. Her five subsequent arrests, many of which were discharged, ranged from fighting to stealing to intoxication. Her problems with the criminal justice system reflect her disenchantment with domestic service, her experience with domestic violence, and her growing dependence on alcohol.[62]

Exploitative domestic labor and persistent, debilitating poverty haunted Payne's life in New York, as it did in Farmville. Payne's migration narrative shows that the working poor espoused moral virtues and taught their children the value of respectability but that, as historian Tera Hunter has remarked, consistent self-discipline "granted them few rewards."[63] Rather than innately deficient in morality, as many black elites suggested, black working-class women sometimes made troubling choices in difficult circumstances in spite of knowing the difference between moral and immoral

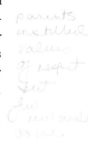

New York's Urban Realities

conduct. Consider, for instance, a social worker's description of a black family in Maryland: the "highly respectable" parents "took a great interest in their children and in their education," but their training did "not show in other members of the family."[64] Payne's parents may have initially been comforted by their son's presence in New York, but they still worried about their daughter's welfare. While they did not condone her behavior, they accepted her son. As an adult, however, she had to fend for herself in New York City.

Migrants like Payne aroused intense anxiety among elite black reformers because of their preoccupation with the presumed moral apathy of the black working class. For different reasons, unmarried middle-class black women were also a cause of concern. Alice Moore had obtained a respectable job and appropriate housing, yet her avid suitor and eventual husband, Paul Laurence Dunbar, was anxious about her being a young woman in the city. Dunbar, a native of Ohio and resident of Washington, DC, was fascinated by New York, making "frequent and prolonged visits to the city," especially to the notorious Tenderloin section.[65] He expressed increasing concern regarding Moore's ability to navigate the urban terrain: "I shall not complain about your being in New York although I do not like it. It is a dangerous place."[66] Dunbar's worries coincided with the sentiments of many other prominent blacks who believed that the city posed moral dangers for all young black women. Dunbar need not have worried. Moore's teaching position and social connections enabled her to benefit from a network of influential and protective friends. Payne, however, faced entirely different circumstances. Domestic work and its concomitant poverty limited her opportunities and influenced the choices she eventually made. A lack of moral training was not relevant to either woman's situation.

Reformers' moral anxieties about single women in the city only infrequently involved any recognition of the many physical dangers these women faced. Black women of every socioeconomic status regularly experienced violent encounters with the police, criminals, and neighbors, as well as their husbands or boyfriends. Writing her fiancé in 1898, Alice Moore expressed her frustration at being robbed a second time in less than a month.[67] In the early twentieth century, domestic violence pervaded many women's private lives, including that of the genteel Alice Moore and the working-class Leslie Payne. Payne later revealed that in 1905, two years after her arrival in New York, when she was just seventeen, she was raped by a thirty-five-year-old man.[68] A dozen years later, her romantic relationship was marred by violence. Although Payne and her neighbors revealed that she fought back consistently, her boyfriend was known to be "quite brutal" and reportedly

AFRICAN AMERICAN URBAN LIFE

"abused her a great deal."[69] In one incident, he "broke most of the furniture in the house and most of the door panels."[70]

Moore's courtship and marriage to Paul Laurence Dunbar were also troubled and volatile.[71] During their 1897 engagement, Dunbar, who was drunk, sexually assaulted his fiancée.[72] Moore's injuries were severe enough that she required medical attention. While her physical injuries healed slowly, Moore agonized about her compromised reputation. Eventually she accepted Dunbar's apologies but was so disgraced by her physician's knowledge of her predicament that she asked Dunbar to lie about their marital status: "The Dr. doesn't do anything especial to make me ashamed. I simply am ashamed to think what he knows of me. But when he sends his bill to . . . me I'm going to send it to you—and let *you* pay him, and I want you to tell a fib for me—simply write him, thanking him for his kindness to *your wife*, will you?"[73] The couple eloped in 1898, but Dunbar's violence toward her recurred. In 1902, after a particularly vicious beating, Moore left her husband for good.[74]

Both women's social standing and economic position failed to prevent their devastatingly violent personal encounters, but their socioeconomic status certainly shaped how they responded to those incidents. Moore, with her connection to black female activists espousing moral purity as a means for racial advancement, was horrified at how her private assault might affect her public image. Her middle-class status enabled her to preserve her privacy in a way that Payne could not. Payne, who found her low-paying and demanding domestic work undesirable, eventually succumbed to a myriad of problems. Many working women struggled with conflicts in their romantic, familial, and social relationships at the same time that they tried to find and maintain viable employment, their most pressing need.

Our Women Bread Winners

Alice Moore's occupational position reflects the deference black educators received as many communities' most prized resource. In 1900, only 4.2 percent of black women were identified as teachers on the federal census. Leslie Payne's situation was more typical: nationally, black women accounted for 86 percent of unskilled laborers, 65.6 percent of laundresses, and 27 percent of servants and waitresses.[75] Industrial employment was virtually closed to them. Many southern migrants discovered that although wages were higher in New York, they also had to pay more for housing, food, and other necessities. Unlike their immigrant and native-born white women counterparts, black women did not experience an improvement in their standard

of living between 1880 and 1920.[76] Their limited opportunities in the workforce shaped their aspirations and the dynamics of black families and communities.

In spite of the rapid expansion of mass-production industries and the
relative ease with which immigrant men and women obtained manufac-
turing jobs, black men and women were relegated to menial positions in
domestic service. Blacks' problems in the labor market stemmed from white
New Yorkers' long-standing belief that "nature intended black people for
servitude rather than free labor."[77] Historian Leslie Harris argues that New
Yorkers' ideological investment in racial slavery and their inability to accept
black freedom before and after gradual manumission influenced how they
treated black city-dwellers and saw them as a "symbol of dependency and
lack of virtue." The stigma of enslavement shaped the gender dynamics and
labor opportunities within black communities. "In the eyes of whites, the
black population as a whole was feminized, politically dependent, and thus
unfit for citizenship, first because of the fact that there were more women
than men in New York City and, second, because black men held a disproportionate number of jobs as domestics."[78] In 1869, the New York Times described the frustrating plight of black men seeking industrial employment:
"If a colored man applies for work at a new job, he always has to wait till
the contractor sees whether he can get enough white laborers for his purpose before he is taken on, and it more often happens that he is at once refused employment, simply on the ground of his color."[79] In 1895, black New
Yorkers still protested, "We only want a chance. Give the young black men
opportunities to learn a business. The trades are closed to them. The trade
unions are against them. They cannot obtain situations or apprenticeships
at the ordinary trades on account of the prejudice against their color."[80]
Racial discrimination in hiring continued into the early twentieth century;
indeed, blacks' relative position in the labor market deteriorated as newly
arrived immigrants were favored over African Americans.

These long-standing discriminatory labor practices shaped the structure
of black families. In 1904, Fannie Barrier Williams succinctly explained why
so many black women continued to engage in wage labor after they were
married: "We know that under present economic conditions the average
home will be poorly furnished and children poorly educated, if everything
depends upon the earning capacity of the man alone. The average Afro-
American can scarcely earn enough to sustain an adequate income."[81] A
nineteen-year-old native of New York whose parents had moved there from
Virginia said that the family "did not have much money." In 1917, her father's
earnings as a janitor were so meager that her mother was "obliged to do day's

work." With both parents working, she had to care for her younger siblings. After she married, she also worked to supplement her husband's wages.[82] Black women entered the labor force as daughters and, unlike many other working-class women, were usually employed full time throughout their marriage to augment the family income.

Fannie Barrier Williams called black women "breadwinners," highlighting the well-known fact that women's employment was central to the financial survival of black families. The 1900 federal census reported that 43 percent of black women were breadwinners in their families. Black women's rates of labor force participation remained constant—at 40 percent or higher—for all black women aged sixteen to sixty-four, while native-born white women and white immigrant women's labor force participation rates declined steadily after they reached twenty-four years of age.[83] Unlike a number of her male contemporaries, Williams not only acknowledged that "in domestic service or as cooks, the demand for Negro women . . . far exceeds the supply" but also emphasized the specific problems black women suffered in the urban labor market. She argued that "prejudice weighs more heavily against an Afro American woman than against an Afro American man." Williams, along with a number of other black commentators, raised the troubling issue of black citizens being bypassed in the labor force because of racist practices that favored European immigrant workers, deploring the fact that immigrant women "with foreign tongue and doubtful patriotism enjoy a monopoly of the right to earn a living."[84] In 1901, a black minister went so far as to say that with the influx of immigrants at the turn of the century, black workers had gone "out of fashion" and African Americans' employment opportunities were "lessening."[85] In 1922, investigators found that among nonprofessional women workers, blacks' weekly earnings averaged only $17.20, compared to $19.15 for whites.[86] Recognizing their inability to alter the institutionalized racism that pervaded the labor market, Williams argued that black workers "must get rid of the notion that [domestic] work is degrading" and instead become more proficient and efficient laborers.[87]

Most working-class black women who, like Leslie Payne, began working as children adamantly disagreed with the idea that domestic work could be anything but exploitative, exhausting, and unrewarding. Some women stated simply that they did not like to work. After two years of toiling in a factory and doing housework, one eighteen-year-old whose husband was able to support her commented that "if you get up in the morning and feel tired it's good to sleep again and then get up later on and go to the theatre."[88] Still, work was an unavoidable necessity, so most women attempted

New York's Urban Realities

to make choices about where and by whom they were employed. A twenty-year-old preferred to wait on tables because she did not like the "dirty, rough work" required of domestics.[89] Many black women shared the sentiments of twenty-one-year-old Alice Knight, who complained that her employer was too demanding. On top of a daily routine that included cleaning and dusting ten rooms and ironing children's clothing, she was constantly expected to perform extra tasks. Her employer complained that she worked too slowly.[90] Whenever it was possible, especially during World War I, black women left domestic work for factory jobs in order to "escape the long hours, the confinement, and the friction of a personal 'boss.'"[91]

Tensions between black domestics and their employers also surfaced in disputes over wages. In 1901, Sarah Vaughn was charged with disorderly conduct and fined five dollars because she refused to leave her former employer's home after she returned to collect what she believed were her remaining wages. Vaughn had worked two weeks out of a month-long arrangement. Her former employer said she paid the domestic, but Vaughn disagreed. Before she was arrested, Vaughn brought a civil suit against her employer, but it was dismissed. Instead of treating Vaughn's individual pursuit of her wages as an employer-employee conflict, the press emphasized that the domestic had been informed of her "right to go to the house and remain there until she was paid." When asked why she refused to leave the residence, Vaughn argued, "De law am wid me. De copper has no right to lay his paws on me when I was sitting wid de law right side of me."[92] Her self-assertion, claim to citizenship rights for her wages, and protest against police brutality shine through the newspaper's stereotypical rendering of her speech in dialect, yet in the end she lost her case.

Poverty required that black women make difficult decisions regarding their priorities. Some women suffered from malnutrition and other health problems. For example, one woman wrote her sister that she "did not want to get so thin again," so she stopped "at the soda fountain every morning [to] get a glass of milk with raw eggs." In the middle of February, she concluded that she could not afford boots because of "what $12.95 mean to a working girl."[93]

While many women suffering financial duress "always worked for a living and never sported on the streets," as a woman of thirty-five put it,[94] others engaged in the sex trade in addition to, or instead of, legal employment. A twenty-five-year-old remarked that she worked but when she got tired she "went on the street."[95] Making this decision often caused emotional stress. A twenty-two-year-old explained, "You don't know what girls like me are driven to do. I didn't do them just for fun life has not been so kind to me I have had to work since I was a small child and coming to a big city like New York with no one to help me made things much harder."[96] At the age of twenty-nine, after twelve years of hard labor, Leslie Payne decided that it was preferable to be a prostitute who could get "$3 or $4 from every man" instead of making just $6 a week as a laundress.[97] Those black working-class women who entered prostitution usually pointed out that sexual labor helped them cope with their impoverished circumstances.

In 1927, a National Urban League study found that out of the 1,225 women investigated, 421 worked in industrial occupations, including as factory workers, laundresses, and pressers, while 733 women were employed in personal and domestic service, by the day, full time, or part time.[98] Black women who obtained jobs in commercial establishments were often relegated to service positions or worked in back rooms out of the sight of customers, and they could be summarily dismissed. In 1913, twenty black women were fired by Gimbel's department store, where they had worked as "dusters" and "maids." The women recalled that they were summoned by an official and told curtly, "You girls will have to resign; so go down and get your pay." The *New York Age*, a black newspaper, noted that the women were sent "out in the dead of winter and without moment's notice." The women were particularly angry because most of them had previously been employed at Wanamaker's, a competing department store, and had left those positions two years earlier because of Gimbel's "glittering promises" of better treatment. The newspaper concluded that "colored help is no longer desired despite the fact that the store has hundreds of colored patrons."[99]

Unlike most migrants, some black women came to New York temporarily, intending to return south. A "middle-aged" black woman explained that "New York is . . . a good place to make money, [but] a better place to leave after one has . . . money."[100] Black sojourners often took seasonal domestic work to help the families they had left behind. Twenty-year-old Bertha Bell came north with her mother and sister because of financial problems. Hoping to take advantage of New York's higher wages, they planned to stay in the city only until they could "help out the situation" in Virginia.[101] Twenty-two-year-old Deloris Jordan and her widowed mother came to the city to work in order to "pay [on their] debt and prevent the loss of property" in South Carolina.[102]

Whether they were native-born, migrants, or temporary residents, black New Yorkers shared the bleak experience of paying more for worse housing than white city-dwellers.

New York's Urban Realities

Housing

Whether they lived in the Tenderloin or Harlem, black people lived in tenements that were overpriced, overcrowded, and dilapidated. In 1890, the Danish American reformer Jacob Riis concluded that blacks "had to pay higher rents . . . for the poorest and most stinted rooms."[103] A 1904 survey of housing conditions reported that "blacks were charged about $2.00 a month more rent than whites for . . . inferior" accommodations.[104] By 1912, blacks moving uptown to Harlem found that they were charged twenty-five to twenty-eight dollars a month for apartments that the white former residents had rented for only twenty to twenty-two dollars a month.[105] In 1917, Leslie Payne paid eight dollars a month for an "old, dilapidated" home in a "very poor neighborhood"; the rent alone consumed one-third of her weekly income.[106] In 1927, a husband, wife, and nine children under the age of twelve lived in two rooms with a sick, elderly woman; in exchange for the wife "looking after . . . the old woman," the family was "given a credit for half of the rent," which was thirty-four dollars a month. In the same year, 48 percent of the black Harlem residents interviewed said their housing conditions were "poor," "bad," or "needed cleaning." Many had made frequent but fruitless attempts to "find more desirable quarters." They complained that their apartments lacked consistent or sufficient hot water and heat and "rats, water-bugs, and garbage" were left unattended.[107] Landlords' neglect of black tenants forced residents to address their problems through especially draconian means. Consider, for instance, the cases of tenants who responded to the stench of "decaying refuse" in their buildings' courtyards by refusing to raise the window "in one and one-half years" and another resident who was forced to "sprinkle lime" in the courtyard "every few days" to "keep down the foul odor."[108]

Although they were aware of racial discrimination in the housing market, social workers sometimes conflated a family's living conditions with their respectability. Some investigators seemed to expect the conditions one field-worker described: "The clothes were piled around everywhere and dirty dishes stood on the stove and table . . . the room is poorly lighted . . . [poorly] ventilated and greatly overcrowded."[109] In other instances, social workers appreciated poor and working-class residents' efforts to create a positive home environment. In a "poor and very noisy" neighborhood, one investigator found a five-room apartment that was "well-lighted and ventilated, and scrupulously clean."[110] The same social worker was "favorably impressed" that the mother of a twenty-seven-year-old drug addict was a "refined superior type of colored woman" whose home was "neat, clean, and attractive."[111]

Poor and working-class blacks, while confined to certain sections of New York City by de facto segregation, were just as concerned about their neighborhood's character and reputation as the reformers who judged them.[112] Emphasizing black people's difficulty in maintaining a respectable existence in the urban environment, one investigator argued that "the tenements are alike in appearance and structure and a church member may live across the hall from a prostitute." "It is a place to live rather than a community life," he continued, and "there is very little knowledge of one's neighbor."[113] Yet working-class women were mindful and even strategic about finding appropriate residences. A twenty-four-year-old said that she "always lived in a good neighborhood" and was paying "a good woman" "$2.50 a week for a furnished room" in Harlem.[114] A nineteen-year-old recalled that her mother "always tried to find good localities for the children to live in." After she married, she lived in Harlem but "did not like [her] neighborhood because there were many fast people and she and her husband wanted to get away and live in the country."[115] Indeed, concerns about disreputable neighbors were shared by the respectable poor.

Exorbitant rents forced many families to take in lodgers. Working-class families of all races and ethnicities rented rooms to non–family members, but black families were especially vulnerable to overcrowding. In 1898, a study found that black families in Manhattan "divided the burden of rent" by living together in one apartment. In the Nineteenth Assembly District, for example, 740 families had 569 boarders, 286 of them male and 27 of them female.[116] These problematic housing conditions followed black families from lower Manhattan to uptown: a 1922 study found that "every apartment in upper Harlem contains as many roomers as it can hold and more than are desirable for health and morals."[117] Scholars have suggested that some black families successfully incorporated lodgers and boarders into their families.[118] One investigator concluded that, "far from being the virtue-devouring ogres they were supposed to be, the lodgers, as a rule, took a lively interest in the children's school progress; and many times on visiting their homes these same lodgers were found helping the children with their lessons."[119] The mother of one eighteen-year-old explained to social workers that her lodgers were "decent respectable men" and she did not allow them to "entertain any women in the house."[120] Yet female residents still experienced problems with male lodgers.

Black women faced sexual and physical dangers as single women living alone when they became the youthful prey of male predators who shared their households. The dreaded "lodger evil" epitomized reformers' fear of these outsiders' immoral influence on the family. Moreover, some reformers failed to recognize the financial imperatives that led families to take them in and argued that lodgers caused overcrowding.[121] W. E. B. Du Bois voiced reformers' most pressing concern: the deleterious effects of male lodgers on "growing daughters . . . left unprotected."[122] Young black women's stories attested to sexual assaults by lodgers. In 1907, a twenty-three-year-old revealed that when the "people were to church," a "drinking man" came to her room and "said he would kill me if I did not do what he wanted" and "tried to ravish" her.[123] She killed the man in self-defense. In 1925, a male lodger was killed when a twenty-seven-year-old woman confronted him "trying to take advantage of" her fifteen-year-old sister.[124] Yet reformers highlighted the danger of inappropriate sexual relationships between male lodgers and young female residents. For example, thirteen-year-old Margaret Hull had sexual relations with her grandmother's thirty-three-year-old boarder and had her first child at the age of fourteen.[125] The social workers involved in her case seemed to dismiss or disregard the criminal actions of the male lodger as they argued that Hull's improper sexual relations with the man as well as her arrest for petty larceny were the result of "little supervision . . . since her mother had nothing to do with her and her grandmother was busy working all of the time."[126] Hull's teenage pregnancy was blamed on her absent mother and working grandmother, not on the dire economic straits that prompted them to keep a male lodger, or on the man's criminal actions.

Though not all young black women migrants confronted such extreme experiences, many found the adjustment to northern urban life difficult. Rural southerners had to orient themselves to their new physical surroundings. Mabel Hampton distinctly remembered that as a young child in the city for the first time "she did not see . . . green grass." New York's buildings, fire escapes, and subway trains made her long for her home in Winston-Salem, North Carolina. "I've always been out in the open, the yard with flowers, . . . chickens, and turkeys. . . . The yard was full of everything, and here I was now, to have none of it."[127] Indeed, housing reports noted that a majority of tenement rooms had "no access to the outer air" and most residents "had but one window."[128] Samuel Battle, Manhattan's first black police officer, remembered that it took time for him to get used to the hustle and bustle of the city: "The elevated [train] made so much noise you couldn't hear. There was so much traffic." He discovered that he had to interact with people differently than he had in the South: "Of course I came from a nice quiet town where everybody spoke to you, but here if you knew somebody and wanted to speak to them they'd think you were fresh or something."[129]

Black migrants had to adjust their social and political expectations to the realities of everyday life in New York City. They learned that segregation prevailed, even though it was de facto rather than de jure. A black minister remarked in 1900: "Our young people, attracted by the alluring tales they have heard of equal rights in the North, come here, expecting to find release from what has held them down in the South. It does not take them long to discover their mistake." As black southerners attempted to gain first-class citizenship rights by moving to New York, they found black New Yorkers struggling, just as urgently, to make sure that their own civil rights were enforced.

The Theoretical Equality of Northern Life

A woman who had migrated to New York City from Virginia pointedly remarked that she enjoyed "the theoretical equality of Northern life."[130] The struggle to realize the promise of civil and social equality was underscored by the controversy over the enforcement of a civil rights law.

In 1895, the New York State legislature, along with Governor Levi P. Morton, passed a law introduced by George Malby, the Republican Speaker of the Assembly, to protect blacks' civil rights. The Malby law, as it was called, was one of a series of efforts to ensure equal rights in the state.[131] The law stated that "all persons within the jurisdiction of" the state should "be entitled to . . . full and equal accommodations, advantages, facilities and privileges of inns, restaurants, hotels, eating-houses, bath-houses, barbershops, theatres, music halls," and other "public conveyances regardless of race, creed, or color."[132] In addition to imposing fines ranging from "not less than one hundred dollars nor more than five hundred dollars," or imprisonment for thirty to ninety days, the statute allowed plaintiffs to collect personal damages of up to five hundred dollars. The provision for civil damages represented a significant departure from previous legislation.[133]

While the law ostensibly protected all New Yorkers, white residents' negative responses stemmed from their agreement with the view articulated in a *New York Times* editorial: "No legislation can . . . establish a social relation which a law higher than all civil statutes declare to be forever impossible."[134] White New Yorkers' response to the Malby law revealed the crux of race relations. Their negative responses were not directed at Assemblyman Malby, Governor Morton, or the legislature. Rather, black people, the perceived recipients of the law's guarantees, were heavily criticized. Newspaper articles bore such headlines as "Comedy in Color," "A Misdirected Effort," "Colored Folk and Their Rights," "Hotel Men Are Worried," "Seeking to Gain Profit," and "Malby's Law Denounced."[135] The *New York Times* editorial opined that "access to the privileges of fashionable restaurants and theatres on the footing of the most favored would be of no benefit to the colored people"; rather, "it harms them to put these notions into their heads." It is "manifestly unwise for negroes and mulattoes to be self-assertive and swaggering in places where Italians, Scandinavians, English, Irish, and Americans bear themselves with habitual quietness and humility."[136] This differentiation between assimilable immigrants and unmanageable black people shaped the discriminatory treatment black New Yorkers continually faced in employment, housing, and urban reform. The very next year, in 1896, the U.S. Supreme Court legalized state laws imposing racial segregation in the *Plessy v. Ferguson* case. While the *Plessy* ruling did not void the Malby law and subsequent civil rights legislation, it did legitimate white New Yorkers' refusal to comply with the law. While blacks used the legal system to fight discrimination, the civil rights protections they won in the legislature had modest bearing on the lived experiences of black residents.

Reports on black urban communities by white and black social investigators illustrate the ways in which black New Yorkers struggled for civil rights and human dignity on an everyday basis. Although their efforts were less prominent than those of the black elite, working-class blacks shared the ideal of social equality and sought to enjoy "a freer and fuller life." Not all reformers got the message. Just as Du Bois and other black activists overlooked the everyday concerns of working-class women, white reformers who attempted to address urban poverty often misread the hopes and desires of black working-class urbanites. Reflecting white prejudices that he had absorbed since arriving in the United States, reformer Jacob Riis asserted that "poverty, abuse, and injustice alike the negro accepts with imperturbable cheerfulness."[137] Contrary to this assessment, black working-class New Yorkers consistently expressed their feelings about race relations and everyday life not only through the black press but also when being interviewed by white people.

In the early twentieth century, several white graduate students at Columbia University conducted small-scale studies of the city's ordinary black residents.[138] Much of their evidence came from observations and interviews. In some instances, researchers revealed the problems they encountered in obtaining information from black residents. Even W. E. B. Du Bois, when conducting his 1899 study of Philadelphia's Seventh Ward, was challenged by black residents at the front door with the question, "Are we animals to be dissected and by an unknown Negro at that?"[139] These white male students' efforts to gather information from black New Yorkers were met with distrust. For black people, an unfamiliar white person intruding into their community and inquiring about their affairs might well mean trouble. Expressing his frustration at the lack of response from black people, a political science student said that after he asked one man a number of questions, the "man told me that if he let me know all of his business I would know as much about it as he did." When the student began asking a black female resident about her life, he was met with frank suspicion. Instead of believing that he was collecting data for a master's thesis, she thought that he "had been hired by the butcher to find out how much wages her husband received."[140]

Many white investigators interpreted their evidence from a perspective that contradicted or dismissed black residents' viewpoints. Despite substantial evidence regarding black people's dismal employment prospects, one investigator stated that the people he interviewed "all claimed they were forced to do odd labor or personal service in order to support their families." He based his assessment, in large part, on the case of an indigent black man who refused to work and whose family was supported by a white charity. The investigator heard about the case after workers from the West Thirtieth Street Mission became "suspicious of the apparent prosperity of a [male client's] family." In their investigation, the charity workers found that various "members of [the man's] . . . family belonged to different churches, receiving charitable help from at least four . . . white churches" as well as the Mission. After discovering this deception, the Mission offered him a job, but he refused it. The investigator waxed indignant, condemning the man as a lazy, ungrateful pauper. He refused to hear, or at least take seriously, why the man rejected the job offer. The pauper's initial statement, "I won't work unless I absolutely have to," may indicate a refusal to work for insufficient wages. As he continued, his philosophy on race relations became clear: "The poor colored people were made slaves by white people for a long time! And now the whites ought to pay for it, and take care of the poor colored man. Besides, Jesus Christ tell all people with money to care for the poor people."[141] Was this impoverished black man's assessment an irrelevant excuse, or did he, in 1912, articulate ideas that were prevalent among African Americans regarding the legacy of slavery, the failure of Reconstruction, the justice of reparations, and the duty of Christians to the poor? Although the black man was dismissed by the investigator, his statement reveals that his socioeconomic position did not hinder his ability to assess his individual situation and that of black people generally.

While black New Yorkers dealt with poor conditions of employment and housing, some of their most difficult experiences stemmed from the myriad ways in which they were disrespected on a daily basis. In 1895, black reformer Victoria Earle Matthews noted that "white people . . . look upon colored people as curiosities. Indeed they know more about the Chinese than about the colored population of this country. They look upon us as they do upon a menagerie of strange animals. It is humiliating to sensitive persons to be so regarded by prejudiced white people."[142] The ways in which whites referred to and addressed black people illustrate the problem. Addressing a working-class black person impolitely was just as insulting as refusing to serve a black middle-class individual in a restaurant. A black nurse from Georgia explained: "It's a small indignity, . . . but an indignity just the same. No white person, not even the little children just learning to talk, no white person at the South ever thinks of addressing any negro man or woman as Mr., or Mrs., or Miss. The women are called, 'Cook,' or 'Nurse,' or 'Mammy,' or 'Mary Jane,' . . . and the men are called 'Bob,' or 'Dilcey,' or 'Old Man.' . . . In many cases, our white employers refer to us, and in our presence, too, as their 'niggers.'"[143] Yet this behavior was not confined to the South, as black migrants found to their distress.

The disrespect that black people experienced not only inflicted personal slights but also shaped power relations between white employers and black laborers and between white and black New Yorkers in public. Conflicts over blacks' distinct sense of entitlement to social and political equality influenced interracial interactions within the criminal justice system as well. Negative preconceptions about black people in general and migrants in particular led to high rates of incarceration. White New Yorkers believed that the increasing numbers of black southerners in the city created irreparable harm. "The metropolis is full of 'vicious and dangerous negroes, whose mere presence in the city is . . . a menace to law and order.'" Many believed in the prevailing argument that linked the legacy of enslavement and allegedly simplistic black peoples' inability to adjust to the complexity of a civilized metropolis. As the *Courier-Journal* put it, "The best place for the colored man is the plantation. He is peculiarly adapted to agricultural labor, and in the country he is not subject to the vicious associations which are his ruin in the city."[144] White New Yorkers' fears influenced how police officers responded to black people. According to historian Marcy Sacks, black residents' arrest rate doubled from 2.5 percent in the 1890s to over 5 percent after 1900, even though black people made up only 2 percent of the city's population.[145] Such disproportionate arrest rates not only reinforced negative sentiments regarding black people but reflected how blacks were treated in New York's criminal justice system.

Black Women and the Criminal Justice System

Officers in New York City's police department felt no need to censor their expressions of cynical hostility toward black city-dwellers, including women. In 1915, social worker Frances Blascoer found that in Harlem and the San Juan Hill district, police department inspectors and captains said, "without mincing their words, that they considered the colored people worthless, and that it was 'useless to bother with them. . . . So long as they did not murder each other,' the police said, they did not pay any attention to them but 'let them do as they pleased.'"[146] Police officers' negative assessments of black women were particularly pronounced. William McAdoo, a former police chief, noted in 1906 that "the vicious and drunken colored woman differs somewhat from her white sister in that she . . . in a paroxysm of passion, and under the influence of liquor, is likely to use a weapon very freely, and not a few of them carry revolvers and razors. . . . There is also, in the Tenderloin especially, a very dangerous band of colored women who prey on white men."[147]

McAdoo's assessment reinforced prevailing ideas that black women were both perennial prostitutes and masculinized, disorderly criminals. Consider, for instance, the anxiety that three fighting black women elicited in 1896 when they turned on officers who tried to end their altercation with one another: "Policeman Brunner attempted to separate the women, but they all turned on him, knocked his helmet off and beat and kicked him. Policeman Rouse came to his assistance and, although he is a six-footer, he fared no better at the hands of the women who made common cause against the blue coats."[148] Policemen viewed black women's actions as suspicious and potentially criminal.

Black New Yorkers, on the contrary, believed that many black women's disproportionate arrests stemmed from racial discrimination and the use of "stool pigeons." Working for the police as decoys, stool pigeons posed as possible suitors or intentionally placed black women in compromising positions. Once these men gained a woman's attention, the police arrived and arrested the woman for prostitution. For instance, after coming home from work, one woman was arrested after opening her door to a detective who proceeded to enter her apartment. Realizing that he made a mistake,

New York's Urban Realities

the detective arrested her even though "he did not find the woman he came after."[149] When Harlem community leaders protested this practice, they warned black women to be careful about the men they interacted with, lest they fall prey to false arrest. The community protests portrayed young black women as "decent, hard-working girls" who were arrested and jailed by a corrupt and racist police force.[150]

Black community members argued that negative attitudes toward black residents influenced the lack of regulation of commercialized sex in their neighborhoods. According to social workers and residents, "the police were neglectful of their duties in colored districts."[151] "Streetfighting, foul language and all manner of indecencies were said to pass unmolested by police interference; and in the blocks having a bad reputation not once was a patrolman found on duty." Many working-class residents devised ways to protect themselves. For example, one mother who "was at home alone most of the time" "kept a wooden club" over her apartment door. A concerned father "stated that so many of his friends had been robbed of their personal possessions that he had formed the habit of placing his 'best clothes' in pawn on Monday morning, leaving them with the pawnbroker until Saturday night."[152]

Concerned Harlem residents frequently requested that the police patrol the neighborhood and protect black women from harassment on the street, but their complaints sometimes led to their own arrest. While one interracial reform organization's May 1911 report noted that black street gangs emerged when black boys defended themselves "against similar gangs of poor white boys" and "colored boys of other streets," it also asserted that the incorrigible young boys had "no place of meeting except the streets." Black residents disagreed, arguing that gang members' "answer to whistle calls and yells at certain sections" were a nuisance and that these unruly young men obstructed and insulted black female residents.[153] After an incident in October that evinced these concerns, the *New York Age* reported that "for no reason whatsoever several law-abiding Negro citizens were arrested on the charge of loitering and fined $1." Earlier that spring, black residents had sent protests to the police regarding a "large crowd of colored ruffians who stand . . . nightly on the corner of 135th Street and Lenox Avenue and insult women." One night when some neighborhood black men "were standing on the corner engaged in conversation, while others were crossing the street," thirty-nine of them were "greatly surprised upon being informed that they were under arrest." The newspaper reported that "the police did not capture one of the rowdies; . . . the rowdies that . . . insult females nightly on the corners are . . . still at large."[154]

AFRICAN AMERICAN URBAN LIFE

At the same time that the police failed to protect black women, they harassed them on the ostensible grounds that they must be prostitutes. Many black women believed they had no recourse when harassed by police officers. Officers could arrest women on mere suspicion. If a woman did not have someone to vouch for her in court, she was likely to be imprisoned in the local jail, workhouse, reformatory, or state prison. In 1915, the National Urban League reported that "the large proportion of colored women arrested . . . is due . . . to policemen not hesitating to accost colored women when their suspicions are aroused."[155]

In an investigation of black women's cases heard in night court, an Urban League representative revealed a troubling but familiar story of police brutality against black women. A seventeen-year-old "weighing less than one hundred pounds" was charged with soliciting and beaten during her arrest. When she appeared in court, after being "in jail two days without attention of any kind," with a "lump on the back of her neck as large as one's fist" and "blood from the wound cover[ing] her clothing," the arresting officer explained to the judge that he had to use his nightstick during the arrest. After seeing the woman's condition, the magistrate "ordered a rigid investigation of . . . her arrest," leading to the dismissal of the charges against her. However, "the officer" who committed the physical abuse "was not reprimanded."[156] The Urban League presented this case as an example of the brutal treatment meted out to black women, as well as of the injustice of their disproportionate rates of arrest and imprisonment.

While black women's urban presence caused moral distress for black reformers, white police officers believed black women contributed to and exacerbated the problems of a city with a rapidly growing population of southern migrants and foreign immigrants. Their concerns were at odds with the needs and expectations of black women in the city, whether they were native-born, migrant, or immigrant.

The desire for a "fuller and freer life" influenced the decisions of many black women in New York City. The problems they encountered, from the difficulties of finding decent employment to their confrontations with the criminal justice system, reinforced the notion that their freedoms were more theoretical than practical. Black women were seen by many black reformers as "excess" as well as problematic and by many whites as exploitable and unimportant. The tenuous existence that black working-class women forged in New York was marked by both intra- and interracial tensions.

Black women vocally protested the problems they experienced. The physically exhausting personal-service positions to which most were relegated paid more than similar positions in the South, but black women kept looking for less-demanding work. Residential segregation required them to pay exorbitant rents for substandard housing. Black women struggled with poverty, domestic violence, and corrupt law enforcement. Their disproportionate numbers in relation to urban black men and their overrepresentation in the criminal justice system created moral anxieties for black reformers, who believed that the image of uncontrollable, single black women could endanger race progress.

W. E. B. Du Bois documented the difficulties faced by all black New Yorkers, whether native-born or migrant, male or female, but he expressed special concern about the presence of so many unmarried women. While describing the gender-specific demands of the northern city's labor market, Du Bois revealed great anxiety regarding the baneful influence of working-class black women on black morality and race progress. He identified the "excess" of black women as the major "peculiarity" of the black population and worried that single women jeopardized the patriarchal order. This view was unreflectively dismissive of urban black women's needs. Despite reformers' contention that the black community's dilemmas were directly linked to the presence and behavior of single black women, they could not ignore how black people's everyday problems in the city were exacerbated by corrupt law enforcement.

The problems that black women and their communities faced with the criminal justice system crystallized in 1900. When a newly arrived migrant's attempt to protect his common-law wife from a white plainclothes police officer ended with the officer's death, interracial tensions in New York's notorious Tenderloin district erupted in riot. The incident reveals the complex nature of black women's protection in early-twentieth-century New York as well as how black women were central to discussions regarding black racial advancement. It is quite telling that, in 1903, when Du Bois highlighted the "Historic Incidents Touching the Negro in New York," he characterized the 1900 melee as the "police riot against Negroes."[157] Du Bois and other black leaders privileged the consequences of the initial physical altercation instead of addressing the underlying issue, black women's protection from the police. May Enoch, the black woman at the center of the dispute, was equally central to the riot's significance.

2

the only one that would be interested in me

POLICE BRUTALITY, BLACK WOMEN'S PROTECTION, AND
THE NEW YORK RACE RIOT OF 1900

> He didn't say nothing to me; he took hold of me—this officer did. Arthur
> stepped up before he had a chance. . . . I judge it was about twenty minutes after
> that that I knew the officer had been injured by some person . . . did I think that
> Arthur did it . . . yes, because he was the only one there with him and the
> only one that would be interested in me.
>
> —May Enoch, August 22, 1900

According to May Enoch's statement about the events that took place on August 12, 1900, Arthur Harris had attempted to protect her from a physical assault.[1] The act of defending his common-law wife from attack in New York's Tenderloin district turned into more trouble than either could have ever imagined. Harris saw a white man assault Enoch and responded by confronting the assailant. The subsequent physical altercation between the two men left both Harris and plainclothes police officer Robert Thorpe injured. Two days later, Thorpe died—a white neighborhood cop killed by a black man who had recently migrated to the city. The news set off a race riot as white mobs attacked black residents. "A reign of terror" of this magnitude, one newspaper explained, had not been seen since the Civil War, when white mobs enraged by the imposition of the draft terrorized black men, women, and children.[2] In analyzing the 1900 disturbance, this chapter explores how black women's problematic encounters with police officers became the catalyst that inflamed existing tensions between black and white Tenderloin residents.[3] The objective here is to facilitate a more nuanced understanding of how working-class women and men relied on the language of respectability to reconfigure their relationship to the state, particularly its legal arm, to challenge myopic portrayals of the black urban body politic as innately criminal, and to enhance their life chances and experiences in a racially repressive society. A central theme of this chapter emphasizes the ways in which black working women's defense of their civil and human rights put them at odds with the state, white society, the black elite, and black working men. Taking seriously black women's experiences of urban violence and their need for protection expands our understanding of the riot's multifaceted meanings and consequences. This perspective emphasizes black New Yorkers' repeated demands for individual and community protection, as well as their efforts to link working-class respectability and first-class citizenship rights.[4]

May Enoch and Robert Thorpe's confrontation and Thorpe and Arthur Harris's altercation illuminate urban communities' and black women's responses to physical violence and police brutality.[5] Black New Yorkers routinely experienced problems with police officers, ranging from apathy and lack of protection to set-ups and harassment. In particular, policemen assaulted working-class women and especially black women like May Enoch with impunity.[6] Regardless of their socioeconomic status, black women struggled to be treated civilly and recognized as respectable. On more than a few occasions, their quest for respectable status and, by extension, the protections of first-class citizenship was aided by men such as Arthur Harris, who based their manhood on their ability to safeguard black women, themselves, and their community.

Concerns about the protection of black women were central to male leaders' ideas about racial advancement, yet directly addressing the experiences of black women in the city presented complex challenges. Living in a society in which all blacks were characterized as inferior and uncivilized, black leaders consistently sought to counter those images, especially as they related to masculinity and femininity, by emphasizing black people's adherence to appropriate behavior. In this sense, the black elite distinguished themselves from the working poor and positioned themselves as race leaders by arguing that they needed to uplift the masses. Racial uplift ideology stressed "self-help, racial solidarity, temperance, thrift, chastity, social purity, patriarchal authority, and the accumulation of wealth," yet respectability was deemed a key element in racial advancement, especially for women.[7] The politics of respectability, through focused attention to public displays of decorum, was thought to help prevent assaults on black women's bodies and character. Yet, as scholar Elsa Barkley Brown notes, "the struggle to present Black women and the Black community as 'respectable' eventually led to repression within the community."[8] Far too often, black women

AFRICAN AMERICAN URBAN LIFE

bore the brunt of this repression. Many incidents involving affronts to ordinary working women—without prominent black leaders and/or white employers to speak for their character—failed to receive legitimate attention as activists sought out the most respectable plaintiffs for their protests against police mistreatment.

The response of community leader Rev. William Henry Brooks to the 1900 riot provides evidence of this problem as well as the direct link between black manhood and womanhood. Brooks claimed that "all men, civilized and savage, protect their womanhood," yet he contended that the 1900 riot began with "bad whiskey, bad women, and corrupt police officers."[9] Although he criticized Harris for being drunk, he emphasized Harris's masculine duty to protect his woman. He extended no such consideration to Enoch, casting her as a "bad" woman rather than a victim of police assault, which forestalled much-needed discussions about police harassment of black women. Brooks's assessment was not unique in that he sought, as did other men of his time, to define black manhood through a Victorian ethos and language of chivalry and a turn-of-the-century emphasis on conquering the uncivilized through virility.[10] Resisting the prominent belief that a legacy of enslavement made black men effeminate, Brooks's statement countered such stereotypes by equating resolute black manhood with that of the dominant and powerful Anglo-Saxon man. Most importantly, Brooks contended that black men intuitively, whether they were savage or civilized, protected a respectable womanhood.[11] This meant that black women's moral behavior was always assessed in relation to a Victorian asexuality that sought to dispel racial stereotypes regarding a natural licentiousness allegedly recognized during enslavement. Living up to these parameters was difficult for working poor women who were often in the street unaccompanied by men—going to or coming back from work, the market, or a restaurant; visiting friends or attending church or group meetings; or simply being outside in the evening—which signaled for many that they were engaging in less than appropriate behavior and not worthy of protection.

When Enoch contended that Harris was the "only one that would be interested in" her, she revealed the challenges black women city-dwellers faced from the state as well as from their community protectors. The mainstream and black press, which devoted a considerable amount of attention to the incident and subsequent riot, focused on the interracial masculine conflict and failed to inquire about Enoch. Instead, they accepted Officer Thorpe's depiction of her as morally questionable and defined her as either a prostitute or the woman whom Harris believed he should protect. Unfortunately, their response to Enoch's assault was anything but exceptional. Black activists usually focused on the moral character of the female victim before addressing the prevalence of state-sponsored abuse. Under such circumstances, black women's most daunting predicaments emanated from their attempts to defend themselves both from physical assaults and from attacks on their moral character by black as well as white community leaders.

Enoch's experience with urban violence was shared by many other Tenderloin residents, male and female. The incident not only illuminates the shadow that the question of respectability cast over black women's protection but also highlights the central role that respectability played in conceptions of citizenship held by black working-class residents of the Tenderloin. Evidence from the 1900 disturbance demonstrates that black leaders and, just as importantly, working-class and impoverished residents protested publicly that their citizenship rights entailed police protection from mob violence. Outraged Tenderloin resident Benjamin McCoy argued that respectable black people expected, and "had a right to expect, to be protected," instead of being victimized by white mob violence and brutal police.[12] A *New York Times* editorial agreed with McCoy, noting that Arthur Harris's individual actions should not be used as an excuse for undermining the "right of orderly negroes to protection" and affirming "the obligation of the police to give that protection" to black New Yorkers.[13] In a distinct but related sense, Enoch's brief public utterance in her court testimony describes Harris's behavior differently. For her, he immediately responded by attempting to protect her from police brutality, which most urban women faced. The incident that triggered both sets of responses as well as the 1900 race riot underlines black women's need for protection from white police officers, while black residents' responses to it demonstrate the broader significance of safeguarding black communities from white city-dwellers.

The Promise of Patriarchal Protection

Responses to Arthur Harris's attempt to protect May Enoch reveal conflicting attitudes regarding the protection of black women.[14] The motivation behind Harris's defense of Enoch's black female body was complicated. The prevailing mythology among many whites, especially the police, portrayed black women traversing the streets as naturally promiscuous. In 1915, a National Urban League report found that the disproportionately high number of black women involved in New York City's criminal justice system stemmed from white officers having "little fear" that arresting and harassing black women without legitimate cause would result in dire "consequences."[15] Women like Enoch endured police brutality rather than enjoyed police protection. Black women in the urban North sought what scholar Farah Jasmine Griffin defines as "the promise of protection" from black men, which would grant "black women at least one of the privileges of femininity" and "restore a sense of masculinity to black men."[16]

African American men's efforts to defend African American women have a long, complex, and painful history. Dominant notions of femininity and of the protections that proper women deserved were inextricably linked to whiteness and often denied to women of color. A middle-class as well as a racialized nineteenth-century construction of what Barbara Welter called "true womanhood" centered on the virtues of "purity, piety, submissiveness, and domesticity."[17] Women's subordination and circumscription by domesticity compelled men to defend their honor and bodies from physical threat and sexual abuse. Indeed, during the late nineteenth and early twentieth centuries, white women's protection from the purported physical and sexual assaults by black men legitimized lynching. Feminist scholars have noted that the protection for white women espoused by the dominant rape-lynch narrative often worked to reinforce patriarchal claims on, rather than to physically defend, their bodies.[18] In contrast, black women's need for protection was, at best, ignored by white society. In the eyes of white men, especially but not exclusively southerners, black women never possessed the innate virtue and moral purity that ladyhood required. Rather, black women were held to be morally depraved and sexually promiscuous, as white women and men blamed the sexual harassment and rape they suffered under slavery on them rather than on their masters.[19]

At the same time that black women's long history of sexual abuse during enslavement and in freedom excluded them from the "promise of patriarchal protection," black men like Arthur Harris felt compelled to defend black women. In protecting black women, black men were asserting their own masculinity and even exerting power over women. While Griffin argues that "black male desire to 'protect' black women [grew] out of a sincere concern for their emotional, psychic, and physical safety," she also acknowledges that this desire stemmed from "the power struggle between black and white men" as well as between "black men and black women."[20] Harris's response to a companion's warning that "a man got your woman"[21] showed how black men's motivation in protecting their women could mirror that of their white counterparts. The act of defending Enoch legitimated Harris's manhood, as he lived up to the credo that "all men, civilized and savage, protect their womanhood." In this scenario, however, Enoch becomes a victim who is protected by Harris from physical assault as well as a dependent possession of her common-law husband. Such an erasure of Enoch's experience

Police Brutality and the New York Race Riot

and agency within the incident highlights how the "promise of patriarchal protection" could, as Griffin explains, "further victimize" black women.[22]

Working-class black women usually endured individual battles rather than receiving collective, engaged responses from black leaders when they experienced and complained of mistreatment by white authorities. Seeking to dispel negative images of black women, community leaders generally posed questions regarding these women's appropriate behavior before directing their queries at the police.[23] Adhering to a politics of respectability that challenged yet reinforced racism, middle-class black leaders stressed that suitable behavior demonstrated black people's morality and legitimized their first-class citizenship rights.[24] Black women's behavior and demeanor were heavily scrutinized by the dominant society as well as within their own communities. Similar to what historian Ellen Ross has revealed about working-class notions of respectability in pre–World War I London, urban blacks believed that "[w]omen . . . *embodied* respectability or the lack of it, in their dress, public conduct, language, housekeeping . . . and, of course, sexual behavior."[25] Symbolically, black women and their behavior were at the center of struggles for racial justice and ideas regarding racial progress.

In this one brief moment, May Enoch's appearance as a black woman on a New York City street challenged prevailing ideas about black womanhood and manhood. Specifically noting that she "had just got done talking with Arthur" when Thorpe "took hold of" her, Enoch described the scenario that set the tone for the two basic assumptions made by Thorpe and Harris. When Thorpe saw Enoch, a black woman, talking to a black man late at night, he assumed that she was a prostitute, failing even to imagine Harris and Enoch as a legitimate couple. Harris saw a white man "place . . . his hand" on Enoch and automatically sought to defend her from physical assault. Both men asserted their racialized masculinity. Thorpe believed that he had the ability to safeguard society from the threat of black women's criminal sexuality. Harris believed that he needed to safeguard a black woman from the threat of a white man's attack. Enoch's womanhood was simultaneously challenged and defended. When he verbally responded to Thorpe, "What are you doing that for? She ain't done anything," Harris voiced his frustration with hasty, racist and sexist policing practices. This interpretation underscored the fact that, whether or not Enoch was then or had ever been a prostitute, at that moment she had not solicited Harris as Thorpe assumed. In the end, Enoch's brief testimony regarding the incident reinforced her vulnerability and how she valued Harris's actions: he was "the only one that would be interested in" her.[26] Harris's interest in her began long before the altercation and had developed into a relationship that propelled the couple to begin a new life in New York City.

The "Negroes of the Tenderloin" and the New York City Police

Like many other black migrants at the turn of the century who encountered de facto segregation in housing, Enoch and Harris lived in the Tenderloin. The couple rented a room from Annie Johnson at 241 West Forty-first Street. Their housing was in close proximity to working-class Irish and German immigrant and poor native-born white neighborhoods, and they also lived in the midst of various commercial businesses such as the American Theatre, which was only four buildings away from their residence.[27] Described by scholars as "the most famous sex district in New York City history" as well as "Negro Bohemia," the Tenderloin was rife with problems that included interracial conflict, police corruption, and a range of behaviors such as "midnight fights, drunken orgies, and foul blasphemies."[28] According to Marilynn Johnson, the area "stretching from Twenty-third Street to Forty-second Street on the West Side . . . housed a strip of saloons, brothels, and dance halls along Sixth Avenue that moral reformers had dubbed 'Satan's Circus' in the late nineteenth century."[29] Newspaper clippings about arrests and trials collected by New York's district attorney show that the Tenderloin was notorious for rampant criminal activity.

Crime in the Tenderloin was often characterized as black crime, although reform activist Victoria Earle Matthews remarked pointedly that "degeneracy is degeneracy, regardless of the color of the degenerate."[30] Indeed, press reports described criminal acts committed by both white and black New Yorkers. For instance, a month before Harris and Enoch moved to the neighborhood, two white women visiting a friend on 553 West Forty-eighth Street at night were robbed by a white, male ex-convict.[31] Yet, despite these and other attacks on women, public discourse increasingly focused on women criminals, particularly black women. In 1899, police investigations of criminal activity highlighted the "Tenderloin Coon Gang," said to be composed of "negro women who haunt certain sections . . . and make a practice of nabbing [white] men."[32] As a result, police officers targeted blacks and women for arbitrary arrest. In June 1900, three white women arrested in the Tenderloin were acquitted when it was discovered that Detective Robert Binning, who declared that he had "arrested 3,000 women within a year," was the arresting officer. Their crime was that they were "found on the street at midnight after having visited" a relative. According to *The World*, Binning had arrested "more women" who had been "discharged than any other plain-clothes man in the Tenderloin Precinct." Though he had often been in court on charges of false arrest, Binning was always acquitted because of techni-calities.[33]

When Harris and Enoch settled among what Paul Laurence Dunbar called the "Negroes of the Tenderloin," the couple had to worry about not only neighborhood criminals but also a corrupt and violent police force. Having already lived in the urban North, Harris and Enoch were well aware of the challenges that surviving in a poverty-ridden and crime-infested neighborhood entailed. Harris had not been convicted of any crimes, but he did admit that he had "been locked up at times."[34] Following the trajec-tory of so many other migrants, they both came to New York City seeking a better life along with more favorable employment opportunities. Twenty-two-year-old Arthur Harris, a Virginia native described by one news report as "a coffee-colored," "slim, alert young fellow" who spoke "good English,"[35] had visited New York but lived in New Jersey. He worked at various jobs as a "cook, baker, carpenter and poolroom attendant" and met May Enoch in 1899. The twenty-year-old Enoch was not a transplant from the South but a native of Philadelphia. Having already left her husband of four years, she became the common-law wife of Arthur Harris a year and a half before they both moved to the Tenderloin.[36]

The district earned its name through its public reputation for graft. When police officer Alexander "Clubber" Williams was assigned to the Twenty-ninth Precinct in 1876, he commented, "I have had chuck for a long time and now I am going to eat tenderloin."[37] Williams's statement illumi-nates the long-standing and mutually sustained relationship between orga-nized crime, then called "vice," and the police. Referring to payoffs he would receive to protect "gambling, prostitution, and liquor interests," Williams knew that working in this neighborhood meant that he could afford the higher-priced tenderloin steak even if he chose not to eat it.[38] Williams's record illustrates how corruption and brutality pervaded policing in the Tenderloin and other working-class neighborhoods. While he was repri-manded for a particularly violent incident in 1879, "over the course of his career he faced eighteen charges of assaulting citizens but was never found guilty."[39]

Plainclothes policing often exacerbated the daily encounters between working-class residents and officers. Instituted in 1853 to "target gangs, vice operations, and other forms of organized crime," "strong-arm squads" had unlimited power to arrest and use clubs against working-class New York-ers. Immigrants and black migrants were special targets of their wrath.[40]

Over the years, officers justified their behavior by noting that they dealt with a very real criminal element, but they also targeted those groups and individuals who rejected unjust policing by filing complaints. Working-class and poor women were usually unable to obtain redress for mistreatment and false charges. In dealing with prostitution, plainclothes officers usually arrested women whom they noticed loitering and talking to men. When one officer was asked, "How do you know that [the] . . . woman is disorderly?" he provided a typical reply, "I know her to be a regular loiterer in the street. I arrested her after she had spoken to two men."[41] The courts generally deferred to the police officers' opinions.

In 1898, Magistrate Joseph Pool challenged the legitimacy of plainclothes policing, arguing that "it was wrong to send the policemen in citizen's clothes to make this kind of arrest" and questioning the dubious or non-existent evidence officers used in court. Pool consistently voiced his dissent and began dismissing charges of prostitution, some of which involved black defendants, because of the lack of credible evidence.[42] Responding to Pool's criticism of plainclothes officers, the Tenderloin's police captain contended that this strategy was "the best way of clearing the precinct of" criminals. "If the men were sent out on this work in uniform, the women would easily evade them." Plainclothes policing allowed officers to arrest more persons, which often led to court fines and/or imprisonment. Defending police practices and indicating his displeasure at Pool's decisions, the captain asserted: "Since I took charge of the precinct I have arrested 232 women of whom 212 have been fined. If you discharge these women you will be undoing my work."[43]

Although police officials emphasized the high numbers of prostitution arrests as proof of urban crime, critics focused on the corruption that arose when officers had the authority to arrest anyone on the street whom they identified as suspicious or disorderly. Most working-class women, particularly black women, were automatically regarded as dangerous, rather than endangered. Historian Mary Ryan argues that women in public were perceived as a threat to the public man, who was implicitly defined as white.[44] Consider Mrs. James Lockett, who, when questioned about her arrest, explained that she "couldn't understand" why she was being charged; the officer had said only that she "looked suspicious."[45] Since the dominant society imagined black women as inherently immoral, many were arrested for appearing disorderly as well as for alleged sexual offenses. Merely living in districts known for illegal activity reinforced prevailing notions about black people's criminality in general and black women's promiscuity in particular.

Assessments of the Tenderloin conflated the region's negative reputation with all of its working-class residents. The *Brooklyn Eagle* remarked sweepingly that the "neighborhood contains an ignorant and impulsive population, including both whites and blacks," and highlighted working-class whites "who loaf about the saloons . . . and . . . live in the tenement[s]."[46] Other newspapers racialized and criminalized black residents. "The metropolis is . . . full of vicious and dangerous negroes whose mere presence in the city is . . . a menace to law and order."[47] The *Brooklyn Citizen* described black men as embodiments of vice and a threat to white society: "The male negro of that vicinity seems to consider it incumbent upon him to go about armed with pistols, razors, or dirk knives, and as he is addicted to the use of bad whiskey, he is a dangerous and dreaded character. He appears to think that part of town belongs to him, and white people have had much to suffer at his hand of late."[48]

Negative press about the Tenderloin influenced how elite and middle-class blacks dealt with the district and its residents. While a number of prominent blacks spearheaded racial uplift initiatives and even patronized Marshall's Hotel, one of the neighborhood's respected saloons, most lived in Brooklyn.[49] In 1898, Alice Ruth Moore pleaded with her fiancé, Paul Laurence Dunbar, to not "go anywhere in the neighborhood." She believed that his presence in the Tenderloin was problematic: "I want you to be dignified, reserved, difficult to access. You cheapen yourself too often by being too friendly with inferior folks, and your wife doesn't want it. You will be better appreciated if you are more reserved."[50] While Moore's request highlighted her class prejudices and personal anxieties regarding her future with Dunbar, it also reinforced a popular and essentialized attitude about the Tenderloin and its residents.

In a letter to the editor published in the *New York Sun* the previous year, Dunbar indirectly responded to his fiancée's persistent concern that associating with "Negroes of the Tenderloin" might mar his reputation. More explicitly, he affirmed his duty to the urban black working class and racial uplift specifically. He argued that the "better-class Negro . . . must lift not only himself, but the lower men, whose blood brother he is. . . . He cannot afford to look down upon the denizens of the Tenderloin or to withdraw himself from them, for the fate of blacks there, degraded, ignorant, vicious as they may be, is . . . his fate." Dunbar was convinced that black migration to New York was creating a host of problems for the race: "The gist of the whole trouble lies in the flocking of ignorant and irresponsible Negroes to the great city. If that could be stopped, if the metropolitan could vomit them back again, the whole matter would adjust itself. . . . For the influx continues and increases year after year."[51] Disregarding the desire of black migrants to "live a fuller, freer life," Dunbar despaired of migrants' dreams, equating these people with their troubles and condemning them as maladjusted, backward, and even uncivilized. "They say that they have not rights in the South: but better the restrictions there than a seeming liberty which blossoms noxiously into license."[52] Dunbar simultaneously blamed black migrants for the predicaments they faced and criticized the urban North's racism for the predicaments black migrants as well as native black New Yorkers confronted.

Victoria Earle Matthews agreed with Dunbar's assessment, but in a follow-up editorial she cautioned him as well as the *Sun*'s readers not to categorize all black New Yorkers as criminals but to remember that many community members were upstanding, respectable citizens. While acknowledging the prevalence of crime and vice among blacks, she complained that "the weaknesses and shortcomings of no race are more paraded and discussed in the public prints than those of the Afro-American." "The conditions described by Mr. Dunbar cannot fairly be confined to the Afro American portion of the Tenderloin." Matthews argued that immigrants—Italians, Irish, Germans, Hungarians, Swedes, and so on—exhibited equal weaknesses even though "these peoples are not tainted with the moral blight of two hundred and fifty years of American slavery to fight against." Invoking the burdensome legacy of enslavement was not an excuse for blacks' illegal behavior but rather a springboard from which to highlight the significant advances by the black race since emancipation. "Why do not writers like Mr. Dunbar make the same effort to show the world the struggles the heart-rending sacrifices of the honest, hard-working progressive black?" Matthews pointed proudly to the "Afro American women" who worked in the recently formed White Rose Mission as exemplars of respectability, showing that the race was "not represented by the 'Tenderloin negro,' a class steadily advancing in the homely virtues and the respect of their fellow men." Instead of placing all of the blame on the inability of impoverished black migrants to survive urban life, she called for more efforts by the "better class of Afro Americans" for racial uplift and attention to the structural problems that Tenderloin residents faced, especially unemployment, insufficient wages, and high rents for squalid housing.[53]

Activists such as Dunbar and Matthews illuminate the myriad challenges migrants encountered. As newcomers coped with issues arising in their transition from the rural and urban South to the urban North, they also dealt with black New Yorkers' interracial and intraracial problems. Both reformers failed to address the dilemmas most black women experienced when they were forced to fight off criminals as well as the police. Black women traversing the streets had countless encounters with violent physical assault. Although black men attempted to protect them, as the case of Arthur Harris and May Enoch shows, they were often prompted, out of necessity, to defend themselves.

Black Women Protecting Themselves

The fact that black women's bodies could be violated with impunity is one of the basic ways in which they were denied protection as female citizens. While scholars have addressed the institutionalized rape of black women in the South during and after enslavement,[54] the historical record in New York City shows that black women continued to be physically assaulted after escaping Jim Crow, not only by ordinary men but also by police officers who could legitimately use force against them.[55] In New York, black women were consistently arrested on false charges and oftentimes violently harassed by police officers.[56] Marilynn Johnson has observed that "for working-class women—and for black women especially—merely being on the street at night made them morally and criminally suspect; their attempts to resist or to protest that stigma sometimes resulted in police beatings."[57] Yet these women were not simply victims; that perspective would underestimate the significance of their attempts at self-defense.

Black women of all class positions, each in her own way, struggled to safeguard their bodies and reputations. Using her writing as public protest, scholar and activist Anna Julia Cooper reported in *A Voice from the South* (1892) numerous "instances of personal violence to colored women travelling" throughout the United States, especially in the South and West. Cooper described the specific dangers black women faced: they were "forcibly ejected from cars, thrown out of seats, their garments rudely torn," and their bodies "wantonly and cruelly injured."[58] In 1883, Ida B. Wells fought back physically against the conductor who was trying to remove her from the "ladies' car," experiencing "rough handling and the tearing of her jacket"; she was thrown off the train only after she had bitten him on the hand. She then fought the Memphis C & O Railroad in court but was disappointed when her legal victory was overturned on appeal.[59] During this period, black women also acted collectively in defense of themselves.

In 1893, the activist and author Frances Ellen Watkins Harper declared that Americans were standing on "the threshold of woman's era" and called upon organized womanhood to defeat both the "lawlessness" represented by lynching and prostitution, euphemistically known as "the social evil."[60] Harper argued that black women's political activism was central to the advancement of the race. Indeed, the formal establishment of the National Association of Colored Women's Clubs (NACW) in 1896 and what became its official newspaper, *The Woman's Era*, illustrated the collective power of black women to protect themselves and the race through uplift work on the local and national levels.[61] Most clubwomen were engaged in professional careers as teachers, journalists, authors, and reformers who publicly addressed and defended the image of black women. They also used the law and components of physical self-protection. Many of these women's attempts to gain civil treatment stemmed from struggles to attain class-based, as well as racially equitable, public accommodations in theaters, restaurants, and stores, as well as on railroad cars.[62] Barbara Welke's work shows how women of color fought railroad companies when they paid for first-class ladies' accommodations and were physically removed when conductors argued that they were not white and therefore not ladies.[63]

Countless unknown black women experienced similar maltreatment at the hands of New York City's police officers. In several instances, these working-class women physically defended themselves when they were attacked. In 1905, thirty-year-old Benita Goode, a domestic worker, stuck a penknife in the arm of a plainclothes police officer after he pushed her in the road and handled her "pretty rough."[64] Twenty-two-year-old Agnes Green explained in 1909 that she assaulted an officer with a hat pin because "he hit . . . me."[65] In a 1926 case, a twenty-one-year-old "nurse girl" recalled that a man on the street asked her, "How old are you and where are you going?" Not knowing that her questioner was a plainclothes police officer who was investigating a house with a bad reputation where she had recently delivered a message, she thought that his questions seemed disrespectful and "very fresh," so she replied, "I am my own woman and you mind your business." The officer arrested her, showing her his badge and telling her, "Shut up, . . . don't get snotty or I'll smack you down."[66] From Wells's 1883 confrontation on the train to this 1926 incident in the street, black women demanded respectful treatment. Without the public platforms that clubwomen such as Cooper, Harper, and Wells commanded, most working-class and poor women faced incidents with police officers alone. While they advocated black women's protection theoretically and were aware of the racialized and gendered pattern of police harassment, black male leaders seldom took up the cause of ordinary black women who were insulted in the street.

In the late nineteenth century, a small number of police brutality cases involving ordinary black women were publicized in the New York press because the arrests called police behavior into question.[67] Although these cases do not indicate any public outrage over the physical abuse black

Police Brutality and the New York Race Riot

women experienced, they show that black women rejected negative stereotypes and claimed that they should be treated with respect. Over one weekend in 1879, the *New York Times* published three cases of police brutality against black women. After leaving a wake "at an early hour" on a Friday morning, Bessie Striker and Maria Simpson, who protested that they were respectable women, said that a police officer "abused them in a shameful manner, and finally wound up his abuse by beating them unmercifully with his fists." Late on Sunday night, Alice Archer said, she was accosted by an officer who "called her foul names, struck her with his fist, and knocked her down." Christine Cousins said she was assaulted on Sunday morning by a police officer who first "beat her with a club about the body, struck her in the face with his fist," and then proceeded to arrest and charge her with "soliciting."[68] Cousins's case was dismissed after she spent a night in jail. Her circumstances, like those of the other complainants, as a lone black woman on the street harassed by a police officer, are similar to what May Enoch experienced in 1900. Police officers' claims that these women were prostitutes played a major role in each case. These women's respectable status within their own communities did not keep them from being assaulted, arrested, and charged with a criminal offense.

Complaints against white police officers that highlighted their mistreatment of black women reflect the officers' presumption that black women were criminal: their very presence in public was disorderly and signified that they were prostitutes soliciting clients. Significantly, the criminalization of all black women must be contextualized within the larger framework of society's tendency to masculinize African American women. Not all, but many, law enforcement officials regarded black women as unfeminine and undeserving of respect. In 1888, patrolman Herman M. Koenig and Dora Coleman were both arrested for disorderly conduct after a fight. Coleman explained that the officer had "dragged her out of the house . . . kicked and beat her and finally fired a shot from his revolver at her." Officer Koenig stated that Coleman, along with another black woman, had attempted to rob him, forcing him to shoot. In the end, the charges were dropped against the officer, while Coleman was jailed for a month because she could not afford her $300 bail.[69] In 1894, Mrs. Jane Abbott complained that plainclothes police officer Joseph Cassidy forcibly invaded her home while he was drunk, looking for a policy (gambling) shop. When Cassidy entered her bedroom, Abbott, not knowing that he was a police officer, was furious and twice asked him "what authority he had to force his way into . . . [her] apartment." Cassidy responded by shouting and pointing a revolver in Abbott's face as well as at her daughter, leaving the home only when Abbott shouted

"Murder!" out her window. Her attempt to get help from a neighborhood policeman proved futile when Abbott revealed that her assailant was a fellow officer.[70]

Adherence to the politics of respectability and class status made no difference when police officers acted on myths about black women's propensity for immorality. In 1886, Mrs. Fannie Belkizer filed a complaint against the police department after she was beaten by an officer with a club and thrown in jail overnight for alleged drunkenness and disorderly conduct.[71] Initially, Belkizer's broken and dislocated jaw prevented her from verbally defending herself in court against the officer's charges; the judge seemed to ignore her when she repeatedly pointed to her lower jaw, which was reportedly "limp and bloody." Her husband, described as a "respectable looking colored man," got her released by paying the ten-dollar fine and then contacted the *Times* to report the incident. According to his wife, she had been attending a society meeting and was on her way home when an officer made an insulting remark to her. When she responded with indignation, he kicked her in the side. As a result of the blow, she lost her balance and fell toward him "to save herself and he struck her on the chin with his club, breaking . . . [her] jaw bone in two places and dislocating it on one side." While in custody, she received no medical attention. Her husband took her to Roosevelt Hospital after she was released. Literally adding insult to injury, the couple was denied service "on the grounds that a dental hospital was the proper place for her." Belkizer was finally admitted to Mount Sinai Hospital, where she was treated—but only after she waited two days for the swelling to decrease enough that her jaw could be properly set. She also faced the possibility of "being permanently disfigured."[72]

Unlike May Enoch and other working women, Mrs. Belkizer was a member of New York's black middle class. Because she was the wife of a "colored caterer well-known to many respectable white families in the city," Belkizer's reputation was defended by several prominent white New Yorkers. Dr. Pallen, a former employer, praised her as a "very estimable and hardworking woman" whose character was beyond reproach and protested that her treatment by the police was reprehensible:

> She has been a servant in my family for years, and I intrusted her with the nursing of my mother when in her last illness. I cannot believe, from what I know of the woman, that she could possibly have been either drunk or disorderly, as charged. The assault upon her was most brutal and what she must have suffered during the night of her imprisonment, with a broken and dislocated jaw, and without any

medical or other means of alleviating her suffering, is simply inde-
scribable. . . . I can only say that what she went through . . . surpassed
everything in the line of the horrible that I have met with my practice
as a surgeon.[73]

Several other white New Yorkers agreed with Pallen's assessment, and "a
number of influential gentlemen" proposed to "secure a hearing" because
"the case . . . was denied that privilege in police court." Although the out-
come of Belkizer's appeal is not known, black women like her found that
when white employers testified about their moral respectability and domestic efficiency, their position in the criminal justice system improved.

Belkizer's experience shows that for black woman, middle-class status
was always precarious. Nevertheless, her situation was mitigated by her
socioeconomic advantages: most working-class black women were unable
to pay fines, receive medical attention, or obtain positive references from
white employers ready to support their black employees. May Enoch's experience on a New York City street was more typical of the cases of working-
class black women like Bessie Striker, Maria Sampson, Alice Archer, and
Christine Cousins—with the significant difference that black male protection was immediately extended to her. Exploring Enoch's experiences brings
into sharper focus black working women's encounters with the legal arm of
the state, as well as a more in-depth understanding of the events that precipitated the infamous race riot of 1900. Enoch and Harris are remembered
not because they attempted to improve their lives and defend themselves in
the city but because their names are associated with the explosive racial and
ethnic tensions of early-twentieth-century New York.

Black Women's Protection, Urban Violence, and the 1900 Race Riot

Most accounts of May Enoch and Arthur Harris attest to the brevity of their
time in the Tenderloin rather than revealing any noticeable character flaws.
Interviewed after the incident, one black resident recalled that he had seen
Harris "in the neighborhood" for "about a week," although he "didn't know
him at that time by name."[74] Edward Rounds, a white watchman at the
American Theatre, noted that he knew Thorpe "pretty well" and he had seen
Harris "in that neighborhood before and knew him by the title of Kid Harris." Rounds routinely surveyed the streets as he stood guard late at night.
"It being a hard neighborhood," he "generally watch[ed] anybody that ain't
right."[75] Yet he did not know or recognize May Enoch. It is not clear how
much the couple knew about the neighborhood or was aware of what it

meant to live in such close proximity to the Twentieth Precinct. Indeed, both Enoch and Harris failed to recognize Thorpe, who was reportedly regarded by black residents as a "terror . . . [who] made it a point to stand near the corner" where the incident occurred "on and off duty and club and abuse black men and women at will."[76] Samuel Thorpe also recalled that his brother had a contentious relationship with black residents, arguing that the officer's behavior was "too antagonistic" and that the "colored people hated him but he did not care."[77] During the two weeks of their residency in New York, the couple encountered no significant difficulties until Thorpe attempted to arrest Enoch for solicitation on early Sunday morning, August 12, 1900.[78]

Like most Tenderloin residents on the night of Saturday, August 11, Enoch and Harris were outside because New York was experiencing one of the hottest days ever recorded. With thermometer readings as high as 95 degrees, along with stifling humidity, many tenement residents headed outside to their stoops and neighborhood saloons in order to find some relief.[79] Harris recalled that he "had bought food for Sunday" but "it was too hot to make a fire" in their room. As a result, the couple changed their dinner plans and at 1 A.M. decided to go to "Dobbins' restaurant." On the way, Harris "stopped at McBride's [saloon] . . . to get a cigar and a drink." Harris emphatically denied drinking alcohol, saying that he got a "ginger ale . . . everyone knows I don't drink whisky or beer." While Harris was in McBride's, Enoch was "waiting on the outside" for him. Impatient with the delay, Enoch attempted to retrieve Harris so they could go on to the restaurant when she caught the attention of a plainclothes police officer.[80]

At about 2 A.M., Officer Robert Thorpe tried to arrest May Enoch, at Forty-first Street and Eighth Avenue. Thorpe apparently had seen her enter McBride's saloon, converse with a man, and then come back outside to wait. He thought she had solicited a customer. Instead, she had asked Harris to leave the saloon. When Harris finally left the bar, a friend immediately pointed out to him that "a man got your woman."[81] Later, arguing that he was unaware that Thorpe was a police officer, Harris said he only saw Thorpe, a white man, harassing his wife by "hunching her . . . with his arm pushing her." Harris then attempted to defend Enoch by questioning Thorpe's actions. "What is the trouble, what are you abusing or assaulting her in this way for?" Harris reportedly asked. Thorpe responded, "It is none of your business. Don't you like it?" When Harris replied, "No," Thorpe then turned, releasing Enoch, who ran home, and repeatedly struck Harris's head with his club. Harris retaliated or, rather, as he argued, defended himself by stabbing Thorpe.[82]

Police Brutality and the New York Race Riot

69

Arthur Harris's attempt to protect his common-law wife had grave repercussions for Harris, Enoch, Thorpe, and black residents in the Tenderloin. Harris escaped the crime scene, left New York City, and was later caught in his mother's home in Washington, DC, where he was charged with first-degree murder. Enoch was arrested immediately after the incident and sent to New York City's House of Detention, a local jail, where her bail was set at $500.[83] The twenty-six-year-old Thorpe was admitted to Roosevelt Hospital at 2:15 A.M. and died at 8:45 A.M. the next day from "post-operative shock." White Tenderloin residents became enraged that their popular white police officer, who was engaged to the daughter of a local police captain, was murdered as a result of being "assaulted by a colored man while trying to make an arrest."[84]

Three days after the incident, at 11 P.M., near Robert Thorpe's home during his wake, a fight between a black man, Spencer Walters, and a white man, Thomas J. Healy, escalated into the notorious New York race riot of 1900. After Thorpe's death, tensions had been running high in the neighborhood between black newcomers and ethnic whites, who were competing for employment, housing, and social space. White residents irritated by the growing black population in the Tenderloin district and incensed by Thorpe's death beat Walters and any other black residents they found on the street.[85] The *New York Age* reported that "every Afro-American who was caught out after 8 o'clock between 29th and 43rd streets and Seventh and Ninth avenues barely escaped death at the hands of the mob and the police."[86] The riot ended at 3 A.M., when an hour-long torrential rainstorm dispersed the rioters from the streets, but there were numerous after-currents in the days ahead.[87]

The ferocious, four-hour riot alerted the nation to the fact that racial violence was not confined to the South. Attention had focused on mobs of white southerners who attacked blacks in Wilmington, North Carolina (1898), and New Orleans, Louisiana (July 1900), but the everyday violence meted out to New York blacks and the urban poor had been disregarded. The intensity of the 1900 race riot and its similarity to southern violence altered that attitude. A number of commentators about the disturbance remarked that the North was becoming "southernized."[88] The Tenderloin riot exposed whites' deep-seated animosity toward blacks. The Reverend Dr. Dean Richmond Babbitt, rector of the Protestant Episcopal Church of the Epiphany, told his congregation sadly, "We thought that race hatred had died in the great convulsion of the civil war. . . . But that race hatred has survived."[89] Newspaper accounts of the riot made the same point:

The reports in this morning's paper of last nights riot in which negroes, regardless of age, sex, or innocence, were indiscriminately attacked by a frenzied mob read more like the account of some fierce lawlessness in the remote regions of the South or Far West than an actual occurrence in the metropolis of the nation. Indeed, common as have been the horrible stories of Southern lynchings, rarely has there come from that quarter an account of a race riot so reckless and inexcusable as that of which the news startled New York this morning.[90]

The extreme violence that occurred during the 1900 Tenderloin race riot contradicted the civilized image of race relations in New York and forced enlightened whites to face the long-standing racial and ethnic tensions in the city. White southerners, angered by the northern press's criticisms of poor race relations and mob violence in their region, pointed out New Yorkers' hypocrisy regarding the "negro problem." Under a headline proclaiming that New Yorkers "Should Condemn [the] South Less," W. R. Carter, editor of Jacksonville, Florida's *Evening Metropolis*, contended that northerners "should say less about alleged Southern outrages and take the beam out of their own eye." Carter commented that the riot "shows that race prejudice exists in New York and that even with her big police force negroes could not be protected there."[91] The *New York Sun* commented that the unrest paralleled the racial violence during the Draft Riots of 1863, but more importantly it described the riot as "a crying disgrace to that civilization which arraigns Southern treatment of the negro; a humiliation to the first community in the land, where the civil and political rights of the colored man have for a generation been jealously defended."[92]

In light of the fact that the police regularly terrorized Tenderloin residents, regardless of their race or ethnicity, the specificity of the brutality against black residents reinforced the notion that the riot was fueled by police officers' retaliation for Thorpe's death and by white native-born and immigrant residents' hostility to the increasing numbers of black migrants.[93] Later official investigations called the night of violence a "negro riot," which would be a misnomer except for the fact that black people were the only victims and the only persons arrested during the melee.[94] After conducting their own investigation, two white observers concluded that "the whole aim . . . was to catch Negroes." Several days after the incident, a man who said that he "had been a leader in the riots and would do it again" told them that the basic sentiment of white rioters was "that the 'niggers' must be treated the same as down South."[95] Thomas Hughes, another white wit-

Police Brutality and the New York Race Riot

ness, stated that "all whom I saw struck were colored persons, and I noticed that as a peculiar fact."[96] Even a white judge commented on the police violence against black residents. After seeing a steady line of black defendants in his court, he began discharging some of them. He concluded: "It seems the white trash of the Twentieth Precinct set upon the negroes last night to avenge the atrocious murder of Policeman Thorpe by a bad negro. Some innocent persons were evidently very much ill-treated. I should like to have before me some of the white persons who participated in this riot."[97]

Many blacks who knew about Thorpe's death had no idea that there would be any type of violent retaliation. Albert Saunders's account indicates how residents were taken by surprise and punished for one black man's actions. "On August 15th I left my work at night and walked up 8th Avenue toward my home. About 38th Street a crowd ran at me, somebody struck me, and I staggered, and then I received another blow that cut open my head and made me speechless. I found myself in the hands of an officer, who took me to the station house, where my wounds were dressed. I stayed there till about four A.M. A number of colored men were brought in by officers, some of them cut, and bleeding, like myself."[98] As the riot progressed, the mob not only attacked blacks on the streets but also entered individual homes. After hearing the rioters near her building, Mrs. Kate Jackson thought rioters would "do her and her children bodily harm, and possibly murder." A terrified Jackson "caught up her youngest child (three years old) in her arms, and in her frenzy and fright jumped out the window on to a shed" and into "the yard."[99] Although no deaths were reported, the mob's anger toward blacks seemed to know no bounds. As Headly Johnson, a Pullman car porter, boarded a streetcar, he heard the crowd shouting, "There's another nigger! Kill him! Lynch him!"[100]

A number of police officers were reported to have protected black residents from mobs, yet other officers chose to ignore the violence. Black residents who sought protection from the police soon learned that their attempts were futile. Despite their knowledge of police corruption and bias, many were surprised by police officers' overt refusal to protect them. A "neatly dressed" black woman who disembarked from a streetcar was surrounded by a mob, "which began to threaten her." Seeing a policeman, she pleaded: "God bless you, Mr. Cop. Let me walk along with you as far as my house. It's only a little way down." Turning away, the policeman reportedly responded, "Go to h—l, d—m you."[101] William and Annie Hamer, who were musicians, were "dragged from the [street]car" and separated by a mob that beat him with "sticks and stones" and struck her in the mouth with a brick.[102] Mr. Hamer recalled that "there were at least a dozen policemen standing around. They did nothing, and made no effort to protect me."[103]

Most citizens' reports noted that police officers were not only indifferent toward black residents but actually participated alongside white rioters. Black men and women bore the brunt of violence from the police as well as the mob.[104] Belle Johnson remarked: "It was a shame when police officers, who were supposed to be protecting peaceable citizens, assaulted them in such a brutal manner."[105] Walter Gregory reported, "I did not know that the people who broke into the house were policemen. I thought they were the rioters."[106] John Wolf explained, "The mob and the police chased me." But Wolf said specifically, "The police hurt me . . . more than the rioters."[107] Officers took John Hains "by the shoulders, . . . feet dragging," from his fourth-floor residence "out into the street." Mrs. Louise Francis, the building's resident housekeeper, described how she had to wash away his blood "from the fourth floor down the staircase to and on each and every landing and including the vestibule."[108] Some bystanders and residents attempted to intervene, physically and through verbal chastisements, but were unable to prevent the assaults. Thomas Hughes, a white resident, remembered that after seeing a black man beaten, he "tried to wipe blood from him" but was stopped by an officer who "spoke roughly and ordered [him] away."[109]

Residents' realization that their civil rights were jeopardized by antiblack violence shaped their responses to the riot. While especially disappointed and discouraged by police brutality, they framed their protests by invoking their strongest argument against assault: that they were first-class citizens rather than criminals and that they embodied respectability.

Black Working-Class Respectability and Struggles for Justice

The black community members most affected by the riot articulated their own sense of respectability and morality in their affidavits regarding the disturbance. Their varied descriptive responses coalesced around these working-class people's everyday attempts to maintain respectability. Their individual testimonies provide explicit details regarding the terrorism they experienced during the riot. They consistently protested that they came from stable backgrounds and upheld moral standards, so they did not deserve the ill-treatment meted out to them. Collectively, these men's and women's statements illuminate the ways in which working-class blacks understood the varied components of respectability. While the doctors, lawyers, ministers, teachers, and businessmen who responded to the riot were generally regarded as moral and respectable, black working-class residents were aware of the stigma associated with their socioeconomic position. They felt compelled to emphasize the respectability of their labor as well as their appropriate and law-abiding behavior, insisting that those factors were important components of their identity.[110] They contended that black urban communities deserved police protection. Their protests against mob violence and police brutality illustrate working-class black activism in turn-of-the-century New York.

While the Tenderloin was seen as a vice-ridden neighborhood, the black activists protesting the brutal treatment of blacks made clear distinctions between respectable working-class blacks and those blacks judged to be lawless and immoral.[111] In this instance, elite black leaders bypassed simplistic renderings of class dynamics that categorized black communities as composed of the morally respectable middle class and elite uplifting the ignorant, immoral working-class masses. While Rev. W. H. Brooks, pastor of St. Marks Methodist Episcopal Church, argued that "colored people who break the laws must not expect sympathy from us,"[112] he supported a communitywide consensus that "insisted that [Harris] . . . was only one man, and that the race ought not to be blamed for his action."[113]

Responses to the 1900 New York riot reveal the complex class dynamics in black communities. Black leaders, instead of making their conventional arguments for racial uplift, recognized, rather than ignored, the fact that respectable, working-class blacks lived in the Tenderloin. Indeed, these leaders emphasized that working-class black people could lead respectable lives even in problematic neighborhoods. Brooks noted that "not . . . a single tough character [was] among the number maltreated but decent, honest, hardworking people."[114] Frank Moss, the white legal counsel for several black defendants, contended that "the dissolute Negroes who are . . . so often seen lounging about the 'Tenderloin' and its neighborhood are . . . not to be found among . . . my witnesses."[115] In his most extreme statement, Moss claimed that police officers planned the riot so well that they notified "dissolute" blacks of the impending racial violence. Instead of acknowledging that he and other leaders chose the most respectable working-class residents as witnesses, he emphasized that black delinquents were "friends of the police . . . and it is . . . quite clear that they had their warning and kept out of the way."[116] Based on his collection of affidavits, Moss argued that only respectable blacks were attacked and injured, while the police deliberately ignored black criminals. By defining the mob victims as respectable, Moss underlined the horror that law-abiding citizens rather than criminals were targeted.

Moss's black deponents provided a wide range of statements about the riot, but all attested that their identity as respectable citizens stemmed from their work ethic. The Tenderloin's working-class residents filled a variety of occupations, although most held personal-service positions. Each statement spoke of their labor as one of the primary sources of their respectability.[117] Whether they signed their statements with a name or with an X, mothers, fathers, daughters, sons, siblings, in-laws, and friends stressed the fact that they worked. They explained how they became aware of the riot, or were caught up in it, as a result of being at work, coming home from work, going to work, or going to sleep before they went to work. John Hains began his statement by emphasizing his status as a worker: "I am a laborer, and am at present employed as a longshoreman at Pier 16. . . . I went to bed as usual at about 9:30 o'clock. About two o'clock in the morning I was awakened by somebody beating me on the back with a club."[118] "Waiters, porters, elevator operators, chimney sweeps, . . . longshoremen," and housekeepers filed affidavits that expressed their belief in the respectability of labor.[119]

Mindful of the neighborhood's notoriety, yet incensed by their ill-treatment, residents emphasized that they were sober, peaceable, and law-abiding citizens without criminal records. While residents who provided affidavits were most likely chosen to strengthen Frank Moss's case against the police force, the ways in which they emphasized their character attest to their awareness that their reputations were always in question. Charles Bennett, a singer who worked at a Coney Island saloon, stated that he had lived in the "City of New York for the past fifteen years" but had "never been arrested before" and had "always been a quiet, law-abiding citizen."[120] Stephen Small said that he was "perfectly sober and was not creating any disturbance, and that the assault by the police officers was . . . entirely unjustified and an outrage."[121] Elevator operator William L. Hall explained that he was a "peaceable, law-abiding citizen and a member of St. Mark M. E. Church."[122] George L. Meyers declared that he was "perfectly sober" and had "never been arrested in his life." He explained that he was downstairs because, as the janitor of the building, "it was his duty to be where he was at that time."[123] When asked if his altercation with the police stemmed from the fact that he might have been "in a fighting mood," cigar maker James Lockett immediately responded, "No, sir; I am no fighting man; I am a working man."[124]

Female victims who filed affidavits recounting the acts of violence perpetrated against them and who were deemed respectable received the community's most heartfelt commiseration. Many affidavits showed that female residents were either married or with a respectable man when they were

This sketch of Lavinia Johnson's beating captures the brutal violence that black women experienced during the 1900 riot. The caption notes: "The mob dragging Lavinia Johnson, a colored woman, from an Eighth Avenue car at Forty-third street. The rioters pelted her with stones and clubs until passengers on the car and the police rescued her."
From The World, *Thursday Evening, August 16, 1900.*

attacked. Mrs. Maria Williams emphasized that she kept house "for herself and her husband."[125] As Judith Weisenfeld contends, these black women were never entirely distinguished from the black men who reportedly experienced the most violence during the riot.[126] Single women like Carrie Wells proved their moral propriety by explaining their background and providing references for who could "vouch for [their] character."[127] In the eyes of black community leaders, the protection of black women was, indeed, predicated on the condition that these women were deemed respectable.

In addition to ascertaining what established black leaders and white people thought about the black women who lived in the Tenderloin, it is equally important to probe what these women thought about themselves. The women's affidavits show that black women did not agree with prevailing stereotypical images of them. While Mrs. Rosa Lewis was beaten by a police officer with a club, she also objected to the fact that the officer spoke to her "in an insulting and ill-natured manner."[128] Female deponents knew that their words were not enough to prove their innocence, however. In the face of long-standing assessments of their supposedly dangerous sexuality and innate criminality, black women understood the importance of establishing individual moral legitimacy so their complaints about the police and the mob would be taken seriously. Among the more than seventy affidavits addressing the violence meted out against black Tenderloin residents, statements by older women, like Mrs. Lucinda Thomson, reinforced the accounts of other women, especially those who were young or single.[129] At the end of Lucy Jones's narrative, in which she recalled one of the most heinous attacks against her neighbor as well as how she was verbally threatened when the mob shouted, "Look at the d—d nigger wench. . . . Shoot her! Shoot her!," she made sure to stress that she "was a widow."[130] Most black women emphasized their marital status, provided references to employers or ministers who could attest to their upstanding character, and explained their commitment to motherhood. Some black women spoke for themselves. Mrs. Irene Wells said that she was "a widow, and the sole support of her five children, by doing general housework, ironing, and washing, etc., and has done so for the past seven years: that she is a thoroughly respectable woman, and is . . . peaceful and quiet at all times, and deems this assault by the police officer . . . an outrage, and without cause or provocation."[131] Wells's statement illuminates her definition of respectability and expresses the outrage that she and most black women felt in response to the attacks on themselves and their community.

In addition to the violent beatings suffered by men and women during the riot, working-class blacks sustained severe economic repercussions. Many residents could barely subsist on their wages, but now they had to pay fines and medical bills. The jail time that residents served as a result of their inability to pay fines placed their jobs in jeopardy. Some were unable to pay for adequate medical care. After going to Roosevelt Hospital three times, fifteen-year-old Harry Reed said, "I don't think I will go any more, but [I] still have to wear a bandage and dress my head."[132] Police officers stole valuables or money when they searched for weapons. Pullman porter Richard Taylor recalled that after the police attacked him in his home, he found that the money that he was saving for college tuition ("between sixty and seventy dollars") was missing; the six dollars that his wife, Mrs. Margaret Taylor, had in her satchel was also missing.[133] Other statements reveal that victims' injuries prevented them from going to work. John Wolf, who was beaten by the police during the riot as well as in a separate incident a month later, reported that in his last beating his "face swelled and mouth almost closed." Wolf declared, "I am poor and cannot work now."[134] William Elliot stated that his "head was swollen half its size again" and he "could hardly open [his] . . . mouth," which made him "unable to work for

Police Brutality and the New York Race Riot

two days."[135] Some bodily injuries were so severe that victims were disabled. After hiding in a cellar the night of the riot and being beaten by the police before he went home the next day, Stephen Small explained that he was "unable to lay flat on [his] back without suffering extreme pain."[136] Women found themselves unable to care for their families. After being beaten on the back with a police officer's club, Mrs. Rosa Lewis said that she was "lame in my back and suffered pain from it for a number of days."[137] "Confined to her bed with shock, fright, and bruises," Mrs. Kate Jackson not only was "lame and unable to walk"[138] but, as her sister noted, was also unable to fulfill her responsibilities as a worker and mother.[139]

Residents experienced psychological ramifications as well. After the riot, many victims were too frightened to leave their homes or temporary sanctuaries. The black press highlighted their concern that "the conduct of the police is . . . a greater menace to the peace and security of the city than the conduct of the mob."[140] After being beaten by the police, Nicholas Sherman, a messenger and mailing clerk for the *New York Herald*, said that he stayed in the newspaper's office "all night, because there was a great crowd around the street and [he] was afraid to go home."[141] James Lockett refused to come down to the police precinct and identify the officers who beat him: "I have never been in any trouble before in my life. . . . I was afraid to go to work, after I got out of jail, because I didn't know what might happen. . . . I didn't know whether the thing was ever going to get over."[142] Lockett's account reveals the emotional quandary that many blacks were in when they realized that, whether the riot had ended or not, they could be subjected to rampant violence at any time without protection from anyone, especially the police. Other riot victims were hospitalized because of the trauma they had experienced. Charles A. Mitchell, a twenty-seven-year-old waiter, was "attacked and clubbed" by a police officer before he could reach the safety of his sister's residence. After his wife took him home the next day, "he became violent . . . shouting in his delirium, 'Devery did it! Devery (referring to the police chief) did it!'" He had to be sent to the "insane pavilion of Bellevue Hospital," where he stayed for almost a week. Mitchell's sister's comments about her brother's injuries also show the extent of his extreme vulnerability during his beating: he was "of very slight build, being only five feet six inches" and "weighing about one hundred and twelve pounds."[143]

The next morning, when antiblack violence on a smaller scale resumed, some residents decided to protect themselves by using armed self-defense.[144] Despite the fact that they reportedly never used their weapons, they likely agreed with an editorial in the *New York Age* that asked: "When the police cease to be the protectors of the personal rights of the citizen and openly assault innocent citizens, or allow the mob to do it, what is the proper course for the citizen to pursue? Shall he defend himself from the assaults of the police or allow himself to be clubbed or shot to death?"[145] Barkeeper Louis Williams went to a firearms dealer and asked for the "biggest gun . . . in the store." After purchasing a revolver "fifteen inches long," he said, "I understand they're knocking down negroes round here. The first man tries it on me gets this."[146] Alfred Bradshaw, who also purchased a gun, said that he had been in the "city for twenty years, and [had] never been arrested before." He armed himself in order to protect his home, rather than from any inclination toward vigilante justice. "I did not show this pistol to anyone after I bought it," he said, "and intended to leave it at the house, as a protection to my family."[147] Headly Johnson, after hearing about the riots, decided to "protect myself from the mob by carrying home with me a revolver."[148] When questioned about why the police found a knife on her husband, Lavinia Lockett repeated her husband's sentiments: "That is all I have got to protect myself. . . . I don't bother anybody and I don't guess anybody will bother me."[149] Many residents were aware of the harrowing post-riot experiences of residents like Alexander Robinson. Robinson and a friend narrowly escaped death when a mob dragged both men from a streetcar, shouting that "two negroes ought to be lynched." After a clothesline was thrown around Robinson's neck, the throng of "fifty or more" men "started for a lamppost" before a squad of police appeared and "with much clubbing dispersed" the mob so the two men could escape.[150]

Alarmed by black residents' decision to protect themselves, the police began to take action to quell post-riot incidents. Sensationalist reporting reinforced police officers' fears of blacks arming themselves by rescripting black self-defense as threatening black offense. *The World* headline read: "Negroes Buying Arms and Cartridges for To-Night's Anticipated Troubles."[151] The *New York Times* noted that "pawnshops were visited, where guns were for sale cheap. All the weapons in pawn were greedily taken out by their owners."[152] In turn, police officers countered complaints against their conduct by arguing that black residents were inciting the riots by their threatening behavior and concealed weapons. Continuing his vigorous defense of blacks arming themselves, lawyer Frank Moss countered that "colored men being denied official protection . . . obtained weapons, and if they were found armed, or if revolvers were found in their houses, then official brutality was redoubled."[153] Police officers intensified their actions, arresting black citizens and confiscating weapons or threatening to

STRUNG HIM TO A LAMP POST

Thousand Men Hanged a Black Boy at Thirty-fourth Street and Eighth Avenue.

ATTEMPTED LYNCHING OF ROBINSON.

Post-riot violence continued with the attempted lynching of Alexander Robinson. Police officers and other citizens stopped the mob. From The World, *Friday Evening, August 17, 1900.*

arrest blacks if they purchased them. At 10 o'clock on the night of the riot, a black woman attempted to buy a pistol. As the weapon was placed on the counter and the woman was about to pay for it, a policeman entered the store. He told her, "You may buy this revolver, but the minute you take it up I will arrest you for carrying a weapon without a permit."[154] Vincent Streets, a painter who was described by the press as a "walking arsenal," argued that he was "entitled to self-protection." When the police searched him, they found "a loaded revolver, . . . a razor, . . . a dirk knife, and a dozen cartridges."[155]

AFRICAN AMERICAN URBAN LIFE

Rev. W. H. Brooks, Arthur Harris, and the Parameters of Black Women's Protection

What are we to make of the statement made twelve days after the riot by Rev. W. H. Brooks, the well-known community leader who became president of the Citizen's Protective League (CPL), blaming the Enoch-Thorpe-Harris incident on "bad whiskey [and] . . . bad women"?[156] His sermon reveals the character of his leadership. "This is a conservative church, and the pastor is a conservative man," Brooks began. "Neither church nor pastor wishes any notoriety, and we hate sensationalism next to sin."[157] Born in 1859 in Calvert County, Maryland, Brooks was educated in public schools, at Morgan College, and at Howard University and then studied for the ministry at New York's Union Seminary, New York University, and the University of Dijon in France. By the time of his appointment to St. Mark's Methodist Episcopal Church in 1897, which had "the largest and wealthiest congregation of any church for colored people in the city," he was a distinguished leader in his denomination as well as in the national politics of black uplift and reform.

As a member of the board of the White Rose Home, the settlement house established by Victoria Earle Matthews in 1897 to protect young black women alone in the city, Brooks was in a position to know about the dangers young women confronted.[158] Yet his description of the Enoch-Thorpe-Harris incident presumed that the presence of May Enoch, who had recently arrived from Philadelphia, was problematic. Although Harris continually argued that he was a teetaler, Brooks believed that Harris's bad behavior stemmed from alcohol. His reference to "bad women" clearly referred to prostitution. The women he singled out for praise were those "'Anglo-Saxon' women who . . . rescued fleeing Negroes by giving them shelter in their homes."[159] In contrast to Brooks's description of the benevolence of a few "Anglo-Saxon" women, the *New York Herald* emphasized the violent language of those native-born and immigrant working women who "took a prominent part in the riot." Characterizing them as "viragoes" who "shrieked vengeance against negroes," the *Herald* noted that even "the police did not like the presence of these women in the mob and were especially active in running them from the streets and avenues, . . . making them leave the district whenever that was possible."[160] In Brooks's statement and the *Herald*'s report, respectability crystallized through criticisms of working-class white women and black women like Enoch.

Brooks and the CPL disregarded completely May Enoch's ill-treatment and subsequent arrest.[161] The organization's pamphlet, *Story of the Riot*, suggests that the political leaders did not believe that Enoch's arrest was legitimate, but no sustained protest was ever initiated on her behalf.[162] The leaders' silence regarding Enoch underscored the parameters within which they believed black women deserved or could obtain protection. Indeed, enacting a politics of respectability influenced how the CPL handled the complicated subject of protecting black women in the city. Like many black reformers, the group believed that black women's appropriate appearance and behavior could be used to counter stereotypes as well as racist treatment. Because black women's morality was constantly in question and that perception was reinforced by frequent arrests of working-class black women, their access to protection from the black community was not guaranteed. Only certain kinds of black working women were deemed worthy of protection. These leaders' response to racism had a strong gender dimension. As historian Michele Mitchell contends, they "emphasi[zed] respectable femininity in women and uncompromised manliness in men and the race as a whole."[163]

Brooks's sermon on the riot emphasized how black men's protection of womanhood reinforced and defined their own manhood.[164] He began by discussing an incident in which a black man from Brooklyn intervened when two white men were assaulting a white woman. Once he knew the woman was safe, the man "ran away, fearing that he would be misunderstood." This incident reveals that black men believed that they had to act with caution around white women in the urban North. According to Brooks, protecting women characterized the behavior of all black men, contradicting the prevailing image of the black rapist. He "declared that colored men would go on . . . protecting defenseless women, white or black."[165]

While most accounts of Thorpe's death indicate that Harris intervened in an attempt to protect May Enoch, Brooks was silent about Harris's motivation. If all men, "savage or civilized," were supposed to protect their womanhood, why did Brooks not justify Harris's actions in those terms? The minister revealed his assessment of Harris by emphasizing the connection between women's protection and the legal system, claiming that respectable black men should protect womanhood "by due process of law." Harris interfered with an arrest and killed a police officer, which, in Brooks's view, made his actions criminal, rather than honorable.[166] Yet he emphasized that if the courts did not address black residents' charges, then "we will make preparations to protect ourselves." Other black male leaders addressed black manhood and appropriate behavior through Brooks's statement. Rev. P. Butler Thompkins focused on the criminal behavior of the mob and the police by citing Proverbs 28:4, "They that forsake the law praise the wicked," rather than criticizing Harris. "What of Arthur Harris?" he asked his congregation rhetorically. "He is innocent until he is proven guilty."[167] Several other black ministers' anger at police brutality influenced their assessment of Harris's culpability.[168]

Not content with verbalizing their dissatisfaction with the ubiquity of police brutality, several African Americans sought to create an institutional structure through which to secure substantive change. On September 3, 1900, black activists and working-class residents formed the Citizen's Protective League. Black leaders believed that the CPL could obtain legal redress. They espoused the stance articulated by Rev. P. L. Cuyler, pastor of the Zion Methodist Episcopal Church, who contended that "we are citizens, even though we are black."[169] CPL president Brooks advocated a nonviolent approach, but other members called for the use of other strategies.[170] On September 13, the CPL held a mass protest meeting at Carnegie Hall attended by approximately 3,500 people.[171] The only woman on the platform, Maritcha Lyons, a schoolteacher and clubwoman who, along with Victoria Earle Matthews, sponsored an 1892 fund-raiser for Ida B. Wells's anti-lynching campaign, spoke for "womanhood," advocating intraracial unity and armed self-defense: "Words are worthless. We must have action. We cannot afford to be silent lest we be misunderstood." The crowd called out in response, "Yes, yes." Lyons continued: "Let every negro get a permit to carry a revolver. You are not supposed to be a walking arsenal but don't you get caught again. Have your houses made ready to afford protection from the fury of the mob, and remembering that your home is your castle and that no police officer has a right to enter it unless he complies with the usages of the law, see that he does not."[172] A Brooklyn resident and the daughter of prominent New Yorker Albro Lyons, whose family left lower Manhattan for Rhode Island after the 1863 Civil War Draft Riots, Maritcha Lyons knew the intimate consequences of racialized violence against black people.[173] Yet her advocacy for armed self-defense and the CPL's call for community protection never took up the problems faced by May Enoch. Nor did she address the predicaments of black working women forced to deal with the repressive power of the urban police. Instead, Lyons replicated aspects of a hegemonic discourse that denied black working women the protections afforded to their middle-class counterparts.

Most activists agreed about protection for respectable women and shared Lyons's and Brooks's concern that some women's behavior could degrade the reputation of the race. Middle-class black women deemed it imperative to distinguish themselves from their less respectable working-class sisters.

Police Brutality and the New York Race Riot

Such distinctions, as the work of Kevin Gaines demonstrates, proved crucial to the construction and public articulation of a refined, middle-class identity. Sadly, these constructions contributed to the marginalization of May Enoch and other working-class women who were routinely characterized as "deviants" prior to their encounters with the legal arm of the state. Thus, for white police officer Robert Thorpe, prevailing notions about black women's licentious and predatory sexuality immediately marked Enoch as a prostitute. A similar reading of black working women emerged from some members of the African American community. For black community leaders, Enoch's presence on the street late at night represented her disregard for appropriate female behavior.[174] As historian Evelyn Brooks Higginbotham has noted, for religious leaders and their congregants, "the street signified male turf, a public space of worldly dangers and forbidden pleasures." From the perspective of Brooks and the black church, "women who strolled the streets promiscuously blurred the boundaries of gender."[175] While carefully outlining the grievances of victimized black men and women, Brooks seemed to accept the police officer's assessment of Enoch. He and other leaders were less willing to parse out the distinction between her questionable or unknown background and the clear fact that she was not soliciting Harris when Thorpe arrested her. Emphasizing the offense against Enoch might have highlighted her less than respectable past and the fact that she was referred to as May Enoch rather than the more honorific Mrs. Arthur Harris. Black leaders preferred to focus the spotlight on those black female residents whose backgrounds could be more easily defended.[176]

Arthur Harris dismissed May Enoch for his own, quite different reasons. After his arrest, Harris recast his story to address the police officer's death rather than Enoch's need for protection. When asked to recount his version of the incident in a Washington, DC, police precinct, Harris expressed regret for attempting to defend Enoch against Thorpe: "If I had known this man was a police officer I would have had no trouble that night, . . . if he had said, I am an officer, and the woman is under arrest, I would have said nothing, as any other man would have done; I would immediately have turned away from him and gone on."[177] Harris ultimately refused to accept responsibility for defending Enoch. His response, however instrumental, failed to stress Enoch's innocence; instead his statement illustrated the tenuous nature of black women's protection. In hindsight, Harris's attitude suggests that black women clearly needed protection in urban spaces, but acting in their defense was contingent on the circumstances. Because of the negative reception of black women's reputations, regardless of class status, black men and white people needed to provide legitimacy for black women's be-

84

havior.[178] As historian Patricia Schechter argues, legalized "matrimony and [verifiable] chastity were . . . key components of gender protection," along with "the idea that husbands and fathers could ensure the safety of women and dependents."[179] Enoch may have understood but been disappointed that Harris recanted in order to protect himself.[180] Ultimately, she would have known that the working-class status and perceived lack of respectability of black women like herself prevented or at least seriously impeded black men like Harris from protecting them.[181] Tenderloin residents were also disappointed when their sustained protest through the CPL and a public police inquiry resulted in no substantial actions taken against the police force or mob participants.

If respectable black women recounted such violent experiences, what about the experiences of those working women who did not file affidavits? Consider, for instance, the case of fifty-two-year-old Emma Gardner, who was seen "discussing the riot at the corner of Thirty-fourth street and Seventh Avenue" the day afterward. When police officers told her to "move on," she refused and was promptly arrested. When officers found a 32-calibre revolver in her pocket, she was questioned, "Why did you carry that gun?" She responded, "Private business."[182] Her use of armed self-defense put into practice the recommendations made by Ida B. Wells and Maritcha Lyons. Yet could women like Gardner preserve their individual and public reputations when they protected themselves? Considering the stigmatization of black women as innately criminal, would their acts of self-defense be regarded as courageously heroic or as an infringement on the manhood rights of black men? Significant praise has been given to Ida B. Wells's call for self-defense, but events surrounding the riot of 1900 demonstrate the interracial and intercommunal consequences of protecting oneself from white aggressors. The politics of respectability failed to afford women of all classes protection from corrupt and violent police officers; for working-class women, like Gardner and Enoch, the strategy intensified intraracial class stratifications and prejudices as well as patriarchal control within black urban communities.

Police Corruption, Urban Black Women, and Judge Joseph Pool

Even before the 1900 riot, New Yorkers were very aware of police corruption and its connections with black women's experience of police harassment and disproportionate arrest. Judge Joseph Pool made concerted efforts to address the problem when black women were brought before his court. In 1898, Magistrate Pool, who had been recently transferred to the West Side

Police Court, began rejecting the increasing number of cases entering his court without proper evidence. Instead of confining his interrogations to defendants, Pool questioned police officers. On August 29, 1898, he dismissed disorderly conduct charges against nineteen women. Pool's "severe examination" of police officers showed how indiscriminate they were in their dealings with black women. The scenarios reported in court of interactions between working-class women and officers mirrored what Enoch would experience several years later. Consider, for instance, the case of "innocent-looking" (according to the press) white Mary Ross, the preconceived judgment regarding her character, and the discredited explanation given to Pool by her arresting officer:

> "Is there any objection to a woman stopping in front of an all-night resort?" asked Magistrate Pool.
> The policeman blushed and fidgeted, but did not reply.
> "What did the woman do?" asked the Magistrate, in a rather high-keyed voice.
> "She stopped men and talked to them."
> "Do you know what she said to the men?"
> "I—I could not hear, but I am sure that it was not proper."
> "Then how do you reconcile this lie with what you swore to positively in your statement?" persisted the Magistrate. "That is the question. In one place you swear to what the woman said and now you say that you could not hear her words."
> "I am positive what she meant," stammered the now thoroughly wilted policeman.[183]

When officers made futile attempts to explain why they arrested certain women, Pool responded with anger, "I have enough of you policemen coming in with prisoners and then not having any evidence . . . to convict them and going away telling everybody that the Magistrate wouldn't convict them and there was no use making arrests."[184] Pool also objected to plainclothes detective work: "Here we have people in this city making arrests without authority. What protection has a citizen when an ordinary man or woman can come along and arrest him? It is a pernicious practice." One court official revealed that various captains around the city "agreed not to arrest any more persons except for serious offenses, and that some of them . . . barred colored persons altogether, because . . . Magistrate Pool turns them loose whether they have a good excuse or not."[185]

The case that set the tone for Pool's courtroom demeanor occurred when the judge arrested a police officer after hearing the testimony of a black female defendant. After discharging Rose Harris from court, Pool decided to support her when she filed assault charges against her arresting officer. As the narrative of the case unfolds, it becomes clear that Pool was not necessarily an advocate of black women's protection; rather, he was a determined opponent of blatant police corruption. Officer Lewis Owens said that twenty-two-year-old Rose Harris was making a "disturbance after midnight" and when he attempted to arrest her for "intoxication and disorderly conduct,"[186] she fought back, necessitating his use of "considerable force" as well as the assistance of his partner. Rose Harris recalled that Officer Owens and his partner decided to "give it to dat brack niggah wench" by clubbing her and knocking a tooth out.[187] After Harris's testimony, the judge permitted her to leave the court to find the tooth as well as character witnesses. Harris brought in two black women, her sister, Alice Sanford, and Marcella Carroll, who attested to Harris's good character and corroborated her story.[188] Pool then discharged Harris. Disregarding the testimony of Owens and his partner, the judge "entertained" Harris's countercharges against Owens. Like the clubwomen and other working-class women, Rose Harris chose to defend her name and body against disrespect and assault. Magistrate Pool eventually told Owens: "Your conduct has been altogether unjustifiable. You have used too much more force than was necessary in arresting this helpless woman." Pool arrested the policeman for "felonious assault,"[189] setting his bail bond at $2,000.[190] "You are a prisoner," the judge explained to the officer; "do not leave the courtroom." Although Owens was placed in the custody of his precinct captain, it is not clear what happened after his arrest. Strikingly, Officer Owens's partner was Robert Thorpe.[191]

Would the lives of May Enoch, Arthur Harris, and Robert Thorpe have been changed if police officers had encountered more magistrates like Judge Pool, who demanded legitimate evidence when charges were made concerning black women's criminal behavior? Many officers in Pool's court district limited the number of persons they arrested because they did not have sufficient evidence for convictions. After 1898, however, Judge Pool's novel idea that officers should present valid evidence against defendants had been set aside, and normal—or, rather, corrupt—police activity resumed. Captain Price of the Tenderloin precinct responded to the court controversy by noting that "he intend[ed] to keep arresting women caught loitering in the streets, irrespective of what Magistrate Pool may do in discharging them for what he calls 'want of sufficient evidence.'" Defiantly arguing against Pool's tactics, the captain foreshadowed the end of Pool's brief influence in the courts and the continuity of police corruption; Price conceded that the "precinct . . . was already much cleaner than it had been." "Let me inform

Police Brutality and the New York Race Riot

you," Price told the judge, "I'll never ask any of the men in my command to demean himself to get the evidence you want nor will I countenance any such action on their part."[192]

Black women traversing the streets of early-twentieth-century New York City discovered that they needed protection both from criminals and from the police. Many women attempted to defend themselves against the physical assaults that frequently preceded their arrests. Black men also tried to protect black women. Arthur Harris's actions were questioned in light of his responsibility for Thorpe's death, but eventually black male leaders created "the Arthur J. Harris Liberation Fund" after he received a life sentence for second-degree murder.[193] After petitioning unsuccessfully for clemency, Harris died in prison on December 20, 1908.[194]

May Enoch's role in the altercation was effaced at the time and by scholars' focus on the racial-ethnic component of the race riot. In 1943, however, New York historian Roi Ottley interpreted the incident differently. He argued that "New York's fourth great race riot, which occurred in 1900, marked the beginning of the wholly turbulent career of Harlem. This disorder was touched off in the Tenderloin by the fatal stabbing of a white man, later found to be a policeman in civilian clothes, who had made unwelcome advances to a Negro woman."[195] In Ottley's view, the race riot became the catalyst for blacks' migration from lower Manhattan uptown to Harlem. Rather than focusing on Arthur Harris, he contended that May Enoch's encounter with Thorpe precipitated the riot. Significantly, Ottley addressed the sexual harassment and brutality that black women routinely faced from the police.

The Enoch-Thorpe-Harris altercation enables us to understand the centrality of police misconduct and black women's protection to the 1900 race riot. The violence stemmed from more than rising racial and ethnic tensions in a working-class neighborhood. Viewing the riot through the lens of gender elucidates the consequences of black men's attempts to defend black women in the urban North.

Viewing the 1900 incident as part of an ongoing attempt by black men to safeguard black women reveals the complexity of black women's protection amid the challenges to black womanhood and manhood at the turn of the century. White policemen acted on the assumption that black women were naturally promiscuous and supported themselves through prostitution. Black women in New York City were, as a result, frequently harassed by police officers and consistently arrested on false charges of soliciting or disorderly conduct. Many black activists believed these arrests occurred because white police officers "had little fear of the consequences if they made mistakes" in dealing with black women.[196] Community leaders primarily worked against these negative images by challenging black women, rather than the police, to behave more appropriately. Black reformers were aware of how the police mistreated black women, but they emphasized those things they believed they could change: the public behavior of black working-class citizens. For reformers, appropriate behavior was seen as black women's saving grace, especially in light of white society's prejudices about their inherent promiscuity.

Black leaders' lack of response to the predicament of May Enoch contributed to her being likened to a prostitute, which was precisely the claim that police officer Thorpe made. The Citizen's Protective League probably worried that addressing Enoch's mistreatment would weaken its case, because her arrest centered on questionable moral behavior. Her common-law relationship with Harris failed to provide Enoch with the level of status and stability accorded female riot victims whose affidavits were taken. Just as Harris argued that he would not have protected Enoch if he had known that Thorpe was a police officer, the CPL's position suggested that bringing Enoch and women like her into the discourse on protection would complicate its case and might ultimately damage its long-term objectives. Black women and their behavior were at the symbolic center of struggles for racial justice and ideas regarding racial progress, even as actual women were marginalized. Struggles for racial justice that focused on antiblack violence and police brutality were conducted by black working-class communities, and through their affidavits one can see that women were vocal about their as well as other Tenderloin residents' plight during the incident.

Tenderloin residents, both male and female, who bore the brunt of the riot responded by arguing that as respectable citizens they deserved protection from the police and the state. Along with elite leaders, they believed that if the police failed to protect them, the legal system should. Lacking the conventional symbols of middle-class respectability in black communities, such as a college education, a professional career, and membership in prestigious civic and social organizations, members of the black working class enacted their own respectability and moral ideals through their commitment to a strong work ethic and attention to appropriate behavior. Indeed, the language of working-class respectability pervades their affidavits. Highlighting the myriad ways in which their respectability was compromised, Tenderloin residents described how debilitating physical assaults by white mobs and the police not only violated their civil rights but also jeopardized their physical and psychological ability to work and take care of their families. From distinct vantage points, questions about how respectability should or could protect men and women from assault permeated black middle-class and working-class discussions regarding race progress at the turn of the twentieth century. The most prominent and public response to the problems urban working-class women faced centered on the southern migrant and activists' attempts to protect black women through preventive moral reform.

Yet the circumstances of May Enoch's migration to New York challenged reformers' blanket characterization of working-class black women's presence in the city. Enoch did not fit urban reformers' image of the young, single, and naive migrant from the rural South who was victimized by unscrupulous labor agents. While Harris's individual attempt to protect his common-law wife failed and her predicament was overlooked in the protests that followed the riot, the efforts made by Progressive reformers, before and after the 1900 riot, publicized black working women's vulnerability to sexual and labor exploitation.

3

i want to save these girls

SINGLE BLACK WOMEN AND THEIR PROTECTORS, 1895–1911

> I was born a slave, and my kin were sold away from me. I dare not raise my hand against a little child I may see in the street, for I do not know but she may be my own kin. . . . I want to save these girls. Their souls are as precious in the sight of the Master as yours and mine.
>
> —Victoria Earle Matthews, 1899

> The need of protecting working women, as a means of raising the standards of living and improving the moral life, is one to which thinkers and workers among the whites are very keenly alive. The need of protecting women who are seeking employment and who are, therefore, exposed to many more dangers because of their lack of money, work and friends, is a newer thought, and one which has a direct bearing on the progress of the Negro race.
>
> —Frances Kellor, 1905

Social welfare campaigns aimed at protecting single, black women in New York underline the significance of black women's urban presence at the turn of the century. Reformers shared W. E. B. Du Bois's fear that "excess" working-class black women caused problems within their communities.[1] While Du Bois emphasized that single black women in the city jeopardized the stability of black families, other reformers responded by invoking the need for black women's protection. Instead of stressing the defense of black womanhood by black men, these reform activists sought to assist and instruct young black women, especially southern migrants, as they adjusted to urban life, thereby safeguarding both black and white communities from a seemingly dangerous element within the black working class.

overview of Progressive reformers' agendas

For the most part, efforts to protect black women looked similar to those undertaken on behalf of immigrant and white women. In the multipronged strategy typical of Progressive Era urban reform, activists sought to reform the labor system through regulation of corrupt employment agencies, train migrant women to be efficient employees, and provide respectable leisure activities as an alternative to dance halls and other commercial amusements, which reformers perceived as immoral and leading vulnerable young women into prostitution. Although these efforts to protect working-class women from economic and sexual exploitation appear similar across racial lines, they actually proceeded from different motives and assumptions and were shaped by black and nonblack women's differing relations to the female labor market.

blk + white Prog reformers have diff't access/imp't.

This chapter explores the crosscurrents of social reform for black women in New York through the distinct perspectives and activities of Victoria Earle Matthews and Frances Kellor. Both used social-scientific investigations in order to secure suitable employment for working-class black women and to prevent their wayward behavior and moral downfall. Race and access to state power distinguished the development and trajectory of their efforts.[2] Without local or state assistance, black reformers depended upon their own community's limited resources to assist migrant women. They believed that addressing the needs of working-class women was part of the collective responsibility of the black middle class.[3] White reformers, in contrast, had amassed significant support from local and state institutions, and their investment in campaigns for black women's protection was an extension of their social welfare work with white native-born and immigrant working-class women.

Victoria Earle Matthews's determination to "save these girls" represented the concerns of many black women activists.[4] Like many black reformers, Matthews was haunted by the legacy of enslavement, which not only influenced interactions among black people but, more importantly, shaped perceptions of black womanhood. When white reformers who were anxious about the alleged increase in prostitution among white native-born and immigrant women emphasized the involuntary character of their sexual exploitation by using the loaded term "white slavery," Matthews and her cohort sought to show that young black girls were also victims of sexual procurers and predators. Although her invocation of religion reflects the influence of nineteenth-century evangelical reform, she utilized social-scientific methods to research social problems, from the convict lease system in the South to "houses of ill-fame" in the North.[5] The latter investigation eventually led her to open the White Rose Mission Working Girls' Home, a black settlement home in New York City. While addressing a pressing need, the Home also fulfilled the black racial uplift endeavor to help the working poor.

Yet black reformers struggled to make their ideological investment in racial uplift succeed on a practical, everyday basis. Securing adequate financial resources to turn their vision of racial advancement into concrete programs was difficult; black social reform was plagued by a chronic lack of funds. When black activists received substantial donations from white benefactors, however, they fought to maintain control over their programs. Conflict between black men and black women influenced reform coalitions as well. Day-to-day racial uplift work was also stressful, especially frustrating when the objects of reform rejected or simply ignored activists' advice and efforts.

Frances Kellor acknowledged that the protection of working-class white women was a long-standing concern among white reformers and that by 1905 some of them were willing to incorporate black women into their agenda.[6] Kellor's academic training in law at Cornell University and in sociology at the University of Chicago, coupled with her critical investigative work in criminology and her close relationships with funding sources, placed her in the mainstream of Progressive reform.[7] The legacy of enslavement influenced white reformers' understanding of the black women who were the objects of their anxious ministrations. In contrast to black reformers, Kellor and her cohort believed that enslavement made all black women less capable of leading moral, respectable lives. Thus, white reformers emphasized changing these women's labor efficiency rather than attempting to transform the racially restrictive practices of the labor market and of social institutions. Kellor's specific focus on black women and the Associations for the Protection of Colored Women that she founded reinforced the prevailing racial segregation of reform in the urban North.

While interracial campaigns shared concerns and drew upon similar ideas regarding protection, the matter of race distinguished how and why black and white reformers dealt with black migrant women. Both groups were deeply influenced by the dominant society's negative image of black women as indolent, immoral, and even criminal. Even those white reformers who chose to work with black women constantly questioned their moral stature. In contrast to many whites, however, they rejected biological explanations of black delinquency and thought that environmental factors contributed to black women's downfall. They attempted to safeguard migrant women through the promotion of domestic work, to train them to be efficient servants for white employers, and to provide them with acceptable leisure activities.[8]

Black activists' approach to helping migrant women was quite different. To them, black women's protection meant inculcating and utilizing self-help and institution building, which they believed were essential for race advancement. Black reformers supported training for domestic workers because a "valorization of work" was critical to their conception of respectability, and personal-service work was the only type of employment readily available to black women.[9] Black migrants needed to be competitive with white native-born and immigrant women, whom employers often preferred. Finally, reformers believed that proper instruction would aid in dispelling the disreputable image of all working black women.

Reformers usually framed their campaigns around the need to shield young women from corrupt employment agencies.[10] Reformers' narratives emphasized that southern black women were "poorly equipped to grapple with [the northern] environment" and often left their homes "without sufficient clothing or money and no information about her Northern home."[11] According to these accounts, young women needed protection from urban inducements; something had to be done to "guard . . . [them] against the dangers of sordid city association, and to surround them with [a] wholesome and religious environment."[12]

In the context of early-twentieth-century "white slavery" scares, these reformers were concerned that black women searching for legitimate work were forced into the sex trade, either as prostitutes or as domestics working in brothels. Activists' narratives detailed how northern and southern employment agencies exploited black women once they reached New York City. Labor agents who traveled through the South promoted northern domestic jobs and had women sign contracts. The terms alone were exploitative; they charged at least twenty dollars for transportation costs that normally totaled seven. When a woman arrived at the northern dock or train station, she faced two scenarios: either her train arrived at a later time than specified, leaving her alone at the station where she was a conspicuous target for criminals, or she was met by an agent who would take her luggage, assuring her that storage was free of charge until she found employment. The migrant was under contract and had no choice but to work as a domestic in questionable homes, saloons, and houses of prostitution. According to reformers, the woman usually worked for two months without pay. If the migrant refused to comply with any of the agent's demands, she was charged a storage fee for her luggage. With no wages, she was left in the city alone, destitute, and without any belongings.[13] Given the prevalence of negative stereotypes regarding black women's sexuality, reformers knew that the image of the black woman as victim might elicit sympathy and support among their peers. Matthews recognized the need to publicize black migrant women's predicament and worked to address it through her club work and her subsequent reform efforts. Her dedication to protecting young black women shaped her political and social activism.

Victoria Earle Matthews: Black Women Protecting Black Women, 1897–1907

Matthews's background provides an interesting parallel to the backgrounds of those she tried to help, for she was a migrant herself. Born a month before the outbreak of the Civil War in Fort Valley, Georgia, Matthews was one of Caroline Smith's nine children. During the war, Smith escaped enslavement, leaving her children behind. Throughout the intervening years, Matthews and her older sister, Anna, were reared in their master's household as if they were white, which tends to confirm the family's belief that their owner was their father. After emancipation, Caroline Smith returned for her children but reportedly was forced to wage a legal battle to regain custody of her two daughters. It is not clear how her remaining children fared.[14] Matthews's migration with her family to New York City was characteristic of that of many black southerners. They traveled from Georgia and lived in Richmond and Norfolk, Virginia, before ending up in New York City in 1873. After she attended only four years of public school, family difficulties forced Matthews to work full time as a domestic. However, she took advantage of her employer's extensive library to educate herself.[15] Frances Keyser, a friend and fellow settlement worker, said Matthews "never lost an opportunity to improve her mind, and by means of lectures, special studies, [and] constant contact with trained persons . . . gratified to some extent her thirst for knowledge and became in spite of her untoward circumstances an educated and cultured woman."[16] After marrying William Matthews, a Virginia native and coachman, in 1879, and having a son, she continued to educate herself and pursued a career in journalism.[17] Another admirer noted that she "did not stop . . . because of obstacles and discouragements, but pushed her way onward, hewing out a pathway for herself; and in this way she . . . [applied] her powers as a thinker and writer."[18]

Black New Yorkers recognized Matthews because of the urgency and energy that she expressed in her journalism and her political activism. Matthews had the "reputation of being one of the most enthusiastic women in town, earnest, and to a remarkable degree a believer in her own sex, and a

Single Black Women and Their Protectors

woman destined to succeed in what she set . . . out to do."[19] Matthews wrote freelance for mainstream newspapers such as the *New York Times*, the *New York Herald*, and the *Brooklyn Eagle*, and for black newspapers such as the *Boston Advocate*, the *Washington Bee*, and the *New York Age*. In 1893, she wrote a short novel, *Aunt Lindy*, which explored how a formerly enslaved woman who was working as a nurse in Fort Valley, Georgia, drew on her Christian faith to resist the temptation to murder her former owner when she had the opportunity to heal him from his ailment — a gesture that epitomized the healing of race relations after the Civil War.[20] Noted as influencing others through its "strong moral and mental powers," her writing served as an arena for the development and expression of her political activism.[21]

Like most black women activists during the late nineteenth century, Matthews was consumed by the consequences of enslavement for black womanhood. In a society that prized a woman's virtue, how did black women, despite their historical experience of sexual harassment and rape, make claims to femininity and the protection accorded the patriarchal Christian family? Those black women who found a public platform consistently addressed the progress of the race since emancipation. In her 1897 speech, "The Awakening of the Afro-American Woman," Matthews addressed black women's perseverance against dreadful odds. "The marvel is not that they have succeeded, not that they are succeeding," she fervently argued to a crowd of white men and women at the annual convention of the Society of Christian Endeavor in San Francisco, "but that they did not fail, *utterly fail*." Matthews emphasized the shameful stigma of rape that formerly enslaved women faced in a society that prized feminine purity. "I believe the God who brought them out of the Valley of the Shadow, who snatched them from the hand of the white rapist, the base slave master whose unacknowledged children are to be found in every hamlet of the Republic, guided these women, and guides them in the supreme work of building their Christian homes."[22] Although Matthews, whose appearance led many to mistake her for a white woman, was a vivid representative of slavery's dark past and freedom's progressive future, she consistently acknowledged her racial background as she promoted her work. In 1902, for example, she explained, "When I speak of the colored people, I speak of people of whom I have my maternal origin." "There is no one so black that is not akin to me."[23] Her work to advance the race focused on teaching young working and poor women the fundamental skills and proper behavior needed to develop and maintain Christian families. While she acknowledged these women's flaws, she argued that "these girls are not to be blamed"; it was the duty of established women to shelter them and instruct them in the responsibilities of Christian womanhood.[24]

Yet women like Matthews experienced criticism from within their own communities.

As a leading spokeswoman for the race, whose "name is . . . a household word wherever the press, and especially the Afro-American press finds . . . its way," Matthews was a target of black male criticism for publicly challenging the boundaries of appropriate womanhood.[25] Reformers dedicated to protecting young women from moral dangers often found themselves characterized by black men and white society as immoral, or at least as morally questionable. For instance, in 1891, an anonymous, "representative" black man contended "that the reading of novels [had] . . . a demoralizing effect on . . . women of . . . [the] race."[26] Matthews responded to this critique by validating black women's involvement in literary production while questioning the reader's moral position as a respectable black man:

I find myself wondering what sort of a man—what kind of home life or associations could produce the conviction from which these objectionable words emanate. . . . To be unequivocal, the charge is willfully wrong, spitefully, narrow and . . . its author is not entitled to leniency we give to the ignorant. . . . I feel commiseration for him, for his enlightening association is as narrow as his expressed views on this question alone, the gentleman is to be pitied more than blamed for his exceedingly rude, not to say unchivalrous judgment.[27]

Single Black Women and Their Protectors

It seems that Matthews's reputation was able to withstand such a public question, but the battles that prominent women fought to be seen as respectable while doing race work were formidable.

Black women reformers struggled to not allow black male criticism derail their political and professional work. Matthews, who promoted both the "value of race literature" and industrial training, maintained a strong working relationship with influential newspaper editor T. Thomas Fortune that eventually led to her association with the powerful Tuskegee Institute president, Booker T. Washington.[28] Those black leaders who publicly rejected the black conservative's accommodationist position, especially after the deluge of white philanthropic support following his 1895 Atlanta Exposition speech, faced negative political and financial consequences.[29] In some instances, however, conflicts with men prompted black women to become more vocal about racial injustice and black male leaders' inability to address those issues effectively.[30] Sometimes women found it desirable to organize independently from men. In supporting the antilynching campaign, Matthews helped to plan a public forum at New York City's Lyric Hall. With cosponsor Maritcha Lyons, a Brooklyn schoolteacher, she organized a benefit that raised $500, enabling Ida B. Wells to continue her antilynching lectures and writings.[31] The successful fund-raiser prompted black women of Brooklyn and New York to form the Woman's Loyal Union on December 5, 1892. The club stressed the significance of having "women coming in closer contact with one another to discuss matters of vital interest to the race."[32]

The Woman's Loyal Union represented the perspective of black, primarily middle-class women,[33] who described themselves as "conscientious, conservative, thinking people." The Union explained that its objective entailed the "diffusion of accurate and extensive knowledge relative to the . . . status of the Afro American" and the "employment of every lawful means to secure and to retain the unmolested exercise of" their civil and social rights. With Matthews as president, the organization welcomed all willing and loyal black women, and by 1893 it had more than one hundred members. From its New York base, the group sought additional branches in Chicago, Washington, Philadelphia, and other large cities.[34] Even though the Union excluded male members, noting that black men "allowed rivalry for supremacy and prominence to make . . . [their] organizations non effective,"[35] members welcomed and often received male support, especially from black ministers.[36]

Other prominent black women addressed issues of racial injustice and social reform by organizing their own women's clubs in Boston, Washington, DC, and New York City. In 1896, in response to a white male editor's vitriolic comments about black women's character, local black women's clubs came together to form the National Association of Colored Women's Clubs (NACW).[37] As the new group's national organizer, Victoria Earle Matthews declared that the NACW's major objective was the "development and protection of our womanhood, our homes and our history, as an integral part of the great American nation."[38]

Matthews and other reformers who focused on working-class women's lives made a clear class distinction between reformers and those needing rehabilitation. Situating themselves as these women's moral and social superiors, black clubwomen were concerned with the effects of working women's urban presence on race progress. Reformers sought to direct young black women into what they regarded as appropriate employment. Unlike some of their peers who acknowledged working-class women's respectability, many clubwomen reinforced socioeconomic distinctions. Clubwoman Fannie Barrier Williams argued that "the club movement among colored women reaches into the sub-social condition of the entire race" and is an "effort of the few competent in behalf of the many incompetent."[39] Clubwoman Addie Hunton's remarks illustrate the manner in which the middle-class distinguished themselves from their working-class counterparts when all black women were characterized as immoral: "Those who write most about the moral degradation of the Negro woman know little or nothing of that best element of our women who are quietly and unobtrusively working out the salvation of the race. Because the Negro women with whom they come in contact exhibit none of those higher qualities that are based upon virtue, it is assumed that these women are typical of all Negro women, and, upon this assumption, an attempt is made to prove the shame of all, a wholesale immorality."[40] These reformers not only were impelled to improve the lives of working-class and poor women but also expressed an equally pressing need to prove that they were of a higher caliber than those they helped. In sum, they focused on the NACW's motto, "Lifting As We Climb," as they aimed to maintain their own respectability while uplifting others.

Matthews was fully occupied with her journalism and club work when, as one friend put it, her son's death in 1895 prompted "her heart . . . [to turn] in a special manner to children and young women."[41] Several years later, when speaking to a group of poor women in Alabama about the "Lord Jesus Christ," she was inspired to expand her activism and began researching black southerners' abject poverty, their severely limited public education, and the problems black parents faced when their young sons were forced onto chain gangs. Instead of establishing a southern organization, Matthews "wanted to come to New York" and expose black southerners' plight and the problems endemic to northern black urban communities.[42] The predicament of black women who migrated from the rural South to the urban North epitomized the linkages between the two regions. Matthews emphasized the moral dangers that naive young women faced as prospective workers in a racially restrictive labor market. While Matthews focused on New York, she understood that southern black women's exploitation was vast. She explained that "by correspondence and personal investigation" she found evidence of corrupt employment agencies in Boston, San Francisco, Chicago, and elsewhere.[43]

When, in 1897, Matthews, with the support of like-minded women, founded the White Rose Mission, she established the first black social settlement managed for and run by black women.[44] The institution's major objective was to maintain a "Christian, industrial, non-Sectarian, Home for Afro-American and Negro working women and girls, where they may be educated and trained in the principles of practical self-help and right living."[45] Matthews argued that it was essential for black ministers to "cooperate in the good work of befriending friendless girls."[46] Black women and black clergy were on the board of directors and were present when the Home was moved to a more stable residence. Rev. Dr. William H. Brooks, prominent leader of St. Mark's Methodist Church and president of the Citizen's Protective League, which was established in the wake of the 1900 race riot, remarked that "considering that the young girls are brought up face to face with the worst kind of vice, he wondered that so few fall, and that so many stand."[47] Matthews also solicited and received donations from several white Christian organizations. The New York City Mission and Tract Society opined: "When God has a special service to be done, we find that He has been preparing a special worker for the work, and we feel He sent us Mrs. Victoria Earle Matthews, an educated Christian woman of experience."[48] Nothing underscored the need for black working-class women's protection more than the praise Matthews received from this organization, which saw urban reform through a Jim Crow perspective: "We hope we are digging the foundation . . . for a great and most beneficent [sic] enterprise, and that friends of the colored race will be raised up to build, and equip, and help carry on, a sort of Hampton Institute right in New York, which shall be to the young colored women what the Y.W.C.A. is to the white girl."[49] The mention of Hampton Institute, a black college established in 1868 by white missionary Samuel Chapman Armstrong, exemplified the national acceptance of industrial education and the ready approval of Washington's concept of a separate caste of black laborers. Matthews understood Washington's influence on white philanthropists and, whenever possible, let audiences know that she had "called the attention of Booker T. Washington" to her mission.[50]

Combining evangelical fervor with social-scientific investigations, Matthews established her settlement on East Ninety-seventh Street. Although black New Yorkers lived on the West Side in the Tenderloin (from the West Twenties to the West Fifties) and San Juan Hill (West Sixties), Matthews identified at least five thousand blacks who had moved from lower Manhattan around Bleeker Street to the Upper East Side because "the Italian population . . . crowded them out." In 1899, Matthews told a Westminster Presbyterian Church audience that she was working with the "most degraded colored population in New York," which helped her secure housing. Upper East Side real estate agent Mr. Philips admitted that Matthews's work was improving the neighborhood's status. In providing her with temporary free rooms that he was unable to rent, he reasoned that "the better the neighborhood the better rents I could get." Matthews often found the work frustrating, since she tried to address the needs of thousands with one small mission. She solicited financial support from various churches and was able to establish nightly meetings with children, mothers' meetings, Sabbath schools, and Gospel services.[51] Although Matthews believed that she and her supporters were sometimes "rejected" by New York's more professional social reformers because they "could not say" they "were trained workers," her work received consistent support from white and black Protestant evangelicals and eventually was recognized by college-educated Progressives.[52]

The White Rose Mission served as a "temporary lodging house for women and girls coming from the South or other parts of New York in search of work."[53] It eventually set up a traveler's aid department to address the city's growing number of southern migrants, which influenced the National Traveler's Aid Society later established by reformer Grace Dodge.[54] As the number of black women arriving in New York from the South and the West Indies increased, the traveler's aid service employed two female dock agents, one to advise departing women in Norfolk, Virginia, and another to receive women arriving in New York City.[55]

While the White Rose Mission provided an employment bureau, assigned migrants a female escort when they began a new job, and offered temporary lodging and meals, the organization's policy was to discourage black women from coming North. Matthews believed that many migrants' naïveté and inexperience made them exceedingly vulnerable, which endangered both individual women and the black community: "If the majority of girls who go North every year understood the condition of the labor market . . . and the kind of work they must expect to do, and . . . the many humiliations they must put up with after they get there . . . it is reasonable to suppose that self-respect would deter hundreds from rushing into a life that only the strongest physically, spiritually, and morally can be expected to stand."[56]

Like settlement houses for immigrants, the Home offered social services and educational programs to black residents of Manhattan's Upper East Side. Although Matthews is best known for her public criticism of racial and gender injustice and her celebration of the black community's accomplishments, particularly its race literature, she believed in industrial training to equip blacks with the basic skills necessary for employment. Matthews wrote Booker T. Washington that the Home sought to prepare young women to find work in families within their congregations, so they would be supervised "by respectable women until they make associations of a proper and wholesome nature."[57] In a letter prompted by a $50 donation from the longtime Hampton Institute trustee Robert Ogden, she thanked Washington for his support and avowed that she wanted to "plant a "minature [sic] Tuskegee" on New York's East Side.[58] In addition to using the library and reading room, young women and men could take classes in "sewing, shoe making, clay modeling, domestic science, chair caning, [and] wood burnishing."[59] Matthews believed that the neighborhood's "young men and boys" should receive manual training instruction. The White Rose Mission also offered specific "lectures in . . . domestic service."[60]

Other clubwomen, as well as their prominent husbands, supported Matthews's vision. The White Rose Mission's annual reports consistently refer to the active support of nationally famous writer Paul Laurence Dunbar, as well as Booker T. Washington. The 1910 report quoted Washington's endorsement: "This is one of the places of good works in which I have been most deeply interested. It represents practical and not imaginary needs."[61] When Frances R. Keyser, who was an assistant superintendent of the Mission, described the Home during an 1897 visit, she remarked with interest that the "kindergarten class is taught by Alice Ruth Moore, later Mrs. Paul Laurence Dunbar."[62] As Matthews's friend and live-in boarder, Moore was the Home's "first kindergarten teacher," who voluntarily taught a boy's class after working all day at Brooklyn's Public School 83.[63] As a fellow Mission worker, Keyser observed that Moore, whom she described as an "attractive young woman, recently from . . . the South," selflessly "gave herself to the work of teaching . . . neglected little ones." Moreover, according to Keyser, Moore's influence on the Home's children also stemmed from her "charming personality in training the children and making them happy in their be-

Victoria Matthews (seated, far left) and helpers at the White Rose Mission, 1899, in a photograph that appeared in the New York City Mission and Tract Society's annual report. Alice Ruth Moore is seated in the first row, center. Courtesy of Columbia University Libraries.

loved 'mission.'"[64] The Home benefited from clubwomen's involvement and their influence on their husbands. Yet the challenges of racial uplift were not simply those of raising sufficient financial resources; addressing the exigencies of the working poor also taxed the energies of black reformers.

Young Black Working-Class People's Response to Racial Uplift

Frances Keyser noted that the Home's recipients were "truly a varied group, some neat, clean and orderly, giving evidence of careful home training, others sadly neglected," while others were "rude and boisterous."[65] In retrospect, when characterizing the Home's Upper East Side neighborhood, Victoria Earle Matthews recalled having encountered "ignorant and almost uncivilized unfortunates" who could be "utterly lawless, . . . with no social considerations to restrain them."[66] It seems that when T. Thomas Fortune, editor of the black newspaper *New York Age*, initially persuaded Booker T. Washington to visit the Home, the Tuskegee Institute president, after seeing the "derelicts who lived in the neighborhood," reportedly said to Matthews, "My friend I wouldn't change fields with you."[67] Alice Moore's experience at

Children of the White Rose Mission, 1899, in a photograph that appeared in the
New York City Mission and Tract Society's annual report. The young children's clothing
reflects the mission's attempt to instill practical domestic skills. But note the child
(front row, second from right) who shows her mischievous side with a
playful mask. Courtesy of Columbia University Libraries.

the White Rose Home reflects various reformers' pessimistic sentiments but also illustrates the physical and emotional toll exacted by practical, everyday race work. Keyser briefly addressed the difficulty that Matthews and her assistants faced with some of the Home's incorrigible children but concluded that they handled their charges with respectable savvy and decorum.[68]

Even though the teaching profession represented one of the most prestigious occupations for black women, Moore readily highlighted the occupation's many challenges. She had a demanding schedule. After teaching a full day in Brooklyn, Moore traveled to Manhattan for the Home's evening classes.[69] Her young charges needed her guidance but also challenged her patience and authority. In one particularly telling piece of correspondence, the educator confessed: "Exhausted? I feel like a dishrag. 62 untamed odoriferous kids all day, 23 fiends in the manual training class to-night."[70] To be sure, Moore worried about her students' poverty: "My little boys had had nothing to eat all day—though they dutifully came in to the mission. I could not help but smile ironically as I wondered how much good all I was trying to teach them would amount to when it was imparted on an empty stomach."[71] At certain moments, she felt guilty about the class inequities that distinguished her middle-class life from that of her destitute students. "When I come back to my dainty little room and sit down to a well ordered dinner, the food actually chokes me at times, remembering those to whom my necessities would be luxuries."[72] The poverty-stricken students, however, challenged her authority and prompted her to describe the pupils in her boy's class as the "toughest, most god forsaken hoodlums you ever saw." Moore also understood that as a woman teaching boys she had to be a fearless disciplinarian as well as an educator. Consider, for instance, how she explained her experience with a particularly rowdy class, which she noted was eventually "dismissed in perfect order."

> My patience endured exactly 57 minutes by the clock, when after an unusually violent break on the part of a stalwart young man of fifteen I reached over another boy, grabbed him by the collar, and dragged him to the center of the floor. One hand was full of papers, so I had only one to manipulate his nibs with. I lectured him in sentences of four or five words, punctuating them with fervent shakes with one hand, while my knuckles made dents in his medulla oblongata. Then I assisted him to his seat rather rapidly, and urged him to retain it with a gentle grip on his shoulder that made him wince with delight— the other hand still holding the papers. One boy whistled, the other looked in respectful silence.[73]

Moore believed that with these students, "it is . . . a pity to be brutal, but it must be." She stressed that her effectiveness stemmed from students being taught or rather threatened to respect her. For example, when one cheeky student asked her if she attended the gym she responded affirmatively, and then told him, "I'm willing to undertake to knock you down if you want." He immediately declined her challenge, and she said he left her class "with respect and admiration beaming all over him."[74] Yet, for all of her bravado, continual confrontational interactions wreaked havoc on Moore's physical and emotional well-being. One troubling day, she noted, "The boys were very bad, and I cried from sheer nervousness when I came home."[75] Black female reformers like Moore, who were struggling to live up to their own standards of respectability and civility, rarely discussed in public how they maintained an image of the racial uplift ideology alongside the myriad difficulties of everyday race work.

Instead of explicitly addressing the troubles they experienced on a day-to-day basis with their charges, reformers concentrated on informing their own communities and possible benefactors about the benefits of racial uplift and the need for financial contributions. For instance, White Rose Home administrators instructed hundreds of migrant women in manners, dress, and domestic skills.[76] Although the women seemed to benefit from this instruction, reformers also imposed regulations on working women's behavior. Black reformers not only trained working-class women to be efficient workers but also attempted to mold them into acceptable representatives of the race.[77]

Black reformers' biggest frustration was the fact that young women appeared to set their own self-interest above racial advancement. Despite their actions, the young women were not unaware of the dangers that alarmed reformers and their parents or other relatives. In most cases, they were aware of their anxieties. From the turn of the century to the 1920s, reformers were at odds with young working-class black women who embraced personal independence and morally questionable coed public amusements and private entertainments.[78] In the 1890s, Victoria Earle Matthews was especially dismayed after meeting girls who explained that they were "going on the stage" or to "Coney Island in the Summer to dance." She attributed these young women's troubling desire to go into the entertainment industry and their knowledge of "all the steps of the cakewalk and the latest coon songs" to de facto segregation in New York. There was no "Christian Association where they can . . . go, no gymnasiums for recreation, no libraries, no reading rooms, and . . . no place for them but the streets."[79] Young women's desire for fun continued in the early 1910s and 1920s. One twenty-three-year-old explained that "she did not care about cabarets and dancehalls, but [was] very fond of house parties and music."[80] A twenty-six-year-old revealed that she loved "drinking and dressing up."[81] One Bedford administrator noted a twenty-two-year-old Maryland native's fascination with the city: she had "not seen much of life yet but has an intense curiosity to see all of it and is not going to settle down yet."[82] In 1922, a young woman reportedly revealed that she liked "gay parties with whisky of which she [drank] plenty."[83] Another twenty-two-year-old admitted that she "went to [cabarets to] have a good time and meet people [she] knew." While she was aware of the "questionable people" who attended the dance halls, she claimed that "she did not talk to them."[84] Not surprisingly, race leaders were horrified at black youths' behavior and attitude. While reformers stressed young people's need to preserve their "mental, moral, and material strength" to be actively engaged in race activism, they failed to see how leisure gave the youth respite from some of New York's troubling social, economic, and political conditions.[85]

Noting that "hundreds of happy youths have danced regularly each week at one or more of New York's great dance halls," a *New York Age* editorial emphasized that young people's pursuit of pleasure came at the expense of the race struggle. "This energy now devoted to pleasure," the editorial contended, "can and must be turned into industrial enterprises, into actual racial advance."[86] Several years later, prominent black minister Adam Clayton Powell Sr. expressed related concerns by opening his 1914 New Year's Sunday sermon arguing that the "Negro race [was] . . . dancing itself to death." Both the *Age*'s editor and Powell questioned particular kinds of dancing, emphasizing how appropriate behavior was a key component in the struggle for racial equality.[87] According to these black leaders, separating the pursuit of individual leisure from racial justice initiatives was not a viable option for black people.[88] This concern was particularly pertinent in light of the racial stereotypes about black women and black immorality.

Believing in and promoting the argument that they were saving women from prostitution, reformers were at a loss when these young black women expressed sexual desire and sexual agency. Consider, for instance, the comment of a sixteen-year-old New York native arrested for prostitution who admitted to "having intercourse with [a man] off and on" but denied "ever [taking] any money from him."[89] In another example, a black social worker recounted her frustration with a young woman who rejected her attempts to provide appropriate, all-female forms of recreation: "I shall never forget the look of frankness on the 17-year-old girl's face nor the sickening sense of horror I felt as I realized the sincerity of her words when she looked me squarely in the eyes and said, 'Lady, I tell you the truth, I never could get along with women folk and I don't try, I deal only with men.'"[90] Reformers and parents responded to these young women's pursuit of personal and sexual independence individually, and, by the 1910s, they turned to the state.[91] Yet in black communities, as reformers and family members constantly fought the negative sexual stereotypes about black people, young black women's expression of sexual agency appeared especially disrespectful, unacceptable, and foolhardy to those separated from them by class, status, and generation. Black reformers also experienced tensions with white sympathizers, as well as other black activists.

Interracial and Intraracial Conflicts in Urban Reform

In 1905, the *New York Evening Post* revealed tensions between white and black reformers. An article titled "White Rose Mission Settlement" explained that the institution served the needs of "the dark-skinned little

Americans who are not very welcome elsewhere." The article expressed surprise at the Home's sustained success, as well as its move from a "notorious neighborhood." The article implied that Matthews hid her reasons for acquiring the house and obtained the lease by passing for a white woman: Matthews's racial identity was "not apparent to the casual observer, and it was possible for her to lease the house without explanation." The article reassured concerned white and black residents that the Home's social welfare work was legitimate and noted that not a single complaint had ever been received from neighbors since the settlement was established.[92]

For black reformers, the most troubling sections of the article asserted that white benefactors' support of the White Rose Home diminished its support from segments of the black community. Highlighting what it deemed to be black elites' moral problems with the institution, the *Post* reported that the White Rose Mission's tolerance of card playing and the development of whist clubs were particularly controversial. Blacks' support for the Home was portrayed as inconsistent, while its ultimate success was explained by generous donations from benevolent white men and women. The article's representation of black community members' attitudes prompted the *New York Age*, a black newspaper, to respond by pointing to the stability and visibility of black female reformers. Matthews was "fortunate . . . in having with her a body of race women as earnest and self-sacrificing as herself . . . [who] have done a vast deal of good and . . . deserve . . . generous support."[93] In its critique of the *Post*, as well as white reformers, the *Age* encouraged forms of interracial cooperation that acknowledged rather than ignored black people's contributions: "We have no sympathy with the organized effort to supplant the White Rose Mission Work being made by some white friends who have become interested in settlement work among the Afro-Americans of New York. There is room for all in the work, and the pioneers should not be shoved aside by the new-comers or for the new-comers. They should rather work together in harmony."[94]

The controversy exposed how black reformers negotiated their own visions of racial uplift while depending on white patronage. They remained conscious of their sometimes tenuous position as long-standing community leaders who appreciated but were also critical of white reformers' power within black urban reform efforts. As an institution that sustained itself through "voluntary contributions," the Home was partly supported both by black community members and by "some of New York's wealthiest families."[95] Matthews understood that the substantial support she received from white reformers might usurp her own power and obscure black activists' contributions. Her sentiments about the centrality of black reformers' presence in racial uplift were well known and respected. White reformer Mary White Ovington, who decided after working primarily with immigrants to devote her activism to black urban reform, wrote W. E. B. Du Bois in 1906 explaining that she was taking up her social work on the West Side of New York because "that [did not] involve any difficulty with Mrs. Matthews."[96] While Ovington's letter failed to explain what "difficulty with Mrs. Matthews" meant, her actions suggest that if there were racial and gendered tensions among New York residents it would not seem peculiar that some of that tension might affect interracial reform.

Matthews's accomplishments were many in her six long years with the White Rose Mission, but the difficult labor of instructing migrants and protecting black women, with constant underfunding and inadequate space, seemed perpetual. Suffering from "exposure and overwork," Matthews entered a "sanatorium for pulmonary tendencies" in 1903.[97] In 1907, the forty-six-year-old reformer died of tuberculosis. The Home did not pass on with her. For the next thirteen years, the White Rose Mission's presidency was filled by Mrs. Mary Stone, the white woman who had served as vice president. A later history of the Home remarked that Stone "was the only white person to hold that position in the forty years of the organization's existence."[98] In 1915, the Home's constitution was amended to stipulate that the seventeen-member board of directors should not "contain more than three white persons."[99] Facing continual financial problems and the staggering number of migrants during the 1910s and World War I, the White Rose Mission, like most black institutions, followed those migrants by eventually moving uptown to Harlem.

While the *New York Age* highlighted black and white supporters of the Home, it declined to address divisions within black urban reform. The issue of protecting black women was a general concern, but the "harmony" that black reformers deemed necessary to achieve their objectives was sometimes absent. Personal and philosophical differences among reformers sometimes obscured the working-class black women whom they sought to assist.

When the limited housing facilities available to black women's lodging forced the Colored Young Women's Christian Association (YWCA) to refuse applicants, Nannie Helen Burroughs, president and founder of the National Training School in Washington, DC, decided to take action.[100] Burroughs complained at a meeting of the Empire State Federation of Women's Clubs and to the *New York Age* that she and two of her students were refused lodging at the Harlem YWCA. At midnight on a rainy night, after several unsuccessful attempts to find accommodations, Burroughs and her students went to the Colored YWCA but were told that there was no more room and that they could go to the Home for Working Girls. Wet and exhausted, Burroughs dismissed this suggestion, arguing that they would probably be turned away again. In Burroughs's account of incident, the YWCA secretary, Cecelia Cabaniss, eventually revealed that the house had "one empty bed" but failed to offer the bed to the women, telling them, "we cannot accommodate you" and suggesting that they go to "The Home for Working Girls."[101] Burroughs made a final call to friends who were unfortunately out of town and unable to help her. She claimed that she and her girls had to walk the streets all night in pouring rain, not finding a place of shelter until the next morning.

By 1914, seven years after Matthews's death, Burroughs argued that social service had become a professional career rather than an evangelical calling; indeed, it was a "fad for a number of women who scorned that old word missionary [and rushed] to become Social Workers. . . . They go into this work to get a decent salary, certain social ambitions and to feed the humble with a long spoon, at other people's weak expense." She concluded: "God forbid that poor, green girls should fall into the hands of one of these faddists."[102] The YWCA's response to Burroughs's complaint suggested that after all of their efforts to assist her with accommodations elsewhere, she had refused them; in their estimation, the entire occurrence was a simple matter of an inflated ego.

This incident was publicized because of Burroughs's prominence and forthrightness. How many other women were turned away from similar settlements because of a lack of accommodations? While surviving organizational records from these institutions depict certain characteristics about black women in need, they would be less likely to allow us to gauge the experiences of women who were not accommodated at all. The best known organizations for assisting black women, the Colored Branch of the YWCA and the White Rose Mission Working Girls' Home, often served dual purposes as temporary residences for respectable women and much-needed shelter for newly arrived migrants. In 1905, assessing her involvement in the matter, Matthews said that "the public was not aroused to the horror of 'girl traffic,'" forcing black activists like herself to "work through colored churches, the preachers' meetings and by writing South to good women in larger centres."[103] Facing continuing financial difficulties, black reformers generally welcomed the efforts of white Progressives in addressing the problems of black urban residents. Frances Kellor's efforts to protect black women were most widely recognized.

In a 1924 speech, Eugene Kinckle Jones, executive secretary of the National Urban League, remembered the impact of Frances Kellor's social activism on behalf of black women. Jones emphasized that Kellor had initially helped working-class and poor immigrant white women adjust to America but eventually recognized the plight of black migrants in large northern cities. The black Urban League executive recalled how she met with a group of interracial reformers and argued that "the only difference between . . . the problems of the white girl [and those of the colored girl] . . . was that there was at least a sympathetic community waiting to give her a chance in the new country while with the colored girls, neither the white community nor the colored community was sympathetic . . . [to] their hopes and aspirations."[104] This memory of Kellor trumpeted her important work with black women while eliding the earlier work of Victoria Earle Matthews. Matthews was often frustrated by this sort of blatant disregard of her mission. In 1905, she wrote an editorial responding to the *New York Tribune*'s claim that "no one meets colored girls from the South but runners for disorderly resorts." The black settlement house founder fervently demanded that "the facts . . . not be overlooked, especially as [such a] statement discredits the work of a struggling band of negro women organized and incorporated to do that very work."[105]

Kellor's assessment of black reformers' community work was incorrect, but her critique of white urban reformers' indifference was more accurate. Her evaluation reinforced the findings of a number of Christian activists that immigrants received more attention than black migrants. In 1902, *Federation*, the journal of the Federation of Churches and Christian Organizations in New York City, criticized their own urban missionaries who chose to address Chinese immigrants' needs and neglected black city-dwellers. "Inasmuch as the Chinese cannot become citizens," it stated, "[and] the Constitution . . . has been specially amended to give the negro the ballot, there is opportunity for an equally honorable missionary effort among New York's blacks."[106] Apathy toward the problems of black migrant women may have stemmed from the disconnect between nineteenth-century evangelically based reform and early-twentieth-century social-scientific Progressivism. An indication of the severity of racial divisions in urban reform is the fact that during Kellor's initial investigations of New York employment agencies' exploitation of black women, she appeared to not have encountered or noted prominently the prior work of Victoria Earle Matthews until seeking more information regarding the problem at scholar-activist W. E. B. Du

Frances Kellor, ca. 1890. Photo by W. H. Ballard. Courtesy of Schlesinger Library, Radcliffe Institute, Harvard University.

Bois's 1905 Atlanta University Studies Conference, which both women attended.[107]

Kellor represented the growing number of young white women who turned their college and graduate school education into professional careers. Some of them extended settlement house work from immigrants to encompass interracial work with black women.[108] Their investigations of urban poverty were not only a means of educating the public; they also hoped to resolve these problems through legislation and governmental action.[109] In 1905, Kellor established local associations for the protection of black women migrating to New York City and Philadelphia. At the same time, she advocated that southern states pass laws to protect black workers from being exploited by northern labor agents.[110] Starting with an effort to regulate the practices of corrupt employment agencies, the associations, which eventually became the National League for the Protection of Colored Women, dealt with the various phases of migrants' adjustment to urban life.

Kellor's focus on poor women as well as black people may have stemmed from her own working-class background. Born in Coldwater, Michigan, in 1873, Kellor, whose single mother was a domestic worker, lived in dire poverty for most of her childhood. Her life changed when she accidentally shot herself in the hand and two local librarians, Mary and Frances Eddy, became her guardians. With their guidance and support, Kellor's education flourished, leading her to attend Cornell University's law school and, later, graduate school at the University of Chicago.[111]

Kellor's professional interest in social reform began in 1898, a year after the White Rose Home opened. Under the direction of Charles Henderson at the University of Chicago, she specialized in criminal sociology, whose purpose she defined as "to investigate crime scientifically: to study its origin and causes, and to determine, if possible, what proportion of responsibility belongs to society and what to the criminal."[112] Like other women in her graduate school cohort, including Sophonisba Breckinridge, Edith Abbott, and Katharine Bement Davis, Kellor used her training as a social scientist to address social problems.

Her first major research project focused on female criminality. Kellor compared the physical characteristics and behavior of female offenders with those of college-educated women and found no significant differences. She was the first sociologist to disprove the theory that physiological character- istics were prime indicators of criminal behavior in women, which was ar- ticulated by Cesare Lombroso, the prominent anthropologist and author of *The Female Offender* (1895).[113] Kellor argued that a person's environment, particularly his or her social and economic background, contributed to the development of criminal behavior. Black people were not constitutionally criminal; rather, the conditions of enslavement prevented them from be- coming civilized. Her subsequent investigation of the southern penal sys- tem, which expanded exponentially after emancipation, demonstrated that its reformatory mission was undermined by whites' disbelief in the possi- bility of moral growth among blacks, as well as states' growing dependence on prison revenue. She pointedly observed that "so long as a State's crimi- nals bring it a net revenue of from $30,000 to $150,000 a year, it is difficult to introduce methods leading to reform and to the decrease of crime."[114]

Kellor's investigation of southern prisons represents her first sustained discussion of gender, race, and criminality, as she began to explore how en- slavement shaped black women's morality and delinquent behavior.[115] While black female reformers such as Matthews stressed the progress made by for- merly enslaved black women as well as prominent blacks' attempts to up- lift the masses, Kellor's focus on offenders emphasized the extent to which blacks needed to catch up to "the Anglo-Saxon race." In some respects, Kel- lor's research coincided with that of prominent black activists who focused on family life as a civilizing force and the problems within the unskilled servant class. Yet her criticisms of enslavement and racial discrimination

Single Black Women and Their Protectors

in the South generally and in the southern penal system specifically characterized black people as without individual agency to improve themselves and to fight for their rights. She failed to consider that it was possible for a black person to develop a moral sense even under the most devastating circumstances, such as those endured by Victoria Earle Matthews. According to Kellor, "There is no race outside of barbarism where there is so low a grade of domestic life, and where the child receives so little training." In her view, black women's immoral behavior was a key problem.[116] In 1901, without considering that women might resist sexual harassment and rape, Kellor stated that "Negro women yield to white men quite as readily as in slavery."[117] Revealing the sentiments expressed by most white Americans and the stereotypes that black activists sought to dispel, Kellor noted that the "negro women and negro girl, judged by civilized standards, are to a large extent immoral."[118] Her experiences with convicts led her to conclude that "there is not yet developed in the race, as a whole, a pride in and honor for its women."[119] Although Kellor thought that blacks were naturally inferior, she believed that in time they could be reformed, a faith that biological determinists did not share. While acknowledging the immoral conditions to which black women were subjected both under enslavement and in freedom, she did not believe that black people had made sufficient progress by the early twentieth century: "First savages, then slaves, with the women in the position of beasts of burden and bearers of future slaves, . . . with scarcely forty years intervening[,] the result [immorality] is inevitable."[120]

In spite of these sentiments, or perhaps because of them, Kellor became one of the leading white advocates for black women's protection in the city. In 1902, a year after publishing her findings about black criminality in the journal *Arena* and in her book, *Experimental Sociology*, Kellor embarked upon a wholesale investigation of urban poverty and unemployment. Her new project was connected to her previous research, since she believed that unemployment led to women's criminality. In the process of probing corrupt employment agencies, she discovered that southern black women migrants who worked as domestics in the North faced equally disturbing labor conditions.[121]

With financial support and fellowships from the College Settlement Association and the New York School of Philanthropy, Kellor examined the practices of employment agencies in New York, Boston, Philadelphia, and Chicago. As historian Ellen Fitzpatrick has noted, Kellor's investigations, which eventually culminated in her second book, *Out of Work*, represented "one of the first studies in the United States to analyze unemployment as a

The Problem of the Young Negro Girl from the South

A City Girl.

Lared Away from Her Rural Home by Unscrupulous Agents to Find Herself Here Confronted by a Choice Between Starvation and Unworthy Associations---Here Is an Opportunity for Practical Philanthropists.

Interior of a Brooklyn Agency. Securing Women as a Sitting room.

A type.

Interior of a South Ave. Employment Agency.

Just from the South.

Exterior of a Brooklyn Employment Agency.

A sketch titled "The Problem of the Young Negro Girl from the South,"
from the New York Times, *March 19, 1905.*

social problem." The unemployed were not characterized as consistently idle or lazy; rather, their predicament was seen as one of the consequences of industrial capitalism. Poverty, race, and ethnicity exacerbated their situation and made them easy targets for fraudulent employment agencies. Working with reformer Mary Dreier, Kellor successfully advocated state legislation to enforce licensure and other regulations. Focusing on the dilemmas women experienced, Kellor worked with organizations to form the Inter-Municipal Committee on Household Research. Her concern about black women's plight stemmed from her investigations of employment agencies that promised them jobs as domestics. Confronting a long-standing issue of black activists, Kellor was most concerned about exposing corrupt agencies that hired young women for domestic service but placed them in what she deemed morally and sexually compromising positions, either forcing them into prostitution or forcing them to work as servants in houses of prostitution.[122]

Single Black Women and Their Protectors

In her research and advocacy work, Kellor expressed contradictory ideas about black migrant women's propensity for immoral and criminal behavior. She pondered whether black women's criminality was southern-bred or stemmed from their association with employment agencies. She believed that the agencies' system of "importing (domestic) help from the South is responsible for only some of black women's criminality."[123] In her view, black women were already prone to criminality before they were influenced by the evil practices of northern employment bureaus. Kellor's claim that black women's migration north to seek employment through labor agents would lead to a life of crime was corroborated by another University of Chicago graduate student, Katharine Bement Davis, superintendent of the New York State Reformatory for Women at Bedford. In conjunction with Kellor's campaigns against corrupt employment agencies, Davis revealed the parallel increase in the numbers of Bedford's black inmates who were migrants. In 1904, the reformatory's third annual report noted that "with the increase in the larceny cases . . . [came] an increase in the percentage of colored women who were primarily brought north by employment bureaus."[124] Neither Davis nor Kellor questioned the influence that legislative changes and corrupt policing had on the rising numbers of migrant women who were incarcerated.

Kellor never quite reconciled her advocacy of black women's protection against sexual exploitation with her belief that these women were already problematic or even immoral before their migration to New York. She emphasized the need to protect black women before they reached employment agencies that taught them "so much immorality, dishonesty, impertinence, intemperance and shiftlessness that they can . . . never be quite reclaimed."[125] Admonishing migrant women against signing deceptive contracts that promised "good wages, easy work, and good times," she disregarded their lack of alternatives. She dismissed the crises that blacks faced at the turn of the century—sharecropping, debt peonage, low wages, antiblack violence, and racial segregation—when she assumed that these women left "happy-go-lucky, cheerful lives in the South."[126] Once migrant women arrived in the city, she seemed unable to account for the fact that "while housework pays . . . good wages at the start the chances of promotion are . . . few."[127] Instead of acknowledging middle-class white women's preference for white or immigrant servants, she blamed black women for their own predicament, noting that their "increasing inefficiency and desire to avoid hard work" led to their being "gradually supplant[ed] with whites" in "the best households and hotels and restaurants."[128] In a significant number of instances, she disregarded the narrative of the "ignorant negro girl brought from the South" needing protection and wondered: "Is it that the Negro woman is already immoral when she reaches our Northern cities?"[129]

Kellor's question reflects white reformers' specific concerns about how the legacy of enslavement affected black women's capacity for a virtue worthy of protection. Unlike Matthews and her cohort, who emphasized a legacy "from the hand of the white rapist" when assessing working and poor black women's morality, white reformers generally believed that these women were more dangerous to society than endangered within that society.[130] After her investigations in the South, Kellor consistently remarked that sexual relationships between black women and white men continued after slavery as "white men have little respect for the sanctity of family life of negroes, [whereas] they would hesitate to enter the Anglo Saxon's home."[131] In 1903, Kellor's view remained unchanged: black women were as culpable as white men for social immorality. "Until Negro women cease to prefer white men, and white men come to respect the rights of Negro husbands and fathers," she asserted, "the immorality of women will increase."[132] The social scientist's assessments never suggested that because "white men had little respect" for black homes that they might in fact have little "respect for the rights" of black women, or that black men, in an era of violent black repression, were unable to protect their wives, daughters, and kin. Indeed, many of the migrants whom Kellor and Matthews encountered may have left the South for personal rather than purely economic reasons. Historian Darlene Clark Hine has argued that many migrants sought to escape from "sexual exploitation both within and outside of their families and from sexual abuse at the hands of southern white as well as black men."[133] Despite Kellor's acknowledgment of white men's inappropriate presence and behavior in black homes, she continued to question black women's virtue: "Negro women are expected to be immoral and have few inducements to be otherwise."[134] Although other Progressive Era mandates regulated sexuality, Kellor did not believe that legislation could address this issue; only a "change in attitude" among black women and white men would remedy the problem. Seven years after the founding of the National Association of Colored Women, Kellor argued in the *Southern Workman*, Hampton Institute's journal, that "Negro women must develop a greater racial integrity, pride and loyalty; and the whites must not only respect it, but assist in its creation."[135] Even an advocate for black women's protection, who in 1906 established the National League for the Protection of Colored Women (NLPCW), believed that black women's capacity for moral reform was limited.

Negative stereotypes of black women's promiscuity influenced most reformers, especially those willing to work on behalf of black women. In 1910, speaking at an NLPCW meeting, white reformer Ray Stannard Baker noted that the rise in black morality since enslavement was remarkable. For many, the idea of equating black womanhood with virtue would always represent a paradox. "For," as the *New York Age* expressed it, "in the South few people expect the colored girl to be moral. Everything is against her morality. In the first place the home life is still primitive. The highest ideal before the eyes of the women in many cases is the finely dressed, prosperous concubine of a white man. Moreover in nearly all Southern towns disorderly houses are relegated to the Negro quarter."[136]

Prejudices about black women's incapacity for moral behavior prompted a number of reformers to make clear distinctions between black and immigrant women and influenced the way in which they sought to improve black women's labor conditions. As she investigated black women's labor in New York City, Mary White Ovington, a settlement house worker and founding member of the National Association for the Advancement of Colored People (NAACP), argued that black women "bereft of home influence, with an ancestry that sometimes cries out her parent's weakness in the counter and color of her face . . . more than the foreign immigrant, are . . . subject to degrading temptation." In language echoing that of her friend W. E. B. Du Bois, she declared: "In their hours of leisure, the surplus women are known to play havoc with their neighbors' sons, even with their neighbors' husbands," resulting in "social disorder."[137] Ovington also highlighted the racially discriminatory labor market that restricted black women to domestic work: "She gets the job that the white girl does not want."[138] Although she answered her own question, "does the attempt to force all women of a race into one industry make for better service in it?" in the negative, Ovington and other white reformers seemed to privilege training more efficient personal-service workers over contesting the long-standing fact that racism precluded black women from other types of employment more suitable to their interests and skill level. While there were some local signs of what scholar Elisabeth Lasch-Quinn calls a "vision [that] rested on a staunch belief in racial equality, mutuality, and integration," there was no wholesale campaign to place black workers in varied types of industrial and skilled employment.[139] With successful legislative campaigns to eradicate child labor and improve factory working conditions and wages, as well as regulate employment bureaus, white Progressives involved with black women's protection seemed more willing to address the consequences of labor discrimination than racial inequity.

These assessments led the NLPCW to encourage black women to remain in the South.[140] In articles designed to garner financial support for the protection of black migrant women, Kellor continually asserted that rural women were totally unprepared for the complexity and dangers of urban life in the North.[141] At one point, Kellor even argued that enslavement was more benevolent than the exploitation found in wage labor: "Between the old Southern master and the slave there was often some genuine human interest, some bond of human sympathy! Between the new master—the employment agent—and the servant, there is nothing but the cold, metallic clink of dollars and cents."[142] This twisted logic shows the way in which white patriarchal power might be hidden behind a face of benign paternalism.

Kellor's investigations of northern employment agencies afforded crucial publicity for the many challenges that black women and migrants faced in New York City. While her research corroborated Matthews's conclusions that black employment agencies were corrupt, Kellor framed her discussion around troubling interracial interactions. In *Out of Work*, Kellor argued that black agencies were problematic because they provided black women with an incentive to leave the South. Characterizing the majority of these agencies as corrupt, she argued that migrant women were "often threatened until they accept positions in questionable places and frequently sent out without knowing the character of their destination." In contrast to her work with immigrants, in which she promoted cross-cultural contacts and assimilation, Kellor expressed concern when she observed that black agencies encouraged young black women to seek better opportunities in the city. "Unlike white offices, negro proprietors really believe they are bettering the condition of these girls by giving them city life and the advantages and the opportunity to mingle with whites."[143] In Kellor's view, white women's use of these agencies to find domestic servants created problematic interracial contact. White women's patronage increased black agencies' legitimacy, but these agencies allegedly sent the innocent women to brothels, where they could "have a good time and make money." She contended that black agencies "reflect the current thought among many city negroes that immorality between negroes and whites is a mark of distinction and is to be encouraged."[144] However, a review of *Out of Work* in the *Southern Workman* disputed her claims, in part by emphasizing how class distinctions within black urban communities accounted for some of her more negative observations: "City negroes are not to be judged by those who visit employment agencies," and Kellor's analysis "applies only to the lowest classes of city Negroes."[145] The reviewer reinforced the class and regional distinctions within black communities that defined and fueled the black elite's program of racial uplift. While Kellor's assessment reflects her inability to recognize complexity

Single Black Women and Their Protectors

within black communities, the response by the *Southern Workman*'s black book reviewer illuminates the tenor of intraracial class tensions, as well as prominent blacks' continual efforts to distinguish themselves from their working, poor brethren.

These activists must have understood the significance of Kellor's activism, which directly addressed those issues she found most troubling in working-class and poor black communities, particularly the plight of migrant women. At a time when racism permeated American society in law and practice, Kellor's sustained effort to improve working conditions for black women was unusual. At a time when the North and South seemed eager to dismiss their previous divisions over the race problem, Kellor's criticism of discrimination was especially significant. Like many white social scientists, she questioned biological explanations for behavior and posited the possibility of rehabilitation. Black reformers understood that attention to the environment and the structural issues of employment, housing, and education complemented their own commitment to a politics of respectability. Kellor's focus on poverty, unemployment, and the exploitation of workers, as well as her critical admonitions about behavior, coincided with the long-standing issues and concerns of many black activists. Along with her access to financial support and government interest, particularly with the passage of the law regulating employment agencies, black elites relied on her research and worked with her when establishing organizations for the protection of black women. Hampton Institute requested information on the dangers of northern city life for black women,[146] and in May 1905, W. E. B. Du Bois invited both Kellor and Matthews to speak at the Tenth Atlanta Negro Conference at Atlanta University.[147]

Led by Kellor, black and white reformers, as well as black churches in New York City, Philadelphia, and Boston, established associations for the protection of black women. In order to monitor migrant women from the time they left the South, the associations reached out to Washington, DC, Baltimore, Norfolk, and Memphis. In 1906, the organization changed its name to the National League for the Protection of Colored Women.[148] Four years later, the group helped to found the National Urban League.

Urban reformers sought to prevent the dangers that black women, especially single migrants, encountered in the city. Their programs developed alongside discussions of black men defending black women and black women's self-defense in early-twentieth-century New York. Urban reformers understood black women's protection as a crucial component of their activism.

Both black and white reformers sought to inform black women of the dangers associated with urban life and offer them alternatives to exploitative employment agencies and commercial recreation. They failed to address the discriminatory employment practices that precluded black women from non-personal-service jobs or the labor exploitation these women faced as domestic workers within everyday households. Instead they sought to regulate working women's behavior by inculcating Victorian virtues and middle-class values with the purpose of improving their morals, employment prospects, and efficiency.

Victoria Earle Matthews and Frances Kellor addressed protection by emphasizing the significance of employment. Both women believed that black women should be well trained and marketable in the domestic-service sector. Matthews was the first woman in New York to address and institutionalize the needs of young black migrant women through her working girls' settlement, the White Rose Mission. In Matthews's view, presenting a respectable working woman would help dispel the negative images associated with black women and aid in uplifting the race. Kellor's national activism built upon Matthews's local efforts, as she institutionalized programs for black working women, especially migrants.[149] Kellor's perspective differed sharply from Matthews's, however, for she thought of the women she served more as objects of rehabilitation than as agents in their own right. For Kellor, training black women reduced the number of victims of corrupt employment agencies and addressed the pressing concern of white employers about untrained working women in the city.

Reformers soon found that their work failed to prevent increasing numbers of black women from landing in prison. The next section explores urban reform and criminal justice through the experiences of black female offenders, white and black prison reformers, and black working-class families. New York's massive waves of newcomers, whether southern migrants or immigrants, worried urban elites, and the Great Migration of African Americans aroused particularly intense concern. In particular, reformers' and prison administrators' anxieties about black women's presence in the city influenced how they dealt with those who entered the criminal justice system, whether they were labeled as dangerous, even violent female felons at the New York State Prison for Women or as sexually dangerous female misdemeanants at the New York State Reformatory for Women at Bedford.

URBAN REFORM AND CRIMINAL JUSTICE

4

colored women of hard and vicious character

RESPECTABILITY, DOMESTICITY, AND CRIME, 1893–1933

> They said I might suffer harm from the convicts for some were
> colored women of hard and vicious character, occasionally violent, and
> I must look out for the blows.
>
> —Madeleine Z. Doty, November 3, 1916

> William Newton . . . a longshoreman, was stabbed to death Sunday by
> his common law wife, Susie Roberts, in their home. . . . He began to beat her, she
> said, and in self defense she took up a knife from the table and stabbed him. . . .
> She had not intended to kill him, she said, only to hurt him sufficiently to
> make him let her alone.
>
> —*New York Amsterdam News*, March 24, 1926

As Madeleine Doty, a white reformer, entered the New York State Prison
for Women at Auburn, she was less concerned with protecting vulnerable
black women than with being protected from black criminals. In her 1916
book, *Society's Misfits*, Doty revealed the grave concerns she had felt three
years earlier as she began her investigation of female felons and the institutional conditions they experienced at the New York State Prison for Women
at Auburn. As a lawyer and a member of the state Commission on Prison
Reform, she embarked on the project by spending a week as an undercover
inmate. She was especially anxious about being imprisoned with physically
strong, sometimes violent black women. The morning before her incarceration, she recalled, she had studied her appearance and wished that she
"looked stronger." The prison warden and commission members who knew
of her ruse also "questioned her strength" and warned her that she "might

suffer harm from the convicts for some were colored women of hard and vicious character, occasionally violent," and that she "must look out for the blows."[1]

A college-educated, middle-class white woman, Doty was seen as distinctly feminine, while the black women she feared were perceived as masculine. From the advent of American slavery, whites refused to recognize black women as feminine; womanliness was an attribute reserved for whites. In the late eighteenth century, femininity was redefined through women's physical weakness and moral strength.[2] In the nineteenth century, the dominant ideology was what historian Barbara Welter called "the cult of true womanhood," which emphasized feminine "piety, purity, submissiveness, and domesticity."[3] As scholar Hazel Carby suggests, those who espoused this ideology believed that a woman's "external physical appearance" reflected her "internal qualities of character."[4] The femininity of native-born white women was regarded as natural, their virtue inherent in their bodies, while black women were seen as the antithesis of femininity because of the sexual violation that their enslaved foremothers had endured. The legacy of enslavement constructed a sharp distinction between black and white womanhood.[5] Carby points out that "strength and ability to bear fatigue, argued to be so distasteful a presence in a white woman, were positive features to be emphasized in the promotion and selling of a black female hand at a slave auction."[6] After emancipation, ideas about black women's masculine strength persisted, but whites thought that physical strength was accompanied by moral weakness, rendering black women as the negative opposite of white women. These ideas still held sway in the early twentieth century, despite the fact that many women—whether they were white, immigrant, or black—failed to conform to this feminine ideal. Black female offenders were perceived through a racial lens as evidence of the "primitive" qualities of the race. Scholar Nicole Hahn Rafter points out that the "bad woman" was usually seen as "dark, large, hairy, aggressive—in a word, masculine."[7]

Racialized notions of femininity influenced how society understood a woman's criminal culpability as well. White women were regarded as deserving of male protection and as constitutionally unable to commit serious crimes against property or persons, especially when associated with violence. At the turn of the twentieth century, social scientists such as Frances Kellor argued that women did not have the "physical capacity for committing crimes of violence," and, as a result, they chose "prostitution."[8] Gendered notions shaped the criminal justice system as well. Female offenders who had committed misdemeanors were seen as "fallen women" in need of moral rehabilitation, including practical instruction in domesticity. Activists believed that these young women's behavior—having been "led astray by" their "own baser instincts or by a male consort"—could be corrected at institutions like the New York State Reformatory for Women at Bedford.[9] In contrast, female felons—who were generally black, immigrant, working-class, and poor—incarcerated in state prisons such as Auburn were depicted by the larger society and criminal justice officials as irredeemable.

This chapter explores the lived experiences of female felons as they reveal some of the ambiguities and contradictions in the construction of womanhood and race.[10] Because powerful tropes defined black women as either the sexually promiscuous Jezebel or the faithful servant Mammy, their struggles with marital and familial relationships were usually ignored.[11] Many black women's appearance, particularly their skin color, and physicality seemed threatening in white people's minds because it connected them to masculinity and crime rather than feminine respectability. The cases of women imprisoned at Auburn, in contrast, highlight a consistent, though underexplored, theme: black working women's struggle to negotiate mainstream society's and their own communities' standards of moral propriety.[12] Vulnerable but not completely victimized, these women's moments of agency sometimes coincided with the commission of a crime.

Auburn inmate records not only indicate the types of felonies these women committed but also suggest how their offenses arose from their situations. Their crimes, such as murder, manslaughter, assault, grand larceny, and arson, reflect the predicaments that poor and working women faced when they received low wages, experienced marital and family problems, challenged police officers and employers, and succumbed to alcoholism and drug abuse. Although from the vantage point of the dominant society of the time, their crimes seemed indistinguishable from men's offenses and outside the realm of femininity, a closer examination of female felons and their actions illuminates the conflicts that working-class women experienced as they grappled with everyday life and the unstable categories of respectability, marriage, and motherhood. Many women who had trouble navigating the urban and domestic terrain did not end up in prison, but these Auburn cases speak to the larger issues black working women confronted. Influenced by the dominant society and their own communities, they nonetheless made their own choices. This chapter examines how Auburn's black female felons incorporated or dismissed the gendered conventions of womanhood.

Doty's initial anxieties about female felons underscored the prevailing ideas of criminal anthropology, which mapped criminality on the black and ethnic body. Criminal anthropologists assessed lawbreaking, Nicole Hahn

Rafter and Mary Gibson explain, "by using the human body as fundamental data."[13] The Italian physician Cesare Lombroso, the well-known founder of criminal anthropology and author of the influential 1895 *Female Offender*, defined female criminals as prime examples of atavism who exhibited inappropriate virility.[14] For Lombroso and other scientists, who were heavily influenced by Darwin's theory of evolution, "criminals were products of bad stock—individuals" who, as scholar Simon Cole notes, "were less evolved than the rest of the population, in much the same way that 'savages' and other indigenous peoples were less evolved than Europeans."[15] In the early-twentieth-century United States, with the simultaneous rise of European immigration, the Great Migration, and national and local concerns about reinforcing Anglo-Saxon Protestant control and white supremacy, this conflation of black and ethnic women with female offenders—who were primitive rather than civilized, and virile rather than feminine—confirmed the idea that white Anglo-Saxon women were not criminal, while racial-ethnic women were deviant. Lombroso contended, "What we look for most in the female is femininity. And when we find the opposite in her we conclude as a rule that there must be some anomaly." He identified the anomaly as virility, which he explained as "one of the special features of the savage woman." Illustrating his point with images of Native American and black women ("Red Indian and Negro beauties"), he claimed that these "primitives" were "difficult to recognise" as women. "So huge are their jaws and cheek-bones, so hard and coarse their features," that one could immediately detect their innate criminality. Lombroso described these women as similar to men in their "stature, cranium, brain," and "muscular strength," a quality that "the modern female" failed to possess.[16]

Lombroso's theories of gender and race coincided with those of French criminologist Alphonse Bertillion, who was also influenced by anthropology's focus on the nonwhite "savage" criminal. In the late 1870s, Bertillion developed a system that used anthropomorphic measurements—quantifying the head, arms, torso, legs, and so on—to identify the criminal body.[17] Lombroso considered this French system "an ark of salvation" for criminal identification, and Bertillionage was practiced in the United States by 1887.[18] Auburn's documentation of all incoming women in an identification ledger mirrored both scholars' theories. Doty observed that "to be bertillioned is to have your photograph taken" and "your body parts measured," resulting in a precise description so an inmate was "easily identified by the police" as a "known criminal."[19] "To criminal anthropologists," Simon Cole contends, "the distinction between using the criminal body as a link to a criminal record and simply reading criminality directly from the body was not entirely clear"; their reasoning seems circular, confirming their prejudice rather than that they were testing hypotheses.[20] Prevailing ideologies about black women's lack of femininity and innate criminality were confirmed in European criminologists' theories. Black women were located at the nexus of sexuality and violence. Black women's threatening presence—except when they acted subserviently—presented a myriad of problems to white people. Within the criminal justice system, black women were delinquent because they were sexually dangerous to unsuspecting white men and physically threatening to the rest of nonblack society. In prison at Auburn, they were characterized as physically threatening to weaker white and ethnic women. Yet the evidence that surfaces regarding black female felons' experiences prior to their imprisonment conveys different and more complex narratives of how these women were intimately engaged in and vulnerable to—rather than detached from—the everyday dynamics of domesticity and respectability.

Twenty-six-year-old Mamie Spencer had never been arrested before she was sent to prison in 1927. With a sister who owned a "hair dressing parlor" and a brother-in-law who had a "newspaper stand," Spencer was a housewife involved in the Eastern Star, the Masonic women's auxiliary; her second husband was a Mason, although the sources fail to identify his occupation. On October 4, 1926, Spencer became incensed when, as she put it, her husband had "been out all night and throwed away the money." The couple's verbal dispute escalated into a "tussle," and Spencer stabbed him, later alleging that she committed the act in self-defense. At the time, neither she nor her husband knew that the injury was "serious," but he died four days later.[21] Spencer was imprisoned for second-degree manslaughter.

It is unlikely that Spencer would have classed herself with Auburn's "colored women of hard and vicious character"; she was a black housewife and mother involved in a domestic quarrel that turned fatal. While Doty worried about how she would survive a week-long self-imposed prison sentence, we must wonder what Spencer worried about when she was given a two-year prison sentence. She had depended on her husband's earnings to maintain the household, and his spending the money on his own pleasures rather than turning it over to her was deeply distressing to her. Spencer's anxieties about money highlight the tenuous financial footing of many working-class black households. The records fail to reveal whether she worked intermittently to help support the household, but her actions suggest that she struggled to attain and maintain a viable domestic role and be recognized as a responsible, respectable citizen, both within her own community and in prison. What anxieties did black women have upon entering

Auburn? How did they deal with the prospect of "colored women of hard and vicious character" who were "occasionally violent" and from whom they "must look out for the blows"? Had Spencer, like Doty, looked in the mirror and wondered if she was strong enough to face prison life? She would be separated from her child and other family members for at least two years. How did she see herself, and would her assessment matter?

Prison reports show that Spencer's actions reinforced the distinctions she made between a female criminal and a woman who committed an act deemed criminal, and her behavior made quite an impression on administrators. Descriptions of Spencer's behavior and character differ radically depending on the official assessing her. According to the head teacher, Helen Stone, she was "excellent most of the time" and showed "greater progress" than Stone had believed she was "capable of making."[22] The shop and laundry attendant, however, said Spencer was "lazy" and "her work was not . . . satisfactory" and described Spencer as "peculiar and egotistical" because she "did not get along with others."[23] Her physician's evaluation echoed the laundry attendant's; he reported that Spencer exhibited "special character defects of egocentrism" and was given to peevish complaining or grumbling.[24] According to prison officials' assessments, Spencer's disinterest in manual labor and her desire to educate herself were problematic. Administrators were aware of Spencer's rejection of her criminal status and saw her confident behavior as incongruous for a black female felon. As Spencer's case illustrates, black women's attempts to negotiate their own sense of domesticity and respectability proved difficult within as well as outside of prison. In both places, she failed to exemplify the societal image of the female criminal incarcerated at Auburn.

Women at Auburn Prison

In 1893, the New York State Prison for Women at Auburn opened to alleviate overcrowding at county penitentiaries across the state, particularly in New York City, and to take advantage of the building made available when male prisoners in the adjacent insane asylum were transferred to a new institution at Matteawan, New York.[25] In the institution's first year, the prison's first matron, Annie Welshe, explained that the prison received 47 transfer inmates from Blackwell's Island and 59 inmates from county penitentiary transfers, along with direct court commitments, for a total population of 106.[26] State officials and prison reformers expressed little or no concern about rehabilitating inmates. As an inspector from the reform-minded Women's Prison Association (WPA) put it, at "Auburn, the murderess, the lowest courtesan, the burglar, the kidnapper, the woman convicted of arson and grand larceny, meet to expiate their crimes through long years of servitude; of course with the hope of reformation, but with the knowledge that it may not always be attained."[27] Prison administrators' and reformers' belief stemmed from the types of crimes felons had committed. In contrast to public-order offenses such as intoxication, disorderly conduct, prostitution, or child neglect, felonies included violent crimes against persons—murder, manslaughter, assault, arson, or robbery—and against property—larceny, burglary, robbery, receiving stolen property, or forgery—that society associated with masculinity rather than femininity. Assuming that these women prisoners were beyond reform, administrators focused on maintaining the institution at minimal expense.[28] Auburn never housed as many of the state's female felons as the institution's planners wished, in part because judges continued committing women to local penitentiaries, so the state Commissioners of Prisons had the 1901 Prison Law amended to require judges to send "all female felons with a sentence of a year or more to Auburn."[29] Inmates were characterized as being as hard and unfeminine as the felonies for which they had been convicted.

Consistent with public and professional expectations, many Auburn prisoners were black or immigrant.[30] Consider, for instance, an 1895 *New York Times* observation of Auburn inmates: "The female convicts are [an] unattractive looking collection. They have hard, coarse faces in most instances bearing the stamp of dense ignorance. . . . A . . . larger percentage of them . . . is colored."[31] The prison's 1895 annual report noted that out of 99 inmates, 25 were "colored" and at least 37 were "foreigners."[32] In 1910, the U.S. census noted that black people comprised just 1.5 percent of the state population, but in that same year black women represented 40 percent of the Auburn prison population.[33] A 1911 description stated that "about one-half of the women at Auburn are colored and a little over one-fourth are foreign born. Three fourths come from the slums of New York City, and they have, as a rule, little knowledge of industry or country life."[34] The prison's 1911 annual report noted inmates' low educational levels: only 3 were high school graduates, 92 had a common school background, and 22 had no education at all. As a result, 60 percent were employed as domestics and housekeepers. The report also noted that, out of a total of 132 inmates, 74 were "colored," comprising almost 60 percent, and at least 32 were "foreigners."[35] Indeed, black women were even more disproportionately represented in the prison in 1911 than they had been in 1895. This trend would continue throughout the prison's existence, even when black women's numbers dropped in certain years.[36] Like most custodial institutions, Auburn's female population was predominantly working class and poor as well as black and immigrant.[37]

The stigma of criminality influenced the type of care women received while incarcerated. State officials and reformers acknowledged Auburn's institutional problems, but, like inspectors from the WPA, they reported difficulties in a pro forma manner and then overlooked many of the prison's deficiencies. While inmates were managed by a matron, the entire institution was controlled by the superintendent of the adjacent Prison for Men. Prison schooling focused on the needs of immigrant women who had little or no command of English.[38] Little attention was paid to health care, as inmates were examined by the physician who worked at the men's prison.[39] In 1900, WPA inspectors described a functional institutional relationship between matrons and women: "The discipline seemed perfect. No conversation is permitted among the inmates, but hope is not crushed out of them, reward for good conduct rather than punishment for evil-doing being the dominant idea."[40] Several years later, the WPA's visitor explained that "for some unaccountable reason, the women employed as matrons . . . are not subjected to State Civil Service examination."[41] Prison reformer Doty later admitted that the matrons' "task was to see that prisoners did not escape. They were not paid to reform convicts."[42] With scanty state funding, the prison's facilities were woefully inadequate.[43] In 1908, following a January visit, the WPA inspector remarked that "the thermometer stood at 14 below zero," yet five women employed outside "apparently enjoyed their work." The "buildings are old and without modern conveniences, but everything showed perfect order and cleanliness."[44] WPA visitors' uncritical assessments of Auburn reinforced the idea that female felons deserved little; maintaining discipline was the institution's sole objective.

In 1913, twenty years after Auburn opened, reformer Madeleine Doty evaluated the institution's conditions in a more in-depth manner. Unlike the WPA visitors who spent between an hour and a day at the prison, Doty and her friend Elizabeth Watson, also a member of the Commission on Prison Reform, conducted a covert investigation that was planned to last a week. Doty was disguised as inmate #933, Maggie Martin, who was sentenced for forgery. Her observations convinced her that male inmates "have a paradise compared to the rigid rules applied to the women."[45] Women were required to maintain silence and follow monotonous routines of eating, walking, and working, and were confined in their cells from 4:30 P.M. to 7:00 A.M. Infractions such as talking or just smiling could mean twenty-four hours or more in a cell with no window, inadequate lighting, no opportunity to bathe, and a daily diet of three gills of water and three pieces of bread.[46] Inmates found it difficult to build communal bonds of support because "any form of greeting between [them was] considered immoral, evidence of what is termed 'lady love,' and promptly punished."[47] Cases of reprimanded inmates offer some clues as to the myriad ways that women negotiated their difficult incarceration.

If an inmate committed an infraction, her jail time was usually increased and her eligibility for parole denied. A twenty-six-year-old was denied release when the parole board chastised her for the number of punishments she had received, denoted by the D on her sleeve. During her parole hearing, a board member remarked, "That is the lowest grade and shows you have been punished 10 times, disobeying rules, using vile language, talking in school, creating disturbances in line, disturbance in hall, etc. Why can't you behave yourself?" She responded, "I will try to behave the rest part of my time."[48] Another black inmate argued that her behavioral problems were "through others" and, when asked whether she could "keep away" from incorrigible inmates, replied, "I am trying to." She lost so much time that in October 1908 the parole board informed her that she would not be eligible for release until January 1909.[49] While many inmates attempted to toe the line with prison officials, other women's patience became strained under the prison's dismal conditions and draconian punishments. When a twenty-five-year-old black inmate who had been denied parole was asked why she turned over a table, she caustically replied, "Thought I might as well do something to be punished for as to be punished for nothing."[50]

In addition to highlighting inmates' concerns and frustrations about Auburn, Madeleine Doty's published story revealed that stereotypical characterizations of female criminals failed to convey their individual or collective experiences.[51] Her experience dispelled some of her preconceived notions about Auburn women's disposition. In the year she conducted her investigation, of the prison's 116 inmates, 58 were "colored," 28 were "foreign-born," and one was "Indian."[52] She observed that "Russian and Irish, colored and Italian[,] scrubwoman and prostitute are bound together by a common misery." Doty also realized that her preconceptions about inmates' character were highly exaggerated. "I thought when I entered prison that being thrown with the type of offenders there I should hear vile language," she wrote, "but during my five days I [heard] only one instance of profanity."[53] To her surprise, she found Auburn's conditions so depressing and oppressive that even she "wanted to curse." "Prison," she remarked, "has a curious way of dragging to the surface all the profanity one has ever heard."[54] After observing a French inmate, Doty admitted that "long ago I had discovered that beauty of figure and fineness of manner are found as often among working women as among women of wealth," yet she was still surprised by the "refinement among convicts."[55]

Doty was particularly astonished that prison administrators failed to see her own refinement. She thought that Auburn matrons would discern immediately that she was different from regular inmates: "I suppose, I thought the matrons ought to have seen I wasn't a criminal, especially when I had on my best manners." To her horror, the prison inspector failed to detect her real character; after she was Bertillioned, he told another officer that she had "all the stigmata of criminality." When prison officials neglected to observe her innocence, refinement, and class status, Doty rejected the criminal anthropologists' premises and contended "that there is no criminal type, no criminal appearance, no criminal manner."[56] Doty's conclusion might seem self-serving, but her revelation coincided with the results of research conducted by Frances Kellor. In 1900, Kellor wrote a series of articles that rejected Cesare Lombroso's theories by arguing that a person's environment contributed more to her criminal behavior than did her biological makeup.[57]

Ironically, the only person who took the time to ask Doty the kind of questions that would reveal her identity was her new black friend, Minerva Jones, "a very tall colored woman." Minerva "skillfully placed me, and finding I was not of the streets, but an innocent thing from home," decided that "I was not to be polluted by bad stories; rather, I was to be protected." When Jones, who called herself "a sportin' lady," defended her, Doty's attitude shifted: "Far from fearing [Minerva] . . . as one of those vicious colored criminals whom I had been warned against, her companionship was the one ray of comfort."[58] Although forced to rethink some of the basic precepts of criminal anthropology and race, Doty still believed in the racialized tenet of womanhood that contended that white women needed protection from a man or someone perceived of as unfeminine. Jones's race and physicality seemed to serve this perceived need. Although twelve years younger than Doty, Jones was almost six feet tall and weighed 168 pounds, while Doty was five feet five inches tall and weighed 130 pounds.[59] Indeed, Doty's reliance on Jones's protection reinforced the prevailing idea that black women were not vulnerable in the ways that white women were; moreover, Jones's ability to safeguard another woman discounted her own feminine vulnerabilities and need for protection. After only four days Doty exposed her feminine weakness. Feeling as if she was "on the verge of a breakdown," she ended her experiment by leaving the prison on the morning of the fifth day.[60] Like many Progressive Era women reformers, Doty held onto those nineteenth-century gender and racial norms that served her interests while tackling modern social problems.

Doty's limited awareness of the complexity of Jones's background prevented her from reflecting seriously on the cultural stereotypes that legitimized the imprisonment of so many black women. From her perspective, Jones was intimidating but gentle, tough but a protector, "a sportin' lady" with a sense of justice, and a criminal with a conscience. According to Auburn's records Minerva Jones was imprisoned for grand larceny; as she explained it, she "went to [a] room with a white man, and . . . took his money."[61] As historian Kali Gross has shown in her work on female felons in early-twentieth-century Philadelphia, Jones attempted to pull off a scam known as the "badger game," using prostitution as a ruse to steal from would-be customers.[62] A Virginia native working as a cook for a white household, Jones told the parole board two years into her sentence that she was "never in trouble before" the incident that landed her in prison.[63] Prior to her arrest, she seemed to be alone; her mother was deceased, although she had a "step mother in New York City." Like many single women whose lives the historian Joanne Meyerowitz examines in *Women Adrift*, she rented a room and took her meals in a restaurant.[64] It is unclear whether the robbery that led to her arrest was her first attempt at the badger game, although most women who were arrested for the scam were recidivists. She had no prior record, which suggests that her actions stemmed from being poor and desperate, and she was apparently a morphine addict.[65] Doty must have seen Jones as something other than a hardened criminal, since she agreed to be Jones's parole custodian a year later.[66]

While Doty publicized her dramatic experience as a white prison inmate, we must wonder about Jones's multiple vulnerabilities as a black woman. Did Jones's imposing physical presence prevent her, as a first-time offender, from fearing female felons "of hard and vicious character"? Who protected Jones, a single woman with no kin nearby, from racial discrimination, urban violence, and sexual harassment, as well as poverty? Doty recognized her fragility when she heard Jones "sighing and groaning" all night; Doty "wondered" whether the imprisoned morphine addict "suffered greatly."[67] Finally, we might consider how Doty's position as a prominent Progressive reformer, rather than a weak and nervous dependent, protected Jones inside as well as outside of Auburn. Doty immediately notified the press about her experiment and, in less than a month, the superintendent of prisons announced he would undertake reforms.[68] Jones seemed to accept the prison reformer's offer to serve as her parole custodian for a number of reasons:

Doty was an older, middle-class, well-educated lawyer and activist who had access to publicity and direct connections to powerful, male Progressives such as prison reformer Thomas Osborne, and she could help protect Jones from racist and sexist scrutiny. The records do not show what happened to Jones after her release. Might Doty's recommendation and guidance have safeguarded Jones from dubious employment? Doty was a vocal, influential advocate for this black female felon as much as she was a critic of the Auburn system, which, she argued, through its "hopelessness," "dreariness," and "ugliness . . . preyed upon" the poor and working-class, black and immigrant women imprisoned there.[69]

Doty declared that her five-day stint changed her irrevocably by compelling her to lose "race consciousness" and prejudice and prompting her to "feel only a sense of companionship" with Jones and other inmates. She offered a trenchant class analysis of an expensive prison system that, she argued, failed miserably in its attempt to address working-class and poor people's problems and conduct. "Hundreds of working people are given to the State's care, and are taught nothing, produce nothing, are ill housed and ill fed, and their time and that of the guards or keepers is wasted," she wrote. "The result is an organization which manufactures criminals, and is maintained at great cost to the State."[70] Instead of ignoring the wretched prison conditions, as many WPA inspectors did, she contended that these conditions created more societal problems. Doty hoped that her readers would be concerned about female offenders' plight, but, in the end, her sentiments were not translated into substantial institutional change.

As was the case with other penal reformers, Doty's emphasis on institutional difficulties neglected the societal problems that led to most women's criminal offenses.[71] Many inmates left Auburn and returned to families, homes, and neighborhoods that had not changed. Inmates' prison experiences had altered their behavior—Doty believed for the worse—but they still struggled to face the everyday issues of economic survival, marriage, and domesticity. Many working-class and poor women were so invested in maintaining some semblance of respectability that the extreme measures they took sometimes became criminal acts that landed them in Auburn.

The Respectable Smith Sisters

In 1910, sisters Harriet and Helen Smith were committed to the New York State Prison for Women at Auburn for infanticide. Their criminal act was listed in Auburn's Bertillion ledger as "child burned in stove."[72] Unlike many infanticide cases, the Smith sisters did not kill their own child. They had not helped their unmarried younger sister, Margaret, abort. Instead, the two sisters claimed that their newborn nephew died of natural causes one hour after his birth and they agreed to "cremate" the infant's body, leaving no evidence of the birth. According to local newspaper accounts and later parole board testimony, the sisters justified their behavior by declaring that they were trying to maintain the family's respectability and reputation. The response from the judge, jury, and community suggests that the sisters' rationalization was understood, although not supported. As the Smith sisters' experience suggests, the ideology of womanly respectability played a significant role even in the most horrific crimes.

Harriet and Helen Smith's offense shows how they responded to the possible dismantling of their carefully cultivated reputation in Poughkeepsie. In 1910, the city had a total population of 27,936, and black people represented a little over 2 percent (699) of its residents.[73] Records indicate that the family, including four-year-old Harriet Smith and her parents, migrated from New Jersey around 1873; by the time of the crime, they had lived and worked in the town for at least forty years.[74] In 1909, working as laundresses and living with their mother and younger sister, Harriet and Helen were characterized by the larger community, black and white, as "very respectable people."[75] Unmarried, childless, and older—Harriet was forty-four, Helen forty—the sisters lived relatively stable lives.[76] Thirty-eighty-year-old Margaret's unexpected pregnancy posed a crucial dilemma for all of the sisters: the disclosure of an illegitimate child would cast doubts on the whole family's reputation, which directly influenced not only their community standing but also their current employment. Arguing that they were "hard working people and were afraid of the disgrace attaching to their sister and to them in consequence fearing the people for whom they worked would not employ them anymore and that since the child was dead and none of the neighbors knew it had been born, they thought it no harm to cremate the little boy and thus avoid public scandal," the Smiths' defense attorney emphasized these black working women's response to the politics of respectability.[77]

Although moral status played a significant role in the trial, the sisters' race was downplayed as a possible contributing factor. Unlike the characterizations of Mamie Spencer and Minerva Jones, the newspaper accounts identified their race but seldom any significant connection between the defendants' race and the crime committed; only one paper used a sensational headline, "Colored Women's Horrible Crime." The prosecution, defense, and judge did not posit race as predisposing the Smith sisters to crime, or even to unwed pregnancy. Indeed, Judge Morchauser emphasized the need for fair judicial proceedings because the defendants were black women. While the prosecuting and defense attorneys were central to jury selection, the judge occasionally questioned prospective jurors by asking, "Do you know of any reason—if you do you would tell me—why you could not sit with this jury and render a fair verdict to this colored woman who has the same rights as any white person?"[78] The court rejected one possible candidate because he had formerly lived in the South, and even after he denied that he was "prejudiced against colored people." Judge Morchauser instructed the jury that the defendant was "entitled to the protection of the law" and that it made "no difference what her color or creed maybe or whether she is surrounded by many or few friends."[79]

Harriet Smith was tried first. Newspaper accounts suggest that, rather than arguing that the crime was the result of natural black female criminality, the prosecution concentrated solely on proving that the women were ashamed of the out-of-wedlock birth, had murdered a healthy infant, and had covered up their crime by burning the evidence. Newspaper excerpts from the testimony of Dr. Powell, the family physician, suggest that he regarded the sisters' words and actions as proof of premeditated murder. According to Powell, when he delivered the child, Harriet Smith said, "This is all wrong, and I won't stand for it." After questioning her statement and asking what she was going to do, Powell claimed, Smith replied, "Get rid of it."[80] The physician told Smith that that would constitute murder, and, according to him, she replied, "Well then I'll suffer."[81]

Reported excerpts of Harriet Smith's testimony, however, recast her meeting with Dr. Powell and the events that led to the crime and illustrate the moral predicament in which the baby placed the family. Smith admitted that she said the child could not stay in the home, but claimed that "get rid of it" meant "getting a home for the infant in some other place," rather than infanticide.[82] She revealed that the newborn was left unattended because the sisters immediately cared for their sister Margaret, who was "very sick and in great pain." An hour after the birth, Helen Smith allegedly found the baby dead. According to the defense, all of the family saw the deceased child.[83] At this point, according to testimony, the older sisters conferred with one another, allegedly without their mother or younger sister's knowledge, and agreed to dispose of the body by placing the child in the stove. The sisters explained that they had not committed a crime but, rather, had chosen an unconventional manner for dealing with a dead infant. Their defense attorneys reiterated throughout the trial that the women were not hardened criminals but, in a sense, victims of circumstance: "If [they were] guilty of any crime it was because in their desire to protect their good name,

138

which was all they had, they made a mistake. . . . The crime they committed, if any, was neglecting to take proper care of the newborn baby."[84]

This contention begged another question: if the physician examined a "healthy, full born male child," and the sisters confessed that they had cremated a dead child, when and why did the infant die? Newspaper accounts of the trial rarely addressed whether the child was already dead when it was placed in the stove or died as a result of being burned. Only one witness spoke to this matter: "Mrs. Smith, mother of the defendant, testified to the death of the child as stated by her daughter and said that she knew the baby was dead for she had it in her lap the night it died."[85] Instead of pursuing this issue, the prosecution emphasized why the sisters committed the crime. An all-white, all-male jury found the sisters guilty of child neglect rather than attempted or premeditated murder. After Harriet Smith was sentenced for manslaughter rather than murder, Helen Smith pleaded guilty to the same charge.

Reinforcing the fact that the community never believed that the sisters were criminals but rather believed they had merely committed criminal acts, the jury asked that the sisters receive mercy during their sentencing.[86] The judge accepted the jurors' petition; he apologetically imposed a sentence for second-degree manslaughter, with a maximum of five years (conviction on the initial charge of first-degree murder carried a maximum sentence of fifteen years). During the sentencing hearing, he explained that the court had "only kindly feelings" toward the well-respected sisters, which reflected the "high testimonials given by those who have known [them] so long." The judge reiterated the prevailing sentiment that in their efforts "to protect the good name of [their] unfortunate sister [they] . . . committed a crime that" could not "pass unpunished." In his final statement, he explained: "To me it is unpleasant to impose a sentence, but the law requires it. A Judge must do what is right in the matter of punishment, however kindly he may feel towards the prisoner at the bar, in imposing the sentence there is nothing of vengeance, but the performance of the duty imposed by the law."[87] The judge's assessment stemmed from the trial testimony and subsequent clemency hearing in which the defendants' respectability was consistently invoked. Community members testified to the family's upstanding position. Mr. James Mullen, who spoke positively about the women during the trial, stated before they were sentenced that "he had known them since they were children. Knew their parents, and grandparents and could testify to their good character, sobriety, industry, and honesty."[88]

The Smith sisters' case shows that these working women were deeply committed to the ideology and politics of respectability. Instead of needing racial uplift from middle-class reformers, these women of "good character, sobriety, industry, and honesty" were seen as exemplars of proper behavior. Their employment as laundresses strengthened their position within the community. In the minds of their black neighbors and white employers, their industriousness revealed their character and helped define them as morally upright citizens. Nevertheless, despite the many years they had lived in the community, the women believed that their reputations were precarious, at best, so they went to great lengths to protect their public image.

The court and the community seemed to understand the sisters' actions. They apparently accepted the defense claim that Harriet and Helen Smith "were suffering more because of the sin of their sister rather than any sin they committed themselves." The sisters' reaction to their sentencing suggests that they had no regrets about their actions. Local newspapers consistently reported that "neither prisoner showed any weakness or tremor before or after the sentence was pronounced."[89] Two years later, the sisters corroborated the newspapers' claims about their rationale for the cremation when briefly responding to Auburn's parole commissioners. They reiterated that, as respectable women, they disposed of rather than killed the infant "to save [their] . . . sister from disgrace."[90] Their actions represented desperate attempts to protect their own reputations as well. In fact, their community and Auburn officials were so convinced about these women's background that they were paroled not to a court officer but to their mother, who ran a laundry.[91]

Usually addressed in the context of social welfare efforts conducted by the black middle class, the issue of respectability was equally salient in the lives of working-class black women. The Smith sisters' lives were shaped—and threatened—by their ability to present themselves as moral black women.[92] Accounts of the incident remain silent about their younger sister, Margaret: neither her feelings about her child's death nor her reaction to her older sisters' actions were ever reported. Yet her presence in court with her mother and sisters suggests that she supported or at least forgave her sisters, although it is unclear how the family treated her as a result of her pregnancy. The Smith family's reaction to an out-of-wedlock pregnancy, whether an act of premeditated murder or child neglect, resulted from their commitment to prevailing notions of womanly respectability rather than the indifference to moral order that reformers attributed to working-class women in general and black female felons in particular. This case raises the significant issue of social ranking within working-class black communities and families and of how relatives sharing a household might respond to concerns about respectability and domesticity differently; moreover, it complicates scholars' middle-class versus working-class binary.[93]

The female felons incarcerated at Auburn were generally assumed to be less respectable than most women, and some inmates fit this description. Yet prison records of women such as Mamie Spencer, Minerva Jones, and the Smith sisters reveal the multifaceted dynamics of womanhood, race, respectability, and crime. Rather than being bereft of morality and femininity, black female offenders had responded to their often dire circumstances by making conscious choices about their moral and domestic lives. Women's vulnerabilities contributed to their lawbreaking: unwanted pregnancy led to infanticide; domestic abuse was followed by assault on, or even murder of, boyfriends or husbands; poverty stimulated theft and prostitution.[94] Poor and working-class women's intimate engagement with domesticity sometimes landed them in prison. Some of the most complicated cases reflect the experiences of women who attempted to navigate the complex terrain of marriage and motherhood.

The Promises and Perils of Marriage and Motherhood

Much like white and black middle-class women, poor and working-class black women believed in the sanctity and significance of marriage, but economic and social factors strained their unions.[95] While the Smith sisters struggled to defend their respectability as single women, Mamie Spencer sought to maintain a level of consistent domesticity within her second marriage. Although social scientists worried about the "excess" of single black women in cities, between 1890 and 1910 the number of unmarried black women in New York City never exceeded that of married black women.[96] Black women and men of every socioeconomic level valued committed, legal relationships. Yet reformers such as Du Bois expressed grave concerns about the status of many marriages: in his view, young migrants who experienced the "peculiar lonesomeness" of urban life formed "chance acquaintances." In Du Bois's estimation, couples "thoughtlessly marry and soon find that the husband's income can not support a family." "Then comes a struggle" that forces wives into the workforce and "often results in desertion or voluntary separation."[97] Women were then left as heads of households that were dependent upon charity and created the conditions for criminal behavior. Influenced by his Victorian sensibilities yet cognizant of the racial discrimination and concomitant structural challenges black people faced in the labor market, Du Bois still argued that working poor women's most available choices could lead to criminality, whether they were single and susceptible to immorality or chose to marry but still became meager bread-winners.[98] Absent reformers' moralizing mission, black women and black couples faced myriad urban dilemmas. The common-law marriage of May Enoch and Arthur Harris shows how heterosexual couples not only experienced financial difficulties but also suffered from their inability to achieve the prevailing norms regarding males as breadwinners and the protectors of women. Furthermore, everyday domestic tensions and disputes could be exacerbated by the tenuous state of race relations in the urban North.

Living in communities where working-class people struggled to survive, black women witnessed the problems that arose when husbands and fathers could not make a family wage. In most families, black women labored along with their husbands in low-paying personal-service positions.[99] Yet many working-class and poor women still envisioned a married life in which the husband would be the primary breadwinner and they could be housewives. In 1913, for example, a black social worker noted that one of her "stupid and sloven" charges lived with three other people in one room "in which the sleeping, cooking, eating, washing and ironing are all done." When the social worker inquired as to why she had stopped working, the young woman responded, "I doan need to wuk no more, I goin' a git married next week."[100] This scenario illuminates as much about the black social worker's perspective as it does about her client: the social worker failed to acknowledge that in the midst of poverty, young black women desired marriage because they hoped it would enable them to withdraw from the labor force.

Black women's strong desire for marriage made broken promises of matrimony difficult to accept. In a particularly interesting case, twenty-eight-year-old Mattie Knight assaulted her fiancé because of the disruption of her wedding plans. In 1911, after borrowing $75 from Knight, her fiancé married another woman. Knight recalled that she was depressed and suicidal when she unexpectedly encountered her ex-fiancé. Knight revealed that her offense was a crime of passion: "I intended to commit suicide, but when I saw [him,] he made me terribly angry and I couldn't help shooting him."[101] This Virginia native had been a widow for eight years. Her loss of a potential life partner was so devastating that she responded with violence.

Working-class black women explained that they had wed for reasons ranging from romantic love or in order to escape their parents to a desire for financial stability. When their husbands failed to live up to their expectations, they often became disillusioned. Many complained that their husbands were "bad providers." Consider, for instance, twenty-two-year-old Daisy Stewart, who recalled in 1920 that "she wanted a home and babies" when she got married in April. Unlike most black women, she made $30 a week as a dancer, while her husband "stayed home read the newspaper and rested." To her dismay, her husband "turned out to be a brute, abused her, failed to support her," and saw other women. Stewart also discovered that another woman was pregnant with his child. A year later, the couple separated. Hurt and angry, Stewart refused "from pure retaliation" to divorce her husband in order to prevent him from remarrying. She believed that her arrest for prostitution was a frame-up so that her husband would have grounds for divorce.[102]

Much like Stewart, a number of black wives became disillusioned with married life. A twenty-one-year-old parolee wrote to her sister, "So I saw my husband the pest but I think he knows now that I will never go back to him and his way of living as long as I live."[103] Thirty-two-year-old Jennie Johnson, a domestic charged with stealing "jewelry from a fur coat," revealed that her "husband was sick and out of work when [she] got into . . . trouble" and died while she was in jail. He had failed to live up to his duties as a husband. "I had to struggle along and do the best I could when my husband was living, and he wouldn't help me," she explained. "Now that he is gone, I can do better and lead a better life."[104] In some instances, black wives' frustrations with their husbands led to threats of violence. Twenty-four-year-old Mary Compton was charged with felonious assault against her husband because she "was trying to clean up their apartment and . . . [he] was in the way." When he refused to leave their home, she "drew a revolver and snapped it at him." He in turn "summoned" the police. When Jack Compton, the superintendent of their 131st Street building, came with a policeman, they found his wife "sitting calmly in a chair." After searching for the weapon, the officer found a "32 calibre revolver in [her] overcoat pocket."[105] The records fail to indicate what transpired before or after Mary Compton's threat, but the incident shows that in some relationships tensions ran so high that the most basic domestic issues, such as housecleaning, could elicit violent responses from aggravated wives.

Marital discord could arise unexpectedly when a woman believed that her husband was not being supportive. Forty-two-year-old black New York native Odessa Crouch set her home on fire when she felt her husband was neglecting her after a series of painful surgeries. Married for twenty-two years, Crouch thought that her marriage was reasonably happy until she became ill. After several operations, Crouch became depressed and accused her husband of "brutal treatment" because she felt abandoned during her long recovery.[106] Her case file does not explicitly reveal her husband's alleged behavior, but it highlights her mental anguish over her declining

Odessa Crouch (pseud.), an inmate at the New York State Prison for
Women at Auburn, 1929. Courtesy of New York State Archives and Records
Administration, Albany, New York (#1513, Series B1273).

health and her spouse's absence. Initially, Crouch planned to commit sui-
cide by setting fire to her home, which was her husband's property. But in a
"spirit of revenge," she changed her mind, walked out of the house, and let
it burn.[107] Although the records do not indicate whether the house was sal-
vageable, Crouch's husband had her arrested and refused to communicate
with her during her imprisonment. Seemingly without any regrets almost
a year later, Crouch told the parole board that upon release she would live
alone as she was "not going back to [her] husband or people."[108]

Most domestic violence cases involved altercations between husbands
and wives, rather than spousal apathy. Women were imprisoned for assaulting their husbands, sometimes retaliating in the course of a dispute. In
1925, Louisiana native Annie Howard killed her husband in an argument
that escalated into violence against her mother. The twenty-three-year-old
recalled that in a dispute over who should be identified as the janitor of
the Bronx apartment building at 555 Southern Boulevard, where they both
worked and lived, her husband argued "that a man was always the head
of the house." Howard disagreed with his patriarchal perspective, coun-
tering that she should hold the title because she was "doing most of the
work."[109] Both Howard and her husband were intoxicated and the disagreement turned violent when he "attacked her mother with a barrage of dishes,
inflicting a severe scalp wound." Howard sought to protect her mother by
using a bread knife to stab her husband, eventually fatally, in the "neck and

Annie Howard, an inmate at the New York State Prison for Women at Auburn, 1925. Courtesy of New York State Archives and Records Administration, Albany, New York (#1353, Series B1273).

body." When she "pleaded guilty to first-degree manslaughter," the court "expressed sympathy." Yet she was sent to prison, as presiding Judge Cohn concluded that "the killing of a human being merits punishment if the killing is not in self-defense."[110]

Domestic violence incidents resulted in manslaughter charges against many women who argued that they had acted in self-defense. Fifty-year-old Washington, DC, native Laura Salem was indicted for second-degree manslaughter after she killed her alcoholic and abusive husband. Even her employer noted that she was "abused," often coming to work "with discolored eyes caused by her husband brutally beating her." The fatal incident occurred after her husband stole her money, leaving Salem and her child destitute. In an attempt to get some of the money back, Salem met her husband, but he refused to pay her back and attempted to cut her throat. In response, she caught the knife he was wielding, "got excited and cut him" in self-defense.[111] In 1926, Susie Roberts killed her common-law husband, William Newton, after a domestic dispute. Roberts explained that she had "suffered constant abuse," "he had a violent temper," and "she was always the butt of his ill humor." On the day of the fatal incident, she recalled, Newton had "lashed himself into a fury over some trifle and a quarrel resulted." Roberts explained that after he began to beat her, "in self defense she took up a knife from the table and stabbed him . . . she had not intended to kill him, she said, but only to hurt him sufficiently to make him let her alone."

Respectability, Domesticity, and Crime

Police officers reported that when they responded to the call they found her "bending over the prostrate form of Newton, imploring him to return to life."[112] In a similar case, thirty-six-year-old Brooklyn native Alice Lansen said that during a fight her common-law husband "hit her" and she retaliated by picking "up a knife to scare him." She had not stabbed him, Lansen explained; her abusive and drunk partner was "coming at . . . me with such force that it went into him," causing his death. Lansen's declaration that she "didn't intend to kill him" was a common response from women who had attempted to ward off an attack but instead committed murder.[113]

Violence also occurred when working-class and poor married women struggled with their parental responsibilities. While the case of Harriet and Helen Smith highlighted the moral burden of an illegitimate child, many other cases of infanticide emphasized the economic burden that unplanned children placed on couples who were barely surviving, even with two incomes.[114] Single or deserted women felt the devastating consequences of motherhood more severely, including poverty, lack of childcare, and their community's moral judgment. In some instances, women turned to local orphanages and state institutions because they could not fulfill their parental obligations.[115] Historian Gunja SenGupta's work on New York State's House of Refuge shows that parents used these institutions as a "material resource to help defray the expenses of supporting dependents."[116] When this option was available at all, it was woefully disproportionate to the needs of poor African Americans. Once these women believed that they had run out of options, their children were usually the injured party.

In Giselle Hopkins's case, the twenty-three-year-old black native of New York committed infanticide after her common-law husband deserted her. According to the district attorney's report, after giving birth, Hopkins "placed rags in the mouth of [her] child, . . . threw it in a pail and . . . buried it in the yard in the rear of her house."[117] Hopkins's sister turned her in to the police. Hopkins was interrogated, and she eventually pleaded guilty to the murder, acknowledging that "being alone without help" prompted her actions,[118] and showed detectives "the spot in the yard where the body had been buried."[119] Her sister's testimony strengthened the state's case against Hopkins even though she confessed to the crime.[120] Her actions in September 1924 seem to have been prompted by her common-law husband's desertion. Yet she may have been in contact with her husband before her April trial, because several months after she was received at the prison in May 1925, Auburn officials discovered that she was in the early stages of another pregnancy.[121]

Hopkins's case highlights the tensions in her everyday life as well as the

Giselle Hopkins (pseud.), an inmate at the New York State Prison for Women at Auburn, 1925. Courtesy of New York State Archives and Records Administration, Albany, New York (#1337, Series B1273).

effects of her actions on her family. Although her file did not contain specific information regarding the father of her child, her actions after his departure are revealing. She later told officials that she believed he would marry her.[122] At the time of the infanticide, she already had a young boy; an employer observed that she seemed "absolutely devoted" to him.[123] After her common-law husband left, Hopkins must have reevaluated her ability to parent her children. She was described as "strictly honest and a good worker," yet she disregarded her own stable qualities. Finding herself in an untenable situation, she seems to have lacked familial support as well.[124] Hopkins stated on several occasions that she was not "on good terms" with the sister to whom she confessed and who in turn informed the police. When parole board members asked if she believed her sister had "done the right thing in telling on" Hopkins, she responded, "not for being a sister."[125] Perhaps because the sister had herself given birth the day after the infanticide, she believed that the baby's murder was inexcusable. After Hopkins gave birth in Auburn to her third child, her mother cared for the baby, although later it was given up for adoption.[126] Hopkins's case demonstrates that family members' distinct ideas about acceptable conduct sometimes resulted in relatives using the state to address what they considered intolerable behavior. It also provides a telling example of how black working women had radically differing interpretations of individual responsibility.

Married women, as well as deserted mothers, made desperate choices re-

Respectability, Domesticity, and Crime

garding motherhood. Eighteen-year-old Lisa Kelly, a black native of Savannah, Georgia, faced dire economic conditions that led to child neglect. Married at sixteen, she migrated with her husband to the Bronx, New York, but soon found that they had "no work or money." Kelly left her baby in her apartment house, where it "became ill and died from exposure."[127] In 1922, she was charged with manslaughter, but the record remains silent about her husband's participation in or response to the crime. During her imprisonment, she corresponded with her husband, who had found a job as a hotel waiter and wrote her every week.[128] Four years later, he requested that Kelly be paroled into his care because she would "be well taken care of and given a good home."[129] It is not clear whether Kelly caused her child's death through deliberate neglect or what happened to the couple after she was released into her husband's care. Her case highlights the desperation of young mothers, married as well as single, who found themselves unable to care for their children.

Those black mothers incarcerated for other types of crimes worried about how their children would be cared for during their prison sentence. Many relied on relatives or close friends, but some used local orphanages and state asylums. In 1906, a twenty-year-old New York native serving time for manslaughter explained that her only living relatives were unable to care for her four-year-old son, who was sent to the Colored Orphan Asylum.[130] In 1909, a twice-married twenty-seven-year-old Georgia native incarcerated for grand larceny decided to put her seven-year-old son in the "Gerry Society until [she] got out." When asked how she planned to care for her son if she were paroled, especially since she decided not to reestablish a relationship with her husband as result of his gambling, she responded, "I want to make home for him soon as [I] can."[131] These mothers must have thought about the impact their absence would have on their children as well as how it would influence their postprison relationships. In 1919, when twenty-year-old Alice Scott was arrested after a domestic dispute in which she killed her husband, Scott's foster mother became her child's guardian. Shortly after Scott was convicted and sent to Auburn, she began proceedings to have her child removed from her foster mother's home. Scott had not heard of any reports of her child being abused or neglected, but she believed that her four-to-thirteen-year prison sentence would cause irrevocable harm to her relationship with her daughter. Moreover, she worried that the growing relationship between her child and her foster mother might replace her child's memories of her mothering. She told administrators that "the child's affections would be alienated and . . . the child . . . would grow to be so fond of" the foster mother "that she would have no affection left for" Scott. Unlike mothers who placed their children in institutional care because of financial difficulties, Scott did so because of her own emotional concerns. She contacted the New York Society for the Prevention of Cruelty to Children, which acted through the Children's Court to place her daughter in the Colored Orphan Asylum. After her release from Auburn in 1922, when Scott attempted to regain custody of her daughter, she assured administrators that she had steady employment but was again living with her foster mother.[132]

Working-class black women struggled with difficult choices when marriage failed to meet their expectations and they became burdened with motherhood as well. In some cases, these women committed violent crimes, but other Auburn inmates had committed crimes against property.

Property Offenses: Rescripting Sexuality and Domestic Labor

The criminal cases against many working-class women show that they committed theft in part because of dire financial circumstances, a verdict on which scholars concur.[133] A thirty-two-year-old black Auburn inmate revealed that her arrest for grand larceny occurred when her husband was "sick and out of work."[134] Women were accessories to their husbands' or boyfriends' crimes, but they also committed crimes individually. A married twenty-six-year-old revealed that she did not know her husband's whereabouts; she was "away from him four years before her arrest for grand larceny."[135] In 1912, a twenty-three-year-old charged with grand larceny for stealing $8 from a man explained that she had been a pickpocket for four years and that her "husband didn't want me to do it, but . . . he did not know."[136] These women grew weary of working at physically exhausting domestic-service jobs that paid badly and of residing in wretched housing. Some admitted they were influenced by "bad company" that convinced them to experiment with drugs, alcohol, gambling, scams, and/or the sex trade. Others attempted to revise the traditional stereotypes that scripted black women as Jezebels and Mammies by using these images to their benefit as they committed theft.

Black women were aware of how they were scripted by white New Yorkers and used the stereotype of the Jezebel, who was sexually insatiable, to their criminal advantage in the badger game. Their property crimes—grand larceny, burglary, and robbery—were often related to their proposed or presumed sexual relationships with white men who were visiting black neighborhoods. In a city where de facto racial segregation clearly defined black neighborhoods, white men's late-night visits to "Little Africa" (the Tenderloin) and Harlem strongly suggest that they engaged in the popular practice of slumming. Such excursions by elite or middle-class white men constituted more than their desire to see how the "other half" lived and played; rather, they sought to fulfill their own ideas about "presumed notions of primitive black sexuality, bawdiness, and obscenity."[137] Black women, who sometimes worked with other women as well as men in the badger game, used their understanding of white men's desire to identify a target and then commit robbery. When these men's visits went awry and they became crime victims, police officers often chose to ignore the question of why respectable white men were in the red-light districts of black neighborhoods.[138] Instead, they focused on the horror of black female criminality. In 1906, former police commissioner William McAdoo contended that "these women rob white men with impunity, especially those who look respectable and well-dressed, because they know the chances are that the man will not care to disgrace himself by appearing in court against them."[139] For example, Fannie Harris, a forty-year-old housekeeper who was accused several times of taking money from white men, was not prosecuted in one instance because the "white man did not want to come forward and deal with the notoriety of being involved with a black woman."[140]

Although Auburn's records show that both white and black women were involved in the badger game, the 1923 case of Augustus Skogman provides a sense of white men's assumptions about black women as well as the type of marks—that is, victims—targeted by black female badgers. While walking on 134th Street in Harlem at 8 P.M., Skogman encountered "an attractive colored girl standing in a hallway" who gave him a "come hither sign." He went to see "what she wanted" and was immediately ambushed by two black men who forced him at gunpoint to the building's roof, where he gave up twenty dollars in cash, a diamond ring, and a gold watch. Several weeks later, Skogman was walking on 138th Street when he noticed twenty-year-old Lucille Tucker. Believing she was the badger thief, he had her arrested, although she denied the crime and her sister and two friends testified that she was at her sibling's house from 5:30 until midnight on the night in question.[141] Tucker's case seems to illustrate that almost any black woman might be identified by a white man as a thief. In June 1900, Rev. Charles Philipbor of the German Evangelical Lutheran Church told a police officer that he had been "attacked by a colored woman" but he "could not recognize the woman who had accosted him" after the officer took him to a house where four black women resided. These women were arrested and literally paid the price for Philipbor's slumming experience, although he was robbed by only one woman. Mary Smith was discharged with a $1 fine because she could prove that she was a "hard working woman," but Lizzie Jenkins, Mary

McDonald, and Lizzie Harris were each fined $5. There was no evidence to indicate that these women had assaulted Philipbor.[142] Although Skogman's 1923 claim centered on his $175 loss, both he and Philipbor tried to conceal the possibility that they were about to cross the color line and engage in the sex trade. White male victims often avoided admitting these thefts, but Skogman argued that he had not immediately notified the police because "he was too frightened to note the number of the apartment"; importantly, he "denied having entered the hallway of his own will." The fact that these victims were seeking prostitutes did not prevent them from retaliating when their intended target turned the tables.

These white men disregarded public scrutiny in order to use the law to punish black women for the crime of theft. Thirty-six-year-old Etta King, who admitted that she was soliciting, discovered that her customer had no problems going public with her arrest for stealing $59 from his pocket.[143] Frank Rice, a cattle buyer from New Mexico who was staying in New York, got caught in the badger game when, at the entrance of a Tenderloin brownstone, a "husky negress," Ann Brandt, asked him for a match. Rice stated that "she seized me by the throat" and was searching his pockets when a policeman arrived.[144] Detective Dockstader's 1904 observations coincided with Lombroso's theories of the atavistic and virile black woman and Doty's initial fears of black female felons; he recognized Brandt's criminality immediately, deciding to follow this "muscular negro woman," "thinking [that she was] the Amazon, who [had] been playing highway robbery" in that neighborhood.[145]

Police officers and the press consistently warned white urban dwellers about criminal black women, but badger cases also reveal the dire social conditions that many of these women faced. Their reliance on the promise of prostitution when they were actually attempting to rob white men discloses the financial instability and physical dangers of their urban environments. Unlike young women who exerted their sexual independence by experimenting with dating and treating, these usually older women used their sexuality for survival rather than for pleasure.[146] Other women may have become badger thieves because they had grown weary of or believed they were too old to engage in the sex trade. For example, a thirty-year-old Virginia native who was being paroled acknowledged that she had "been soliciting on the streets for about six years" before her grand larceny arrest for taking "money from a man."[147] Supplementing or rejecting employment in domestic service, these impoverished women were often constrained by circumstances to make choices that disregarded the gender conventions of respectability and moral propriety.

Respectability, Domesticity, and Crime

At the same time, black women understood how domestic service might provide a legitimate disguise when they intended to commit a theft. These women seemed to count on and use to their advantage prospective white employers' image of black women as the perennial servant or Mammy figure. In these cases, black women would go to white households explaining that they desperately needed work, find that they were immediately hired, and then proceed to steal from their new employers. Nineteen-year-old Gertrude Willis used white homeowners' acceptance of black subservience to her advantage. In 1922, the Wilmington, North Carolina, native went around the Bronx offering her "services at very cheap rates." When the "lady of the house" who hired her left the home or was "out of sight," Willis "would take whatever valuables she could find and disappear." She allegedly committed twenty-five burglaries in seven months.[148] Eighteen-year-old Mrs. Margaret Briggs, the wife of a mail carrier, worked as a "by-the-day maid" and was arrested in 1925 for stealing over $5,000 worth of money and valuables from at least six Bronx housewives.[149] Briggs's case reinforces the fact that neither marriage nor the low wages of domestic service could provide the financial stability that many women needed for everyday survival.

The unique case of twenty-six-year-old Evelyn Pitts provides a window into a black woman's history of poverty, theft, and institutionalization at both Bedford and Auburn. From her Auburn file, we might surmise that she turned to theft just as her marriage began to dissolve; however, her Bedford records indicate her longer connection to stealing. According to Pitts's husband, they married in 1916; she was a nineteen-year-old New York native whose parents had migrated from Virginia, and he was a twenty-two-year-old migrant from Virginia. Although their relationship survived her imprisonment in Bedford on a false charge of soliciting, it fell apart following her parole. He commented that his wife was "weak" while he was "strong," and he prayed to "God for the day to come" when she would "make up her mind to got [sic] strait." After her husband established various short-lived businesses, including an employment agency and a fruit stand, Evelyn Pitts allegedly rejected his attempts to support her and even, he argued, sabotaged his efforts. He wrote two explicit letters to Auburn's parole board explaining that he wanted to buy a home outside of New York City, away from urban temptations, but she encouraged him to abandon those plans and return to the city.[150] She informed the Auburn prison physician and warden that her husband was an alcoholic and that she often left him and "went to her mother." This statement represented a radical change in perspective, because previously she had said that she "was bad before" the marriage but "her husband is not responsible for it."[151] Her husband made a substan-

Evelyn Pitts (pseud.), an inmate at the New York State Prison for Women at Auburn, 1925. Courtesy of New York State Archives and Records Administration, Albany, New York (#1328, Series B1273).

tial revision of his attitude toward his wife as well. In his initial letter he had said that he would "give her a chance as his wife to redeem herself, be a woman and live within the law," but in his final letter he declared, "I have washed my hand. I give up."[152]

While Pitts's early conviction for soliciting was questionable, her convictions for theft were the culmination of a long history. As an adult, she had a typical modus operandi: she entered homes, usually with the owner's consent, and attempted to steal from them. If she was caught before the robbery, she would "always state that she had rung the doorbell or knocked on the door" and decided to let herself in, but then pleaded that she was a poor "widow out of employment with a sick child" and needed "any kind of work she could find." If homeowners believed her story, she did domestic work until they left her alone, and then she stole their property. Apparently she was quite persistent in her attempts. In 1926, when Pitts was finally paroled from Auburn, several warrants were pending against her in various New York boroughs as well as in New Jersey.

Records indicate that Pitts had begun stealing as an adolescent. In 1911, when she was thirteen, she was arrested four times between March and May for stealing "sums of money from the homes of neighbors."[153] When she turned fifteen, her mother decided that her incorrigible behavior had become too much to handle so she had her committed to the New York State Training School at Hudson for three years. Although Pitts was labeled

Respectability, Domesticity, and Crime

a criminal and imprisoned for a considerable portion of her young life, an alternative perspective on her case might be more appropriate. During the year before she was sent to Bedford, Pitts dealt with a series of traumatic and life-altering incidents: her father died in November 1916; she married in December; she had a miscarriage in February 1917; she contracted a venereal disease from her husband in April; and she was falsely arrested for prostitution after taking her husband dinner at his night job in August.[154] Because she was black and poor, Pitts was assumed to be innately criminal. Yet, as historian Elaine Abelson has shown, certain types of theft such as shoplifting were considered "an ancient, if not honorable, art."[155] During the nineteenth century, when a family's class status became more directly connected to the wife's ability to purchase consumer goods, Abelson argues, the anxieties middle-class white women experienced in the city were eventually labeled as a mental disease that was manifest in kleptomania. "Since ladies could not be called thieves, the medicalization of shoplifting provided an alternative and maintained the illusion of respectability." This label, Abelson argues, allowed these sick white women to be "removed from moral judgment," to avoid public embarrassment to themselves, their husbands, and their families, and to escape imprisonment.[156] Despite her long history of stealing, Pitts was not labeled a kleptomaniac; her racial, class, and gendered position precluded her from being considered a respectable lady or medically ill. Indeed, women like Pitts succeeded in part because homeowners wanted to believe that cheap domestic labor had arrived on their doorstep—until they realized that a woman posing as a domestic had stolen their property. Thus, both white middle-class women and poor black women played on gendered and racialized constructions of womanhood. At the same time, they faced different consequences for their behavior. Black domestic workers continually dealt with employers who accused them of stealing property and had them prosecuted whether they were guilty or not. Women perpetrating scams reinforced ideas about the confluence of race and crime that all black women had to confront.

Ruth Brown and the Deadly Consequences of Disreputable Behavior

Although some female felons faced challenges while trying to attain respectability and domesticity, others chose to ignore or reject conventional gender ideals. These women reinforced whites' fears regarding black women's imposing physicality as well as their seemingly unfeminine responses to their offenses. The stories of those whom others considered "colored women of hard and vicious character" are especially compelling.

154

Some women failed to see the benefits of living a respectable life and holding onto domestic ideals when they were exposed to wretched living conditions, performed hard labor for low wages, and suffered myriad emotional disappointments. Until they were arrested, they found living a life of easy money and illegal fun as more appealing. They appeared to stop caring about what others thought of them. In 1928, for example, a twenty-eight-year-old parolee allegedly reneged on her promise to improve her behavior and became a disruptive lodger in her friend's home. The troubled friend wrote Auburn's parole board that the parolee was "no good. . . . She done me a dirty trick. She came to my house . . . and I made her welcome and she got drunk and tried to break up my home, and I put her out." A long list of complaints followed: "she took some clothes of mine. she ain't nothing but a prostitute and if she aint very careful she is going back to prison. I really feel hurt for the way she done me. . . . I am through with her for life. I am a hard working woman and I have good white people to speak for me and I try to carry myself up."[157] This statement illustrates her attempt to distinguish herself—through her work ethic, respectable behavior, and white employers' approval—from the impudent Auburn parolee. Just being openly disreputable could land women in prison.

The case of Ruth Brown shows how a woman who appeared to be of "hard and vicious character" could come to face the death penalty.[158] Widowed for two years, the twenty-four-year-old Virginia native had a six-year-old child who lived with her husband's family in the South. In New York, Brown had worked as a domestic but was unemployed and, according to court papers, was always intoxicated. She frequently purchased liquor at speakeasies, where she became rowdy and threatened other patrons and was forced to leave. On May 21, 1931, she visited a black-owned speakeasy on 311 East 99th Street and used such "vile language" that she was asked to leave. When she refused and was ejected, she allegedly threatened, "You mother fuckers, I'll be back tomorrow and put you on the spot."[159] Brown arrived the following night with John Dawson and Theodore Ryan. Soon Dawson encountered Eli Hutson, with whom he had had a prior disagreement that had nothing to do with Brown. They began arguing, and Dawson fatally stabbed Hutson. Witnesses said that Brown, who "had a knife in her hand," urged Dawson to "finish him up." She was convicted of first-degree murder and sentenced to be executed in Sing Sing's electric chair along with Dawson.[160] Theodore Ryan, who witnesses said had a gun and threatened customers during the stabbing by shouting, "Don't know [sic] goddamned body leave here," was charged with manslaughter for providing Dawson with the knife.[161]

Respectability, Domesticity, and Crime

Brown's case shocked New Yorkers because no woman had been convicted of first-degree murder in forty years.[162] Brown, who had no criminal record and was not directly involved in the stabbing, was arrested and indicted because witnesses remembered her troubling character as well as her standing by "with a knife warning away any persons attempting to interfere" with the altercation.[163] Unlike the Smith sisters' actions, the defense of which highlighted their respectable background and their neighbors' testimony about their "good character, sobriety, industry, and honesty," Brown's disorderly behavior was deemed normal. Her own testimony confirmed the fact that she was "cursing and carrying on" the night in question, but she also had been so intoxicated that she, at times, failed to remember details that could support her case.[164] Her defense team spoke for her. Her attorney contended: "We will show you that she had been put out of that place so often it became a habit with her, and that there was absolutely no ill feeling between the defendant . . . and the man who put her out."[165] During the defense's summation, another lawyer reminded the jury that the whole case was based on the testimony of black people, whose words were questionable. To discredit the state's witnesses, he argued that black people were either "faithful, honest, devoted and hard-working or . . . the other type . . . shiftless and untruthful." According to his argument, Brown was not guilty of murder because there was no evidence to support such a claim, but she was deficient as a result of biological and environmental factors. "Ruth Brown is not very highly endowed mentally," he asserted. "She is a stupid woman, a southern woman, coming from a strata of colored people from the South who marry young. . . . Instead of bucking up to the situation, she succumbed to the use of liquor. The kind of liquor you get nowadays is bad enough, but in these sections of the city where the colored people live the liquor is exceptionally vile. This girl was constantly drunk before and after the occurrence."[166] Brown's lawyer argued that "through her weakness and love of pleasure, she got into bad company."[167] In 1932, his characterization of Brown echoed the assumption, long held by reformers and prison administrators alike, that black female migrants were incapable of handling urban life. Even by her defense counsel, Brown was presented as a "colored woman of hard and vicious character."

Brown was convicted of first-degree murder and given the death penalty. Her execution was scheduled for the week of June 6, 1932. In the end, New York State governor Franklin Roosevelt agreed with Brown's defense attorney's assessment. He observed that "the evidence in the record leads me to believe that the proof of premeditation and deliberation . . . was not sufficiently established."[168] He commuted her sentence to life imprisonment.

John Dawson's appeal failed, however, and he was put to death on June 7, 1932. Brown served one year before being transferred from Auburn to the New York State Reformatory for Women at Bedford.

Forty years after the Prison for Women opened, the declining financial support received from the state and the increasing number of male inmates at Auburn prompted the transfer of female felons to Bedford's reformatory prison for wayward girls. This move signaled an end to the nineteenth-century reformatory movement for women.[169] In 1933, the separate system of custodial and reformatory prisons officially ended. Both the public and administrators had come to believe that the reformatory prison, which was plagued by disciplinary problems, failed to rehabilitate wayward young women.

Female felons contradicted prevailing notions about what it meant to be a woman. Many late-nineteenth-century reformers believed that women were not capable of criminal acts, or at least not felony offenses. Their gendered conception of crime led to the conclusion that women who were prostitutes but not women who had committed crimes against property or violence against persons had the capacity for reform. The realization that black and immigrant women were disproportionately represented among inmates in custodial prisons like Auburn reinforced the idea that felons could not be rehabilitated.

While black female felons were excluded from the concept of proper womanhood, their lives, as documented in prison records, indicate a constant negotiation with feminine gender conventions. Indeed, poor and working-class women's intimate engagement with respectable domesticity influenced their actions and sometimes landed them in prison. Some women expressed acute concerns about the parameters of moral propriety, and their crimes occurred as a result of their fear of being exposed as disreputable. Other women's entry into crime stemmed from the ways in which they were perceived or scripted: they chose to use negative perceptions of black women to their advantage in the commission of certain crimes. Poor and working-class black women negotiated not only urban life but the rocky, and sometimes violent, terrain of domesticity.

The dynamics of the Smith sisters' case and the case of Ruth Brown demonstrate that women's standing within their communities heavily influenced legal outcomes. The respectable Smith sisters, who admitted they had cremated an infant, served no more than two years in Auburn. In eliminating the evidence of their sister's immoral conduct, they also eliminated the evidence that could have been used against them. Ruth Brown, who was admittedly disreputable, was convicted as an accomplice to murder because of the alleged threats she made before and during the fatal incident and received a death sentence that was commuted to life in prison. While race was a significant factor in the criminal justice system, class status and respectability within the community also affected the court's final verdict.

Eventually, social welfare organizations such as the National Urban League began to address these issues. The economic exploitation of black women's bodies and, at least implicitly, their sexual exploitation became part of these groups' platform. While stressing that appropriate behavior was essential to racial advancement, they knew on a practical level that their social welfare efforts had to extend beyond the efforts of Progressive reformers like Victoria Earle Matthews and Frances Kellor. Many reformers ignored female felons and women incarcerated in local penitentiaries or workhouses; they focused on prevention, reaching younger women whose lives could be shaped and who seemed both more vulnerable and more manageable than female offenders. Yet black women, whether first-time offenders or recidivists, were arrested more often and had fewer opportunities for probation and other rehabilitative services. The work of Grace Campbell and Judge Jean Norris demonstrates how race, gender, and criminal justice affected black women, their communities, and interracial relationships within reform organizations.

5

tragedy of the colored girl in court

THE NATIONAL URBAN LEAGUE AND NEW YORK'S
WOMEN'S COURT, 1911–1931

Of course the lure of the north for southern colored woman is just the same for
the southern white woman who hopes to obtain employment here. But where there
is protection for the white girl there is not so much for the Negro.

—Grace Campbell, 1911

The colored girl lacks the right interest from her people both in and out of court.

—Judge Jean Norris, 1925

Dominant narratives of the troubled female migrant emphasized grave
moral dilemmas. All too often, these stories overlooked the legal problems
that many black migrant women endured. Sixteen-year-old Faith Towns's
experience shows how some migrants ended up in prison. A native of Lenoir,
North Carolina, she arrived in New York after a prospective employer paid
for her transportation.[1] In less than a week, Towns presented her employer
with a letter (which, it was later revealed, was written by Towns herself) indicating that her mother was ill and she was needed at home. Her employer
immediately rejected her request. Towns had not worked long enough to
cover her expenses. She then stole $17 from her employer in order to re-
turn south. Having underestimated the train fare, Towns stayed at a friend's
apartment until she could acquire the remaining cash. The police arrested
her there. After filing an insurance claim, her employer was advised by an
agent to press charges against the former domestic, which she did. When
a social worker suggested that the employer be more understanding about
the young girl's predicament, she responded, "You couldn't treat niggers like

other people."[2] Towns was sentenced to the New York State Reformatory for Women at Bedford.

Towns's experience brings to the surface several issues that reformers' narratives frequently neglected. While the young woman was naive about northern life and quickly decided to return home, her difficulties were with her employer, not an unscrupulous labor agent. Her case shows how race relations in New York resembled those in the South, as white employers wielded power over black domestic servants and were able to prevail in the criminal justice system. Black women like Towns got into trouble with the law because of their immaturity and financial instability, not their lack of morality. Reformers like Victoria Earle Matthews and Frances Kellor failed to address the growing number of black women who were incarcerated; those who dealt with criminal cases understood the problem better. Black women, whether they were native New Yorkers, southern migrants, or West Indian immigrants, faced overwhelming odds once they became caught up in New York's criminal justice system. Nineteenth-century prison activists established reformatories so that youthful offenders like Towns would not be imprisoned with Auburn's "women of hard and vicious character," although when released they had a criminal record. In addition to being vulnerable to poverty, black women were subject to a racially segregated, oftentimes corrupt criminal justice system. This chapter examines this problem from two reformers' standpoints. Grace Campbell, a black probation and parole officer, emphasized the "tragedy of the colored girl in court" who received little or no state-sponsored preventive care and was seldom granted probation once she was arrested. In contrast, white municipal Judge Jean Norris believed that the real tragedy stemmed from the black community's apathy toward delinquent girls and women.

Comparing the professional biographies of Grace Campbell and Jean Norris raises a number of critical issues regarding gender and criminal justice, as well as urban reform and race. Unlike their predecessors, these women benefited from the work of Progressive reform that stressed government responsibility and legislative solutions for social problems. Both women expressed concerns about the inadequate services for delinquent black women, but they disagreed about the state's responsibility. For Campbell, working with black women was a constant, uphill battle that she fought with insufficient state resources and mounting conflicts with her working-class clients and professional colleagues regarding how to handle young black women. Influenced by the racial uplift ideology of an earlier generation, Campbell found that her vision of helping and protecting young women and black people was compromised by pervasive racism and class inequities. Like many activists of her time, she joined the vanguard of the radical black activists that responded to the disappointing discriminatory treatment in the criminal justice system during World War I and the spate of postwar antiblack violence by calling for self-protection and rejecting the hollow promises of American democracy. For Norris, New York's first female judge, the black women who appeared in her courts seemed neglected, not by the state but by the black community. She sympathized with black women's plight but argued that the black community needed to take a more proactive stance in dealing with its own. Her perspective reinforced the fact that racial segregation not only influenced employment and housing but shaped the vision of urban and penal reform. Norris followed the long-standing arguments of nineteenth- and early-twentieth-century white re-formers whose gendered perspective on female rehabilitation developed from the premise that the best hopes for inculcating the Anglo-Saxon ideals of feminine domesticity in working women was through those native-born white and immigrant women of European, rather than African, descent. Although both Campbell and Norris worked in New York City's criminal courts, there is no evidence that they encountered one another.

Grace Campbell: The Problems of Interracial Coalitions and Probation Work, 1911–1925

In 1911, a journalist celebrated an exceptional figure in New York's criminal justice system, writing, "Grace Campbell is her name, and at the criminal courts building she is known as one of the most successful probation offi-cers. She is the first and only one of her race, and she has attracted a great deal of attention by her work in the Tombs." A fellow officer enthused: "Miss Campbell is doing fine work here, and there isn't any one who won't respond to her sympathy. She is an ideal disciplinarian." Along with her skill as a probation officer, the article suggested, Campbell's "large, soft, brown eyes" contributed to her success. Campbell was not only efficient but approach-able. "It is her eyes that make the most eloquent appeal, although her soft, well-modulated voice is almost as persuasive."[3]

Such positive reviews of Campbell raise serious questions about race, gender, and the criminal justice system. Why were there no other black pro-bation officers six years after probation was instituted? Because of white social workers' and prison officials' hesitancy about working across the color line, black women in the New York court system failed to receive adequate—or, in some cases, any—state-sanctioned services. Campbell's career illumi-nates the crisis that unfolded as reform groups such as the National League

*Grace P. Campbell, n.d. Courtesy of
Photographs and Prints Division,
Schomburg Center for Research in
Black Culture, The New York
Public Library, Astor, Lenox
and Tilden Foundations.*

for the Protection of Colored Women (NLPCW), which attempted to safe-guard young urban women, realized that those women who found them-selves in the courts and prisons lacked such basic services as probation and access to local and state rehabilitative institutions.

Campbell, originally an NLPCW employee, publicly acknowledged that the league's work to protect southern migrant women and assist in their transition to urban life coincided with her own goals. Like most preven-tively oriented social reformers, she believed that the black working class, especially young women, needed guidance and instruction to navigate the urban terrain. Her ideas and objectives mirrored the concerns of black re-formers, especially clubwomen, who recognized racist practices in the court system but also believed that disreputable behavior could hurt racial ad-vancement. Campbell was influenced by Victoria Earle Matthews, though it is not clear that the two ever met. She saw her work as an extension of the legacy of black reformers. Newspaper clippings show that she was well con-nected with black social welfare networks. For instance, she attended a 1909 Woman's Loyal Union reception to honor antilynching activist Ida B. Wells-Barnett.[4] In 1911, the racial uplift message she articulated in relation to criminal justice echoed Victoria Earle Matthews's turn-of-the-century ad-vocacy of preventive reform. "The majority of people forget that the colored race is not naturally vicious or shiftless," Campbell asserted. Like Matthews, Campbell believed that blacks' lack of development stemmed from a "lack of proper training" that resulted from their long oppression.[5] As a court officer, Campbell showed concern for all urban working women needing assistance, yet she understood that "where there is protection for the white girl there is not so much for the Negro."[6] She focused specifically on migrant women as she addressed the problems that black women faced in New York City.

Campbell was well aware of the challenges associated with black female migration. Her father was from the West Indies, and her mother was born in Washington, DC. While she and her family clearly represented the successful side of the migration story, she could understand the problems that black native-born migrants and immigrants faced. Her father was in the ministry, so the family moved frequently, from Georgia to Texas and then to Washington. She attended her parents' alma mater, Howard University, and after graduation worked as a kindergarten teacher in Washington, DC, and Chicago. She later explained that she was "drawn to the work" of social reform through her interest in teaching. In 1905, Campbell settled in New York.[7]

Campbell's earliest documented connection with preventive social work began with the NLPCW. Strikingly, the executive board of this interracial organization included white men, white women, and black men, but no black women, even though it focused on young, single or unattached black women migrants.[8] The group differentiated between "those seeking education who are able to take care of themselves" and the "green inexperienced working girl." They worried most about the working woman who, they argued, sought "more liberty and, without money or friends, [found] herself stranded in a new world of cold strangers."[9] It is not clear when Campbell joined the NLPCW, but by 1911, when Frances Kellor left the organization to focus on the Americanization of immigrants, she was working for the organization, making $65 a month, in two distinct capacities: at the docks, where she assisted women arriving from the South, and as a probation officer working with black women in the courts.[10] Alongside Traveler's Aid Society workers, Campbell met many of the boats coming into New York. She also made sure that black female migrants were taken to their destinations in the city and were referred to suitable settlement houses or homes for working girls until they adjusted to urban life. Like Victoria Earle Matthews and Frances Kellor, Campbell lamented that "the temptations of . . . innocent colored girls from rural districts are great," stressing that "the lost address to a friend or a decent lodging house is one source of a girl's downfall."[11] Campbell and the NLPCW discovered that a "girl's downfall" was not simply a moral issue but, as the case of Faith Towns showed, often became a legal problem. Black migrant women were arrested for vagrancy, prostitution, theft, incorrigibility,

The National Urban League and Women's Court

and other offenses. Campbell's dual roles increased her efficiency, as she explained: "My work at the docks puts me in touch with many of these girls, for I am not at the court the whole day."[12]

Her work for the protection of black female migrants extended from the moment of their arrival in the city through their involvement with the courts to their release on probation. Campbell became the court advocate for black women and, unlike the majority of white court officers, willingly agreed to supervise them on probation in their neighborhoods. "The girls who find their way to the night courts are often victims of these spurious employment agents," Campbell maintained. "If they could be reached in time, a few words [would] put them on the right road." For instance, between October 1, 1911, and February 1, 1912, the NLPCW handled eighty-nine cases of women migrating to New York, twenty of whom were on probation.[13] As the number of poor and working-class women experiencing problems with the law increased, Campbell concentrated on her work with black women in the criminal justice system.

Campbell became preoccupied with her responsibilities as a probation officer, which led to conflict that left a mark on urban reform, interracial coalitions, and intraracial power struggles. Once again, black women were the victims of internecine strife. In response to Campbell's actions, some NLPCW members questioned the direction of her work and argued that the organization was established for preventive reform, not criminal justice. Elizabeth Walton, in particular, objected to Campbell's shift in focus. Like many other white female reformers who took an interest in the welfare of urban blacks, she came from an abolitionist family and, as a woman of means, believed she should devote her life to serving others. Walton complained that Campbell failed to spend enough time helping women who might have been in danger at the docks and "never found as many cases as" her predecessor. When Campbell went on vacation, Walton orchestrated a scheme to assess her efficiency at the docks by comparing her performance with that of her temporary replacement. Walton explained that she wanted to know whether "in . . . Campbell's absence, . . . there really [were] fewer cases by her boats, or whether . . . Campbell being so much more interested in the probation work [could not or would not] get them." Although later Walton openly expressed the opinion that the black social worker's activities failed to align with the objectives of the NLPCW, she apparently did not want her scheme exposed; she asked the black executive director, George Haynes, to be discreet as he carried out her experiment, masking her own power in the organization.[14]

Walton's undercover tactics in August 1911 not only reveal the diverging ideological positions within the NLPCW but also indicate the organization's discomfort with Campbell. Walton believed that "prevention work on the dock . . . is much more fundamental and must be done thoroughly."[15] Campbell, on the other hand, envisioned probation work as preventive: young women were monitored in their home and community by a court official, but not imprisoned. Walton's underhanded attempt to discredit Campbell, just months before the organization became a part of the National Urban League, foreshadowed subsequent tensions between Campbell, Walton, and other reformers over the proper strategy for assisting black women, which had long-term repercussions.

In October 1911, the formation of the National League on Urban Conditions Among Negroes (later the National Urban League) through the merger of three separate organizations, including the NLPCW, marked a significant break from urban reformers' attempts to discourage black migration.[16] The convergence of the Committee for Improving the Industrial Condition of Negroes, the Committee on Urban Conditions Among Negroes, and the National League for the Protection of Colored Women shows that southern migrants' insistence on taking hold of the opportunities they believed the urban North held reshaped the types of services that reformers offered. While reformers still questioned black southerners' ability to handle city life, they now worked to address the problems that northern blacks experienced in terms of employment, housing, and social work rather than argue that migrants were too uncivilized or ill-equipped to navigate the urban environment.

The NLPCW eventually became the Committee for the Protection of Women (CPW).[17] Campbell continued concentrating on probation. By giving talks at various organizations, including Harlem's Young Women's Christian Association (YWCA), she advocated increased attention to probation as an alternative to incarceration.[18] In 1912, the municipal court judges with whom she worked acknowledged her success as the CPW's new probation officer. After meeting with the CPW's chair, Elizabeth Walton reported that Campbell had done such "effective work" that the judges strongly encouraged that she be officially appointed as a regular probation officer of the New York Court of General Sessions.[19] Campbell used her growing expertise in the courts to push the Urban League to address black women's plight in the criminal justice system.

At Campbell's urging, the CPW investigated the social and criminal justice services available to black women, compiling information about the increasing numbers of black women in custodial local jails rather than in rehabilitative institutions.[20] As a result, the CPW wrote the judges of the Court of General Sessions to express concern regarding the small number of black women placed on probation and the state's responsibility to provide financial support for probation work.[21] The Urban League understood the severity of the issue after its student research fellow, Ellie Walls, completed a master's thesis on "the delinquent Negro girl in New York." Walls emphasized the "mental effect which knowledge of no place for commitment had" on young black women.[22] These women were aware that racism limited their rehabilitative possibilities as well as their time in custody. One woman stated that upon leaving a white institution a matron told her to tell the court officer not to "send any more colored girls out here, I have no place for them, and I don't know what to do with them," providing evidence that black women were less likely than white women to be admitted to local rehabilitative institutions. The case of two "unmanageable" young women highlights black reformers' dilemma. A probation officer told the young girls severely, "If you don't conduct yourselves properly I will have to report you to the Court, and if I do you will be committed." One girl replied, "They aint got no place to commit us, the Training School [Hudson] is full and they don't want us at the House of Mercy, so I'd like to know where they are going to put us."[23] In 1913, the CPW sent a letter to the board of managers at New York State's two female reformatories, Bedford and Hudson, regarding the low numbers of black women in those institutions. The committee demanded that action be taken to obtain additional accommodations for black delinquents.[24]

Although the CPW supported criminal justice work alongside preventive social work, the chair, Elizabeth Walton, continued to question the value of Campbell's probation work.[25] Campbell made it clear that her main objective was to deal with the growing number of women who were already in court, not to wait at the docks for women in need of guidance. From the end of 1912 to the beginning of 1913, Walton expressed her displeasure with Campbell to another important committee member. In her correspondence with the National Urban League's secretary, L. Hollingsworth Wood, she said that because of a public "row . . . over careless probation work," Campbell was being given more probation cases.[26] In January, she stated that she was "of the opinion that there are too [many] quiet investigations" and that she needed Wood to support her position by coming to a CPW meeting to "speak . . . from the point of view of the larger work."[27] Walton continued to define Campbell as problematic. In March, when Campbell was praised by court officials, Walton grudgingly admitted that those instances "make one feel Miss Campbell's investigations were worthwhile."²⁸ Yet Campbell's work was not the real problem; Walton, who was formally her supervisor, believed that she could not control Campbell.

As Campbell received accolades from the courts and in the black press, her relationship with Walton and key members of the CPW deteriorated. The black assistant director, Eugene Kinckle Jones, eventually requested Campbell's resignation. Although Walton attempted to hide her role in the dismissal, Campbell knew whom to call when seeking an explanation. Walton, who later said that Campbell had "given her a long song and dance over the telephone," remarked that Campbell should not have been surprised at her firing. Writing Secretary Wood in May 1913, Walton noted, "I told her she knew this had been going on for over a year and we had talked it over as much as a year ago, and decided the time had come to halt, as she could not fall into line." Campbell insisted on a public hearing. When Wood agreed, Walton made it clear that she did not "think it best" for her to see Campbell alone, and she did not want the larger organization to know about her involvement in Campbell's dismissal. Instead, she said, "for the sake of example . . . I should not assume . . . authority"; she wanted other members to think that the executive committee had taken this action.²⁹

While Walton acknowledged that she felt threatened by Campbell's presence, Assistant Director Jones expressed completely different sentiments. Jones supported Campbell's dismissal but argued that it was a "matter . . . of discipline" and would "give [the CPW] . . . momentum for further office efficiency."³⁰ He saw Campbell as a "subordinate, [who] lacks respect for authority" and contended that "at times" she tried to "domineer the whole office staff." Jones asserted that she had overstepped her bounds, thought too highly of herself, and "subordinates the work of the entire Committee, to her fractional part of the movement." He touted his own ability to handle business conflicts more effectively, reducing the conflict between Campbell and Walton to bickering between women rather than identifying it as a legitimate struggle over ideological and methodological differences. Revealing his own sense of power to another black member, George Haynes, he remarked, "I think . . . personally, I [could] manage her." He was equally dismissive and critical of the white "office staff," who "as a whole" struck him as "retarded." Because "the members . . . continually complain of [Campbell's] . . . attitude . . . I really do not see how we can do justice to the League and continue her in office," he added.³¹

Campbell's problems in a male-dominated, interracial organization were typical of those encountered by other direct, determined, and successful black female activists. Ida B. Wells-Barnett's forceful personality and forthright speech often rubbed whites the wrong way.[32] According to Wells-Barnett, Mary White Ovington played a central role in the decision to leave the antilynching activist off the National Association for the Advancement of Colored People's founding Committee of Forty. Although Ovington denied playing any role in this decision, she revealed how she felt about Wells-Barnett's type of leadership: she was a "powerful personalit[y] . . . fitted for courageous work, but perhaps not fitted to accept the restraint of organization."[33] Black clubwoman Fannie Barrier Williams remarked that while she never experienced problems working with interracial coalitions, she "soon discovered that it was much easier for progressive white women to be considerate to one colored woman whom they chanced to know and like than to be just and generous to colored young women as a race."[34] Although Ovington praised the diligent work of the National Association of Colored Women, Wells-Barnett and Williams may have felt vindicated and insulted had they read some of the white reformer's observations about black clubwomen. "Negro women enjoy organization," she observed. "They are ambitious for power often jealous and very sensitive. But they get things done."[35] Ovington's comments illuminate the very narrow confines within which black women's activism was deemed acceptable by white reformers.[36] These attitudes affected not only black women activists but also the black people who needed social welfare services. Campbell's final experiences with the Committee for the Protection of Women and the National Urban League exemplify this conundrum.

On June 11, 1913, the executive board of the National League on Urban Conditions Among Negroes held a special meeting to consider dismissing Campbell. The director, George Haynes, and the assistant director, Eugene Kinckle Jones, expressed alarm over Campbell's independence, which in their eyes diminished her ability to work with others. Elizabeth Walton stated her own reasons for recommending her colleague's dismissal. Board members pondered whether Campbell was "able to get along with the office Staff and the Protective Committee." The minutes do not reveal the board's official statements or Campbell's responses to their questions. Campbell was dismissed, not for inadequate work, but in the interest of maintaining the "harmonious work of the League's forces, and the order and discipline of the office." League officials noted their "appreciation of [her] . . . high efficiency and real ability." When Abraham Lefkowitz proposed a motion to pay Campbell two weeks of salary because she "had taken no vacation while in the employ of League (2 years)," Walton was the only member to vote against the motion.[37]

While Campbell's verbal or written response to her dismissal fails to ap-

168

pear in the historical record, her insistence on a hearing forced the League to admit publicly that they simply did not like her. While the board believed that Campbell disrupted the League's work, community members expressed surprise at her dismissal. When the Empire State Federation of Women's Clubs met that week, they protested Campbell's "summary dismissal," expressing "indignation" at "the manner" in which Campbell was discharged.[38] Campbell was able to obtain employment a month later as the superintendent of the Empire Friendly Shelter. This settlement home for black delinquent women provided temporary housing for those who were awaiting trial or needed a place to stay after being discharged from prison and finding "themselves without friends and in desperate circumstances."[39]

In retrospect, much of the problem, at least as it related to Campbell, stemmed from the inability of white men and women and black men to see black women as their equals. Historian Nell Irvin Painter succinctly describes the dilemmas inherent in interracialism: "No matter how patient the Negroes or well-meaning the whites, cooperating interracially in a segregated world that assumed black inferiority imposed strains on both sides."[40] Assumptions about race and gender influenced how Campbell was treated by the League. Her colleagues failed to accept her as an equal just as she was becoming a leader in criminal justice. They could only imagine a black woman as in need of supervision, not as competent to supervise others. Campbell, a college-educated, well-respected professional, was characterized in the same terms as the black female migrants she helped. In the same way that society labeled urban black women as immoral and in need of policing, reformers' references to Campbell as "not able to fall into line,"[41] an "insubordinate" who "lacks respect for authority,"[42] and a difficult employee who disrupted the "order and discipline of the office"[43] defined her as a problem that needed to be excised from the National Urban League. While they never claimed that Campbell was sexually degenerate, she was characterized as dangerous to the success of the organization. In many ways, restrictive gender and racial codes influenced how Campbell did her work and how her work has been viewed historically. While she is known for her later activism in the socialist and communist movements and the black nationalist African Blood Brotherhood (ABB), the histories of the National Urban League fail to acknowledge her critical role in the organization.[44] As her organizational affiliations changed, her work with black female offenders continued.

Campbell's role as a superintendent of the Empire Friendly Shelter coincided with her new position as parole officer for the New York State Prison for Women at Auburn. Although working in the same capacity as any parole officer, Campbell was officially identified as the prison's "acting parole agent for colored female prisoners."[45] Black women at Auburn immediately requested Campbell's services, yet they were not always pleased with her supervision. Though her charges welcomed her sympathetic attention to their positions in the criminal justice system, they were less accepting of her qualities as a "disciplinarian."[46] She generally believed she knew what was best for her parolees, but some failed to agree with her recommendations. Returned to Auburn for violating parole, a twenty-one-year-old black inmate committed for grand larceny explained that Campbell sent her to "some colored folks" and that she left the position because of the "way [she] . . . was treated." When Campbell refused her initial request for another job, the parolee simply left.[47] A thirty-one-year-old Auburn parole violator arrested for grand larceny had similar problems with her residence and employers. When the parolee told Campbell about her predicament, she reported, "Campbell said if I didn't stay . . . she would send me back" to Auburn.[48] Another parole violator convicted for grand larceny left New York to be with her mother in Virginia. When standing before Auburn's parole board a second time, she revealed her dismay in having Campbell as her parole officer and indicated that she would choose Maud Booth of the Salvation Army instead; Campbell had been unresponsive to her complaints that the "work was too hard."[49] There were many indications of tension between Campbell and her charges, indicating a fundamental disagreement over the direction of their lives and employment under parole. These black women rejected Campbell's vision of reform; in return, Campbell must have seen many parolees' demands as unrealistic and unreasonable.

In 1917, Campbell was officially appointed parole officer for the Parole Commission of New York City, while continuing to run the shelter for "unfortunate" black women and serving as a social investigator for the Board of Child Welfare.[50] At that point, she developed a documented connection with the New York State Reformatory for Women at Bedford. Consistent with her mission, she provided training and guidance to young black girls and women in trouble with the law. She believed that even in the "most stubborn cases" of delinquency, "sympathy and the proper kind of discipline" were essential.[51] Other reform organizations, such as the YWCA, recognized her skill and sent to Campbell women whom they "could not handle."[52] Her career in the criminal justice system reinforced her direct connection to racial uplift ideology. She consistently responded to what historian Evelyn Brooks Higginbotham calls the politics of respectability: black reformers' strategically emphasized proper behavior and conformity to middle-class values as a means to counter racism.[53] Campbell's evaluation of the prospects of rehabilitating particular female offenders was influenced by this standard, and her emphasis on appropriate behavior affected her ability to provide services to black women.

Campbell championed respectable behavior at the Empire Friendly Shelter, an institution that became an extension of her reputation. In one case, she dismissed two young black women in her care who disregarded basic rules of decorum. Campbell reported that she was willing to supervise the two women on probation, but pending their court investigation, "they had been . . . noisy and difficult" and "exceedingly hard to manage." They "used profane language, called people from the street, . . . [were] unpleasant with other inmates, and each on a separate occasion . . . attempted to start a fight." According to Campbell, although both women had "some good points," they were "uncouth." To maintain order at the shelter and prevent neighbors' complaints, she recommended they be committed to Bedford, as she believed "both are plainly in need of strong discipline." Campbell said that "if she had a Home in the country she would have taken the girls herself but in the city it was impossible to handle them because they were so troublesome and could not be properly restrained."[54] Despite Campbell's concern and caution, she was unable to secure enough financial support to keep the Empire Shelter open, and after she worked there five years, the home was closed in 1918.[55]

After 1918, it might seem that Campbell embraced left-wing views, yet her social and political activism always involved new, innovative strategies for black freedom. Despite the silences in the record regarding Campbell's familial and personal background, her dismissal from the Urban League, her concern about how the disruptive behavior of residents would affect her institution, and her long-standing employment with New York State provide a portrait of a determined public activist who used myriad means to address oppression. Like many black Harlem activists, she became more radicalized after World War I and increasingly made vocal public criticisms of the U.S. government and the capitalist system. Many of her peers, while criticizing W. E. B. Du Bois's argument that black people should "Close Ranks" and support the war effort, would have endorsed the ideas and angry defiance of his famous postwar *Crisis* editorial, "Returning Soldiers," with its critique of lynching, disfranchisement, and labor exploitation and its call for black veterans to "return fighting."[56] Racial discrimination in social welfare initiatives, white violence against black veterans, and the "Red Summer" of race riots in 1919 all prompted the activism of a group of black socialists, known as the "New Crowd Negro," who demanded full citizenship rights.[57] Through her work with the urban poor, Campbell had come to understand the vulnerabilities of black communities, particularly black women, more clearly than most Progressives, who sought to reform society without challenging industrial capitalism. Campbell became one of the first black socialists in Harlem, but unlike many black radical activists, she eventually espoused communism. She frequently spoke at public forums and, according to a Federal Bureau of Investigation informant, "condemns all other forms of governments but the Soviet, which she claimed is . . . the only hope of the workingman."[58] She also ran for the State Assembly on the Socialist ticket in 1919 and 1920 and became a prominent member of the African Blood Brotherhood.

Campbell's postwar politics grew out of her frustrations with the status quo and her determination to seek new avenues for fundamental social change. As an urban reformer, criminal justice officer, and director of a settlement house for delinquent black girls, Campbell seemed to follow a trajectory that mirrored the work of Victoria Earle Matthews. But her militant stance against racial discrimination moved her rapidly to the left. She was the only woman who joined the ABB, which shows how much she was respected as a community organizer and her skill in negotiating gender tensions. The group, organized after the 1921 Tulsa race riot, "called for armed resistance to lynching, unqualified franchise rights for blacks in the South, a struggle for equal rights and against all forms of discrimination, and the organization of . . . [blacks] into established trade unions."[59] Explaining that the ABB was a "Peace-loving, but Red-Blooded Organization," the *Crusader*, a radical black newspaper that promoted self-determination and later the objectives of the ABB, explained that the group stood for the "IMMEDIATE PROTECTION AND ULTIMATE LIBERATION OF NEGROES EVERYWHERE. . . . No loose-talking. No cowardly compromises. No servile surrender of Negro rights. No illusion about the task before us. No attempt to operate without a program."[60] While under constant surveillance as "one of the prime movers of the organization," Campbell was never fired from her position as a state employee.[61]

As an avowed socialist and later one of the first black communists in Harlem, Campbell knew from professional experience that her political activism must address working women in general and the plight of black working-class women in particular. Campbell argued that women were "being driven to prostitution and other evils by the low scale of wages," and she "promised to work hard among . . . women, not only of her race but all of the women."[62] Nonetheless, in 1925, as in 1911, "the number of colored women and girls convicted . . . was relatively larger than white," because "the colored woman, and especially colored girls, are the least protected group."

Although all working women were more likely than middle-class women to face the criminal justice system, white working women received preventive and social services that were not available to black women. As a court officer, she emphasized that "white women . . . are oftimes sentenced to private institutions which refuse colored girls—as they might have to occupy the same dormitories, or eat at the same table." Campbell criticized the "degradation of putting unfortunate young colored women in the workhouse with hardened offenders" rather than in reformatory institutions and concluded that "the loss of self-respect and vice learned by" black women in those prisons "is appalling."[63]

Campbell cultivated a remarkable ability to remain involved in a myriad of groups that used different strategies for black freedom. Her affiliation with the ABB did not derail her career as a municipal and state worker, nor did it disentangle her from various prominent black female leaders in Harlem. In addition to her demanding job and political party work, she was also called on to demand justice for the long-standing problem of police brutality against black women. In 1925, Campbell was one of several "prominent fraternal women" who directed the district attorney to begin an investigation into the police shooting of a black woman. Two officers had "forced their way into" Mrs. Mary Lee's home and "when she objected to them searching her premises, one of them opened fire." Lee was shot in the stomach.[64] It seems that Campbell's work as a community activist—involved in distinct and in some ways competing organizations—was never done. As long as injustice remained, she stood up for the oppressed in the same way that Judge Jean Norris saw herself guiding female defendants charged with sex-related offenses.

Judge Jean Norris and the Female Offender, 1919–1931

Grace Campbell seems never to have encountered Judge Jean Norris, but the veteran probation officer would have heard about the prominent magistrate. Both women were concerned about the deleterious effects of modern urban life, as popular amusements such as movies, amusement parks, and dance halls; premarital sex; and youthful economic independence transformed the behavior of young women. While Campbell worked as a court officer, Norris presided in the Women's Court, which was established in 1910 to "rid the city of prostitution, to prevent the spread of venereal disease," and to "rehabilitate women coming before the Court."[65] As the first female judge, Norris had the opportunity to clean up the Women's Court, which had a pattern of convicting women of solicitation despite insufficient evidence, and used her feminine judicial perspective to extend activists' efforts to rehabilitate young women. The *New York Times Magazine* proclaimed, "First Woman Magistrate Judges Fallen Sisters."[66]

Jean Norris was appointed to the New York City Magistrates' Court on October 27, 1919. A native of New York and a graduate of Fordham University and New York University School of Law, Norris had served as a prosecuting attorney. She was assigned first to the Domestic Relations Court and then to the Women's Court. Norris advocated moral reform and argued that young delinquent women should be given an opportunity to rehabilitate themselves.[67] As a member of the Women Lawyers' Association, Norris, along with five other women, "lobbied" to become "volunteer defense attorneys for . . . alleged prostitutes" who were vulnerable to plainclothes cops and an all-male court system.[68] Almost a year after her appointment, the achievement of women's suffrage had removed bars to women's full, active citizenship, and educated women were seen as "capable of filling the highest positions." Norris's appointment underscored a growing sentiment that a women should preside over the Women's Court.[69] Amy Wren, president of the Brooklyn Women's Bar Association, declared: "It was our dream that someday a woman would hold the position you occupy and I am glad our dream has been realized."[70] Norris had been elected to leadership positions in a host of organizations, including the National Woman Lawyers' Association, the Women's City Club, and the New York State Federation of Business and Professional Women's Clubs. She served on the boards of the Florence Crittenton League, the House of Good Shepherd Auxiliary, and the National Probation Association as well as the National Conference of Catholic Charities.[71]

Norris ardently supported the concept that women should reform women and argued that a woman magistrate should always be present in the Women's Court. She contended that "there are so many phases of . . . [women's] cases . . . that a man [could not] handle, simply because he has no conception of the difficulties" women face.[72] Female offenders appreciated having another woman in a position of authority. "The girls who are brought into the court are not antagonistic to our interest," Norris argued, "as some have declared they would be, for they see at once that we are there to help them."[73] Norris took a special interest in the cases of unmarried mothers and, in several instances, helped them obtain employment with her philanthropic friends who were willing to assist young women as they attempted to make a "fresh start."[74]

Norris's reform agenda crossed racial lines to include black female delinquency. When interviewed by the black press, Norris expressed grave concerns about the black community's apathy toward the plight of black female offenders. In a meeting with the *New York Age*'s editor, Fred R. Moore, Norris argued that black communities were relatively complacent about black women's behavior in general and black female delinquency in particular. "Colored people," she asserted, "should render more assistance to these girls by a larger cooperation with the welfare and social service agencies, and even the court itself."[75] Praising the value of social workers, despite the fact that whites rarely took black cases, she suggested that more black social workers were needed. A year later, when she was questioned about the relationship between young black women's delinquency and the racial segregation in state-supported homes for working girls, Norris replied, "Rich colored people . . . should establish homes and respectable houses where a girl may get wholesome food without a large amount of money." Norris also said that black "churches could do an enormous amount of good."[76] Norris's lack of contact with black New Yorkers meant she was unaware of the efforts that activists, settlement houses, social reform organizations, and churches were making in the black community. Unlike Frances Kellor, Norris never felt compelled to inquire about black social welfare reform.

Like most educated, middle-class white woman involved in urban reform, Norris focused on the plight of working-class native-born white and immigrant women. In doing so, she followed the direction of many of her nineteenth-century predecessors who, while holding nativist sentiments, believed European ancestry and its connection to civilization gave these poor working women the capacity to be rehabilitated and eventually assimilated into American society. European immigrants' experiences, however difficult, contained the possibility of upward mobility and first-class citizenship. African Americans failed to enter this narrative. In this sense, nineteenth-century reformers, as Gunja SenGupta argues, imagined "a white nation in which people of color were invisible."[77] Early-twentieth-century urban and penal reform mirrored the dictates of a racially segregated New York that made Norris's ideas about black people's responsibility for their own fate a common perspective.

Many white reformers who worked with primarily working-class immigrant groups acted as if, as Mary White Ovington put it, "the Negro was non-existent."[78] Ovington, best known for her later work with the National Association for the Advancement of Colored People, was a thirty-eight-year-old native New Yorker when she discovered "the Negro and his problems"[79] after attending a 1903 lecture by Tuskegee Institute president Booker T. Washington. Once she committed herself to addressing racial discrimination, she recalled, many of her white friends commented that "the

Negroes should support their own charities."[80] Ovington probably would have agreed with this assessment before she investigated conditions within black communities and developed working relationships with black activists such as Du Bois. Her research, summarized in her 1911 book, *Half a Man: The Status of the Negro in New York City*, led her to conclude that effective social work needed solid and consistent financing, which most black organizations and communities lacked. Ovington had come to understand the predicament of black reformers, while Norris, like many other white reformers and activists, never developed a real understanding of black people's situation and concerns.

Norris's position regarding the black community's responsibility toward young women might also have stemmed from the cultural and political lessons she learned as an Irish American. While the Irish held prominent positions in Democratic Party politics at the turn of the twentieth century, during the nineteenth century they had been the target of nativist hostility from white Anglo-Saxon Protestants, who characterized them as "indolent, improvident, and immoral" and as similar to black New Yorkers.[81] The immigrant group's rise in social and political mobility—seen in the makeup of the city police force and local elected officials, as well as Norris's court appointment—illustrated the positive consequences of assimilation. Occasionally, successful Irish Americans were reminded of their immigrant group's humble beginnings. For instance, one Protestant male journalist "portrayed Norris as an Irish American woman with unwarranted pretensions and ambitions." He highlighted what he deemed as Norris's class pretensions when "he mocked her 'frequent use of an obviously Oxonian accent'" and observed that "twice in her excitement she slipped back into her native language."[82] Yet Irish Americans might well have compared their immigrant group's relative success with native-born blacks' constant struggle. Norris's blind eye to state funding for racially segregated religious and secular public institutions suggests that she believed black people's problems stemmed from apathy rather than racism. Moreover, her assessments might also come from long-standing tensions and apprehensions—which could be seen in the 1900 race riot and other minor and major altercations—between the two groups.

Unlike Grace Campbell, who argued that black women's high conviction rates stemmed from racist policing and social service practices, Judge Jean Norris believed that black women's downfall resulted from community indifference. In her view, the "tragedy of the colored girl in court" could be addressed by black people becoming more involved and cooperating with the police and social workers. Contending that "the colored girl lacks the right interest from her people both in and out of the court," Norris disregarded the work of black social workers and organizations that addressed the protection of black women. In 1925, seemingly unaware of Grace Campbell's long service as a probation officer or the National Urban League's fourteen-year commitment to training black social workers, Norris told a black interviewer: "You should have . . . a colored social worker who would take an active interest in the welfare of your girl; visit her home, and take her out of her environment if it is a wrong one." The fact that after six years as a Women's Court magistrate concerned about young women's rehabilitation she was not cognizant of the Colored Young Women's Christian Association, the White Rose Home, and the Empire Friendly Shelter illustrates the enormous task of reformers working for black women's protection. Indeed, her suggestion that "there should be a well authenticated list of exceedingly respectable homes which would give [black women] board, lodging, and a chance for recreation at a moderate charge"[83] reinforces the notion that she was determined to remain uninformed.

Like many white reformers, Norris supported rehabilitative, state-funded, and racially segregated programs for immigrant and white women. She failed to propose that working-girls' homes and settlement houses accept black women. Indeed, when asked about the possibility of their admitting black women, she reinscribed prejudiced institutional policies by explaining that they were "very limited in accommodation," and because girls had to share "rooms and a common table for meals, . . . as a rule the colored girl was not sent to them."[84]

Norris presented a race-neutral discussion of her vision of female reform; only when she was questioned about programs specifically for black women was its racial exclusiveness made apparent. In an article explaining that the spirit of the court was one of a "genuine service," seeking to reunite "the young girl with her family" and assist in "her rehabilitation and restoration to society," the young black woman disappeared.[85] Describing Catholic, Protestant, and Jewish organizations' programs and working-girls' homes, Norris implied that all young women could be saved and rehabilitated. Norris presented a distorted image of her work as a judge and reformer, emphasizing the court as guiding and training young women so that they could be "made physically and morally well again" but failing to acknowledge that these services were seldom available to black women.[86]

Black defendant Mabel Hampton's experiences belie the judge's benevolent intent and mirror the problems that most women, black and white, faced in Norris's court.[87] Looking back on when she was sentenced on a prostitution charge in 1924, Hampton recalled an uncompromising judge.

The National Urban League and Women's Court

Uninterested in Hampton's claim that she was innocent but had been framed, Norris declared that the "only thing I can say is Bedford." Hampton argued that in court Norris "railroaded me" because, as she put it, she had "no lawyer, no nothing."[88] Hampton's assessment of Norris is corroborated by the judge's record. She "gained a reputation for harshness" and "severe jail sentences" with "few acquittals."[89]

At the beginning of her tenure, Norris tended to dismiss prostitution cases with "insufficient" evidence, but over time she began to defend the city's vice squad.[90] The reasons for her shifting views are not clear from the record. Although other magistrates highlighted improper police activity, contending that officers "unlawfully entrapped" women into criminal behavior, Norris argued that these men were simply doing their job to alleviate the "prostitution evil." "The police methods are by no means perfect," she said, "but they are the best so far. Today the detectives use a legitimate trap that is recognized by law."[91] Unlike Justice Joseph Poole, who at least two decades earlier had condemned police officers for their dubious conduct, Norris characterized them as family men "of the utmost trustworthiness and responsibility." Indeed, Norris was a reformist judge who worked to wipe out prostitution, but her cultural background might well have shaped her court decisions. While their noted excessive drinking and property crimes indicated a need for reform, Irish women were less likely, as Hasia R. Diner has argued, to enter the sex trade.[92] This may account for why the judge consistently allowed the violation of female defendants' rights in order to sanction working-class and poor women's violation of middle-class moral standards.[93] Norris never questioned the practices of the vice squad, even when the officers arrested women without sufficient evidence of their crimes.[94] Several of the officers, in fact, were subsequently convicted of and jailed for perjury.[95]

In 1931, during retired judge Samuel Seabury's investigations of the magistrates' courts and police conduct, Norris's actions were publicly dissected. Many magistrates were accused of abuses, especially complicity in allowing police officers to use informants (stool pigeons) to procure shady evidence against women. Norris's position as the first woman magistrate of the Women's Court made her behavior more egregious. Scholar John Peretti notes that in over 5,000 cases "overwhelmingly related to prostitution and disproportionately involving African American defendants," Norris handed down 40 percent more convictions than her peers.[96] Some of the policemen whom she defended in the 1920s were just as corrupt. In addition, in violation of the ethical rules pertaining to her court position, she endorsed and appeared in her judicial robe for an advertisement of Fleischmann's Yeast, a move that many believed was "contrary to the essential dignity of the court office." Later she was found to own stock in Equitable Casualty and Surety, a bonds company that profited from defendants in her court.[97]

The Bodmer case illustrates Norris's use of illegal means to enforce her moral ideals. When a twenty-five-year-old woman who was living with a man was arrested as a wayward minor on the complaint of a local deaconess, Norris argued that she was saving the woman from a life of sin by sentencing her to Bedford reformatory. When the woman was "decently married," Norris believed she had done her job.[98] However, the judge's decision in the case was later questioned, since the young woman was arrested without a warrant and when sentenced had no lawyer. The testimony on which she was convicted was later deemed "insufficient in law and almost exclusively hearsay."[99] Judge Seabury severely criticized Norris's use of the courts to maintain moral standards instead of legal justice. The investigation revealed that Norris attempted to cover up her questionable tactics by having some of her more "prejudicial remarks" removed from the courtroom transcripts.[100]

Twelve years after her appointment, Judge Norris was removed from the New York City Magistrates' Court because of her "severity, . . . unjudicial conduct and . . . callous disregard of the rights of defendants in the Women's Courts."[101] Norris believed that a woman magistrate could make a significant difference in the lives of wayward and delinquent women because she understood women's problems. Her critics condemned her overbearing use of moral standards and particularly her mistreatment of young women.[102] A *New York Times* editorial contended that Norris had fallen short as a role model for women in high positions: "She must be true to her oath of office and to her own conscience in conducting herself with perfect integrity and all the efficiency of which she is capable, and at the same time never forget that she is a representative of her sex in political affairs and as such must be especially scrupulous lest any failure of hers lower the repute of women in public life."[103]

While Norris was singled out because of specific gendered concerns, the majority of the magistrates in the Women's Court violated young women's rights under the wayward minor law. Judge Seabury's investigation never questioned the validity of the law that allowed the arrest of a girl "who habitually associates with dissolute characters, or who is expressly disobedient of the commands of [her] parents." He focused only on the matter of sufficient evidence or a proper trial.[104] In a separate case during the Seabury investigation, police stool pigeon Chile Mapocha Acuna told the court that in eight of nineteen cases "patrolmen had arrested women on immorality

charges though the policemen were informed that there was no evidence."
Acuna, who was paid $5 per arrest whether or not he had sufficient evidence,
told of a number of experiences in Harlem. He explained that one black
woman was arrested "in an apartment house hallway and charged with misconduct in an apartment which she had not yet reached."[105] Although these
practices were in force throughout the 1920s, it was not until January 1931
that the problem received public attention. The ensuing investigation revealed that seventy-seven women were unlawfully imprisoned at the New
York State Reformatory for Women at Bedford, for terms ranging from one
to five years, by seven judges. Norris had sentenced sixteen of those cases.
At the time of the investigation, fifty women were still imprisoned, fifteen
others had been paroled, one had died, another had been transferred to an
insane asylum, and at least three had been discharged.[106]

The personal and professional biographies of black probation and parole
officer Grace Campbell and white municipal judge Jean Norris illuminate
the ways in which race shaped the public services that black women received
and how they fared in the criminal justice system. Norris's mistaken perception that the black community neglected its young women underscores
the difficulties faced by black activists. Despite their consistent efforts, the
private facilities they founded were overcrowded, underfunded, and short-
lived. Campbell's efforts were frustrated by many white and some black reformers' inability to deal with her forthright personality and her political
radicalism. Despite her contentious relationships with other activists and
the government surveillance to which she was subjected after World War I,
she maintained a successful and uninterrupted career in the civil service.
Campbell always stood her ground.

Judge Norris sympathized with the "tragedy of the colored woman in
court," but she urged the black community to take responsibility for providing the services and guidance they needed, rather than advocating the
integration of the state's reformatory institutions. She seemed willfully unaware of the sustained efforts of black organizations and of interracial organizations such as the National Urban League. Norris's dismissal from the
Women's Court after revelations of her abuses of defendants' rights and
collusion with the police reveals the multiple challenges black women faced
within the criminal justice system. Whether arrested because they committed a crime or because of a frame-up, black women were entering an
arena that was tainted with corruption, all the way from the police on the
beat up to the magistrates. These women encountered equally daunting cir-

cumstances when their own family members' anxieties about their attempts at independence led to them to seek recourse in the wayward minor law. The next chapter explores how working-class parents and relatives attempted to use the statute proactively to regulate the behavior of their daughters, nieces, and kin.

6

in danger of becoming morally depraved

SINGLE BLACK WOMEN,

WORKING-CLASS BLACK FAMILIES, AND

NEW YORK STATE'S WAYWARD MINOR LAWS,

1917–1928

> Whenever any woman or girl of the age of sixteen or over . . . is found
> in a reputed house of prostitution or assignation . . . is found associating with
> vicious or dissolute persons, or is willfully disobedient to parent or guardian,
> [she] is in danger of becoming morally depraved.
>
> —New York State Law, 1920

> I am asking you why are you all keep my . . . daughter so long [there.] I would
> like very much for the Board to discharge her, so she could be out to work for her
> children as I am getten almost under able to be work for her children. . . .
> [S]he was not put their for anything that was bad.
>
> —Letter from inmate's mother to Bedford, 1927

In 1923, after attending a Fourth of July party, Gail Lewis missed her curfew. Instead of coming directly home, the black seventeen-year-old New
York native decided to stay out all night and face her parents the next day—
especially her father, whom she feared would be angry. By the time she returned, her parents had already notified the police. Lewis's violation of her
parents' rules, in their estimation, indicated that she was at risk of engaging in inappropriate behavior. Although school officials had reported that
she had a few skirmishes with her classmates, Lewis was considered well
behaved and not a juvenile delinquent.[1] When notified about her arrest,

Lewis's pastor replied in disbelief: "I was never more surprised. . . . I am certain that there must have been some evil influence in her straying away."[2] Her parents "entered a complaint" against her for violation of New York State's wayward minor law.[3] This statute criminalized female disobedience and actual, alleged, or feared sexual delinquency as a proactive means of protecting young women from urban "vice." Lewis was arrested and imprisoned in the New York State Reformatory for Women at Bedford for being "willfully disobedient" and, more important from her parents' perspective, for being "in danger of becoming morally depraved."[4]

This case points to an important but unexplored issue in the history of early-twentieth-century urban reform campaigns: black families' anxieties about single women's moral behavior and their proactive attempts to keep them from going astray. Black working-class families actively participated in the effort to protect and, ultimately, to control young women. The records of the women sent to Bedford reveal that their families sought to monitor their activities and guard their reputations. The single black woman was not always a lone southern migrant or independent urban dweller who was in need of moral guidance from strangers; many young women lived with their families.[5] Black working-class people's commitment to conventional standards of morality and respectability, as well as their efforts to maintain stability in their households and communities in spite of their impoverishment, were accompanied by a belief in their entitlement to state services. As they navigated the city's dangerous terrain, young women's parents and relatives sought social support from the state. Unfortunately, their efforts to utilize public institutions for their own ends often had unexpected and, in many cases, negative consequences.[6]

Some black working-class families deliberately turned to the courts to regulate what they defined as the transgressive behavior of their female relatives.[7] Clashes between young women and their elders over what was viewed as appropriate behavior caused tremendous conflict within black families. The legal, and ultimately unequal, relationship between young black women, their parents and kin, and the state dramatically affected black families' expectations of and experiences with public institutions.[8] Why did some families turn to the state for support? How did New York State reformers and administrators respond to the needs and requests of working-class and poor black families? Finally, in light of the prejudices that reformers held against working-class persons, how did the race-based choices reformers made affect black people's abilities to use the law to protect young women? The fifteen existing case files of black women sentenced to Bedford between 1917 and 1928[9] challenge many of the general claims made about working-class black families' composition, concerns, and ability to assert their own moral voice.[10]

The Wayward Minor Laws

New York State's wayward minor laws[11] date back to an 1882 municipal law that was "designed to control those girls from fourteen to twenty-one who, charged with being prostitutes, had professed a desire to reform" by committing them to reformatory institutions.[12] In 1886, the state legislature amended the law to include "incorrigible girls." The 1886 law enabled parents and legal guardians, as well as the police, to commit young women whom they believed were delinquent by testifying in court. Young women indicted under the law were committed to private reformatory institutions. Eventually, magistrates could sentence women as young as twelve upon a finding that they were discovered in a "reputed" house of prostitution, "frequenting the company of thieves or prostitutes," "associating with vicious and dissolute persons," or "willfully disobedient to parent or guardian, and in danger of becoming morally depraved."[13]

Legislators repeatedly modified the statute, and in 1923, the legislature amended it for "the commitment, custody and control of wayward minors."[14] Under the "wayward girl" statute, women aged sixteen to twenty-one could be committed under the same conditions as under the incorrigibility statutes, with the addition of their being "habitually addicted to the use of drugs or the intemperate use of intoxicating liquors." When the statute was extended to cover young men in 1925, court officers and administrators reinforced the idea that, like young women who had been subject to the law since 1882, young men were not seen as having "committed serious offense against the law, but they were certainly entering on the road which would eventually find them in its clutches."[15]

While defining the parameters of inappropriate female behavior, the laws encouraged parental and community monitoring of young women by providing a means to discipline morally wayward and rebellious girls through the courts. The laws from 1882 to 1920 provided that local private reformatories, like the Protestant Episcopal House of Mercy, the Roman Catholic House of Good Shepherd, the New York Magdalen Benevolent Society, and the Jewish Protectory and Aid Society, could serve as the sites for young women's moral rehabilitation.[16] Although Bedford received incorrigible young women as soon as it opened in 1901, it was not until 1920 that the state legislature revised the incorrigibility statute to allow courts to send the most troublesome young women to Bedford. Young women who caused continuous disciplinary problems or were deemed unfit to benefit from "the discipline and training" that the reformatories offered were returned to court and then sent to Bedford for up to three years.[17] This change marked the Bedford commitment as the final, and most serious, stage in the institutional reform of young women charged with wayward behavior.

State legislators and reformers used the incorrigible girl and wayward minor laws to regulate what they saw as improper parenting within working-class, native-born and immigrant, white and black families.[18] When family members brought their female kin to court for repeated disobedience, it underscored legislators' assumption that working-class parents were deficient. Reformers' and administrators' definitions of incompetence ranged from immigrants' inability to assimilate American customs to the families' inability to discipline their children. For instance, an administrator noted that a young woman deserved to be institutionalized because her parents, "although good people . . . with a good home, were not able to control" their daughter.[19] Probation officer Patrick Shelly of the New York City Magistrates' Courts articulated the widely shared belief that "at the root of all delinquency is an improper home environment, which includes a lack of religious teaching of any kind, and bad example or downright indifference on the part of parents."[20] State officials concluded that adults' incompetence contributed to their problem.

Both white and black reformers assumed that the black working class was prone to immorality. Black activists committed to social uplift sought simultaneously to assist and to distinguish themselves from those individuals they believed were in need of guidance.[21] Victoria Earle Matthews's concern for black prostitutes was motivated in part by the concern that white society would take "for granted that all black people—all Afro-Americans are naturally low." She believed that the black elite had a responsibility to address the problems endemic to working-class and poor black communities: "The public must be convinced that there is another class than is represented by the depraved class commonly met with on the streets and in certain localities. The common standard of life must be elevated. . . . Corrective influences must be established in the infested centres."[22]

In contrast to black reformers like Matthews, who emphasized how far black people had advanced since enslavement by reinforcing intraracial class distinctions, white reformers questioned all black people's moral capacity as a result of their African ancestry as well as the legacy of slavery. While they may have agreed with nineteenth-century abolitionists' arguments that enslavement created dissolute domestic conditions, early-twentieth-century

Single Black Women and the Wayward Minor Laws

white reformers never quite believed that black people, particularly black women, were civilized enough to possess a moral compass. Frances Kellor's investigations of southern criminality only reinforced these views. As she saw it, slavery had placed blacks "several centuries behind the Anglo-Saxon race in civilizing agencies and processes."[23] Black families were not stable patriarchal structures, she argued, because black women had to work outside the home and black men did "not discourage it."[24] White reformers' assumption that black women lacked moral propriety extended to entire communities. In 1911, Jane Addams of Chicago's Hull House argued that "one could easily illustrate lack of inherited control" among blacks, especially when comparing "the experiences of a group of colored girls with those of a group representing the daughters of Italian immigrants, or of any other South European peoples." Italian mothers, she asserted, "seldom" gave their daughters "permission to go to a party in the evening, and never without chaperonage." In Addams's view, Italians partook of the "social traditions which have been worked out during centuries of civilization" and, along with other "new groups," had the capacity to be "assimilated into civilization." In contrast, black women, without the "protection" of social restraint, "yield more easily to the temptations of a city than any other girls." Addams assumed that immigrants could be assimilated because their behavior, however problematic, was rooted in European culture, whereas blacks, because of their African descent and the legacy of American slavery, lacked the same capacity for cultural improvement.[25]

These perceptions influenced the ways in which reformers used the wayward minor laws to compensate for what they perceived as inadequate black parenting. Reformers saw delinquent black women as troublesome because their families lacked both the ability and the authority to address immoral behavior. Those working-class black family members who resorted to the wayward minor statutes because of their fear that female relatives were "in danger of becoming morally depraved" found that their own behavior was also called into question. However, this scrutiny failed to translate into appropriate criminal justice services for young black women, whether probation or admission into state-sanctioned private reformatories.

Black Working Women and Their Families

Black families were not uniform but had quite varied aspirations. Bedford inmates' case files reveal that they grappled in different ways with the behavior of their female kin. The records of girls found to be incorrigible and wayward show the disparate definitions of appropriate standards of conduct held by black working-class women and their families.

The women charged with incorrigibility and the families who sought state intervention represented the diversity of New York's black working class. They were natives of northern states (New York, New Jersey, and Massachusetts), southern states (South Carolina, North Carolina, and Maryland), Washington, DC, and the British West Indies. Some of their families were familiar with urban life, while others were still adjusting to New York City. These women had all received at least a fourth-grade education and were employed at the time of their arrest as domestics, laundresses, or factory workers. Most had been committed by their parents, single mothers or fathers, or extended family members—grandmothers, aunts, sisters, and cousins—who were their legal guardians. These family members worked primarily in personal-service positions and in factories. Only two of these women had spent any time in juvenile institutions before arriving in Bedford. They and their families were affiliated with Baptist, Catholic, Methodist, Pentecostal, Presbyterian, and Seventh Day Adventist churches. Most families struggled to maintain modest homes, while others were considered financially "above the average [for] colored people." All strove to be regarded as respectable within their communities.[26]

Working-class and poor black people concerned about the moral respectability of their community often attempted to move out of black neighborhoods when they were threatened by instability. Keenly aware of the moral dangers young black women faced on a daily basis, especially saloons, dance halls, gambling, and prostitution, black working-class families were concerned with protecting the reputations and monitoring the activities of their young women. This concern influenced how family members understood and responded to their positions within particular neighborhoods.[27] Many believed that living in predominantly black neighborhoods exposed young women to unsavory influences that were not so evident in white and primarily immigrant communities. Mainstream reform efforts, as historian Kevin Mumford notes, focused on moving criminal behavior out of white neighborhoods but ignored or failed to address crime when it migrated to predominantly black neighborhoods. When they could, some black families moved to what they deemed more respectable neighborhoods. A sixteen-year-old inmate who lived in a predominantly Italian American neighborhood explained that her mother "always tried to live in a good neighborhood, so that she would not meet bad girls."[28] A seventeen-year-old woman explained that her parents "always tried to get in a good neighborhood for her sake" and that she had "never lived in a distinctly colored neighbor-hood."[29] In describing her neighborhood as a "very good residence section in [the] Bronx" and emphasizing that "there are no colored people in this vicinity except one colored janitress [on the] next block," she reinforced the notion that black neighborhoods were inherently problematic. However, problems were not exclusive to black neighborhoods: when this inmate's family had moved into a "bad neighborhood, where a great many Italians of a poor class lived," they left as quickly as possible.[30] In some cases, families moved to what they hoped were better neighborhoods but once there real-ized that not all white working-class neighborhoods were freer of baneful moral influences.

The stigma attached to black neighborhoods increased families' concern about young women's moral and physical well-being. While Jane Addams and other white reformers believed that the prevalence of red-light districts in black neighborhoods created disastrous conditions for young women be-cause their families were "least equipped with social tradition [and] forced to expose daughters to the most flagrantly immoral conditions the commu-nity permits," the case files tell another story.[31] A twenty-year-old inmate commented that, although she lived in a good neighborhood, she was not allowed to go to movies and public dances without being accompanied by her mother.[32] An eighteen-year-old said that she was "brought up strict." Her older siblings, who served as her guardians, never allowed her to "play in [the] streets" but encouraged her to attend activities at the local YWCA. She, too, could not attend movies or public dances without an older sister.[33]

Working-class families' concern about their daughters and young female kin was shaped by their specific perceptions of their neighborhood's repu-tation. When young black women rejected their family's attempts to protect and guide them by establishing clear rules, some elders made their private concern about these young women public and sought to utilize the wayward minor laws.

Probation, Local Reformatories, and Bedford

Once they entered a complaint against their female kin, most families, black and white, believed that the young woman would be reprimanded in court, given probation, or, in extreme cases, sent to a local reformatory for a short time. Many assumed, as did the parents of one seventeen-year-old, that the "scare of bringing her into court would be enough punishment."[34] How-ever, black women were not placed on probation at the same rate as white women and were often rejected from social welfare programs because of the discriminatory policies of court officials and local reformatories. The justice system handled black women's minor moral and social transgressions very differently from those of their white counterparts, as the support mechanisms that encouraged preventive rehabilitation rather than punitive incarceration were less available to black women.

Even though reformers and the courts that carried out their objectives supported the criminalization of young women's behavior, they advocated probation and generally discouraged treatment within custodial institutions. They believed that these women were too old for juvenile court but too young to be incarcerated with adult offenders. Reformers were convinced that custodial sentences, in which adolescent girls would be incarcerated with "confirmed prostitutes, shoplifters, and petty thieves," offered little help to these young women.[35] Probation addressed delinquent behavior by suspending court sentences or deferring charges and releasing the offender into a rehabilitative program, treating minors as wayward so they would not suffer "the stigma of the conviction of crime."[36] Women were allowed to live with their families under the supervision of a probation officer to determine "whether [they could] live in free society without breaking the law."[37]

Probation posed a number of problems for black women, however. In 1914, an investigative report on the Jefferson Market Night Court undertaken by the National League on Urban Conditions among Negroes found that probation officers appointed by the court, local jurisdictions, or local religious organizations often neglected black women's cases. According to the report, "Although provision has been made at the Night Court for the maintenance of a Jewish, a Protestant, and a Catholic worker, . . . very little protective, preventive, and reformative work is being conducted among [black] women." Probation officers' "chief interest" was the supervision of white women.[38] The limited availability of probation for black female offenders meant that a higher proportion of them were incarcerated in private and state-run custodial institutions. A study of female delinquents in New York published in 1920 found that probation was largely unavailable to black women because of the "meager facilities for supervising colored girls" because "several of the private institutions in the city refuse to take colored women."[39]

Superintendents of local reformatories cited several reasons for their exclusion of black women. Administrators' prejudices against black people and stereotypical notions of black sexuality pervaded reports that justified the exclusion or separation of black women from white native-born and immigrant women. Administrators were concerned about how black women's sexual and criminal nature would affect white women. Anxiety about delin-

Single Black Women and the Wayward Minor Laws

quent working-class women was temporarily, and conveniently, shifted to race.

Administrators particularly feared that interracial, same-sex relationships would develop among inmates. One superintendent explained that "the colored girls [possess] an unwholesome physical attraction for the white girls and . . . it is better for both races that they be kept apart."[40] Within this institutional setting, the commonplace fear that black men represented a sexual threat to white women became displaced by anxiety that the presence of black women would cause social disorder among white women inmates. This view did not take into account the existence of intraracial same-sex relationships and the problems administrators encountered when white inmates actively sought out relationships with black women.[41]

Private institutions also rejected black women because they feared that an interracial inmate population would generate violent antagonisms. Although the House of Good Shepherd had a separate "home for colored girls under sixteen, it [did] not [accept] those over sixteen, claiming that the white girls [would] make it unpleasant for the colored girls, and that they could not afford to mix them."[42] These arguments implicated black women's presence as disruptive to the real objective of rehabilitating wayward and rebellious young white girls.

The exclusionary policies of private institutions limited black women's access to state-sanctioned rehabilitative services. In 1913 *The Survey*, a leading periodical of social progressivism, revealed in its support of the Sojourner Truth Home, a facility for young, delinquent black women established by the National Urban League, that the odds were "at least five to two" that young black women "would find no door open to them."[43] In 1917, an eighteen-year-old's probation officer who believed that the young woman's behavior might improve if she were removed from her "mother's charge" noted, "The Episcopal House of Mercy cannot receive any colored girls at present and the Magdalen Home does not receive them at all; the only place that defendant could be sent would be to [Bedford]."[44]

Black women were not denied admittance into all local reformatories, but their reception depended on the subjective decisions of particular administrators rather than institutional policies. In 1911, Ellie Walls, a National Urban League research fellow and a member of the Committee on Urban Conditions Among Negroes at the New York School of Philanthropy, reported that the "House of Good Shepherd and the House of Mercy, which formerly received colored girls, no longer accept them, although these institutions describe themselves as being open for the help of all friendless women, regardless of race, color or religion."[45] Some decisions seemed quite arbitrary; one black woman was refused admittance in 1917, but in 1922 another was admitted for a similar charge.[46]

Limited resources within the black community exacerbated the problems of probationary and local institutional care. Few social workers were dedicated to working with delinquent black women. Grace Campbell represented one member of this small group of reformers who were always overextended. The institutions for black delinquent women, such as the Sojourner Truth Home and the Empire Friendly Shelter, did not enjoy reliable financial support and were unable to remain open. The small number of white reformers who supported efforts to rehabilitate black women clung to racial segregation. The Sojourner Truth Home worked only with delinquent girls under the age of sixteen, but older women needed services as well.[47] An interracial committee composed of a number of social welfare advocates reported that the "small and inadequately run House" used for black women was "now entirely without funds to continue the work," and it acknowledged the need to "establish a Home for friendless and wayward colored girls such as Waverly House and Florence Crittenton House for white girls."[48]

Judges and police officers were "at a loss" in deciding what to do with those women who "should not be locked up with criminals" but "should not be turned out on the streets with no one to care for them." The reformers' push for "a place of temporary abode where colored girls can be cared for under conditions favorable to mental and moral improvement" illuminates their concern for black women's rehabilitation and reveals their segregated vision.[49] The committee's black members welcomed white assistance despite their promotion of a separate institution for black women.

As early as 1913, frustrated black reformers criticized the racism underlying mainstream efforts on behalf of delinquent black women. An editorial in the *New York Age*, titled "The Sisterhood of Woman," criticized the Conference of Organizations for Assisting Young Women, which included representatives from many local reformatories and institutions that did not accept black women or did so only on a limited basis. The *Age* editorial disagreed with the conference's statement that a home for black women should garner support because "few if any colored girls can or should be received in homes for white girls." Agreeing with the conference's contention that black female offenders needed social services, the editorial argued that if social welfare reformers stopped making racial distinctions in their private and state institutions there would be no need for a separate home for black women. The editorial concluded, "We need such a home because the State of New York and the private charity organizations which receive such delinquent girls at the expense of the county or the State, have deliberately denied to Delinquent Colored Girls Sisterhood with Delinquent White Girls."[50] This statement reinforced the fact that the state willingly provided resources for nonblack women's rehabilitation but forced those working with black women to depend on self-help initiatives and charitable or philanthropic contributions. These sentiments were underscored ten years later when another black reformer argued that it was "hard to understand the policy of the great State and City of New York, willing to spend hundreds of thousands of dollars in the attempt to reform girls, but unwilling to spend a few thousands to protect, help and eventually save the underprivileged colored girl." In 1923, Mrs. Edwin Horne explained in the *New York Amsterdam News* that young black women needed "sympathy, encouragement, help, direction and guidance." Horne expressed her frustration that, despite protracted efforts, "there are plenty of such institutions for white girls, but there is not one for the unadjusted colored girl."[51]

The long-term consequence of the segregationist practices in New York's criminal justice system was an increased population of young black female inmates in state, rather than local, reformatory institutions. Reformers' decisions to assist women based on race reinforced the stereotype that black women were inherently criminal. Young black women who were sent to court for disobedience were subjected to harsher treatment in the criminal justice system than their white counterparts.[52] Black working-class parents and guardians, who were primarily concerned with the disruptions these rebellious young women caused, were often unaware of these circumstances until it was too late.

Geraldine Jones's case highlights the dilemma that many black parents faced when they turned to the state believing that the worst-case scenario for their daughter would be probation or a short sentence in a local reformatory. Jones's parents sought assistance from the court after she ran away from home with a suspicious black couple who lived in the same rooming house as the Jones family;[53] they were particularly worried because the woman "was known to be a procurer of girls."[54] When Jones returned home four days later, her father had the couple charged with "white slavery," a term commonly used to refer to the forced prostitution of young white women. The Joneses' fears about their daughter's vulnerabilities to the city's sexual dangers illustrate black families' attempts to prevent what reformers called the "black side of white slavery."[55] After several disputes with her parents, the seventeen-year-old became increasingly difficult to manage.[56] Finally, she disobeyed her father and stayed out all night with a woman her father claimed had a "questionable" reputation. After making a complaint against her, he took a police officer to the woman's house, where Jones was found and arrested.[57]

Initially, Jones was sentenced to the House of Good Shepherd, a Catholic reformatory seen as more of a reform school than a prison that carried less of a stigma than a reformatory. After Jones's parents consented to her commitment, however, they were notified that she would be sent to Bedford because at that time the House of Good Shepherd did not accept black women. Jones's parents protested, saying that they felt "very badly because she was sent" to Bedford.[58] They did not want to be seen as "an object of charity," and they did not expect the state to act as their child's parent.[59] Their simple plan of going to court to intimidate their daughter had backfired. Jones's father explained that "he did not intend to have her sent away but simply wanted to scare her so she would know she must obey" him. Her parents were surprised that the court's ruling, coupled with institutional racism, undercut rather than buttressed their assertion of parental authority.[60]

In light of the inadequate probation services and private facilities for black women, many of them were automatically sent to Bedford. A respected state rehabilitative facility, Bedford represented one of the final stages in the reform of young women who violated probation or the policies of private reformatories. When white women were sent to Bedford, they had usually violated probation and had spent time in local reformatories. Black women, in contrast, were usually sent directly to Bedford. In one case, when Bedford administrators discussed admitting an inmate who had no prior offenses, they acknowledged that she "would have been given probation if there [were] more adequate provision for colored girls."[61]

In Bedford's early years, its reputation was based on the idea that it could reform wayward girls.[62] While Bedford's mission centered on adolescent women, the institution held moral offenders in addition to misdemeanants and a small number of felons.[63] Beginning in 1920, those women deemed "unfit to benefit by the discipline and training" of local reformatories, such as the Wayside Home and the House of Good Shepherd, were also committed to Bedford.[64] Rather than obtaining care that met the objectives of the wayward minor laws, a woman sent to Bedford after 1920 was held to the same regulations as the Bedford residents who had committed more serious offenses.

Many families believed that young women would benefit from being at Bedford. In letters to the superintendent, a number of inmates' family members praised the institution's emphasis on rehabilitation. One mother, inquiring about her daughter's infrequent letter-writing, told Superintendent Helen Cobb that she understood her daughter was "well taken [care] of with good people."[65] Parents, as well as black reform organizations like the National Urban League, pushed for higher numbers of black women to be admitted to Bedford, because even a Bedford commitment was not guaranteed.[66] Bedford offered rehabilitation that most black women would not have received otherwise. It seems highly unlikely that black parents and guardians would have filed complaints against, and in some cases refused probation of, their female relatives if they knew the full context of segregationist policies in the rehabilitative services available to young black women. To these black families, Bedford represented the best solution for dealing with rebellious and easily influenced young women.

Wayward Minors

Varying forms of parental disobedience, from broken curfews to out-of-wedlock pregnancies, headed the list of transgressions resulting in wayward minor commitments. Parents and kin had a clear sense of what they expected from young women, as well as the state, when they had their female relatives arrested. Inmate's case files suggest that it was only when preventive measures and home discipline failed that working-class families turned to state laws to address the issues that created the most conflict: labor, leisure, and sexual propriety.[67]

The women charged with violating the wayward minor laws voiced a variety of responses to their commitment to Bedford. Many inmates came to understand their relatives' apprehensions, admitted fault, and worked to improve themselves while institutionalized. Other inmates were angered by their imprisonment and felt betrayed by their families. For example, one woman, when she learned that the aunt who had her committed wanted to reestablish their relationship, dismissively responded that she was an independent woman who could take care of herself without the frustrations that such a contentious custodianship entailed.[68]

Case files illustrate the range of working-class black family members' everyday concerns rather than the concerns of the wayward minors themselves. Young women were considered "in danger of becoming morally depraved" when they disregarded their curfews, became truant, spent too much time with their boyfriends, or ran away, or when their family members reached a general consensus that they had become unmanageable.[69] While regulating young women's behavior addressed working-class families' desire to enforce morality, these commitments were also used to address intrafamilial disputes regarding a young woman's assertion of independence and her contribution to the family's financial stability.

Constance Mimms's case suggests that a conflict with extended family members was construed as a battle over respectability and led to her arrest. Mimms, a sixteen-year-old native of South Carolina, was arrested on charges filed by her cousin, who subsequently moved to North Carolina for a teaching position.[70] Orphaned at the age of six, Mimms had lived with one aunt in Florida. When she turned fifteen, she moved to New York to live with another aunt.[71] Convinced she was being treated unfairly, Mimms ran away from home.[72] Later she complained that on several occasions, "her aunt took her money to buy clothing for her cousin."[73] Initially working as a live-in domestic, she eventually turned to day work and moved in with a female friend. Mimms's mixing with "a bad crowd of girls and boys" led her cousin to report her to the police, and she was arrested on incorrigibility charges.[74]

Another case illustrates the difficult transitions that a family experienced after the death of a parent and social workers' efforts to use the law to compensate for parental inadequacies. Seventeen-year-old Mabel Smith was institutionalized by her father several times before her Bedford commitment.[75] Her father and two younger sisters moved from Boston to New York City after her mother's death. During this transition, Smith's disputes with her father increased and, in his estimation, her behavior deteriorated. Smith's father twice took her to court for incorrigibility. She was given probation first, and then sent to the Sojourner Truth Home and the Salvation Army Home. When her father remarried, he allowed her to come home, but a year later Smith was sent back to the Salvation Army Home.[76] As was the case with many parents who believed that young women should attend to household responsibilities and contribute to the family budget, Smith's father believed that she should give him her wages. Smith had been doing very well at the Salvation Army Home when her father demanded that she give him her wages and threatened to take Smith and the institution to court if they refused his request. Smith was later asked to leave the Home when she refused to abide by the rules. Upon her father's fifth complaint, which he lodged when she returned home after running away for a month, Smith was sent to Bedford. Smith's life was marked by a history of institutionalization and parental conflict. As her probation officer saw it, "The girl has been under supervision since she was ten years of age and all who have worked with her and tried to help her have failed. As she is colored there is only one institution where she can be sent and that is Bedford."[77]

When black women were given probation, disgruntled relatives sometimes rejected the court's decision and requested institutionalization.[78] "Fearing that she would come to harm through her bad associates," Daisy Mason's aunt and legal guardian filed a complaint and had the seventeen-year-old arrested as a wayward minor.[79] Mason pled guilty, and the court offered probation, but her aunt "absolutely refused" to take her home, so she was committed to Bedford. Mason was raised in a financially stable, two-parent home, but her problematic behavior stemmed from her rebellion against her strict upbringing. Mason refused to continue her education because she claimed that she wanted to work,[80] yet she was never consistently employed and complained about her working conditions. She left both a factory job and a position at a five-and-dime store because she claimed that it was "too hard standing on [her] feet all day."[81] Without permission, she stayed out very late at night to visit friends and go to dances and parties.[82] Her aunt initially contacted the Church Mission of Help, a social service agency, for advice in handling Mason's repeated lies about her activities and to express her fear that the girl was "drifting into bad company."[83] But all her aunt's "efforts to guide [and] discipline [Mason] . . . failed." Mason's probation officer concluded that her aunt was "a very kindly, conscientious superior old negress—probably . . . [a] servant in a very fine family in the South." The officer, who was quick to note the deficiencies in working-class parents' childrearing practices, liked Mason's aunt, who "impressed" her.[84] Ultimately, Mason's aunt attained her desired result: her niece's commitment to an institution. The fact that Mason's aunt unhesitatingly turned over her responsibility to guide Mason's moral behavior to the state illustrates how working-class black families and communities became socialized through their interactions with state officials or state-sanctioned representatives, such as the Church Mission of Help, to accept certain ideas about what constituted illegal behavior and female criminality.

The Bedford cases bring to light these families' perspectives on out-of-wedlock pregnancies. As with other types of disobedience, the families of young single mothers believed that they needed to control the women's behavior. One black woman had her younger sister arrested and committed because she "habitually associated with dissolute persons" and "became pregnant with child although unmarried."[85] Although scholars agree that black parents and kin cared for, rather than ostracized, the children of single mothers, they have not sufficiently appreciated the direct and personal effects of out-of-wedlock pregnancies on working-class families. An analysis of the case files of single mothers sent to court and later to Bedford suggests the need to reconsider the consensus that black families and communities were more likely than white families and communities to accept out-of-wedlock pregnancies. The case files contain evidence that challenges scholars' arguments that black families failed to attach special stigma to inappropriate female behavior and illegitimate births.[86] Single motherhood created moral and financial tensions that affected the lives of both the young mothers and the family members who cared for them. Although black families usually accepted the children of single mothers, they did not condone the behavior that led to the pregnancy. Out-of-wedlock pregnancies, like other forms of legally questionable behavior, became a point of contention between women and their relatives.

197

Case files of women committed for out-of-wedlock pregnancies demonstrate that families struggling to survive financially resented the additional burden created by the sexual behavior of their young female members. Janet Green's mother, for example, requested the state's intervention because she could not adequately support her daughter's successive illegitimate children.[87] Green's mother brought her to the Women's Court because "she was mad" that, at seventeen, Green was pregnant with her second child. After Green was arrested and examined at a local hospital, her mother refused to take her home and requested that she be committed to an institution.[88] Her mother cared for her first child while Green had the second child in Bedford.[89] After being released on parole, Green was sent back to Bedford because she violated parole by marrying "without permission" from Bedford administrators.[90] When administrators discovered that Green was pregnant with her third child, they asked her mother to care for her second child, but she refused and asked that the child stay at Bedford. She explained that she was "already paying [$6] per week to the woman who cares for [the older] child during the day and that she does not feel she can assume any further financial responsibility." She was "at a loss to know what is to become of [Janet] and her babies" after her discharge "and asked . . . whether some arrangement could not be made whereby [Janet] would remain in [Bedford] for another year."[91] Unable to care for two children on her own, Green's mother took advantage of Bedford's legal responsibility to care for her daughter, which included supporting the children who were living with Green there.[92] Janet Green challenged her mother's assessment. She stated that she had "no sense of guilt" regarding her behavior, and she refused to go back to her mother's home (perhaps in the hope that she would be allowed to live with her husband), and subsequently requested parole work as a live-in domestic.[93]

Some families initiated charges when a young woman's out-of-wedlock pregnancy threatened the moral standing and financial stability of the home. Annie Dillard, an eighteen-year-old native of the British West Indies

Single Black Women and the Wayward Minor Laws

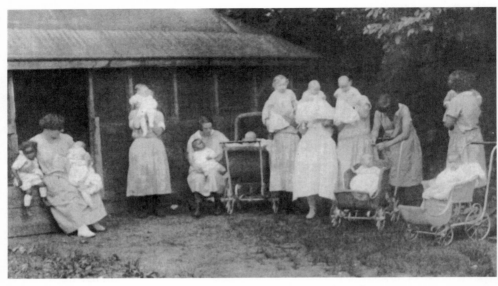

"From the Nursery," a photograph that appeared in Salient Facts
about the New York State Reformatory for Women, Bedford Hills *(1926).*
Bedford's interracial nursery shows how New York State became responsible for
the children of incarcerated mothers. Courtesy of the New York State Library,
Manuscripts and Special Collections, Albany, New York.

who was living with her sister and brother-in-law after her parents' deaths,
was arrested as a result of the problems her pregnancy caused.[94] She had
been raised in a "religious atmosphere" and was affiliated with the Pentecostal Reformed Church,[95] but after she became pregnant, her sister condemned her as promiscuous and felt Dillard was untrustworthy. Because
her sister's work schedule as a domestic meant that she was only at home
in the evenings and on Sunday, Dillard was often unsupervised, with ample
opportunity to meet with her boyfriend alone. Her sister later surmised
that Dillard's "difficulties were the result of over indulgence"; Dillard was
the youngest of four children, and "it seems that her brothers and sisters
. . . all united in spoiling her." Her pregnancy threatened a relatively stable
working-class home by creating additional financial and familial responsibilities. Her sister and brother-in-law worked hard to provide for Dillard and their own four children, who ranged in age from six months to
seven years.[96] Equally important, Dillard's pregnancy served as a constant
reminder of her outright disobedience and, according to her family's religious beliefs, her sin. In her family's estimation, only marriage could redeem her. When Dillard's boyfriend reneged on his promise of marriage, her

sister filed a complaint and had Dillard committed to Bedford. It is not clear whether Dillard's family filed charges against her boyfriend, but he would not have been charged as a wayward minor because this law did not apply to young men until a year after Dillard's 1924 Bedford commitment.[97] Dillard, however, could not "say whether or not [Bedford was] the place for her"[98] and, after her parole, she continued to experience problems with family members, who constantly reminded her of her moral shortcomings.[99]

Some families used the wayward minor laws when a young woman's behavior was seen as a negative influence within their community. Ellie Davis's promiscuity and successive pregnancies, for example, not only affected her family's reputation but were seen as troubling examples for other young black women in her small upstate New York town. The twenty-year-old had two children by the time she was committed to Bedford. Her first child was illegitimate.[100] She had married the father of her second child, but he was arrested and imprisoned for grand larceny charges.[101] When her mother died a year later, Davis's father said that she "could come home with her two children and keep house for him" and a younger sister and brother. Her father, a longtime employee of an electric company, promised to "provide for her if she kept straight." This arrangement did not last long. Six months later, Davis's father went "to the Police Magistrate, signed the complaint, and asked to have [her] sent away" because she "had been running out nights with different men" and was expecting her third child. Reminiscent of the gendered expectations in Mabel Smith's case, Davis's recently widowed father's concern about her behavior coincided with his practical need for someone to run his household and take care of his children. Davis's pregnancy created both a moral and a domestic dilemma. The local agent for the State Charities Aid Association agreed that Davis should be imprisoned, since her sexually promiscuous behavior was "extremely dangerous for the rest of the girls and for her younger sister." Her behavior was scrutinized more carefully than it would have been in an urban environment. In the end, social workers and her father argued that Davis needed to be sent to Bedford for the benefit of the community, rather than for her own rehabilitation. Her behavior jeopardized the morality of other young women and the stability of the community.[102] Davis later stated that her commitment to Bedford was "maybe a good thing," as she had to learn the "lesson to leave men alone."[103]

These cases illustrate the varied responses of black working-class families to young women whose behavior they deemed problematic. Unaware that rehabilitative services were not available to black women, parents and guardians used the wayward minor laws when familial discipline had

Single Black Women and the Wayward Minor Laws

proven ineffective. As members of black working-class communities, they coped with the everyday difficulties of surviving in single-parent, nuclear, and extended families. Faced with the unexpected pregnancies of their female kin, these families forcefully rejected the moral and financial burdens that would inevitably come with single parenthood. They sought to use the services of the state and hoped that this alliance would bring their wayward relatives into line.

Did the Law Help Black Working-Class Parents?

Commitments to Bedford had consequences that black families had not expected. Relatives often sought a young woman's release from Bedford when they believed she had learned her lesson, but families and the state rarely agreed on the terms of incarceration and probation. In many instances, relatives believed that a young woman's arrest or court appearance would be enough to prompt her to change her behavior. When they sought to halt the criminal justice process, many were told: "I don't see how [you] can control her any better now than before."[104] On the other hand, some family members disagreed with what they saw as a rather permissive parole policy. One father wrote to Bedford officials after his daughter had come up for parole after seven months: "It was not my intention to have [her] released to[o] shortly. But as much as your Board of Managers has seen fit to grant her a Parole and on the conditions as stated in your letter I will gladly receive her. I beg to [thank] you and [Bedford] for having aided me."[105]

Families' loss of authority to the state became clear when they sought to reverse or end their female kin's Bedford commitment. Many families needed the young women at home to help with domestic responsibilities. Second thoughts about their commitment often arose when families encountered hard times because they had lost a wage-earner. Consider the case of Miranda Edmonds, a seventeen-year-old native of North Carolina, who was committed to Bedford after her first act of disobedience.[106] Edmonds stated that after migrating to New York with her mother and two younger sisters while her father remained in the South, she received private tutoring until the eighth grade but decided to go to work because all of her female friends had jobs. Edmonds was employed in general housework and in a candy factory, but her troubles began after she spent three nights with her boyfriend. When she returned home, her mother had her arrested. According to Edmonds, the court gave her six months' probation but her mother said, "Send her away."[107] Edmonds was committed to Bedford as a wayward minor in February 1926. By June, Edmonds's mother needed her at home and wrote Bedford pleading for her release.[108] During Edmonds's imprisonment, her mother became the guardian of two orphaned nieces and nephews who had recently arrived from the South, and her health and financial position deteriorated as a result. Edmonds's mother's "doctor advised her to give up doing laundry work," which had been the family's primary source of income "for years."[109] She wrote to Superintendent Amos Baker, "I imagine you have my picture, and can reali[z]e what it is to be father and mother for three children. . . . Please let her come and help me [so] I can rest a little. . . . I am feeling very bad both physical and mental. My physical trouble is I am al broke down from hard work and need help very bad." Bedford officials denied her repeated and increasingly desperate requests for her daughter's release. Edmonds's mother's letter, like those many other families wrote, explained that she had done what she thought she was supposed to do and she believed her daughter had learned her lesson: "I fel she has ben punish enough. The cort told me she would be sent there three months and then be return back to me on probation If she did not prove good they would take her back for the remain of the three years. It was hard but for her disobying me and staying out . . . with bad company I th[ink probation is] best for her."[110]

Seventeen-year-old Harriet Parker was committed to Bedford for disobeying her parents' rules, staying out all night, and refusing to return home.[111] Less than a year into Parker's sentence, her mother requested that she be paroled, but her request was denied.[112] Six months later, she wrote again: "[I am] begging you to let me have my child [so] she may help to brighten my days on this earth. . . . I am now confined to my bed. . . . I ha[v]e a good comfortable home but I need [someone] with me as [my husband] has to go to work and my daughter and son-in-law . . . are gone all day. Oh I hope and pray that you will grant me my child and god will ever bless you."[113] Disregarding her plea, the Bedford superintendent explained that Parker's best interests would be served by her staying: "[Your daughter] has been with us only a little over a year, and while I realize that you probably need her help at home, I feel that [she] should have [the] opportunity for further training in [Bedford] before being tried on parole. I am glad to report that she is doing very well and has a good record with us."[114]

The mother of a young woman who had violated parole and was imprisoned under several superintendents' administrations believed that, after four years, her daughter should be released: "I am asking you why are you all keep . . . my daughter so long. . . . She could be out to work for her children as I am getting almost under [caring for them. My daughter] was not put [in Bedford] for any thing that was bad."[115] Yet the state placed its percep-

Single Black Women and the Wayward Minor Laws

tion of a young woman's interest over her family's immediate need for her presence in the home. These sad cases reveal the unequal power relations not only between the state and the working class but also between young women and their families. In addition to their expectations regarding young women's behavior outside of the home, these families had specific, gendered expectations regarding young women's domestic responsibilities.[116]

Other case files reveal that family members believed their kin had served enough time. Two years into seventeen-year-old Lynette Moore's sentence, her mother went to Bedford in order to secure her release. The superintendent denied her mother's request because of Moore's improper conduct at Bedford. After her mother sought legal counsel, the superintendent remarked that Moore "was not able to make good when she was with [her parents] before and [that she] very much doubt[ed Moore's] ability to do so now." Moore's parents found that after they had consented to their daughter's imprisonment for training and rehabilitation, their parental rights were jeopardized.[117]

Most working-class black families expressed mixed feelings about the effects of the wayward minor laws on their female relatives' behavior. Imprisonment and, in some cases, probation presented alternative disciplinary options for relatives concerned about these young women's rebellious and disrespectful behavior. By placing them in institutions that focused on rehabilitation, most relatives felt assured that these young women would benefit from a more regimented environment. But these families failed to realize that invoking the law constituted an admission of their own incompetence in the eyes of the state. The state's ambivalence toward working-class families' capacity for parenting can be seen in administrators' responses to families' attempts to modify or end their female kin's institutionalization. In focusing primarily on how they could reform young women, state administrators failed to think seriously about the needs of the families that these women would rejoin.

Black families attempted to uphold and enforce their moral principles by taking advantage of the services provided through the state's legal system. The charges they filed against young women for disobedience, including out-of-wedlock pregnancies, challenge prevailing assumptions that black working-class communities were culturally accepting of unwed mothers and their children. At the end of one woman's commitment for becoming pregnant, for example, her sister pushed for the baby to be paroled into her care. At the same time, however, she emphasized that she would deal with her convicted sister only if she "distinctly understands that she must conduct herself properly and keep off the streets at night."[118]

Nevertheless, racism within the criminal justice system undermined the efforts of the relatives who used state intervention to stabilize family relationships. Moreover, it reified stereotypes about black women's innate criminality. When they were denied services geared toward women who were considered "in danger of becoming morally depraved," black women were sentenced, usually as first-time offenders, to state institutions that served as the last resort in most white women's cases. In some instances the state addressed parental concerns successfully, but the unequal power dynamics between the state and the black working class resulted in parents and guardians losing their natural and legal authority over their female kin.

Conflicts within black communities were not simply the result of tensions between elite reformers and the masses but the result of the fact that working-class families had their own ideas and expectations about black women's respectability and morality that, in many instances, conflicted with what these women wanted for themselves. Although the wayward minor laws provided family members with a means to protect young women from very real urban dangers, they also provided them with an opportunity to regulate young women's behavior. Conflicts between the two generations were often shaped by families' assumptions that young women should be responsible for household duties. The perverse combination of familial and state authority meant that these young women's gestures toward social, economic, and sexual independence were interpreted as criminal. Consequently, black women were usually imprisoned in state institutions, rather than given probation or detention in local rehabilitative institutions.

While wayward minor case files reveal the power struggles within some black working-class families, they also attest to relatives' deep concern about the welfare of their female kin. After a former Bedford inmate disappeared and violated her parole, her aunt wrote to the prison's superintendent, "I am still worred about her I have not herd one word." She knew that her niece was safe when she was at Bedford, but she worried when her whereabouts were unknown: "I don't know whether she is sick" or "she is dead."[119] Unlike reformers, black families had a distinct and personal investment in the perceived or actual downfall of young women. To their relatives, these women were more than professional case studies or representatives of the race; they were their daughters, sisters, nieces, and granddaughters, and their actions affected their entire family. The next chapter explores the experiences of those women whose experimentation with sexuality caused consternation, not only to their parents, but also at Bedford.

7

a rather bright and good-looking colored girl

BLACK WOMEN'S SEXUALITY, "HARMFUL INTIMACY," AND
ATTEMPTS TO REGULATE DESIRE, 1917–1928

Says that she has never prostituted. She was raped when she was 18 years old
by a friend who was visiting her sister. Since then she has had sexual intercourse
with three different friends but has never taken any money from them. They have
sent her presents, and have taken her out to dinner and the theatre often. She says
that "in a way prostitution is the worst crime anybody can commit because you
have to do things that take away your self-respect."

—Information Concerning Patient, Bedford Inmate #2480, June 23, 1917

The most undesirable sex relations grow out of . . . mingling of the two races.

—Report of the special committee to investigate the charges made against the
New York State Reformatory for Women at Bedford Hills, 1915

Mabel Hampton's experiences in Harlem never quite measured up to the
popular image of the black neighborhood. Visitors from other parts of the
city would go to "the night-clubs . . . and dance to such jazz music as can
be heard nowhere else."[1] Elite and middle-class white voyeurs, finding confirmation for their own ideas about the authenticity of primitive black culture, enjoyed Harlem's "'hot' and 'barbaric' jazz, the risqué lyrics and the
'junglelike' dancing of its cabaret floor shows, and all its other 'wicked' de-
lights."[2] As the black writer and activist James Weldon Johnson put it, after
"a visit to Harlem at night," partygoers who practiced slumming believed
that the town "never sleeps and that the inhabitants . . . jazz through existence."[3] Hampton's everyday life was strikingly different from the romanti-

Black Women's Sexuality As It Appears in Bedford Prison Records

Incarcerated women offer a perspective that places black working-class women's own ideas about and experiences with sexuality at the center of the discussion. While historians have explored the sexuality of white working-class women, the sexual experiences of black working-class and poor women have rarely been examined.[9] Female offenders' viewpoints vividly underscore the complexity of the black working class. Black women understood, experienced, and expressed heterosexual and same-sex desire at the same time that they had to deal with others' perceptions of and attempts to regulate their sexuality.[10] Looking at this dynamic from the perspective of a specific group of working-class women responds to Evelynn Hammonds's call to consider "how differently located black women engaged in reclaiming the body and expressing desire."[11] Scholarship on black women's sexuality at the turn of the twentieth century has emphasized that black women refrained from discussing sexual desire and advocated behavior that rejected stereotypes that defined them as sexually promiscuous or deviant. Black female activists promoted what Evelyn Brooks Higginbotham calls the "politics of respectability"; decorous behavior was a defensive response to gendered images of black immorality as well as to civil and political inequalities.[12] Black women enacted what Darlene Clark Hine calls a "culture of dissemblance," creating "the appearance of openness and disclosure but actually" fashioning a silence about their personal and sexual lives that protected them "from their oppressors."[13] Hammonds argues that the "politics of silence" worked so successfully that black women eventually "lost the ability to articulate any conception of their sexuality."[14] The most significant exception was the blues singer, who expressed sexual desire through explicit lyrics and performance.[15]

Black women confined at Bedford include both those who practiced a "politics of silence" and those who openly expressed an identity as sexual beings. Answering the explicit questions that Bedford administrators asked all women during the admissions process, black domestics, laundresses, factory workers, and children's nurses between the ages of sixteen and twenty-eight revealed a range of sexual experiences that occurred as a result of desire, ignorance, or abuse.[16] In some cases, administrators became frustrated when black women acknowledged their involvement in the sex trade but were reticent about conveying further details. For example, a twenty-year-old Virginia native was characterized as "pleasant" and "truthful" but provided officials with "little information about herself."[17] White female administrators (and one white male superintendent) documented black inmates' sense of propriety when they refused to talk about their sexual experiences or said they complied with moral proscriptions by rejecting pre-marital sex.

Female offenders' responses to prison administrators might be seen as evidence of the state's intrusion into black women's lives and an attempt to construct and reinforce derogatory racialized images.[18] Yet black women understood administrators' skepticism when what they recounted did not coincide with long-standing stereotypes. Consider, for instance, the sexual history of one inmate who revealed that she had been raped and had pros-tituted herself twice but adamantly denied that she was promiscuous. The administrator seemed to dismiss the woman's difficult circumstances by focusing solely on her demeanor, noting that the woman's "better education" had given her a "superior manner" and her "distant and haughty" attitude kept her from having an "attractive personality."[19] Indeed, what administra-tors thought, as well as what they observed and chose to hear from black women, shaped the information recorded in all the case files.[20] But these partial transcripts also show how inmates challenged the public discourse that characterized all black women as pathologically promiscuous. These women's responses were particularly influenced by their attempts to negoti-ate Bedford's indeterminate sentencing; depending on how an administra-tor assessed an inmate's behavioral improvement, she could be given a mini-mum sentence of several months or a maximum sentence of three years.

In analyzing offenders' responses to questions about sexual behavior, this study takes seriously the possibility that black women who felt compelled to silence outside the prison walls may have seen the admission interview as an opportunity to articulate their desires as well as to reveal sexual abuse. Some women described experiences that ranged from romance to partici-pation in the sex trade. Others revealed the dangers encountered by young women alone in a large city. Understanding that white society believed that black women were complicit in their rapes, these inmates may have viewed administrators' direct question about whether their first "sexual offense" was consensual or rape as a chance to address their abuse in ways that may not have been possible with friends, family members, community leaders, or the police. Administrators' decision to label young women's first sexual encounters as criminal offenses reminds us of their moral position on pre-marital sex and makes clear their preconceived notions about working-class women.

Officials also observed and documented what they called "harmful inti-macy": interracial relationships among the women incarcerated at Bedford.

In 1917, "the disciplinary records of 175 women were studied for information as to the amount of harmful intimacy reported of officers . . . and it was found that these inmates were frequently punished for such offenses."[21] While acknowledging the prevalence of same-sex desire among white inmates, administrators were most concerned with attachments between black and white women. Records of conduct violations in white women's files, described variously as "fond of colored girls" or "seen passing notes to black inmates," provide evidence of these relationships.[22] Black women also received conduct violations, which indicates that they actively participated in interracial liaisons. Administrators, however, portrayed "harmful intimacy" as white women's heterosexual attraction to black women whose dark skin color represented masculine virility rather than same-sex desire.[23] Officials attempted to ignore black women's participation in romantic relationships with other black women.

Prison officials overlooked their own evidence of black women's varied sexual experiences and instead based many of their evaluations on powerful racial stereotypes. Centuries-old preconceptions that defined black women as immoral and pathological deeply influenced their perceptions. As historians Deborah Gray White and Jennifer Morgan have shown, seventeenth-century male Europeans depicted African women's bodies as savage, lewd, and unfeminine, and unleashed Christian condemnations of "uncivil" cultural practices, such as semi-nudity, polygamy, and dancing, that eventually justified the slave trade.[24] The association of lasciviousness with Africans shaped the development of slavery.[25] As Sander Gilman has argued, Europeans eventually viewed black men and women's bodies as "icon[s] for deviant sexuality."[26] Southern slaveholders accepted the notion that enslaved women were sexually insatiable and depicted white men as victims of dark temptresses.[27] The direct connections that southerners made between black women, immorality, and promiscuity remained vivid in popular culture long after slavery's demise.[28] In 1904, when one southern white woman commented that she could not "imagine such a creation as a virtuous black woman," she articulated the sentiments of many late-nineteenth- and early-twentieth-century white Americans.[29]

When black women were imprisoned for sex-related and other minor offenses, prevailing stereotypes influenced Bedford prison officials' assessment of their culpability. Administrators' physical descriptions of new inmates resonate with these notions. Such written comments as "true African type . . . inclined to be somewhat vicious looking" and "a typical African cunning calculating eyes" indicate the depth of their prejudices in evaluating individual women.[30] Observations were always qualified by race, ranging from "refined looking pretty colored girl" to "very inferior looking colored girl."[31] More positive appraisals, such as "appears intelligent for one of her race and station" and "has little moral sense but appears more decent than the average colored girl," reveal officials' belief in black inferiority.[32] Regional biases are also apparent in initial interviews. Administrators observed the marks of southern origins—"peculiar way of speaking, a drawl and a typically Southern way of pronouncing words"—and questioned migrants' level of intelligence, fitness for urban life, and predisposition to criminality based on their diction.[33]

In 1924, Mabel Hampton, described by Bedford superintendent Amos Baker as a "small, rather bright and good looking colored girl," complicated Bedford officials' assumptions. Administrators never questioned the validity of her arrest, despite her fervent denials of solicitation. Yet they acknowledged that Hampton seemed unique. Her comportment impressed prison officials. They found her "alert" and "composed," with a "pleasant voice and manner of speaking." In another interview, they noted that Hampton's "attitude and manner seem truthful" and that she talked "freely and frankly conceal[ing] nothing." Although administrators found Hampton personable and honest, they still imprisoned her. Ignoring their own observations regarding her credibility, officials judged Hampton based on their preconception that, even when black women had not violated the law, their sexual misconduct could be attributed to their innate susceptibility to "bad company." Hampton explained her altercation with the police quite differently, calling her arrest a "put up job."[34]

The "ill-feeling" that Hampton expressed "toward her accuser" mirrored the sentiments of many black women and community members who contended that police corruption rather than women's behavior accounted for high numbers of prostitution arrests.[35] Caught in a house raid when her employer of two years took an extended European trip, Hampton was most likely arrested because she was "between jobs."[36] The fact that Hampton had access to her employer's home shows that she was trusted, but Hampton had no one to vouch for her reputation in court.[37] Her arrest resulted from the fact that the legislature and the courts had expanded the legal definition of vagrancy, which had applied only to public drunkards and persons "with no visible means of support," to include anyone who "in any way, aids and abets or participates" in the sex trade.[38] A plainclothes detective charged Hampton with being an accessory to a sex crime by alleging that she permitted a female friend to use her employer's apartment for the "purposes of prostitution." According to Hampton, on the night of the arrest, she and a friend were waiting for their dates, "who promised to take them to a cabaret." Shortly after the men arrived, the police raided her employer's home and arrested both women.[39] Hampton denied ever prostituting herself, contending that she had been seeing her date for a month and he "wanted to marry her." Hampton's perception of her boyfriend changed when she surmised that her date worked as a stool pigeon or police accomplice and arranged for her arrest.[40] Hampton's evening excursion led to her imprisonment because in court, the police officer's word was deemed more legitimate than a young black domestic's.

The Dangers of Black Working-Class Leisure

Young black working women who sought entertainment and companionship found themselves exposed to myriad danger. Not only could they be harassed by men at cabarets and dance halls, but they also could be arrested in a police set-up. In 1923, Harriet Holmes, a laundress making $15 a week, argued that she was falsely arrested when leaving a popular dance hall. It is not clear whether she arrived at the function with friends, but when she left at half past one o'clock in the morning she was alone. The twenty-three-year-old said that when she was walking to her apartment on West 133rd Street, a car stopped at the curb and four men claiming to be police officers pulled her into the car "without any reason . . . [and] declared that she was guilty of prostitution."[41] In a similar case, a twenty-two-year-old left a cabaret alone at half past one o'clock in the morning but followed her sister's advice to "always take a taxi" home after dark. When she got in the cab, "two men stepped in with her." She fought them, thinking they were robbers. Instead, they were policemen, who took her to the police station and arrested her for prostitution.[42]

Young black women found that the cheap and pleasurable practice of visiting friends' homes could also be a dangerous form of leisure.[43] A number of women were arrested for solicitation while enjoying the company of friends in their tenement or boardinghouse rooms. Twenty-four-year-old Millie Hodges, for example, had separated from her husband of nine years and decided to leave Chicago and come to New York. She was visiting her friend's boardinghouse on 132nd Street when it was raided and its occupants were charged with "being disorderly."[44] Her denial that she had been soliciting and her assertion that she had never been arrested did nothing to change her fate; she was convicted and sent to Bedford simply for visiting her friend's home at the wrong time. Young black women in Harlem enjoyed

Black Women's Sexuality and "Harmful Intimacy"

the freedom to partake of commercial and informal amusements, but the stigmas attached to working-class and black communities meant that their behavior was regulated on a discriminatory basis.

Some black women made entertainment choices based on the short-term benefits of pleasure rather than thinking through the implications of associating with men and women with morally questionable backgrounds. They found themselves in a variety of situations, ranging from those in which they misjudged the character of their acquaintances to those in which they knowingly associated with bad company and were led into dubious, and sometimes illegal, activities. Having lived in her furnished room for two weeks before her prostitution arrest, twenty-four-year-old southern migrant Sarah Woods claimed that she believed that her West 140th Street boardinghouse was run by a "respectable" colored woman. Woods later discovered that the house had been raided, and her landlady was described by the police as a white woman in an interracial marriage with a previous arrest for running a disorderly household.[45] While Woods may have suspected her landlady's racial identity, it is less likely that she would have known of her previous arrest record, which illustrates how some women became caught up in unforeseeable circumstances.

Alice Kent's case illustrates how young women's associations with bad company could be fun but lamentable. When she arrived in New York, the twenty-year-old Philadelphia native immediately made friends with people who shunned legitimate employment but enjoyed Harlem's nightlife. Kent's troubles began when she and a friend attended the Savoy Dance Hall on Lenox Avenue and met two men with whom they eventually cohabitated and who partially supported them. While social workers contended that she prostituted during her New York tenure, Kent fervently denied her culpability and later wrote to a friend (in a letter that was confiscated by prison officials and never mailed) admitting her mistakes: "I was furious for a time, having the knowledge of my innocence. But I am now coming to the conclusion that it was more or less my fault for staying there, knowing what was going on. We are always judged by our companions. This has taught me a lesson. . . . I will always remember my (A.B.C.) that is to avoid bad company."[46]

Twenty-two-year-old Wanda Harding, a native of the British West Indies, acknowledged her misconduct in terms drawn from her Pentecostal background, recognizing her "great weakness and craving for the attractions of this world" and remarking that "everybody . . . is a born a sinner."[47] Harding was acutely aware of her mistakes and struggled to face their consequences. Stating that "her father and mother were devout Christians" and concerned about her moral quandary, Harding's minister concluded that "through bad company she went astray [and] through good company she will be brought back again to the narrow way."[48] Relatives and black community members believed that young women should socialize only with respectable people and under appropriate circumstances.

While black people were aware of rampant police corruption, they expressed serious concerns about young women's naive or wayward behavior. Even though they sympathized with those who had been falsely arrested for prostitution, they also questioned these young women's decisions to attend unsupervised dances, associate with unsavory people, or walk unaccompanied late at night. The families of young women were especially anxious. The mother of an eighteen-year-old Long Island native declared: "Her going to the bad was going to dances and then being led by others older than herself." This mother protested that she worked diligently to safeguard her children: "I have tried to bring my children up in a [C]hristian way [and] have done the best I knew of, but you know the world has to[o] many charms for young people of today."[49] Working-class parents shared reformers' belief that "silk and electric lights" and other "evil influences" such as dance halls and saloons caused young women to go astray.[50]

Black Working Women's Sexuality

Although they were acutely aware of black people's second-class citizenship and of racial discrimination, many young women simply wanted to enjoy Harlem's social life. While they understood their relatives' anxieties about its temptations, they sought diversion after they had worked all day. Many had been employed since they were twelve or thirteen years old. As a nineteen-year-old domestic from Washington, DC, asked: "Why shouldn't I go out some times if I worked?"[51] These women hoped that the easy pleasure of commercial leisure would temporarily transport them from their everyday drudgery and the constant struggle to make ends meet. When they had extra money or they had a date, they spent their time in dance halls, gyrating enthusiastically to popular tunes. To the horror of most of their parents and community members, young women quickly learned popular dances, such as the "turkey trot" in the early 1910s and the "black bottom," the "mess around," and the "Charleston" in the 1920s. In 1914, Rev. Adam Clayton Powell noted that young blacks' fascination with music and dancing was evident "not only in their conversations but in the movement of their bodies about the home and on the street."[52] This anxiety about the unrestrained black female body epitomized the black community's con-

parents
disapprove
of yp's
behavior

cerns about individual women's welfare, in addition to their belief that respectability was essential for a stable family life and a viable strategy for racial advancement.[53] Attending dances, cabarets, and movie theaters was not the most pressing problem or seductive inducement, however. Socializing within smaller, unsupervised, mixed-sex groups and the concomitant romantic and sexual interests alarmed adults and excited young women. Young women in prison disclosed the reasons why they rejected or became involved in premarital sexual relationships. Some were seduced by the promise of marriage, were led astray by curiosity, were too ignorant to understand the situation, or were willing to barter sex for nice things; others were subject to coercion.

Relatives constantly sought to prevent young women from acting independently and hoped to guide their moral lives. They chaperoned their young women, set up strict curfews, and encouraged them to devote their leisure time to church activities. In some instances, their efforts were successful, as a number of women prisoners adamantly denied ever having premarital intercourse.[54] Relatives dealt directly with the consequences of young women's disobedient behavior. A twenty-three-year-old Cuban immigrant, for example, explained that after she became pregnant at the age of fifteen, her aunt forced her to marry the baby's father.[55]

Miranda Edmonds's experience illustrates the tensions within families over leisure activities and sexuality. When recalling her first sexual encounter, the seventeen-year-old North Carolina migrant said that she was "partly forced" to have intercourse with her boyfriend. While she blamed the troubling experience on her "ignorance," she was "clear in opinion" that her parents were also at fault because the incident "would not have happened if she had had sex instruction." Edmonds raises a critical point that suggests how the "politics of silence" could injure young women even though their relatives believed that they were protecting their kin. Moreover, many working-class black parents agreed with the tenets of racial uplift's concern about sexual purity and reproduction but, in certain instances, chose not to be as open or explicit about "sex instruction" as the etiquette, sex, and home manuals that black leaders provided for black community members.[56] Edmonds's position also highlights the complex consequences of her inexperience and her disregard for family rules regarding respectability: she was sent to Bedford by her mother as an incorrigible case because she stayed away from home for two consecutive days with her boyfriend.[57] Edmonds suffered from the gap between the adult behavior young women thought they exhibited when they dated and became sexually active and the maturity they actually needed to live as independent adults.

Many black women acknowledged that ignorance and curiosity fueled their sexual encounters. One twenty-five-year-old divulged that she had sex at fifteen but still "had no idea why."[58] A twenty-year-old noted that her first encounter occurred because "she was [simply] foolish."[59] A number of women admitted that they had intercourse because they "saw other girls do it" or that they were "curious to know what sex experience was."[60] In another case, a nineteen-year-old revealed that she consented to sex with a boy because he was someone "she had known for some time," suggesting a degree of trust.[61] These accounts convey these women's youthful lack of forethought about the physical and moral dangers of sexual relationships.

The promise of marriage prompted a number of single women to engage in premarital sex. As romantic relationships transitioned into more intimate contact, young men, whether they were sincere or not, negotiated with girlfriends about the meaning of sex in relation to the couple's courtship and future commitment. For example, a nineteen-year-old baby nurse explained that she consented to sex because she "liked the man" and he "promised to marry her." In another case, a twenty-one-year-old unmarried waitress noted that she had her first sexual relationship at eighteen because she was "engaged."[62] These women's expectation that marriage would follow their decision to have premarital sex was quite conventional.[63] A boyfriend's refusal to marry a young woman in the wake of an unplanned pregnancy challenged her beliefs about courtship. Some women, however, continually emphasized that their first sexual encounter occurred with their husbands.[64] Twenty-one-year-old Ohio native Lena Jones, who was characterized by prison administrators as a "thoroughly decent woman," stated that she began intercourse at age sixteen with the man whom she later married.[65]

In the early twentieth century, young women's sexual activity was becoming more than a precursor to marriage. Some working women engaged in consensual and noncommercial sexual relationships outside of serious courtships. Scholars have highlighted the phenomenon known as "treating,"[66] in which women bartered sex or sexual favors for goods or commercial amusements rather than accepting money for intercourse. A nineteen-year-old black domestic, for example, emphasized that she took "presents from the men she went with but . . . never accepted money."[67] Evelyn Pitts, who was also nineteen, claimed that she never prostituted herself but did have sex "off and on with two or three different men since she was 17." Like many other young women, she stressed that she "never [took] . . . money for it."[68] The terms some women used to refer to their sexual partners, such as friend, sweetheart, or lover, suggest these women's distinct perceptions of acceptable heterosexual relationships.[69] Participating in the early-twentieth-century youth culture of amusement parks, movies, and dances, working women across the color line found "treating" a means to satisfy their desire for romance and pleasure.

Women who accepted these nontraditional sexual arrangements understood that others expressed strong objections to their behavior. A twenty-four-year-old domestic, who grew up with a mother who was "strictly Methodist and insisted that . . . [her] children go to church regularly," defied her mother after she arrived in New York. Even after she started earning her own money, "her mother would not let her go to a dance or theatre because she thought it was wicked." When she finally left Washington, DC, she declared, "no one [could] to tell her what she could do . . . [and she] began to go out nearly every night." She consistently denied soliciting but acknowledged that during her five-year residence in New York she had intercourse with "three different friends." Her experience with treating garnered her presents from lovers that included "candy, theatre tickets, and invitations to dinner."[70] Relatives, reformers, and prison administrators viewed these women's situations quite differently; for them, treating represented a new form of female sexual delinquency. Young women's frequent admissions to being "immoral" suggest how they responded to administrators' specific questions about their premarital sexual practices. Like the twenty-three-year-old who disclosed that she had been "immoral" but denied that she had "ever practiced prostitution," these working women insisted that they had made an independent choice to engage in sex solely for the enjoyment it provided, not for income.[71]

Not all black women's sexual relationships were consensual, however. Young women recounted experiences of sexual harassment, rape, and abuse by employers as well as within their families. Mabel Hampton, for example, recalled that when she was eight years old her uncle had raped her;[72] and when she was working as a domestic, men in the household "would try to touch" her inappropriately.[73] Like most women, Hampton understood that in any disclosure of sexual harassment, her credibility, not her assailant's would be questioned.

Some black women were abused by men they knew. A twenty-one-year-old told how she was raped by "the husband of her foster parent,"[74] and a twenty-four-year-old disclosed that she was raped by a "friend who was visiting her sister's house."[75] Even seemingly innocent interactions between young women and men could lead to horrific consequences. A twenty-three-year-old domestic recalled that she was forced into intercourse at fifteen when she and a boy "were playing school" and then a game called "Mama and Papa," which she "did not understand" until it was too late.[76]

Even as they were indicted for sexual offenses themselves, these women disclosed that rape committed by a family member, friend, or neighbor had made a huge impact on their lives. In this forum with prison administrators, where they knew their stories would be recorded, black women revealed their harrowing experiences. They understood that administrators would not take legal action against their abusers, but they believed that speaking of their trauma was important enough to provide details about it. Some may have sought to mitigate administrators' negative view of them as well. Twenty-three-year-old domestic and Colorado native Sally Bruce seems to have blamed herself for her abuse when she explained how she dealt with her rape. She revealed that her "first time was at 20 years [old] without her consent" but decided to continue with the relationship, rationalizing that "she was a woman, no longer a child and intended to marry" her abuser.[77] Indeed, Bruce's belief that she had no other options highlights the difficult choices working women made when negotiating their sexuality in light of the long-standing pernicious belief that black women could not be raped.[78]

Black women's decision to enter the sex trade represented a difficult choice for those who did so to supplement their paltry salaries as personal-service laborers. Highlighting the contrast between the inadequate wages paid for menial labor work and the higher earnings brought by solicitation, Heather Hayes, a twenty-six-year-old New York native who toiled as a cook and chambermaid, acknowledged that she had "practiced prostitution off and on since she was seventeen" to supplement her income.[79] This sort of testimony was corroborated by a 1914 Women's Court investigation that concluded that black women's "meager salaries and uncongenial surroundings tend to produce a state of dissatisfaction which sometimes leads . . . to prostitution."[80] Unlike the twenty-two-year-old laundress who admitted to being a "habitual prostitute," many black women claimed that they solicited only infrequently.[81] For instance, a twenty-three-year-old acknowledged that she "prostituted with 2 men in 3 years" but, while conceding that she had been "immoral," denied "being promiscuous."[82]

Black women's behavior after arrest suggests that they struggled with the psychological consequences of their decision to solicit. The 1914 Women's Court study indicated that when questioned during admission interviews, twenty-four out of fifty-six women stated that they were single and alone in the city "without near relatives." At least eight of these women "admitted having mothers" in New York but refused to provide their addresses to court administrators because they did not want their relatives "to know where they were." The investigation concluded that most of the women came from "poor but respectable homes" but eventually buckled under the pressures

Black Women's Sexuality and "Harmful Intimacy"

of inadequate wages and bad company. Charting their moral downfall, the study traced their transition from legitimate employment to prostitution: free "from all restraining influences they lodge in questionable districts; associate with questionable people; work for a while; then both solicit and work, finally ending by giving up their regular employment in order to solicit."[83]

The lure of easy money led some young women to enter the sex trade full time. A seventeen-year-old domestic earning $7 a month claimed she was able to make "about $10 a week" as a prostitute.[84] A few women needed money to support their drug habit. And a small group of women claimed that they solicited because they enjoyed sex and needed money for material possessions. The same year that one sixteen-year-old domestic consented to have sex with her "boy-sweetheart," she also began prostituting herself for "money and pleasure."[85] Another woman entered the sex trade because "she saw other girls with nice things and wanted them too."[86] Twenty-year-old laundry presser Christina Greene explained that she grew up in New York neighborhoods where prostitution took place and "associated" with sex workers "without entering their profession," although as a "young child" she "used to envy them because of the money they made." According to Greene, her aunt, who consistently "kept her back," made sure that she stayed out of the sex trade. "After many years of trouble with [her] husband and poverty," however, she ultimately "succumbed."[87]

Poor black women who made a difficult but definite choice to work in legitimate jobs understood the impact of prostitution on their lives all too well. Often living in the same neighborhoods where the trade thrived, they negotiated their moral stance against the sex trade on a daily basis and contended with the generally accepted notion that black women were its natural participants. Although most black reformers expressed their frustration with prostitution in a public forum and incorporated their concerns in their work, like-minded working women must have also talked with one another and their families about their anxieties. One twenty-four-year-old domestic told prison administrators that "prostitution is . . . the worst crime anybody can . . . commit because you have to do things that take away your self-respect."[88] Women like her made a conscious choice not to prostitute and were frustrated that they were consistently mistaken for and often arrested as sex workers. Relatedly, they made specific distinctions between immorality and promiscuity. During the period of what scholars have defined as the early-twentieth-century sexual revolution, where working-class women "self-consciously rejected Victorian mores," they understood their elders' condemnation of premarital sex and would agree that having sex before marriage and with men they did not intend to marry was immoral.[89] Their making a choice to engage in premarital intercourse, whether they considered themselves promiscuous or not, was quite different than their being innately drawn to sex because of their racial and socioeconomic status. Indeed, black working women were in a tenuous position as they negotiated their perceived as well as actual sexual identities. These women's concerns about prostitution reflected the negative consequences they feared and experienced when they exposed their sexual desires within their community.

Regulating Black Women in Harlem

During the 1920s, Harlem was the site not only of a renaissance in black cultural production but also for the open expression of various forms of sexuality.[90] Many black residents and community leaders expressed grave concerns about the confluence of popular entertainment and nonmarital sex. They were particularly concerned about the growing visibility of same-sex relationships. Many were aware of the lesbian references in songs like Gertrude Ma Rainey's "Prove It on Me Blues" and the popular, sexually explicit parties held in Harlem.[91] Within many working-class communities, however, the public expression of sexual desire—of heterosexual desire, not to mention same-sex desire—was discouraged. With relatively few exceptions, black churches enunciated and attempted to enforce conservative gender and sexual norms.[92]

Ironically, some black ministers were discovering, or rather exposing, their own gay congregants during this time. Denunciation of these relationships conflated two distinct issues: same-sex desire and ministers who preyed on young male congregants. Rev. Adam Clayton Powell of the Abyssinian Baptist Church lamented that young women were increasingly involved in same-sex relationships, although he did not distinguish consensual from predatory relationships. "Homosexuality and sex-perversion among women," he thundered, "has grown into one of the most horrible debasing, alarming and damning vices of present day civilization." According to Powell, homosexuality was "prevalent to an unbelievable degree" and "increasing day by day." Powell's conflation of same-sex desire with the sexual abuse of children gained strong support from his colleagues as well as his congregation, whose responses on the day of his sermon indicated that his "opinions were endorsed and approved without limitations."[93] Mabel Hampton would have understood the minister's sentiments as representing the views of most Harlem residents, since she hid her sexual orientation in her neighborhood but participated in private rent parties. Many Harlem-

Black Women's Sexuality and "Harmful Intimacy"

ites gladly paid to enjoy a night of food, bootleg liquor, music, and dancing while helping a neighbor pay the rent. According to Hampton, partygoers might eat "chicken and potato salad," "pig feet, chittlins," and black-eyed peas and "dance and have fun" until the wee hours.[94] But Hampton partied exclusively with other women, which some black Harlemites would not have accepted. Explaining her predicament in retrospect, Hampton revealed that as a young woman in Harlem she experienced a "free life" where she "could do anything she wanted," but publicly expressing her desire for women was out of the question.[95] "When I was coming along everything was hush-hush," she recalled. She and women like her felt safer meeting at house parties, "private things where you'd go with" a woman without fear of reprisals.[96]

Hampton's recollections indicate that black women who desired women usually disguised their feelings in public, in order to avoid both the police and other black Harlemites. When women attended all-female parties, "very seldom did any of them [wear] . . . slacks . . . because they had to come through the streets." Instead, they played it safe and dressed in women's suits. "You couldn't go out there with too many pants on because the men was ready to see . . . and that was no good," Hampton stated. "You had to protect yourself and protect the woman that you was with."[97] Scholars have suggested that Harlem's working class might have been more accepting of gay men and lesbians than its black middle class, but Hampton's personal experience belies this perspective.[98] It is unlikely that she was apprehensive about encountering Powell in Harlem; she appears to have been most concerned about her working-class neighbors. The range of black working-class political and social ideologies meant that some poor urban dwellers could be more accepting about her choices, while others, especially religious groups, mirrored a moral conservatism that, Evelyn Higginbotham argues, was "more effective than middle-class reformers in policing the black woman's body and demanding conformity to strict guidelines of gender roles and sexual conduct."[99] Hampton's case also suggests that lesbians were less accepted in black neighborhoods than gay men, regardless of the residents' socioeconomic status.

Hampton did not reveal whether she had experienced repercussions from exposing her attraction to women, but her fear prompted her to take precautions. She managed by limiting her contact with people who were not "in the life." Much later, she told a friend that even during the height of the Harlem Renaissance "you had to be very careful," which meant that Hampton and her friends "had fun behind closed doors."[100] Going out to bars was too much of a hassle because, as she recalled, "too many men was [tangled] up with it; . . . they didn't know you was a lesbian . . . [and] they didn't care. . . . You was a woman . . . [so] you had the public [and] you had the men to tolerate." Although she met a number of girlfriends when she was working as a dancer in Harlem cabarets such as the Garden of Joy, she eventually stopped dancing because, in her experience, it required exchanges with men. "I gave up the stage," she explained, "because unless you go with men you don't eat."[101] As a gay rights activist later in life, Hampton spoke about herself as having embraced lesbianism directly and publicly as a young adult, yet when she was arrested for prostitution in 1924 she was not forthcoming about her sexual orientation. Her arrest stemmed from an ostensible heterosexual double date gone awry. Her later characterization of her arrest for solicitation as absurd because she was considered a "woman's woman" reveals little about how she addressed her feelings for women and men at that time.[102]

Hampton's same-sex inclinations were shared by other women, black and white, but urban reformers and criminal justice administrators focused on regulating the behavior of heterosexual working-class women. During World War I, the federal government attempted to prevent the spread of venereal disease, not only by distributing condoms to the troops, but also by appropriating funds for at least forty-three reformatories and houses of detention that confined and treated "women and girls who, as actual and potential carriers of venereal diseases, were a menace to the health of the Military Establishment of the United States."[103]

The increased scrutiny of single working women's sexuality directly influenced black women's treatment in the social welfare and criminal justice systems. Seventeen-year-old Amanda B. was originally arrested for incorrigibility when her parents "could no longer keep . . . her from attending dances and associating with bad company." But her harsh Bedford sentence stemmed from social workers' discovery that she had refused treatment for a venereal disease at "the City Hospital."[104] Because of the heightened alert about the supposed connection between working-class women and venereal disease, Amanda's family's concerns about her inappropriate behavior led to her imprisonment in a state institution rather than in the local rehabilitative home and a permanent arrest record. Caught in a moment when their experimentation with leisure and sexuality was perceived as a national security threat, young women found their behavior deemed suspect. Thus, public and police perceptions of black women's supposed innate promiscuity and criminality shaped their arrests.

Ruby Brooks's case shows how reformers' as well as the federal government's anxieties about working-class women's sexual behavior and venereal disease continued after the war. When the thirty-year-old domestic worker

Black Women's Sexuality and "Harmful Intimacy"

was walking home one evening in 1924, she was approached by a man who asked if he could go home with her. When she responded, "No, I have no place to take you," another man appeared and arrested her for prostitution. Brooks, who had no prior criminal record and a solid work history, believed that her arrest was a frame-up and contended that she would not have been sent to Bedford if she had not been adamant about keeping "her arrest from her family," with whom she still lived. Other evidence in her file, however, indicates that her imprisonment more likely stemmed from the fact that she had tested positive for venereal disease. Brooks's claim that she had had intercourse only with her fiancé was recorded but ignored, as he was investigated rather than clinically tested. For prison administrators, regardless of Brooks's verified background and upstanding fiancé, her medical condition posed a danger to society, justifying her year-long imprisonment and multiple postponements of parole until she was cured.[105] Brooks saw her arrest and imprisonment as unjust and believed that she understood the parameters of moral and legal behavior. Bedford officials felt differently; their objectives entailed rehabilitating and controlling the purported sexual deviancy of women, regardless of their sexual orientation.

Racial Segregation and Interracial Sex at Bedford

Bedford's goal was to reform young women by instilling morality and restraining sexual conduct. The institution opened in 1901, just when perceptions of aberrant female behavior were changing from the nineteenth-century idea of the "fallen woman" to the twentieth-century notion of the sexual delinquent. During the 1870s, reformers concerned about the growing number of young women in custodial prisons pushed for segregating women under thirty from older women because they believed that young first offenders had the capacity to be reformed.[106] During Bedford's initial years, administrators believed that working-class women's delinquent behavior could be addressed and even eliminated through proper training. Bedford's first superintendent, Katharine Bement Davis, stated that the women who entered the institution were "capable of . . . education and industrial training" that "would restore them to society, self-respecting and self-supporting."[107] City magistrates and some state legislators, however, found the reformatory's operation too expensive, and it was consistently underfunded. Reformers argued that expenses related to rehabilitation far outweighed the consequences of being apathetic about urban crime. Bedford officials agreed. "The cost to the State of allowing [young women] to lead dishonorable, and perhaps criminal lives, . . . [perpetuating] their kind in succeeding generations in an ever-increasing propensity to evil," they declared, "is so very great [that] reformation . . . is the cheapest means of securing the public welfare."[108]

Reformers advocated practical programs of reform with varying degrees of success. Over the years, the institution ensured that inmates were constantly occupied, through industrial classes, religious services, or extracurricular activities. Instead of prison cells, women resided in individual cottages with matrons who encouraged family-style relationships. Some inmates seemed to enjoy this arrangement, as a number of paroled women wrote Bedford for permission to return to visit their friends.[109] Inmates were separated by age in 1901. By 1924, when Ruby Brooks and Mabel Hampton were admitted, Bedford was segregated according to inmates' psychological diagnosis and race, with cottages designated for a range of inmates from "feeble-minded" white girls to newly admitted black girls.[110] Still, inmates pointed to interactions that may have been detrimental to their reformation; one inmate claimed that she learned about sex from "Bedford girls."[111] Other women tried to convince administrators that they should be discharged to escape other prisoners' influence. Brooks was so worried about how other black inmates' behavior would affect her release that she wrote prison administrators: "I was not brought up to fight and curse and I am willing to take any kind of [parole] job . . . as long as I get away from here."[112] Brooks's trouble with unruly roommates in racially segregated housing attests to the problems Bedford administrators experienced in implementing reform.

Administrators agreed that the advent of probation, in which a woman was supervised in her community rather than being imprisoned, changed the type of inmate they received.[113] Introduced in 1901, probation slowly parceled out the most redeemable female offenders and left the institution populated with probation violators, recidivists, and uncontrollable women.[114] Katharine Bement Davis identified these inmates as the major impediment to Bedford's rehabilitation process. In 1906, Davis argued that if Bedford was to "receive so large a proportion of 'difficult' young women, whom probation and private institutions . . . have failed to help, the public must recognize the task" Bedford had before it.[115] Since black women had more difficulty obtaining probation, their disproportionate representation in the institution's population increased as its reputation as a model reformatory declined. Black women who were first-time offenders, like Brooks and Hampton, were admitted along with white women whose behavior failed to warrant probation or who had violated probation. More young women were also being committed to Bedford, which led to overcrowding.[116]

Bedford's problems led to a 1914 State Commission of Prisons inspection and a scathing report, followed by public hearings a year later.[117] While inspector Rudolph Diedling's report noted myriad problems with Bedford, ranging from its rural location to the fact that it could be more self-sustaining because it held "several hundred able-bodied young women delinquents whose labors should suffice for their maintenance," the report focused on the institution's inability to maintain discipline.[118] During the public hearings, investigators noted that the most troubling issue involved same-sex romances between black and white inmates. Bedford's administrators publicly disclosed that the institution's primary disciplinary quandary stemmed from "harmful intimacy," or, rather, interracial sex.[119]

When the State Board of Charities' special investigative committee addressed Bedford's "harmful intimacy," it focused on the fact that, unlike most women's prisons in the North or the South, Bedford was racially integrated. When questioned about this policy, former superintendent Katharine Davis explained that she did "not believe in segregation by color in principle and [had] not found it to work well in practice."[120] The committee strongly recommended segregation. With Davis no longer the superintendent, Bedford's Board of Managers agreed with the committee's final recommendations, which pronounced segregation to be the most viable solution to inappropriate interracial relationships.[121] Denying any accusation of racism, the board declared that "most undesirable sex relations grow out of . . . mingling of the two races."[122] The board defended its right to segregate inmates against the protests of those who argued that racial segregation was "contrary to the equal rights of all citizens under the Constitution."[123] Explaining the discretionary power given to them by the State Charities Law, the Board of Managers argued that "individual rights are not disturbed by the separation of delinquents into groups when such segregation is likely to promote reformation and prevent undesirable relations."[124] In 1917, Bedford institutionalized racial segregation with two cottages "set apart" for black women.[125] Superintendent Helen Cobb explained that, in addition to disciplinary concerns, the separate cottages were established as a result of written requests by black inmates.[126] During Mabel Hampton's and Ruby Brooks's imprisonments at Bedford, black women were categorized as "recently admitted," "younger," "more unruly," or "quiet" and housed in cottages accordingly.[127] Ironically, even after racial segregation was established, administrators failed to acknowledge publicly that "harmful intimacy" persisted as inmates continued to pursue relationships across the color line.[128]

The actions of Bedford administrators and state officials coincided with the views of psychiatrists and prison reformers. Generally, psychiatrists and prison reformers addressed the issue of female homosexuality by emphasizing, to the virtual exclusion of other romantic or sexual attachments, the problem of developing relationships between white and black inmates.[129] They portrayed white women's participation in same-sex, interracial relationships within the confines of the prison as a longing for masculinity.[130] The psychologist Margaret Otis voiced the opinions of many scientific observers when she argued in the *Journal of Abnormal Psychology* in 1913 that whether viewed as "an affair simply for fun and . . . lack of anything more interesting to take up their attention" or as a relationship of "serious fascination and . . . [an] intensely sexual nature," this kind of association had a racial and gendered character.[131] "The difference in color," she added, "takes the place of difference in sex."[132] Much like Cesare Lombroso's 1895 linkage of black women's color and physical features with masculinity and criminality, Otis's explanation of same-sex desire equated black women's darker skin color with virility. Moreover, these relationships could be described as an example of what Regina Kunzel calls "racialized gender inversion."[133] For example, a white woman to whom Otis referred in her article "admitted that the colored girl she loved seemed the man."[134] In 1921, a Bedford official explained that black women's "abandon and virility . . . offered" white women "the nearest substitute" for the opposite sex.[135] According to her, black women functioned as masculine substitutes who fulfilled white women's heterosexual desire. Psychologists and prison administrators characterized white inmates' attraction to one another as nothing more than crushes. In their courtships, according to one report, women "vow that they will be friends forever, dream and plan together, confide their deepest secrets," and there is no serious connection to homosexuality.[136] White inmates, whether or not they were aggressors in these affairs, maintained a normative heterosexual status. In this sense, administrators failed to address same-sex desire directly, but rather constructed their explanations so that, as Kunzel remarks, "homosexuality was heterosexuality; the unnatural was natural."[137] In contrast to white inmates, black women at Bedford were rarely portrayed as initiating relationships, although they may have done so.[138] Administrators did not characterize black women as responding in like manner to the attentions of white women, or as experiencing crushes among themselves.[139] By and large, black women's romantic attachments, whether heterosexual or homosexual, were ignored.[140]

Black Women's Sexuality and "Harmful Intimacy"

Although officials noted numerous instances of intense and sometimes even violent romantic relationships among white women, they continually focused on the impact of interracial sex. Assistant Superintendent Julia Jessie Taft defined the disciplinary problem as stemming from "colored girls [who are] extremely attractive to certain white girls; . . . the feeling is apt to be more intense than between white girls alone."[141] When questioned about the disciplinary problem, Taft agreed that black women had an "unfortunate psychological influence" on white inmates.[142] One white woman's attraction for black women, for instance, was noted as being so "extreme" that she was staring at "the temporary object of her affection as an animal might watch its prey, oblivious of all that was going on about her."[143] Yet these interracial cases were outnumbered by similar incidents among white women.

What did officials find so damaging about interracial same-sex relationships? Siobhan Somerville suggests that in reformatories, they highlighted "two tabooed sexualities—miscegenation and homosexuality."[144] During the 1915 State Board of Charities inquiry, investigators raised concerns about both "harmful intimacy" continuing beyond the women's release from Bedford and the possibility of white women living in black neighborhoods.[145] Bedford administrators had imposed racial segregation, but their decision failed to address the "harmful intimacy" that thrived among women living in different buildings. Indeed, the Board of Charities investigators ignored Taft, who testified that she dealt with same-sex relationships "all the time" and stressed that these romantic attachments usually occurred between women "in separate houses."[146] Racial segregation would not solve the problem of same-sex relationships, but it did address institutional and national anxieties about interracial sex. Indeed, the institution's emphasis on maintaining a Jim Crow ideology superseded their fears about same-sex desire and shaped how inmates' romantic and/or sexual interactions— whether interracial or intraracial—were racialized; moreover, their focus on working-class white women's behavior indicates that while they believed in rehabilitation, they understood that it would be impossible to redeem these women's moral propriety.[147]

Between 1916 and 1918, psychiatrist Edith Spaulding of Bedford's Laboratory of Social Hygiene conducted an extensive and well-documented study of several inmates that provides more information about "harmful intimacy." Spaulding examined women who were deemed psychopathic, and she concentrated primarily on white inmates. Although she diagnosed some black women, a number of the black inmates whom she scrutinized were associated with the hospital only because they were assigned to work there as

laundresses, housecleaners, and cooks. Unlike administrators in most institutions, Bedford officials argued that black inmates were the passive rather
than aggressive parties in homoerotic relationships. Spaulding's findings
reinforced administrators' premise that the attraction white women felt for
black women stemmed from the fact that black inmates seemed masculine.
Amanda B., the seventeen-year-old who was charged with incorrigibility
but imprisoned because she had contracted a venereal disease, was seen as
a problem because white inmates desired her. Eventually, she was removed
from the hospital because of the "infatuation which two white girls showed
for her and the resulting disturbance caused by their jealousy." In Spaulding's view, Amanda, a "young colored woman with thick lips and very dark
skin," appeared virile, which accounted for her popularity among white inmates. Amanda was "not unattractive in personality and always ready for
fun, [but] she readily supplied through her racial characteristics a feminine
substitute for the masculine companionship [white women] were temporarily denied." Spaulding implicitly assumed that Amanda became a potential partner for white women because of her "racial characteristics." She rejected the possibility of genuine and mutual interracial, same-sex desire,
maintaining that only "feebleminded" white inmates became "attached to"
Amanda. Interestingly, Spaulding portrayed Amanda as an unwitting and
thoroughly desexualized object of desire who was "fairly passive in the affair" although "she enjoys the situation keenly." Since Spaulding focused her
work on white inmates, there is little evidence to suggest what Amanda enjoyed about the situation. Her Bedford commitment for incorrigibility was
based upon her refusing municipal treatment for venereal disease and her
"attending dances and associating with bad company," which meant that
she would not have been ignorant about either same-sex or heterosexual
desire.[148]

White inmates were also attracted to Emily J., a black inmate with
"thick lips, [and] deeply pigmented skin." Imprisoned for solicitation, the
seventeen-year-old reportedly elicited an "emotional disturbance" among
white women; in Spaulding's estimation, "unstable white girls were uncon-
trollably attracted to [Emily] . . . because of her color."[149] Spaulding never recorded observing Amanda or Emily actively pursuing white women, but she
also failed to think beyond her own racial concerns and acknowledge that
these black women may have engaged in these interracial relationships because of their inability to pursue the heterosexual relationships that landed
them in Bedford.

The attraction that white inmates expressed for black women like

Amanda and Emily was usually diagnosed by administrators as mental deficiency, which they described variously in terms that ranged from feeblemindedness to psychopathology. When defending Bedford from charges that the institution fomented interracial, same-sex relationships, the president of the Board of Managers, James Woods, conflated women's working-class status with deviant sexual behavior, arguing that women initiated these kinds of associations before they entered the reformatory. Addressing the problem without direct reference to black women, Woods remarked that this behavior was "not uncommon among the people of this class and character in the outside world, and when inmates addicted to these practices come into the institution it is practically impossible to prevent them finding an opportunity in some way or other to continue them."[150] Woods's assessment shows how administrators attempted to deflect responsibility for an escalating disciplinary problem by suggesting that these relationships should not be solely defined as "situational homosexuality," that is, the consequence of incarceration among women.[151] Indeed, Woods's perspective highlighted what administrators had already discovered: that homoerotic relationships were also emerging in the larger society, both black and white.

While officials framed these relationships as a result of aggressive white women pursuing passive black women, their observations contain evidence of black women's individual sexual agency. Black women appear to have been active participants in interracial romances. Spaulding observed a black inmate's overtures to a white inmate: "While the girls were at chapel, a popular colored girl was reprimanded for talking to the white girl of her affections. When asked to change her seat the colored girl became defiant and there ensued an unpleasant episode in the midst of the service, in which she had to be taken from the room for striking the matron who had spoken to her."[152] Examples of conduct infractions noted in black women's files include "passing a note" and "2 girls in room with door closed. In room indefinitely." The fact that these reports were written in race-neutral language suggests the existence of intraracial romances.[153] For instance, the disturbance that Spaulding noted was caused by the "deep affection" of one black inmate for another black woman mirrored the problems that she observed with white inmates. Apparently more concerned with whether these women had finished their tasks as hospital laundresses, Spaulding at first dismissed the sexual implications of their behavior but in the end explained the altercation in racial terms, calling them "two tigresses" and noting that "primitive fires of that kind do not die down."[154] Spaulding provided no sustained analysis of the detrimental moral effects or intense, romantic nature of such attachments among black women. Instead, these black inmates' behavior seemed to confirm prevailing beliefs about black women's innate promiscuity and sexual deviancy.

While not contradicting societal stereotypes regarding black women, the case of Lynette Moore shows how a black woman's behavior and appearance challenged prison administrators' premise regarding "harmful intimacy." According to one Bedford superintendent, seventeen-year-old Moore did "fairly well" while imprisoned but had a "great attraction for . . . white girls," making her a "troublemaker." Initially, Moore's physical appearance attracted as much attention from officials as her incorrigibility; they described her as a "colored girl with . . . light skin and rather pretty, wavy hair." A physician concluded, "I have an idea" that "she has been rather good looking and considered clever by her set and has managed to get off with a good many things." Given their general apathy toward black inmates' romantic relationships, the attention administrators paid to Moore was striking. Her behavior on one occasion even prevented her from corresponding with her parents, as the superintendent wrote her mother that Moore was in "punishment for improper actions with another girl."[155] A black woman whom even prison officials found physically attractive, rather than virile, Moore consistently pursued "undesirable" relationships with white women, both at Bedford and after she was paroled.

Moore's case illustrates the fluid nature of sexuality: some women desired men as well as women. As Evelyn Hammonds notes, "Desire between women and desire between women and men [could occur] simultaneously, in dynamic relationship rather than in opposition."[156] Moore married and became pregnant after being discharged, but she stayed in contact with Connie Carlson, the white inmate with whom she developed an "undesirable friendship" in Bedford. After Moore became estranged from her husband, the two women began living together. At some point, an anonymous letter was sent to a charitable agency informing it that Moore had become a beggar and Carlson was "usually with her."[157] In contrast to Mabel Hampton, who attempted to keep her romantic relationships private, Moore did not conceal her romance—and suffered the consequences. Five years later, Moore was arrested for gun possession and again sent to Bedford. Bedford officials refused to keep her, but they did interview her. Moore explained that while working as a nightclub hostess she had continued to experience relationship problems, as she wanted to marry her boyfriend but had not divorced her first husband. Her second case file documents her continuing tie to Carlson. Although neither woman could support the other or Moore's infant and they stopped living together, Moore acknowledged her continued connection with Carlson.[158] Moore's reference to Carlson as a friend indicates that she boldly defied Bedford's continual attempts to keep the women apart. Yet the institution was simply another conduit for enforcing a respectable domesticity and de facto racial segregation. Both women were married with children; Moore lived in Manhattan while Carlson resided in Long Island. Moore's simple but bold actions provide us with a hint of the struggle that she and Carlson faced as they attempted to maintain a connection with one another.

Mabel Hampton's experience complicates prison officials' essentialized portraits of homoerotic relationships. The story of her lesbianism, which was never directly mentioned in her case file but revealed through her subsequent social activism, challenges Bedford administrators' premise about "harmful intimacy" and highlights many of the institution's evaluative discrepancies. In Hampton's brief account of her Bedford experience, she openly acknowledged the prevalence of same-sex relationships and affirmed her participation in them, though she did not indicate whether they were interracial or intraracial.[159] She remembered these relationships as comforting. After she and another prisoner revealed their attraction to one another, Hampton recalled, the woman "took me in her bed and held me in her arms and I went to sleep."[160] Although Hampton was attracted to women and dated men before her imprisonment, her Bedford experience may have provided her with an opportunity to embrace her same-sex desire more fully. Like Moore's, Hampton's looks did not fit administrator's characterizations of a black woman likely to become involved in "harmful intimacy." Superintendent Amos Baker described her as feminine rather than masculine in appearance. Because of her dissembling, Hampton never received any conduct violations. Her family members, however, worried that she was being influenced by "bad company" and found her affection for women troubling. During her parole, her aunt wrote to Bedford officials that Hampton was "very much infatuated with a middle-aged colored woman, with whom she became acquainted a short time before her arrest, and whom she [the aunt] thought was not a good influence on the girl."[161] Hampton's case suggests the extent of administrators' indifference to black women's sexuality within the prison.[162] Yet Hampton's post-Bedford life as a lesbian was in some ways an open secret: she and her black partner, Lillian Foster, who met in 1932 and remained together until Foster's death in 1978, "negotiated the public world as 'sisters.'" As Joan Nestle notes, referring to themselves as sisters protected them from unwanted attention and allowed "expressions of affection" that "demanded a recognition of their intimacy."[163]

Other black women also attempted to maintain intimate liaisons, especially during their parole. Ironically, Bedford sought to create a familylike atmosphere in prison but penalized parolees for interacting too closely with one another once they left the institution. Social workers found twenty-one-year-old Addie King was living with another black parolee and a "masculine sort of woman known as 'Alec.'" When they decided to rearrest her as a parole violator, they discovered not only that she lived intermittently with another Bedford parolee and three other women but also that these women shared an apartment with ten men.[164] The nature of King's associations with the black women and men with whom she lived seems to be economic, although this cannot be confirmed, but other evidence indicates that she attempted to maintain an interracial sexual relationship. When King worked as a live-in domestic, her various employers complained that she disregarded her curfew, returning late in the evening or even the following morning. In one instance, King brought a white Bedford parolee to her white employer's house and "tried to keep her there all night unknown to the family." When King's employer discovered her companion, the woman was asked to "get up and leave." King's employer believed that the interracial friendship was inappropriate but was even more disturbed when she realized that the relationship was not platonic. Underscoring societal anxieties about interracial romantic relationships and same-sex desire, the employer reportedly described the affection between the women as "disgusting."[165] With the pervasiveness of Jim Crow ideology in the urban North, this case illustrates the enormous challenges that women in "harmful intimacy" liaisons faced as they struggled to spend unfettered time together.

Same-sex desire was not simply situational.[166] Some Bedford women gave up on same-sex intimacy or became more adept at hiding these relationships from their employers and social workers, but others continued to have homoerotic relationships outside the prison. More importantly, some women managed multiple and simultaneous relationships with both men and women. Social workers noted that black parolees remained in contact with their prison mates, whether those relationships were interracial or intraracial. Sometimes their relationships were discovered when former inmates obtained permission to visit Bedford. A confiscated letter in one black parolee's file explained how the former inmate "walked up to the Nursery" and picked up her white girlfriend's child, asking "her if she didn't know her own daddy." Reportedly "all the girls [in the nursery] laughed."[167] While some inmates began same-sex relationships as an act of rebellion, rejecting the control of Bedford administrators, others entered into them seeking a true connection.[168] They strove to maintain relationships developed in Bedford, and some may have desired women before their imprisonment.

Mabel Hampton's experiences in Harlem and at Bedford as recorded by prison administrators and her subsequent reflections upon her life provide a unique lens through which we can view black women's sexuality. She was neither a reformer advocating the "politics of respectability" nor a blues singer expressing sexual desire through performance. Rather, her life shows the complex ways that young women acknowledged the importance of decorum at the same time that they participated in consumer culture and popular amusements. Women faced enormous challenges as they sought to establish their independence in a society that simultaneously offered uninhibited opportunities for pleasure and was threatened by working-class women's sexual behavior. Relatives, community members, and the police monitored young women's sexual expression and generally supported the rehabilitative objectives of state institutions like Bedford.

The case files of black women at Bedford give us a sense of the language that ordinary black women used to describe their sexual experiences. Although the information found in prisoners' case files has been mediated through prison administrators' biases, we can discern the stories that black women chose to impart behind officials' responses to those narratives. The sexual experiences that are documented in Bedford's records range from premarital heterosexual intercourse and same-sex desire to rape and prostitution. The concerns of black women's relatives and community members often conflicted with what black women wanted for themselves. In their interactions with the community residents black women acted as cautiously as they did around representatives of the state. Mabel Hampton's reflections about Harlem highlight how she dissembled in her neighborhood. Black women who were attracted to women "had to be careful" and "had fun behind closed doors."[169]

Although Hampton seems to have hidden her relationships with women when she was incarcerated, other women, black and white, flaunted their attachments. Bedford claimed that the majority of their disciplinary problems stemmed not simply from same-sex relationships but from "harmful intimacy," that is, intimacy that crossed the color line. Prison administrators' anxieties about interracial relationships mirrored the national preoccupation with interracial social and sexual relationships. Instituting racial segregation did more to assuage their racial anxieties than to address the issue of "harmful intimacy." When some officials acknowledged that young women brought same-sex romance into the institution and that same-sex relationships might not be a consequence of imprisonment, they illuminated the fact that sexual expression took many forms both within and outside Bedford. Expanding our focus from how black women in New York navigated the myriad pleasures and dangers of sexuality, we now examine the challenges they faced as they negotiated relationships with their families, their communities, and state officials.

REHABILITATION, RESPECTABILITY, AND RACE

8

i don't live on my sister, i living of myself

PAROLE, GENDER, AND BLACK FAMILIES, 1905–1935

> This is business I want to talk with you like a woman. . . . Dr. Baker tell
> your officers to stop call up to my sister concerning of me. . . . I am working for
> my living. . . . I am my own woman I live before so many women officers interfere
> in my business. . . . I am working, I report; let hence wise be sufficient.
> I don't live on my sister I living of myself.
> —Lucy Cox, letter to Bedford, 1924

> I think it would be best for you to take [Carrie] . . . back to Bedford, she has
> gotten out of my control will not obey me. [S]he prefer the same [type] of criminals
> which she class herself with in New York. . . . She is my sister as true, we all
> have nothing against her but the class she keep company with.
> —Carrie Hall's brother, letter to Bedford, 1927

Lucy Cox was angry. In 1924, the black North Carolina native admitted that she had made mistakes, one of which landed her in the New York State Reformatory for Women at Bedford for prostitution. But Cox believed that at the age of twenty-four she could take charge of her life, deal with her missteps, and learn from them. She was frustrated that her release from prison was contingent upon continued surveillance by an approved custodian as well as her parole officer. Her strong will and sense of independence made her resent the fact that her relatives were responsible for reporting on her behavior. Cox's anger about the parole process provides insight into black women's relationships with their relatives. More importantly, her demand that she be allowed to "talk" with the prison superintendent "like a woman" demonstrates how black women parolees attempted to voice their concerns

237

about the parole process and to negotiate difficult relationships with family members and parole officers who believed they lacked the ability to take care of themselves.

Black women like Cox who were paroled from Bedford or the New York State Prison for Women at Auburn between 1905 and 1935 negotiated with state representatives and family members over the conditions of their parole. Race influenced prison administrators' assumptions about parolees, and the differing expectations of parolees and state officials complicated the parole process. In a significant number of cases, working-class black families handled black female parolees by cooperating with the state. Family members appealed to the state, often ambivalently, in a city whose influence on young women often defeated their attempts to sustain a cohesive, though struggling, family unit. The agents of the state may have regarded black people as an essentialized racial group, but families saw themselves as uniquely concerned with their particular—not necessarily racial—needs.

Parole records disclose prison administrators' racial, class, and gender biases. Black women were often held to different standards and subject to different judgments from white and immigrant women. In particular, black women's treatment was shaped by administrators' fundamental disapproval of the black community. Their distrust was often the determining factor when they denied black women parole or cited them for parole violations; their decisions were often different when the parolee was white or foreign-born. Black women not only bore the ordinary burdens of parole but were also sent into domestic service rather than factory jobs. And although administrators promoted marriage for white parolees, they believed that matrimony for black women would produce more financial insecurity than stability.

Expectations and Realities of Parole

Parole represented the final phase of rehabilitation, when offenders were released after imprisonment.[1] Parole extended the state's control over the offender when she was no longer under the surveillance of the prison matron and attendants.[2] Parolees remained under the state's legal custody and supervision until they either completed their sentence or were given a final discharge from their sentence for good behavior. A family member, spouse, or employer with the prerequisites of stable employment, respectable community status, and suitable housing had to convince a parole board that they could supervise the former inmate and would report any violations. Auburn superintendent Cornelius Collins warned departing inmates: "The police will watch you. . . . We will watch you, your friends will watch you. A slip on your part will bring you back to prison."[3] In fact, anyone—including other former inmates—could jeopardize a parolee's standing by informing officials about any type of questionable behavior.

Auburn and Bedford, while distinct in the makeup of their populations, had similar philosophies regarding the relevance of parole and its relationship to rehabilitation. Both institutions used the prospect of parole to promote good behavior within the prison.[4] Whether they had been felons in a custodial institution or misdemeanants and felons in a reformatory institution, inmates were considered for a final discharge provided they had not violated parole rules. Regulations stipulated that parolees keep a curfew and document their wages and expenses. By fulfilling these requirements, inmates could prove their readiness to be law-abiding citizens.

Because they had distinct expectations of their parolees, Auburn and Bedford implemented parole quite differently. At Auburn, which housed both men and women, the superintendent told parolees to behave as "you know you ought to" and instructed them not to "keep evil associations," frequent disorderly places, or drink alcohol. Tellingly, he added, "It seems so much easier for a woman to keep her parole than a man. It does not seem as though she is exposed to so many temptations."[5] In contrast, Bedford's administrators, who anticipated their inmates were likely to succumb to temptation, presented exact guidelines for resisting vice: "You are to keep good hours. If you are located in the country, it does not seem necessary to remain out at night later than 10 P.M. If you wish to do so, special permission must be received from the Institution. If you are located in the city, it does not seem necessary to remain out later than 11:30 at night. If for any reason you must remain out later, permission must be obtained from the Institution."[6] An inmate was required not only to report her wages but also to send portions of her wages back to Bedford. She was instructed to open a savings account, consult her parole officer, who determine her budget, and make regular monthly deposits.[7] Regulations regarding wages reflected the centrality of work; the first phase of parole involved obtaining and maintaining employment.

Employment

An inmate's release on parole was contingent on her finding appropriate employment. Officials at both Auburn and Bedford assumed that, as Auburn's superintendent Cornelius Collins told parolees, "nobody who is working steadily has any time to commit crime."[8] Many women obtained jobs through social service and religious organizations such as the Salvation Army, Catholic Charities, Episcopal City Mission Society, Church Mission of Help, Christian Science Prison Committee, and Jewish Board of Guardians.[9] Other inmates found jobs on their own or with the aid of family members and friends.

Most inmates worked as domestic servants. Bedford used a modified version of the nineteenth-century juvenile indenture system, in which young women were given domestic employment with a family, preferably in a rural area. In this environment, the wife and mother continued the institution's training and served as a role model for parolees developing domestic skills.[10] It was presumed that within a white middle-class household, a working-class woman would be supervised and protected from the moral dangers of urban life such as sexual exploitation and prostitution.[11] This system contained inherent weaknesses, however. Most employers were less interested in rehabilitating the inmate than in taking advantage of a cheap, controllable labor force. Inmates were often overworked and underpaid. Twenty-one-year-old Mabel Hampton found her position onerous and threatened to return to Bedford to protest what she deemed unfair employment conditions. In 1926, she described her exhausting routine to Superintendent Amos Baker: "I have ten to cook for, and 8 beds to make and there are 14 rooms in all to be clean. . . . There are three straight meals to get and full one's too. . . . When I get through it is 8:30 and nine o'clock." Hampton decided that unless her wages were increased, she would serve out her term at the reformatory, because there was "too much work and no money." She concluded, "The people in the country here dont like to pay, for all the work that they wount done."[12] After being paroled to "some colored folks," twenty-eight-year-old Anita Jones requested a transfer to another position. She reported unfair treatment, including her employer's expectation that she would "sleep in a dirty place, and in the dining room."[13]

Many parolees found live-in domestic service just as constraining as imprisonment, especially when employers tried to control their personal lives.[14] Employers monitored their phone calls and social visits and opened and read their mail.[15] Twenty-six-year-old Lilly Gordon, for example, confronted her employer's family when she discovered that they were reading her mail; she had "found a letter addressed to her opened in the wastebasket" in her employer's bedroom. After a heated argument in which the employer called Gordon "impudent," Gordon was fired. The employer had a parole officer put Gordon out of her house.[16] On the other hand, some employers proceeded with caution when notifying prison administrators about what they deemed questionable behavior. Marion Long's employer notified her parole officer about the eighteen-year-old's correspondence with a married man, implying that she may have been involved in an immoral relationship, yet the employer requested anonymity in the matter because she "did not want to antagonize" Long.[17]

Prison administrators, who were interested in expanding women's job options beyond domestic service, commented on employers' paradoxical views of parolees. Katharine Davis, Bedford's first superintendent, remarked as early as 1903 that families consistently desired parolees for live-in domestic positions; Bedford even had a waiting list. It proved much more difficult to place parolees in other occupations. Davis remarked: "It is a curious illustration of the peculiar working of the human mind that . . . [employers] refuse to give a chance to the girl based on . . . the moral ground of unwillingness to run the risk of contaminating the other employees—while the same [employer] will gladly receive the same girl into his own family as a maid to come . . . into much more intimate relations with his own children."[18]

When an employer complained about his or her employee, the parolee's criminal background was frequently noted as an issue of significant concern. One employer was infuriated when a parolee requested her back pay. The employer's comments mirrored a growing consensus within society that parole was a failure and that Bedford was too lenient in dealing with criminals.[19] "After all I went through with [her]," the employer complained, "I am inclined to believe that something is due to me. . . . She was as insulting and impudent as any one I've seen. The state may feel that to make [her] better, it is necessary to coddle her . . . but in my opinion if the girls were coddled less they would come out better. . . . Frankly I am so disgusted I feel I never want to see another Bedford girl!"[20]

Employers continued to request parolees for domestic service, especially black parolees, who were not readily hired elsewhere. The problem was a lack of supply of controllable nonincarcerated domestic workers. Believing that domestic work was a less desirable occupation, in large part because it allowed them little autonomy in their free time, white women increasingly chose factory work over household work. Holding similar views but relegated to domestic work by racial discrimination in the labor market, nonincarcerated black women sought domestic positions in more respectable households, and if they were not treated well, they quit.[21] Because they had to comply with institutional regulations, parolees provided employers with consistent and somewhat malleable labor. Even though employers could easily fire parolees, parolees had the limited option of requesting another equally demanding position or voluntarily returning to prison.

Parole, Gender, and Black Families

Two cases handled in the same year reveal that prison officials reinforced racially discriminatory hiring practices. For example, Bedford administrators could not understand why Sarah Finch, a white native of New York City, rejected a position as a switchboard operator at an insurance company and requested a job in domestic service. The twenty-year-old had three years of office experience, but she revealed that she was in "too nervous a condition to take a position as . . . a switchboard operator or" to do "general office-work." Despite Finch's request for employment with a private family, her parole officer continued to argue that "it would be much better if she would take a [clerical] position . . . where the work would be very simple for the first few months but where she would have a chance of advancement."[22] Lucy Cox, on the other hand, wanted an office job instead of domestic work. Having normal-school experience and having taken a course in a local business school, Cox decided to take a "nice little [domestic] job" until she could get a typewriting position.[23] Cox desired an office job that utilized her training and aspirations, but Bedford superintendent Amos Baker thought her "queer" for desiring something other than domestic work. While assuring Cox that he was trying to find her an office job, Baker told her parole officer that she "did not impress one as being very ambitious and has rather high ideals of her own ability."[24] These black women were sent directly to domestic employment, while white women of the same class were expected to take advantage of their wider, and marginally better, employment options.[25]

Maintaining an Appropriate Lifestyle

Regardless of their race, parolees' behavior was closely monitored. Administrators of both Bedford and Auburn emphasized that "parole does not mean freedom; [and] that the girl is still a ward of the State and under . . . obedience to the Board until her discharge papers are granted to her."[26] The basic rules included keeping reasonable hours, avoiding disorderly houses, evil associates, and alcohol, and maintaining a positive relationship with parole officers and the institution.

Parolees and parole officers often had different ideas about supervision. White parole officers' assessments of black parolees were frequently influenced by stereotypes. One parole officer expressed her frustration in dealing with black parolees who, she noted, "always [have] some sort of excuse." She was troubled by her "difficulty in dealing with colored people." She found it "almost impossible . . . to [know] when they [were] telling the truth." "I should very much prefer to believe [them]," she added, "but I do not know."[27] Inmates often complained about parole officers' oversight. When officers questioned parolees' actions either in person or through their neighbors or relatives, parolees became suspicious and often angry. Believing that she was treated unfairly, black inmate Tessie Ford wrote to Superintendent Baker, "I am trying so hard to keep out of trouble and it seems as if [my parole officers] are trying to frame me or something I haven't did any wrong I only want to be to myself."[28] Lucy Cox expressed a similar sentiment when parole officers suggested that her sister monitor her church attendance. In her second letter of complaint to Baker she argued, "I am my own woman I live before so many women officers interfere in my business. . . . It is nothing just the matter want to keep grown people down; and had audacity to tell my sister to take me to church just like If I was two years old." Superintendent Baker replied that he would look into the matter and assured the disgruntled Cox that the parole officers were "sincerely interested in [her] welfare and did not . . . want to interfere . . . or make it hard" for her."[29]

Susan Brooks's unique parole case reveals how assumptions about race also affected prison administrators' assessment of an inmate's parole custodian. The white twenty-three-year-old was a difficult inmate and an even more problematic parolee. In 1919, the Indiana native was charged with grand larceny after stealing $1,000 worth of money, jewelry, and clothing from her employer. In 1925, after years on parole, she was re-arrested and returned to Auburn when she quit her job and moved without the parole board's permission. Brooks's problem did not end there: she came under increased scrutiny when it was revealed that she was "living with a Colored Family and was to be married to a colored man."[30] Brooks's marriage plans did not work out, but she continued to live in Harlem and associate with black people. Unable to obtain permission from her parole officer to live with a respectable black couple, Brooks wrote Auburn superintendent James Long about her predicament. She explained that she "liked colored people and [had] chosen to live [her] life among them," since, after being orphaned when she was only eighteen months old, she had been adopted and reared by a "well to do colored family."[31] She felt more comfortable living with blacks than with whites. When she did not receive an immediate response from Long, she wrote another letter. "These people," she asserted, "care a great deal for me and will help me. . . . The only thing is the color of the skin and our skin is very small matter considered with our happiness."[32] Only after intense scrutiny of the couple in question was it determined that the two met the standards of propriety established by the parole board. Although the father and husband worked for the U.S. Customs Department and was a lieutenant in the army, prison officials voiced considerable concern that a white woman wanted to be paroled to a black family; they saw her request as "peculiar."[33]

Brooks's case illuminates how racial bias shaped prison administrators' assessment of black and white inmates' projected success as parolees. Although black women were routinely paroled to and supervised by whites, administrators doubted whether a white woman could maintain an appropriate lifestyle while living with equally respectable blacks. Auburn's superintendent had enormous difficulty thinking past the race of the people with whom Brooks wanted to live in his evaluation of their fitness as supervisors. In his final recorded response to the issue, Superintendent James Long continued to question whether Brooks could be "persuaded to give up her desires" to live with the black couple.[34] Long may not have acted in a blatantly racist manner, but his reservations about the black couple's ability to provide a wholesome environment for a white parolee mirrored the racism of Brooks's parole officer.

Most prison administrators contended that marriage improved a woman's moral and financial stability, but in the parole process, marriage was a complex issue. Parolees could not marry without the permission of the board or the Commission of Parole. Some inmates felt marriage would be beneficial, but they were often unwilling to go through their institution's voluminous red tape. A twenty-two-year-old parolee who had married without Bedford's permission contended that marriage would keep her out of trouble: "I know that I haven't done what was right by getting married as I did, but why I did it was because I thought it would be for my better I mean it would keep me from going out anywhere that I shouldn't go and maybe I would keep my parole more better . . . for it has given me a desire to keep away from bad company."[35] Bedford officials discovered that another black inmate had married without permission when an administrator saw her wedding announcement in the local newspaper.[36] If a parolee wanted to get married, the prospective husband had to be investigated. A parolee who sought Bedford's permission had to wait for a parole officer to investigate her fiancé's background. For black women this process could be lengthy because few parole officers were willing to deal with black women's cases.[37] In some cases, administrators believed that an inmate's husband was the source of her delinquency. Even if husbands did not lead wives into crime, their inability to ensure a parolee's financial support and social stability weighed heavily against them. One black inmate's fiancé tried, unsuccessfully, to influence the board's decision, explaining that he was an acceptable, conscientious marriage candidate who was willing to play a major role in his fiancée's rehabilitation:

> Mr. Baker I wish you will give me permission to marry [Hattie] be-
> cause I am working everyday and I am able to take care of her and put
> her in a home. . . . And if you want my Boss to write you why I will
> have him write to you and let you no more about me. . . . Mr. Baker
> the reason I want to marry [Hattie] I want to make a different woman
> out of her. You see if I marry her I will have her around my sister and
> she will have to do what is right and they will make her go to church
> on sundays.[38]

Even when parolees observed all the prison's rules and regulations, officials dragged their feet. In December, an angry black parolee complained: "I have aske you permission to get married . . . [since] last April I was told that it would go before the Board in July and now it is December and I have not hear one word from the Institution in my behalf. . . . Now . . . you can see that I am trying to do what is right for I have waited all this time for your answer when I could have goten married all ready."[39]

Marriage did not necessarily guarantee parolees' social or financial stability, however, particularly for black working-class couples. According to parole boards, living with unstable husbands denied women the opportunity to rehabilitate their lives. For example, Tessie Ford, a mother and the wife of a blind itinerant street singer eighteen years her senior, was paroled to a job as a live-in domestic. At the time of her arrest for prostitution, Ford was twenty-one and had been with her husband for ten years. The couple had met in Georgia when she was eleven, and they married when she was thirteen. After they came to New York, she worked as a domestic and factory worker to support him and their children. When the couple was on the road, their children lived in Alabama with her in-laws. According to Ford's parole officer, her disabled husband never adequately supported his family. When investigating his apartment, she reportedly found him intoxicated, "reclining on a bed at eleven o'clock in the morning, his clothing in considerable disarray, [with] a couple of women and children in the room . . . [and] the phonograph going vigorously." Consequently, the officer decided against paroling Ford into his care. When Ford later left her job to live with her husband, violating her parole, she was sent back to Bedford.[40]

Long before Evelyn Pitts's husband decided to give up on their marriage, he was denied parole custodianship when she was paroled from Bedford. A black World War I veteran, he was optimistic that, having protected his country, he would also be able to provide for his wife. He wrote Bedford officials: "Having been in uniform for over four months, and gladly done my bit for Uncle Sam during the emergency, I trust that when I receive my discharge from the Army, that you will be willing to grant my wife a parole."[41] Nevertheless, his postwar employment was unstable and his salary inadequate, which influenced Bedford's estimation of his ability to provide a proper home. In order to fulfill administrators' domestic standards, Pitts's husband requested a portion of her government allotment—money that was sent to families in order to buttress households while the missing breadwinner was away at war. When Bedford denied his request, he initially decided to leave New York City and return to his native South.[42] Pitts's parole officer concluded from his seemingly hasty decision that "he is not fit to be made responsible for [her], and that he doesn't care a great deal about her anyway."[43]

Pitts's husband decided against moving back to the South and worked consistently to have his wife paroled into his custody. After he wrote several letters regarding Pitts's release, Bedford offered him another opportunity to prove his overall financial and social fitness: "We have the impression that you have not arranged to provide . . . a place for [Evelyn] which we could consider permanent or satisfactory, [that] . . . you are making frequent changes in your work, and that there is nothing very definite as yet regarding your income upon which you or we in placing [Evelyn] could depend. We have, therefore, decided to give you sufficient time, that is, several months, to locate permanently . . . your business and residence before we shall consider allowing [Evelyn] to go with you."[44] Echoing the postwar protests of the New Negro movement, which demanded that the United States grant blacks first-class citizenship rights, Pitts's husband argued that if Bedford continued to deny his requests he would sue the institution: "You know that you did wrong you cannot keep me from my wife by law. . . . I tell you now . . . it is know slave time with colored people now. I will take this case to court and we will find out if you can keep me from my wife or not."[45] When he obtained a lawyer, the Treasury Department's Bureau of War Risk Insurance was notified, and Bedford officials were forced to give him Pitts's remaining funds.[46] This proved a pyrrhic victory. When Bedford officials finally released the money to him, they refused to parole Evelyn into his custody or reveal where she was employed. Like Tessie Ford, Evelyn Pitts left her job to live with her husband and was sent back to Bedford.

Twenty-one-year-old Lena Jones's positive record and a capable lawyer outweighed the handicap of her being black. In Jones's case, a marriage, a home, three young children, and a solid legal defense made all the difference in her husband's obtaining parole custody. Jones's husband owned a trucking business and a six-room house and could afford a competent lawyer. Jones, who was in prison for third-degree assault, claimed that she struck another woman on the head with a bottle and bit one of her fingers in an argument when the woman disrespected her home and ignored her requests to temper racy discussions with Jones's young sister-in-law. Her lawyer, in his attempts to have Jones paroled early, said that the board of parole should consider the fact that Jones was a first-time offender, attended church regularly, and had a good reputation in her community. While reiterating her husband's financial stability and moral probity, Jones's lawyer emphasized her role as mother and homemaker. The board, he said, should seriously reconsider the fact that "she is the mother of . . . young children," one of whom lived with her in Bedford, and "that she has a home to take care of," which was being "destroyed by her absence." His plea on behalf of motherhood and domesticity worked, despite the fact that Jones had committed a felony, punishable by imprisonment for more than year. Nevertheless, convicted in June 1926, Jones was released and paroled to her husband three months later, in September 1926.[47]

The parole process, in which racial and class expectations played a large part, was highly subjective. While few parolees experienced a smooth transition, maintaining a lifestyle deemed appropriate by the state was particularly difficult for black parolees. The precarious nature of urban life influenced administrators' opinions about women's ability to live upstanding lives within black communities. The conflicts both between black inmates and their families and between families and state representatives reflect the familiar struggle of working-class communities under an oppressive state system. Historians easily recognize this antagonism. But black families did not always array themselves against the state; intrafamilial conflicts were also prevalent within black communities.

Family and Community Surveillance

Working-class black families cooperated with the state penal system in a number of ways: they committed their young daughters for morally wayward behavior, they reported on paroled relatives who rejected or ignored their authority, and they demanded that erring inmates paroled to their care be re-institutionalized, going so far as to report criminal activity knowing it would result in women's re-arrest.[48] The correspondence in black parolees' files reveals that families often asked for administrators' assistance in dealing with their troubled charges. Family members consistently distinguished the offender's behavior from their own and worried that the woman's incorrigible behavior threatened the family's stability. Considerations of race intersected with considerations of family respectability and solidarity when families dealt with troublesome female relatives.

In most cases, conflicts arose between a family and a paroled relative from the confluence of tensions that flowed from family members' need to preserve their position as respectable members of their communities and to maintain a sound home environment. For example, parolee Carrie Hall's brother, a police officer, reported her parole violations while she was under his supervision in Philadelphia and asked that she be re-institutionalized: "I think it would be best for you to take [Carrie] . . . back to Bedford, she has gotten out of my control will not obey me. she prefer the same tipe of criminals which she class herself with in New York. . . . She is my sister as true, we all have nothing against her but the class she keep company with."[49] In another case, the sister of inmate Rita Lowe wrote to a parole officer at Bedford Hills not only to express her anger at her twenty-one-year-old sibling's outrageous behavior toward her but also to explain that she was unable to deal with her recurring drug addiction. In her despair about helping her troubled sister, she reveals her concern that her sister's behavior will irreparably damage her own reputation: "I am writing to you once more this time to ask you in the name God, please come and get my sister as quick as possible. For she . . . [has] made a perfect disgrace of me and my house. She came over here to-night under the influence of drug and challenged me for a fight and used me like any dog. And went out in the street and walked to the corner fell out in the street unconscious under that dreadful drug. Please I ask you in gods name to come get her."[50] The mother of another black inmate wrote: "I think Bedford will be a good place for her for a while. I hate to have her go back there but would rather have her there and I would know she was safe. The last 3 years has most turned my hair white in worry over that girl."[51] In other instances, relatives sometimes disagreed about the state's role in rehabilitation. While Sadie Brown's father continually questioned administrators about her parole release, her aunt believed that she had "seen a great difference in [Sadie] since she has been [at Bedford] . . . as she is doing so good it be ashame to move her."[52]

In a number of cases, parents struggled with the delicate line between believing that they could care for their female relatives and accepting the devastating reality that they could not control them. The mother of Geraldine Jones expressed a mix of guilt and fear and then a renewed commitment to managing her troubled daughter. Jones's parents had used the wayward minor law to have their seventeen-year-old daughter arrested. Rather than receiving probation or being cared for in a local facility, Jones was sent to Bedford. Jones, who was epileptic, was also prone to seemingly uncontrollable fits of anger. During her parole, after a particularly frightening encounter with her child, Jones's mother wrote Bedford's Superintendent Helen Cobb, "Will you please send for . . . my daughter as soon as possible? I am so sorry to do this but I am sure she is insane and I am afraid she will kill me." But she also asked that Bedford not let her daughter know that she had turned her in. The next morning, Jones's mother wrote: "I hope that I am not too late to change request. . . . I am willing to give her another chance I am afraid that it will kill me to part from her. It is my place to care for my own child anyway and I think I can manage her."[53] Two years later, when Jones was less than two months from her final discharge, her mother wrote to express her fears that her unmanageable daughter had decided to leave home. Jones's mother did not believe that the twenty-year-old was mature enough to care for herself, and, because of her epileptic seizures, "she had to be watched always." Feeling at a loss regarding what to do with a daughter that she clearly loved, Jones's mother made another desperate plea to a social worker: "Could you advise me what to do with her? I am sick and she is a great care." Reluctantly admitting her own limitations as a parent, she revealed how much her daughter's welfare affected her own sense of well-being: "I cannot manage her anymore and I don't want her to go to the bad."[54] It is not clear what happened to Jones or her mother's perpetual worries after she was finally discharged three years after she was arrested.

In an unusual case, inmate Suzette Elliot's father, who was an immigrant from Trinidad, simply gave up when Elliot continued to reject his authority while she was on parole, requesting that she be deported at his expense. Elliot's father strongly believed that her prostitution conviction threatened his position as a naturalized citizen.[55] His correspondence with Bedford administrators reflects his attempts to separate her illegal actions from his status as a law-abiding citizen. In his first letter to Superintendent Amos Baker, he emphasized his social and moral standards, explaining that although he was a native of the West Indies, he was a "trusted government employee, a Catholic and a citizen of this Great Country"; he was "one . . . who believes in obeying the law and liv[ing] a good life for the benefit of [his] soul."[56] In response to his nineteen-year-old daughter's parole, he argued that his daughter's actions should not influence Bedford's assessment of him. In fact, he contended that once Bedford officials met him, they would likely be puzzled at his daughter's behavior. "As a trusted servant of our War Department," he wrote, "I think you ought to see and talk to me, so that you could be convinced that my daughter . . . should not have been in a place like Bedford."[57] Elliot's father, a strict disciplinarian, was never satisfied with his daughter's behavior and was always suspicious that she was immoral. When Elliot ran away from home after less than a month on parole, her father reported that she had "quit my residence and protection" and encouraged her deportation: "I am sorry to inform you, she is my daughter and I am absolutely through with her. I wish as soon as she is arrested and returned to your institution that you do me the favor to recommend to the Board that she be deported back to Trinidad BWI where she was born. The cost to be borne by me—3rd class passage." At the same time, however, he was severely critical of Bedford officials: "I thought Bedford would reform her but in my opinion she is worse now. I will do my level best to assist you to locate her, . . . and will not stop until she leaves the U.S."[58] Although Elliot's father contacted immigration officials at Ellis Island, Bedford officials decided to ignore his requests and paroled Elliot to a social worker.[59]

In some cases, relatives emphasized their commitment to parolees' rehabilitation. Mabel Hampton's aunt, for example, was concerned about Hampton's late nights and her plans to return to her former "immoral" life in New York City after her prison discharge. After five months of trying to deal with Hampton's independent and troublesome behavior—from her refusal to pay rent to her unauthorized trips from New Jersey to New York City—her aunt notified Bedford. Highlighting several conflicts, Hampton's aunt pointed out that she had attempted to deal with Hampton's behavior before requesting assistance: "Although I have been very broad and liberal in my actions—in fact too much so—I have had my hands full, for she [is] wild and wayward and does not like to be admonished and respectable. . . . The truth is—[she] does not want to stay in my home—[because] she must try to do right and behave around me. For she knows when she get too high I will report her."[60] Because relatives seemed to be protecting their reputations as much as the interests of the parolee, parolees resented their prying. Parolees often responded to their relatives' actions by rejecting them. Hampton, for one, had the last word, at least with her aunt. A year and a half into her two-year parole sentence, she escaped her family's control by voluntarily returning to Bedford. Hampton's decision to return to prison was a conscious rejection of her family's standards of respectability, a rejection that was later compounded when she agreed to be paroled as a live-in domestic under the supervision of a white employer.[61]

Other parolees experiencing familial disagreements returned to Bedford because of financial crises as well as unresolved moral dilemmas. An eighteen-year-old returned to Bedford because she could not survive on her own as a single mother. Failing to live up to her family's expectations, she decided to live alone with her infant. She soon found single motherhood financially impossible and decided to return to Bedford with her child voluntarily. "I see I must return to the Institution," she wrote to Bedford superintendent Baker regarding her decision. "I havent got the money to come and am asking you please send for me, I wants a job where I can have my baby wit me. Dr. Baker I tried very heard but can't make it, I have no one to help me, my family don't want me because I have brought a disgrace on them I am an outcast it is bitter for me to come back."[62] Ostracized by her relatives, facing single parenthood as well as poverty, this parolee felt despair about her predicament but was clear about the state's responsibility toward her and her child.

The ambivalent interactions between black families and the state reveals the differentiated experiences of working-class black city-dwellers. While many black families experienced difficult relationships with various arms of the state, they proactively chose—or felt entitled—to use state services to discipline their female relatives. These relatives used the state's assistance to resolve many distinct and personal predicaments. In most cases, family members made numerous attempts to negotiate positive relationships with their paroled relatives before notifying the state. Yet what most relatives did not realize was that once they notified the state, they relinquished their authority over the parolee as well as any right to question the state's actions toward the parolee. Black families were aware of the state's racist practices, but they also believed that some state policies mirrored their own ideas about appropriate moral behavior.

Focusing on parole cases yields insights into the conflicts between administrators and parolees' employers and the ways in which black women negotiated power relations within the criminal justice system. When parolees had the opportunity, they asserted their independence. The instability endemic to urban life influenced the way in which administrators handled women's rehabilitation, restricting further black women's already limited opportunities in New York.

Yet black women's relationships with state representatives present only one perspective regarding parole. Black families and communities were very involved in the parole process, and not always in concert with their female relatives. Black families held their own ideas of propriety, which were influenced by traditional gendered expectations but were enacted on an individual basis. Black families used the power of the criminal justice system to enforce their moral standards, even when that meant re-institutionalizing

Parole, Gender, and Black Families

a female relative. In their distinctive ways, black families invoked the state in shaping their destinies.[63] Those institutions often presented the face of the state in black communities because poverty and racial discrimination frequently landed New York blacks in penal institutions.

Examining black women's parole reveals the varied thoughts, desires, and ambitions of a small segment of the black masses. Like other working-class communities, the black working-class community used the state for its own purposes;[64] however, working people's use of the state was often problematic. Wayward minor cases show that using the state to control young women had different implications for black communities, who were also dealing with state-sanctioned racial discrimination in housing, employment, and leisure, as well as in the criminal justice system. Nevertheless, those black women subjected to state and familial control still attempted to improve their lives as they sought to obtain a level of independence.

While prison administrators gave the impression that parolees were treated equally, an inmate's racial identity definitely influenced how they handled her rehabilitation. Responding to anxiety about dangerous and endangered black women in the city, after 1922, administrators began requiring more and more black women who were southern migrants or had relatives living in the South to serve their parole in the South, where they believed black people belonged.

9

she would be better off in the south

If you had never left Georgia, you wouldn't be in prison. You are not the
type of Colored person who can stand the North. You got a vile temper, and you
drink, and you are headstrong. You should never have come out of Georgia.
If you will go back there, we will cooperate with you.
—Parole board commissioner Moore, Auburn, 1932

I wrote you. . . . hardly any money making in Charleston. . . . you can get work
but hardly any money in it people want you to cook nurse and everything in the
house for 2–3–4–5–6 dollars a week and that is know money for your expense.
—Elsa Cook, parolee, to Bedford superintendent, 1924

Parole board commissioner Moore's comments about a southern migrant at
Auburn reflect New York State prison administrators' anxieties about black
women's presence in the urban North.[1] Moore's attribution of twenty-six-
year-old Carrie Green's criminal offense to her innate inability to handle
living in the city underscores the subjective nature of the parole process. He
deemed her "headstrong" and believed that in the South she would be kept
in line. Moore's 1932 comment was reminiscent of white and black reformers' arguments about race and civilization at the turn of the century, which
emphasized that working poor black people were rooted in preindustrial
southern slave society and lacked the aptitude to adapt to modern urban
America. By the time the National Urban League was formed in 1911, most
reformers had incorporated their specific concerns about black women's
protection into their concerns about black people's larger political and eco-

nomic struggles, especially during the postwar period. Unlike their earlier directives that emphasized the need for blacks to remain in the South, activists focused their efforts on helping migrants adjust to the city by tackling the municipal problems that these newcomers faced. Yet the doubts some white activists and state officials still held about black women in the city were reflected in Moore's statement. The commissioner invoked slavery's lasting legacy, now through Jim Crow laws, as the twentieth-century remedy to controlling black bodies. Moore and his fellow officials thought they could identify "the type of Colored person who could not stand the North" and use southern parole to prevent her relapse into delinquency.[2] Moore's anxiety about Green's presence in New York City mirrors the concerns of reformers nationwide. In New York's criminal justice system, prison administrators' moral panics in the 1920s and the early 1930s often led them to parole black female migrants, including some native New Yorkers, to the South.

In early-twentieth-century New York, social reformers' focus on black women involved two simultaneous and competing concerns: the desire to protect black female migrants from urban dangers and the drive to protect urban society from criminal black women. The southern parole program was based on the assumption that black female migrants represented a threat to the legal and moral order.[3] The prevailing stereotype that deemed all black women naturally criminal as well as promiscuous led many administrators to be more punitive than rehabilitative in the parole process.[4] They saw black women as more dangerous to white citizens' safety than endangered by the proliferation of violent crime and prostitution. In 1932, Moore's ultimatum—accept parole in the South or serve a full prison sentence in New York—reinscribed whites' conviction that the South provided a solution to regulating black women's behavior.

The main similarity between southern and northern parole was that black women were placed with a family that shouldered the responsibility for their supervision and rehabilitation. In this context, "family" meant not simply reconnecting with black relatives but also reentering the white-dominated, supposedly paternalistic society of the South. Ironically, the image of the antebellum slaveholder as a benevolent father who would protect his slave children was strengthened rather than eroded after emancipation—at least in the minds of northern whites. By the turn of the twentieth century, this scenario had been reinforced by vagrancy laws, the convict lease system, and disfranchisement. Thus, racial and class hierarchies were reestablished through segregation. Northern prison administrators believed in the South's legitimacy as a default parole custodian because they recognized that "certain conventions associated with slavery"—such as "the use of physical violence to make slaves obedient and submissive," seen in lynching and other forms of antiblack violence, as well as "the unquestioned right of owners to use the people they owned in whatever ways they wished," seen in sharecropping and peonage—were still being used against black people.[5] Jim Crow laws not only shaped white employers' views of black labor but also underlined their coercive power. Northern whites understood that the respectable, mother-centered, affectionate, and nurturing family ideal that had prevailed in wayward women's rehabilitation since the Victorian period was quite distinct from the paternalistic familial order of the South. Parole administrators counted on the fact that white southerners "knew" black people and that black people understood the consequences of stepping out of their place. As historian Nell Irvin Painter has remarked, "Violence is inseparable from slavery." The "long-standing ideals of obedience and submission, the values of slavery and the acceptance of violence as a means of enforcement" shaped the early-twentieth-century South as well.[6] This fact underscores the social, economic, political, and psychic costs black parolees paid when they were sent below the Mason-Dixon line. These myriad costs—including sexual exploitation—prompted black women to reject the legacy of enslavement through migration. However, many migrants, like Carrie Green, were forced to return to the South. Sadly, many migrants failed to escape brutal treatment in New York as they often suffered from the pervasiveness of violence in the form of domestic abuse.[7]

The hearing transcript that reveals the commissioner's ultimatum also provides a window into Carrie Green's experience. Her criminal behavior stemmed from a volatile and abusive marriage. Two issues, her previous arrest for a felonious assault on her husband and a conviction for second-degree manslaughter, dominated her parole meeting. Green argued that she killed her husband in self-defense: "He said I cut him, but he is the one that cut me." Disregarding her domestic abuse, the parole board believed her actions were a consequence of her migration from Savannah, Georgia, to New York. Green's scarred face, a visible remnant of spousal violence, caught the parole board's attention for only a moment: when asked by one commissioner, "How did you get that cut on the side of your face?" Green replied, "My husband hit me there." For her, the scar from an injury inflicted in 1927 was a constant reminder of the precarious nature of everyday domestic life and had nothing to do with her living in New York City. While the parole board believed that returning Green to Georgia under her elderly aunt's care would be a positive step forward, Green must have thought that her ten-year parole was another prison sentence, as she would return to many of the same problems that prompted her departure from the Jim Crow South.[8] For black women, southern parole was not a solution but a problem.

Examining the complex dynamics of southern parole, this chapter investigates the motivations of prison administrators and the responses of black working-class women and their families and communities. It addresses how New York administrators—with racial and, with declining state funding, economic concerns—came to see the South as an appropriate place for black women's parole and how parolees reacted to state officials as well as their own families; moreover, it explores black family members' involvement in the parole process.[9] The experiences of black women paroled from the New York State Reformatory for Women at Bedford and the New York State Prison for Women at Auburn demonstrate that while the racially specific policing practices of southern parole illuminate New York State's agenda for black women, the responses of parolees and their families reveal working-class blacks' shared, conflicting, and gendered visions of respectability.[10]

The manner in which administrators dealt with black parolees changed after the Great Migration. Between 1901 and 1920, the New York State attorney general seemed to discourage out-of-state parole.[11] In the 1920s, however, the continued migration of southern blacks as well as restricted foreign immigration after 1924 raised grave concerns about New York's growing black population.[12] Between 1920 and 1930, the city's black population more than doubled, from 152,467 to 327,706.[13] After 1920, both Bedford and Auburn paroled black women to the South. Black women sent to the South were usually southerners—from Maryland, Virginia, the Carolinas, Georgia, and Alabama—or had southern relatives willing to take on the responsibility of serving as their parole custodians. Most black women had migrated to New York to improve their and their families' economic circumstances, and southern parole forced them back into low-paying domestic-service jobs and the strictures of segregation.

The rise in southern parole for black women in New York coincided with widespread moral panics about single working women's sexuality in urban America during the 1920s. Administrators were convinced that black women's downfall resulted from their exposure to city life. In this instance, discourses about race and civilization made black people's purported innate promiscuity or deviant sexuality and their primitive criminality seem a dangerous combination for native-born whites who resented and feared the influx and influence of immigrants and migrants. Prison officials agreed that, whenever possible, black women should be removed from Harlem and

New York City, not to rural upstate New York as they had previously advocated, but to the South. Superintendent Amos Baker argued that "it is better for . . . colored girls to be away from New York City," because "they invariably drift back to Harlem and [become] . . . involved in difficulties again."[14] Baker's general assessment is reflected in Bedford's and Auburn's unofficial parole policies. At Auburn, one prospective offender's parole was delayed, she was told, because she was "not the kind of girl [who could be] safely [placed] in . . . New York City."[15] Prison administrators stipulated that those women who were paroled to the South and returned north would be apprehended as parole violators.[16] At the same time, prison administrators vigorously maintained that native-born white women were better equipped to handle urban life and continued to be paroled in New York.[17]

Psychological evaluations of black women that supported southern parole ignored migrants' attempts to be independent citizens and reinforced the idea that black people were too crude and unrefined to navigate the industrialized North. For instance, a Bedford physician described a black inmate's case as "the not unusual development of the southern negro with inferior mentality who comes north and has too little supervision in the new environment in which she enters."[18] Black inmates' psychological examinations and treatments reflected the consensus that southern blacks were incapable of successfully dealing with urban life. A black inmate transferred to the Matteawan State Hospital for the Criminally Insane, for example, was diagnosed as a "constitutionally psychopathic individual and one who would always require considerable supervision." The final diagnosis referred explicitly to this inmate's migrant status. The inmate's examining doctor wrote, "I have felt . . . that she like many other young colored girls, would have been able to adjust herself fairly successfully if she had remained in the South and had not been exposed to the disorganizing influence of our great northern metropolis." He suggested that the inmate be "given parole" if she was sent to her "home in Virginia": "If she could be kept in Virginia, and away from the State of New York, I believe that both she and the public would be benefited. For this reason, I suggested her for a parole in order that she might go to the South and be placed again under the supervision of her parents, sister and other relatives who should be able to look after her and insure that she keep the provisions of her parole."[19]

In their assumptions about the moral value of rural life,[20] administrators stressed that family members in the southern countryside could quell the delinquency born of black women's exposure to the city. A prospective parolee was told, "The salvation of you is to get you down to Alabama." Administrators worked diligently with southern social welfare officers to identify a residence that could be adequately supervised and an appropriate parole custodian. One woman was told that her parole was conditional upon her returning to her proper place: "We are trying to give you a chance, but we are going to place you down there because your family is there and they got room for you. That is where you belong."[21] Like reformers involved in campaigns to protect black women, prison administrators viewed the South uncritically, never considering why black women had felt compelled to migrate north. Rather, southern parole and the need to put black women where they belonged stemmed from more than administrators' anxieties about immorality. It also grew out of the resurgent racial and ethnic intolerance of the 1920s, which was evident in anti-immigrant legislation and the rebirth of the Ku Klux Klan.

Southern parole coincided with prison policies regarding foreign-born offenders. Both Bedford and Auburn deported a number of inmates and designated others for Americanization,[22] wherein, as a part of the rehabilitation process, prison schools focused on teaching immigrants the English language and American customs.[23] For instance, in 1928, a thirty-five-year-old Italian woman was denied parole twice when Auburn officials concluded that, after six or seven months, she had not yet learned enough English. At her second hearing, the inmate was told: "You have to learn English before the Board of Parole is going to look favorably upon your case [and] . . . you will have an opportunity between now [December] and January to show us what you can absorb of the English language."[24] Like white immigrants, many black women were initially given the chance to redeem themselves as parolees in rural New York State and, in some instances, New York City. Cases of southern parole indicate those instances when administrators believed a particular woman's past behavior, institutional record, and family background called for her removal to what they deemed a more stable South.

As prison administrators sought to control white immigrant and black migrant populations, they sometimes ideologically equated paroling black offenders to the South with deporting immigrants. Parole officers and superintendents referred to black women as if they were not U.S. citizens and referred to the South as if it were a foreign country. In this sense, southern parole's linkage to deportation highlights its punitive implications rather than ostensible rehabilitative purposes. It also illuminates the assumption that black women had no citizenship rights that white institutions had to respect. One parole officer wrote to Bedford's superintendent, "I am anxious to know whether you would approve my referring . . . [two inmates] to the State Board of Charities for deportation."[25] The superintendent responded,

"I agree with you concerning . . . deportation . . . to North Carolina and Georgia respectively."[26] When the parolee or their relatives could not afford train fare to southern locations, prison administrators notified officials at the Bureau of State, Alien and Non-Resident Poor, who provided funds. Reminiscent of those in charge of deportation at Ellis Island, this agency, which was associated with the New York State Department of Charities, was used when prison administrators wanted to assign travel attendants to parolees to ensure that they actually returned to the South.[27]

The Ironies of Southern Parole

Prison administrators ultimately learned what black migrants had long known: the South had its own urban problems. After parolees were relocated, the southern social welfare and criminal justice systems presented New York administrators with new difficulties. Penal reform was only beginning in the South.[28] The administrators who cooperated with Bedford and Auburn were located in southern cities rather than rural counties. Ironically, southern administrators rejected a number of New York parolee cases because their residences were rural and too difficult to supervise. Most black parolees were sent to cities, where officials grappled with their own problems with wayward women.[29] Prison administrators viewed southern life as simple and free of the dangers and temptations of New York, yet this vision failed to acknowledge the existence of a rapidly growing urban South. For those blacks who lived in cities, the South replicated many of the problems—such as poor housing, inadequate sanitation, overcrowding, a lack of municipal health services, and unregulated vice districts—present in larger northern cities.[30]

Northern administrators, while naively expecting the South to be less vice-ridden than the North, were clearly aware of the racially restrictive practices of Jim Crow; indeed, that system enforced their own ideas about policing black women's behavior. Nevertheless, administrators encountered a myriad of problems. Some southern states either entirely lacked or were in the initial stages of developing institutionalized social welfare services. In these particular cases, New York administrators questioned the wisdom of paroling inmates there. For instance, in 1923, when Superintendent Amos Baker wrote Roba, Alabama, for assistance, he addressed his letter to the state social welfare agency. He received an immediate reply from the local postmaster, who "took the liberty" to open the letter and inform Baker that "no board . . . was in operation." The postmaster served as a self-appointed case worker by "confering [sic]" with the woman's in-laws and, in closing, asked Baker to inform him about Bedford's decision and when he should expect the parolee to arrive.[31] Bedford's decision to parole the inmate in New York likely stemmed from the fact that Roba had no social welfare system in place.

In the South, many black female offenders were housed with men and forced to work on chain gangs and fulfill convict lease contracts along with men.[32] Because southern institutional facilities were racially segregated, no attempt was made to rehabilitate black female offenders. Young black women in trouble with the law were often housed in local jails with older and habitual offenders, rather than receiving rehabilitative care in a women's reformatory. Given state administrators' neglect of black inmates, the black community played a crucial role in southern social welfare efforts. Black clubwomen founded homes and reformatories for delinquent girls and wayward women.

Under the leadership of Janie Porter Barrett, the Virginia State Federation of Colored Women's Clubs established the Industrial School for Colored Girls in Peake, Virginia. Raising over $6,000, clubwomen bought a 147-acre farm and opened the facility on January 19, 1915.[33] Plagued by financial problems, the institution struggled for its first three years. During World War I, the Virginia state legislature and the federal government, attempting to police female promiscuity and sexual relationships with soldiers in local communities and nationwide, provided the institution with financial support.[34] In 1920, the state legislature officially took over the reformatory's financing.[35]

While the school received consistent state funding, it never had its own parole officer. In annual reports to the state legislature from 1920 to 1939, Superintendent Barrett made continual requests for a parole officer. In addition to running the school, Barrett shouldered the responsibility of supervising parolees. In some instances, the State Board of Welfare provided the institution with assistance by investigating the homes of prospective employers. Barrett's argument to the Virginia legislature that "this very important work can be done most effectively by a parole officer connected with the institution" was never effectively addressed, even as the institution received public accolades.[36] But even with the lack of state social services for southern black women, parole records show that southern administrators consistently complied with New York administrators' requests for supervision of black parolees. It was only when the residences of New York parolees were located in rural counties that southern administrators refused to help. Southern administrators explained that their reluctance to supervise New York's black parolees stemmed from the difficulty of following the activities of black people in rural areas rather than from their adherence to racially restrictive policies.[37]

Southern administrators' concerns about vice in the urban South belied New York administrators' notion that the South was the safest place for black women.[38] As southern administrators faced the social dilemmas associated with urbanization and industrialization, they had their own problems with and anxieties about young women. When a parolee was sent to her home in Lynchburg, Virginia, the Associated Charities representative wrote Bedford's parole board about the woman's employment: "This work will be near the girl's home and we think it would be safer . . . than a position in the city would be."[39] Superintendent Barrett expressed grave concerns about the black women who were paroled in cities. "The girls who have left us and gone on parole into country homes," she wrote in an annual report, "are doing well[.] It is always with a heavy heart that I send a girl to the city, for in far too many instances she goes under; the temptations are too great. She is simply swept off her feet."[40] Since promoting and even imposing southern parole gave prison administrators a way to address their anxieties about sexually promiscuous black women in New York, these kinds of comments fell on deaf ears. While it is clear why New York prison administrators advocated southern parole, it is uncertain why southern social administrators proved so willing to accommodate this practice, particularly given their own anxieties regarding urbanization and delinquency.[41]

Southern and Urban Experiences

The rural environment that New York administrators envisioned as the perfect means to quell urban degeneracy often relegated black women to low-wage domestic employment or, in some cases, unemployment. Black women who were returned to the South found themselves in socially and economically oppressive situations. Consider, for instance, the predicament of twenty-one-year-old Alice Jenkins, who was imprisoned for vagrancy in New York City and "deported" to her parent's home in North Carolina.[42] When Jenkins's mother learned of this plan, she requested that Jenkins find work in New York because of the "difficulties at home" and because she "wouldn't be able to work as there is . . . no work."[43] When this request was denied, her mother asked that prison administrators allow her daughter to work in New York for four months in order to purchase clothes before returning home.[44] A month later, Bedford released the unemployed Jenkins to her family in Edenton. The ideological connections between the legacy of enslavement and the economic as well as sexual exploitation that black

Southern Parole

southerners were forced to endure were no more evident than in Edenton, the birthplace of Harriet Jacobs, author of the autobiographical *Incidents in the Life of a Slave Girl*.

Initially Jenkins encountered a dismal job market, but eventually she found stable employment as a cook for the family where her father worked for twenty-five years. Although Jenkins's family became her official parole custodians, her employer's family reported on her behavior to a county worker and eventually became responsible for "look[ing] after her wants and . . . influenc[ing] her moral life." White employers and social workers exerted complete control over Jenkins's employment and social life between 1928 and 1930. When reporting on Jenkins and her family, a county official expressed a widely held white conviction about black people when she explained, "They are fairly good servants if you know how to manage them and do not expect too much from them."[45] Jenkins wrote New York administrators that she was "getting along fine," going to church every Sunday, limiting her extracurricular activities, and "still working"; however, her wages in 1929 totaled only four dollars a week.[46] Because she was a wage laborer, Jenkins's actions were completely regulated by her "white" southern family—her employers—rather than by her own relatives. Her meager salary is evidence that parolees were forced back into the position that many had sought to escape.

Many black women paroled to the South requested new positions in New York because they received low wages for backbreaking work in domestic and personal-service jobs. When responding to parolees' letters containing these kinds of requests, prison administrators usually expressed skepticism about parolees' financial and employment difficulties and reiterated the idea that the South was the best place for black women to be rehabilitated. Superintendent Leo Palmer responded to one complaining parolee: "I rather think you underestimate the wages down there when you say you would be paid but $2 a week, for we know something about what girls can earn there, and if one is well qualified she can get more than that. . . . You found that in New York . . . big wages did not keep you out of trouble."[47] Administrators often contended that parolees were to blame for their own economic predicaments. Twenty-two-year-old Elsa Cook made several requests to move back to New York because of limited employment and meager wages.[48] Superintendent Baker's response was typical. "I am sorry you have not been able to find any work," he wrote. "It would seem to me in a city like Charleston that there would be many places open for a girl. . . . I am sure if you persist, you will find something suitable and profitable."[49] At one point, Cook sounded desperate: "Now Dr. if I break my parole don't you or anyone else say anything because I have asked permission from you. I always like to do the write thing but I see where it don't pay all the time."[50] Two years later, Baker continued to dismiss Cook's pleas, writing insensitively, "I think if you could see our very deep snow drifts, you would be glad you are in the sunny South."[51] Baker's attitude reinforces prison officials' commonly held notion that black southern labor in white households and businesses would lead to a more appropriate rehabilitation. Cook was finally discharged from parole five months later.

Black parolees' experiences illuminate the distinct meanings that southern parole held for administrators and for black women. Prison administrators viewed southern life as free of the dangers and temptations of New York, but black women encountered many of the same problems in southern cities as they did in the urban North.[52] As in the North, black women faced with dismal job prospects sometimes engaged in prostitution, either full time or to supplement their low wages. Parolees' emphasis on inadequate wages in their correspondence with prison administrators suggests their anxiety about entering or reentering the sex trade in the South.[53] Family members shared parolees' concerns about southern employment conditions and their moral effects on black women.

When they could, black families attempted to shield parolees from the moral dangers of personal-service work and from harsh working conditions. A sixteen-year-old parolee who was returned to a relatively stable home life in Maryland wrote Bedford's superintendent in 1926: "I am getting along fine but still have no job and I really don't expect to get any, as these people do not pay over $2.50 a week. My mother says that I do not have to work [because] they [employers] work you to death." While this example illuminates why many women believed that New York's higher wages were worth the troubles associated with migration, it also highlights a family's concerns about the circumstances under which young women should work. Her family considered the southern labor market objectionable and had the economic resources required to keep her at home.[54] Superintendent Baker advised the parolee to reconsider her position: "I wonder if it is best for you to stay at home and not work at all because the wages are small. Even though your parents are able to support you that way, it seems best that your time should be occupied rather than you should be idle. Busy people are not so likely to get into mischief as idle ones. I realize, of course, that wages in that part of the country do not compare with those in New York."[55] In this case, Baker disregarded not only the parolee's concerns about southern employment conditions but also those of her family. Indeed, he and other administrators saw labor for white employers, rather than a parolee's family's protection and control, as the best way to regulate black women's behavior. While concerns regarding appropriate behavior and particularly about women engaging in the illegal sex trade led to the removal of black parolees from New York, employment became the most salient issue once parolees reached the South. Administrators, however, consistently ignored the connection between the lack of employment opportunities, inadequate wages, and illegal sex in the South.

Black Family Members Debate Appropriate Behavior

When possible, black women parolees behaved according to their understanding of New York administrators' and familial expectations of proper womanhood. A twenty-six-year-old woman from Danville, Virginia, who felt that her eight-year sentence for the second-degree manslaughter of her common-law husband would bring shame upon her family sought to keep her criminal record from them. Paroled for four years in New York and in poor health, she asked Auburn's superintendent for a discharge so she could go home. Asking to return to Virginia without parole supervision, she revealed that her "people did not know anything about [her] downfall."[56] Twenty-year-old Carrie Hall, convicted of petty larceny, immediately wrote her Bedford matron when she realized that she would be sent to her native Anderson, South Carolina. "I do appreciate . . . the kindness of the board in being so lenient with me," she said, "but you know I do hate to go . . . [home] as they all know I'm in trouble and it seems so bad, because I made one mistake in New York it does not mean that I will continue to do so."[57] Although administrators appeared to be irritated that Hall, who they said was "conceited" and had dealt with them in a "high-handed manner," her "black curly bobbed hair, brown eyes, light brown skin . . . good looking teeth," and "a nice smile" apparently tempered their response to her. One administrator explained that Hall's "appearance and conversation would lead one to estimate her intelligence at a much higher level than it actually is."[58] Aware of the impression she made, Hall used this knowledge to make her case for staying in New York before facing her southern family and community's high expectations. "Now if I should be fortunate enough to get a job and get on my feet," she wrote, "why then I won't mind returning to my mother, but to go home now, as I am why I'd be a disgrace to her and myself." Her request that the cottage matron "please help . . . and advise . . . me" worked, as administrators eventually paroled her to a brother in Philadelphia.

When thirty-eight-year-old Katie Simms, a Virginia native, addressed Auburn commissioners, she explained that her criminal behavior was

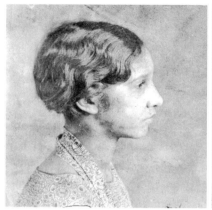

Carrie Hall (pseud.), an inmate at the New York State Reformatory for Women at Bedford, 1926. Courtesy of New York State Archives and Records Administration, Albany, New York (#4087, Series 14610-77B).

a betrayal of the respectability of her sister and brother-in-law and persuaded the board to allow her to remain in New York. She admitted her faults, noting that at one time she "worked six months and was idle for four months." Emphasizing that her sister worked in a legitimate service position and that her brother-in-law served as "postmaster," Simms argued that her sister would only tolerate a certain type of behavior and would therefore be an acceptable parole custodian. She recalled, "When I went into the street, my sister would have nothing to do with me." Appealing to the parole commission's sense of moral propriety, Simms promised that instead of soliciting, she would "stick to laundry work." "She will take me with her only if I behave," Simms emphasized.[59] Simms effectively used past disagreements with her sister over proper behavior to her advantage. Eventually she persuaded the parole board to allow her to live with her family in New York rather than paroling her to Virginia. Simms's success was exceptional. The case files of inmates originally destined to be paroled to the South suggest that the parole board was not easily convinced by prospective parolees.

Administrators' basic premise that familial surroundings would ward off vice failed to account for disagreements within black families over what qualified as appropriate behavior. Tensions often resulted from conflicting generational ideas about respectability and gender, a family's desire to shield female relatives from the temptations of city life, and young women acting out their social and economic independence. While many families welcomed returning parolees, others expressed concerns about their ability to care for their charges. Parole records show, however, that family mem-

Southern Parole

bers made numerous attempts to negotiate positive relationships with their paroled relatives before notifying the state.

Seventeen-year-old Mabel Smith's situation is a case in point. Paroled to her aunt and uncle in Atlanta, Georgia, after she failed to mend her ways while living with her widowed father in New York, Smith felt out of place in Atlanta. She was not "delighted with the south" but hoped she could "get used to it." Adjustment proved difficult not only for the parolee but also for her relatives. Smith's aunt, frustrated by her unsuccessful attempts to "mold [Smith] into a christian woman," told Bedford superintendent Baker, "If there should be anything that goes wrong I will inform you."[60] Three months later, she notified Baker of her growing concerns about Smith. She noted that her niece dated various men, broke her curfew, and refused to work. Her "conduct," the aunt said, "has been very unsatisfactory. . . . I had hope for an improvement [but] I have come to the conclusion that my efforts are futile." Smith's aunt's amicable correspondence with Baker reveals that some black family members believed that some state policies reinforced their own ideas about moral conduct.[61]

Smith's aunt's correspondence also indicates the parolee's disenchantment with her aunt and uncle's custodianship. Indeed, according to her aunt, Smith not only acted inappropriately but accused her aunt and uncle of agreeing with the community's negative assessment of her. "We have been good to her regardless to what she may tell," her aunt explained; "my conscience is clear. She accuses me of listening to what other people say. . . . Notwithstanding the different things that I have heard[,] *I have seen* enough myself without anyone telling me anything to know that she is an undesirable character." Smith's aunt was so committed to upholding respectability that she was willing to cooperate with the state: "I see no hopes for improvement I am desirous of giving her up. . . . I am sorry that it is necessary for me to write you all this but I felt that it is my duty to do so."[62] Seven months later, Smith reported to Baker her niece's consistently inappropriate behavior: "I am really sorry that I consented for her to come down here to us. She has caused so much trouble. I sure do wish something could be done to get her back there and unless she changes greatly from what she is now it would be good if she could be kept in some place of confinement."[63] By this point, the Atlanta Family Welfare Society had also requested that Smith be sent back to New York.[64] Smith's aunt's statement shows how state authorities reinforced her and her family's ideas about respectability and discipline; it also shows her belief that imprisonment, or at least reformatory care, would best protect her niece from the dangers of the city, South or North. The conflict between Smith and her aunt stemmed from their distinct perspectives regarding how a young woman should conduct herself. Respectability and attention to appropriate gendered behavior were not simply middle-class preoccupations enforced by social reformers and prison administrators on parolees.[65]

Despite administrators' claims, the southern environment failed to prevent a northern-born black woman like Smith from violating her parole. Nor did it rehabilitate twenty-two-year-old Sally Jones, who was paroled to her native Charleston, South Carolina, after her parole with her mother in New York did not work out. A parole officer admitted that while "it would scarcely seem advisable to allow [Jones] to return to New York City where she has in the past made so many disreputable associates . . . [i]t seems obvious that her mother [who also returned to the South] is quite unable to supervise her properly."[66] Nevertheless, Bedford officials approved her parole to South Carolina, where she lived with her parents and her sister and brother-in-law and their child. Initially, according to a county social worker, Jones appeared to be "comfortably settled."

Jones ran afoul of traditional moral conventions when, less than a year into her parole, Jones was seven months pregnant and living with the father of the child.[67] While fully aware that after repeated attempts, Jones could not obtain a divorce from her estranged husband, state officials frowned upon her acceptance of financial support from her boyfriend and her subsequent common-law living arrangement. Her family appeared supportive of Jones's choices, acknowledging that she was in a stable relationship but noting the added strain that another child would pose on the household's resources. Administrators never changed their negative assessment of her family's ability to handle her parole, but they made no attempt to return her to New York and subsequently discharged her for good behavior.

Three months after her final discharge, Jones became involved in a violent altercation in a club and stabbed another woman. According to newspaper accounts, on the night of the stabbing, Jones returned to the family home, still carrying the bloody knife used in the fight, and rushed to see her mother, "who had been failing in health." The sight proved too much for her mother, who died "from the shock."[68] After her mother's death, Jones apparently moved back to New York, was arrested for vagrancy-prostitution, and was recommitted to Bedford for two years.

Jones's case underlines the real problems with the strategy of southern parole. Rather than curbing her tendencies to "associate with disreputable" people, Charleston proved to be just as problematic as New York. Although Jones committed her most serious crime after she was discharged from Bedford, she had violated the conditions of her parole with her boyfriend without having to deal with the consequences of that decision. The moral panic that convinced New York administrators to send women like Jones to the South failed to sway them when these women replicated the behavior administrators had found so troubling. In their eagerness to make southern parole the solution to dealing with black women in New York, prison administrators ignored the region's economic and social problems, not to mention the dangers awaiting women in southern cities. Ultimately, New York administrators' imaginings of southern life never coincided with black women's experiences, and in that discrepancy lay the root of much material suffering and moral harm.

There were other signs that the reform ideals that shaped female rehabilitation strategies were becoming less relevant to legislators and officials. With declining state funding came the end to nineteenth-century reformers' vision of rehabilitating younger working women by segregating them from older and hardened female offenders. In 1933, one year after Carrie Green's parole hearing, the Prison for Women at Auburn was closed and female felons were imprisoned with younger misdemeanants at Bedford. This inmate transfer illustrates how the project of rehabilitating all working women was excised from criminal justice initiatives.

Southern parole reveals complex ideas about race, rehabilitation, and respectability. With the advent of immigration restriction statutes, prison officials not only deported immigrants back to their native countries but also "deported" black women to the South. Southern parole was a response not only to an overall anxiety about the dangerous working classes but also to administrators' specific beliefs that black people simply could not handle the urban North. Instead of using a traditional parole system in which middle-class housewives inculcated domestic respectability, administrators depended on the power of Jim Crow to regulate rather than reform black women. Whereas prospective New York parolees were required to have jobs and suitable living arrangements before their release, southern parolees found that the availability of a relatives' custodianship and a viable social welfare system constituted the necessary prerequisites for their prison release. Additionally, while the notion of domestic respectability was a minor concern of administrators, it permeated the lives and experiences of working-class black families. While administrators enforced a legalized view of respectability, black parolees and their families acknowledged the law but held fast to their own fashioning of moral propriety.

Southern parole also coincided with a national anxiety about expanding racial and ethnic urban communities. Moreover, concerns about all working-class women's sexuality affected black women specifically when prison administrators began to envision southern parole as one solution to the problem of black female delinquency. For reformers, black women's presence in New York fueled moral panics because there seemed to be no plausible way to rehabilitate black women, whom they believed were easily tempted by urban vice. Instead of emphasizing the need to protect the endangered, vulnerable southern migrant, prison officials argued that these women were too dangerous and immoral to live in the urban North. Sending black parolees to the South, where administrators believed Jim Crow laws would regulate black bodies, provided a means to address black women's threatening presence in New York.

The fact was, southern cities, where most black women were paroled, had their own moral and social problems that offered just as many temptations. At the same time, southern society provided fewer opportunities for economic autonomy and the rehabilitation of paroled black women. Yet most New York administrators disregarded black women's welfare once they reached the South.

Black women paroled south, however, negotiated power relations within the criminal justice system and their communities. The records show that when parolees had opportunities, they asserted themselves regarding their living and employment conditions. Some women attempted to manipulate administrators' decisions. Others protested their predicaments by writing to prison officials. In their correspondence, including their required monthly missives to parole officers, black women pointedly questioned the authority of prison administrators, employers, and family members. Finally, these women not only dealt with the regulatory practices of the state but also responded to the authority and individualized renderings of moral propriety within their own families and communities.

conclusion

THANK GOD I AM INDEPENDENT ONE MORE TIME

I am sure glad you are still good.
Hope you haven't forgotten your home teaching and religion.

—Relative to paroled Bedford inmate Constance Mimms, July 27, 1923

I have lived sixteen bad years, but I am a good person. Because my life
has been hard, I am very tired. It isn't just being a good person that has made
me tired, but being any kind of a person at all. No matter how good most
of the people I know live, their lives are hard.

—Harriet Jones to John Langston Gwaltney, 1980

In the early 1970s, sixteen-year-old Harriet Jones told John Langston Gwaltney, a black anthropologist who was interviewing ordinary African Americans, "I don't see myself or most people I know in most things I see or read about black people. . . . I wish I could read something or see a movie that would show the people just, well, as my grandmother would say, drylongso. You know, like most of us really are most of the time—together enough to do what we have to do to be decent people."[1] Jones speaks for many of the working-class black women who are the subjects of this book. Although she was never incarcerated, Jones had to deal with an alcoholic mother and a cruel absentee father. Her neighbors supported and took pride in her "civil, principled survival in the face of maddening provocation" but understood that the physical and moral dangers in their urban environment continually challenged Jones's steadfast determination to be a "good person"—or, indeed, "any kind of a person at all"—and led her to lament, "My life has been hard."[2]

Throughout the twentieth century, black working women's words and actions have testified to their struggle to defend themselves and to maintain their own distinctive sense of respectability. The case of Constance Mimms shows the resourcefulness young women exhibited as they sought to be "good" people amid the myriad challenges of the city. Like Jones, Mimms was taught to value respectable behavior by her family and community. In 1923, Mimms's relative reminded the Bedford parolee of her "home teaching and religion." Her urgent letter stressed that, whatever difficulties the Columbia, South Carolina, native encountered in New York City, she should apply that instruction to her everyday life and "Trust God for all things." Charged with incorrigibility by another set of relatives, Mimms entered the criminal justice system because of familial conflict, rather than any alleged failure to negotiate the obstacles posed by urban life. Several years later, Mimms explained that she had incorporated her moral upbringing into her adult identity: "I'm able to take care of myself now . . . and also made a woman of myself." Responding to her relatives' continual questioning of her behavior and life choices, she stressed her maturity and independence: "I know write from rong . . . I am not a child anymore."[3]

Although working-class people's sentiments about morality and respectability seldom appear in the scholarship on early-twentieth-century racial uplift efforts, the poignant declarations made by Mimms and other incarcerated black women and their relatives reveal that working people labored diligently to uplift themselves and their community. Half a century later, Harriet Jones's commentary about ordinary black people's day-to-day struggles to survive and maintain a level of respectability in a volatile and unforgiving urban environment underlines the same point. Jones was frustrated by the proliferation of racial stereotypes that stigmatized and criminalized all impoverished black people, and she yearned for some public acknowledgment of the determined efforts of those who were "together enough to do what we have to do to be decent people." Confronting the long-standing conflation of the working poor's socioeconomic status with their ethical stature, she explained that under her grandmother's tutelage she learned to validate ordinary people's moral compass while disparaging the dominant society's negative assessment of black people. Harriet Jones's struggles with familial tensions and gendered expectations as she sought to make a respectable life for herself are representative of those of black working women living in New York City between 1890 and 1935.

Although the women in this study were incarcerated, they understood the parameters of what it meant to be good, decent people, an understanding they shared with the proponents of racial uplift. Scholarship on racial uplift generally focuses on how the black middle class worked to improve the moral stature and daily existence of the black masses in order to advance the race. When we examine the lives of working women who struggled with issues of moral conduct, however, we find that ideas about appropriate behavior came from these women's own families and communities rather than from middle-class activists. Many families sought to impart a strong work ethic, the value of thrift, and attention to gendered notions of proper demeanor. Many working-class blacks believed that these standards would provide stability in familial and community structures that were battered by institutional discrimination in housing, employment, and public accommodations, as well as the criminal justice system. Indeed, familial tension often resulted when young women disappointed or defied their relatives and, as they saw it, betrayed the moral standards they had inculcated. At the turn of the twentieth century, these private disputes evolved into public and state-influenced conflicts when reform initiatives increasingly regulated the behavior of urban working women.

The state's reforming role as an intrusive as well as invited presence in the lives of working-class people shaped this group's own conceptions of respectability and criminality. In the mid-nineteenth century, reformers convinced legislators that ameliorating the conditions of poor children should become a state responsibility rather than simply the duty of evangelical reformers. Activists' concerns about young women stemmed from their fears about growing female independence under industrial capitalism and the changing social norms connected to leisure that resulted in more and more unsupervised heterosexual interactions. Another pressing fear was the state's inability to eliminate prostitution. From reformers' perspective, the home environment was the "root of all delinquency." Working parents who attempted to survive through their long hours of backbreaking labor were accused of improper parenting and neglect, which were regarded as the root of the newly defined social problem of juvenile delinquency. The wayward minor law gave police power to parents, guardians, and court officers, who could define particular kinds of behavior as putting a young woman "in danger of becoming morally depraved." While families used these state resources to protect their female kin from urban dangers and to reinforce the significance of domestic respectability, reformers saw this use of the law as evidence of their incompetence. With the confluence of mainstream society's assumption about black women's promiscuity and their relatives' concerted efforts to protect them, their behavior was stringently regulated. Conduct—such as truancy, broken curfews, and disobedience—that many would not have deemed "serious offenses against the law" landed many black women in a local or state reformatory for rehabilitation. The racially

Conclusion

discriminatory practices in local rehabilitative institutions forced young black women into Bedford, where they would be treated like criminals who had to prove that they had "reformed" through parole. In many instances, black families who believed their intervention would prevent their female kin's downfall helped to reinforce the state's ideas about working-class and black people's criminality.[4]

While the state's policies served to regulate social behavior, its use of the parole system to employ women as domestic servants illuminates not only its emphasis on feminine domesticity but also young women's rejection of this ideology. In the early twentieth century, industrialization expanded the employment opportunities available to nonblack women and created a crisis for white middle-class women whose leisure time was dependent on, and whose status was based on, their keeping servants. As immigrant and native-born white women left these demanding, often demeaning jobs, black women, and especially southern migrants, filled them.

Although paroled black women had no choice about where they were employed as domestics, they were able to articulate their displeasure with their employers. Constance Mimms was repeatedly sent back to Bedford because her employers found her an unsatisfactory servant. One woman noted that she was "stupid and cannot grasp anything." In one instance, when Mimms was told to wash the front door panels and she asked what she should "put the water in," her employer replied that she could use "anything that she could find," and Mimms took a tea-kettle rather than a bucket or large pan. Clearly, her actions demonstrate that she disliked housework and feigned ignorance when she was told to clean.[5] After all, the sixteen-year-old had worked as a domestic, nurse girl, and waitress before her arrest.[6] Reformers characterized Mimms's behavior as a rejection of domestic employment rather than of her employers, which reinforced their ideas about a problematic working class.

At the turn of the twentieth century, the urban elite—black and white— regarded black migrants as an undifferentiated mass of poor people who were incapable of adjusting to the city. Increasing rates of black criminality—whether it be vagrancy, petty theft, prostitution, or assault—were blamed on the rising black population. Black working people thought differently. While black and white reformers believed that the legacy of slavery made black people unable to handle the fierce competition that characterized the modern metropolis, black migrants showed how much they valued their freedom as wage laborers and citizens. Black southern migrants, Afro-Caribbean immigrants, and native-born black New Yorkers alike fought to make the "theoretical equality of northern life" a reality, even as European immigrants gained rights that they were denied.

Members of the black working class sought to utilize public resources to protect their female kin, not because they considered them dangerous, as did the state. While they claimed that the state should protect them from antiblack violence and racial discrimination, they also felt entitled to those state services that would enable them to rehabilitate their female relatives. The same working-class blacks who sought redress for the police brutality and mob violence they experienced in the 1900 race riot felt equally compelled to protect their female kin by using social welfare services funded by citizens' tax dollars for probation, parole, and institutional support. Even though female kin may have shocked or angered them, relatives held fast to the idea that their citizenship rights entailed reinforcing their working-class respectability by using public institutions. The exclusionary policies of state-sponsored institutions and criminal justice services illustrate how black women were increasingly criminalized rather than rehabilitated. These policies, along with black people's continued mistreatment in the wake of World War I, propelled some reformers into political radicalism that buttressed their community activism. Probation and parole officer Grace Campbell, for example, was involved in the African Blood Brotherhood, which allowed her to criticize the state and seek new paradigms for freedom and equality.

The state's stance toward young black women changed dramatically during the early twentieth century, from viewing black women as simultaneously endangered and dangerous to simply defining them as dangerous during the 1920s and 1930s. Although white evangelical reformers would admit that black women were just as vulnerable to urban risks as white women, they often excluded them from the rehabilitation programs they established. At the turn of the century, Victoria Earle Matthews was the first black reformer to institutionalize black women's protection and link the problem to northern migration. Like most black activists, she had two main concerns: that women were morally endangered within the city and that their behavior would reinforce a dangerous image of black people. Both concerns, she believed, could be addressed by racial uplift, which initially encouraged black women to remain in the South. During the Progressive Era, reformers' initiatives were shaped by a continual influx of southerners. Activists not only sought to save endangered women but began to help migrants adjust to the city, as the formation of the National Urban League shows. White Progressive reformers also established laws that increasingly isolated those potentially dangerous young women in rehabilitative institutions like Bedford. Initially, black women, like most of the other working women, were paroled in New York State. During the 1920s, however, when the fear of the working class also prompted immigration restriction statutes, prison officials began to contend that black women needed to be sent back to the South. Although they argued that the city and particularly Harlem had a bad influence on young women, they defined these women themselves as the real problem. The women chosen for southern parole were considered too dangerous to maintain a respectable and orderly existence in New York. Reverting back to turn-of-the-century inclinations, officials also argued that the South was where black people belonged. Most working women's experiences show how poverty, family disruptions, and changing legal definitions of criminality made women in the North and South ever more vulnerable.

The early life of Ella Fitzgerald, the famous jazz singer, is representative of the plight of young black women living on the precipice of poverty and their never-ending struggle to survive and thrive in urban America. Like so many other young black New Yorkers, Fitzgerald experienced a familial and financial crisis. When her mother died in 1932, whatever stability she had known was disrupted as her stepfather was unable to care for her and she chose not to stay with an aunt for long. Fitzgerald got by in the borderline jobs that reformers worried about—as a numbers runner and a police lookout for a house of ill repute. She was eventually placed in the Colored Orphan Asylum, and after she ran away she was arrested and taken to the New York State Training School for Girls at Hudson, New York. Her talent as a singer and her indomitable determination led to her relationship with Chick Webb's jazz band, which became her parole custodian. After a long, difficult struggle, Fitzgerald was able to make a living in her profession. When Hudson reformatory's last superintendent was interviewed about Fitzgerald, he responded: "How many Ellas are there?" While recognizing that "she turned out to be absolutely one of a kind," he stressed that all the other children at Hudson started out the same way, "[as] human beings, too. In that sense, they are all Ellas."[7] Indeed, before Fitzgerald's "success" she was considered one of the many young black women who needed institutionalization to control their wayward behavior.

Fitzgerald was one of the countless black working women who confronted the poverty and racism that restricted their access to housing, employment, and social space. She and a number of women were able to parlay their talent and skills into recognized "success." Others succumbed to their adverse circumstances. But most of the women in this study were like

Harriet Jones, simply "drylongso," "together enough to do what" they had "to do to be decent people."

Lucy Cox, whose request to "talk with you like a woman" represents the central themes of this book, has the last word here. Cox admitted that her mistakes led to her imprisonment, but she refused to believe that her misstep had blighted her life chances. In the six-page letter she wrote to her parole officer expressing her anger and resentment over being forced to answer to the state and her sister when she had taken responsibility for the actions that led to her incarceration, she captured the sentiments shared by many women caught in similar predicaments. Like these other working women, she defined her character and ambition differently from the society that judged her. Cox simply wanted the opportunity to live up to the ideals that her family imparted to her and to work toward the objectives that she set for herself.

> It makes me dad blame angry to be under my people and the law is behind you. Before I got in trouble I was getting along fine. . . . They didn't know me before I got in this trouble now the world want to bother you in your business. . . . If they want talk let them see me[;] and further more no law in the world cant make a grown woman stay with her people like baby. It is nothing just the matter want to keep grown people down; and had audacity to tell my sister to take me to church just like If I was two years old. I live before I saw such places[.] [W]hat in dadblast do these people know about me[?] I want the whole world keep they mouth of[f] me. . . . I am not going to be under foot of no one before I'll suffer to go to hell first. I Thank God I am independent one more time. . . . My sister didn't get in trouble: It was me.[8]

notes

ABBREVIATIONS

AU   Auburn Correctional Facility, Records of the Department of Correctional Services, Division of Parole, New York State Archives, State Education Department, Albany, New York

BH   Bedford Hills Correctional Facility, 14610-77B Inmate Case Files, ca. 1915–30, 1955–65, Records of the Department of Correctional Services, New York State Archives, State Education Department, Albany, New York

COF   Committee of Fourteen Collection, New York Public Library, Rare Books and Manuscripts Division, Astor, Lenox, and Tilden Foundations, New York, New York

DAP   District Attorney Indictment Papers, New York County, Court of General Sessions, New York City Municipal Archives, Records, and Information Services, New York, New York

DAS   District Attorney Scrapbooks, New York County, New York City Municipal Archives, Records, and Information Services, New York, New York

FIF   B0054 Female Inmate Identification File, 1909–33, Auburn Correctional Facility, Records of the Department of Correctional Services, Division of Parole, New York State Archives, State Education Department, Albany, New York

GHC   George Haynes Collection, Fisk University, Special Collections, Nashville, Tennessee

HNCF   Hampton University News Clippings File, Hampton University, Hampton, Virginia

LHWC   L. Hollingsworth Wood Collection, Haverford College, Quaker and Special Collections, Haverford, Pennsylvania

MHSC   Mabel Hampton Special Collection, Lesbian Herstory Archives, Brooklyn, New York

NULP   National Urban League Papers, Library of Congress, Manuscripts Division, Washington, DC

NYCMA   New York City Municipal Archives, Records, and Information Services, New York, New York

NYPL   New York Public Library Rare Books and Manuscripts Division, Astor, Lenox, and Tilden Foundations, New York, New York

NYSL   New York State Library, Cultural Education Center, Albany, New York

PF   Auburn Prison Female Inmate Case Files, 1920–30, Auburn Correctional Facility, Records of the Department of Correctional Services, B0050 Division of Parole, New York State Archives, State Education Department, Albany, New York

PM   Minutes of Meetings of Board of Parole, 1905–52, Auburn Correctional
      Facility, Records of the Department of Correctional Services, Division of
      Parole, New York State Archives, State Education Department, Albany,
      New York

SCH   Schomburg Center for Research in Black Culture, Manuscripts, Archives,
      and Rare Books Division, New York Public Library, New York, New York

TNCF Tuskegee Institute News Clippings File

WRC   White Rose Mission and Industrial Association Collection, Schomburg
      Center for Research in Black Culture, Manuscripts, Archives, and Rare
      Books Division, New York Public Library, New York, New York

INTRODUCTION

1. Mary Helen Washington, introduction to Cooper, *Voice from the South*, xxxi–xxxvi; Elizabeth Alexander, "'We Must Be about Our Father's Business.'"

2. Inmate #3521, History Blank, September 20, 1923, BH. I have used a pseudonym for inmates' names but have retained original case numbers.

3. Cooper, *Voice from the South*, i–ii, 31. See Deborah Gray White's discussion in *Too Heavy a Load*, 37–39.

4. See Deborah Gray White, *Too Heavy a Load*, 21–55.

5. Inmate #3521, letter from Inmate to Superintendent Amos Baker, May 1, 1924, BH. Cox wrote two prior letters regarding her parole and how she envisioned her independence as a young woman. See Cox's letters of April 13 and April 29, 1924.

6. See Jones, *Labor of Love*; and Hunter, *To 'Joy My Freedom*. Exciting recent research on working-class and poor black women includes Wolcott, *Remaking Respectability*; Rhonda Y. Williams, *Politics of Public Housing*; Gross, *Colored Amazons*; Levenstein, *Movement without Marches*; Orleck, *Storming Caesar's Palace*; and Nadasen, *Welfare Warriors*.

7. Cooper, *Voice from the South*, xxix–xxx.

8. The Bedford records provide an incredibly detailed portrait of working-class women's lives, yet no inmate case files from 1901 to 1916 survived. The remaining records, which vary in documentation, represent a perspective of the women, prison officials, and institution from a different time period.

9. On the history of African Americans and race relations in New York City, see Wilder, *Covenant with Color*; Wilder, *In the Company of Black Men*; Harris, "Slavery, Emancipation, and Class Formation"; Harris, *In the Shadow of Slavery*; Foote, *Black and White*; Leslie M. Alexander, *African or American?*; Sacks, "'To Be a Man and Not a Lackey'"; Sacks, "'To Show Who Was in Charge'"; Sacks, *Before Harlem*; Osofsky, *Harlem*; Scheiner, *Negro Mecca*; Watkins-Owens, *Blood Relations*; San Gupta [SenGupta], "Black and 'Dangerous'?"; and SenGupta, *From Slavery to Poverty*.

10. Peterson, "Contesting Space," 67.

11. U.S. Bureau of the Census, *Negro Population*, 51.

12. "Mission of the White Rose," Seventy-fifth Annual Report, New York City Mission and Tract Society, Woman's Branch (February 1898), 23–24, in Guichard Parris Collection, Box 30, Rare Book and Manuscript Library, Columbia University, New York.

13. U.S. Bureau of the Census, *Negroes in the United States*, 15.

14. Logan, *Negro in American Life and Thought*.

15. George Henry White, "Farewell Speech to the U.S. House of Representatives,

Notes to Pages 1–7

Washington, D.C., January 29, 1901," abridged from the *Congressional Record*, 56th Cong., 2nd sess., 34, 1:1634–38, in Justesen, *In His Own Words*, 206.

16. See Ryan, *Women in Public*, 58–94; and Carby, "Policing the Black Woman's Body," 739–40.

17. SenGupta, *From Slavery to Poverty*, 5. See also Hannah Rosen, *Terror in the Heart of Freedom*, 11–16.

18. SenGupta, *From Slavery to Poverty*, 5, 15.

19. Mitchell, *Righteous Propagation*, 57.

20. See, for example, the important work of Gaines, *Uplifting the Race*; Mitchell, *Righteous Propagation*; and Gross, "Examining the Politics of Respectability." Mitchell addresses the black aspiring class that she notes was distinct from the black elite: "From seamstresses to small proprietors to teachers to skilled tradesmen, the black aspiring class was comprised of workers able to save a little money as well as those who worked multiple jobs to attain class mobility; significantly, it included self-educated women and men as well as those who had attended normal school or college" (9).

21. See Lasch-Quinn, *Black Neighbors*, 9–46.

22. See Painter, *Standing at Armageddon*, xii. She notes, "Much historical writing . . . presents a tableau in which middle- and upper-class people—the well-educated—are the main actors, because historians write from written sources, which educated people produce"; yet she argues, and her work shows, that "working people have also created history."

23. Gaines, *Uplifting the Race*, 14–17.

24. Wolcott, *Remaking Respectability*, 4–5. See, for example, Bailey "'Will the Real Bill Banks Please Stand Up?'"; Rosenzweig, *Eight Hours for What We Will*; and Ross, "'Not the Sort that Would Sit on the Doorstep.'"

25. Higginbotham, *Righteous Discontent*, 185–229.

26. Wolcott, *Remaking Respectability*, 6–7.

27. I use the terms "working class" and "working poor" interchangeably, not because I do not recognize any socioeconomic distinctions between them but rather to emphasize that the poor worked and held the same substantive ideas about respectability that the more stable working class did. Similarly, Gretchen Lemke-Santangelo (*Abiding Courage*, 46–47) notes that World War II–era black migrant women were influenced by their sharecropper parents: "The values they acquired from their elders—family loyalty, frugality, self-sufficiency, cooperation, reciprocity, and respect for education—came directly from sharecropping roots."

28. Wolcott, *Remaking Respectability*, 7–8. Also see Harley, "When Your Work Is Not Who You Are."

29. For a perspective on conflicts within the black working class, see Higginbotham, "Rethinking Vernacular Culture."

30. See Brenzel, *Daughters of the State*; Freedman, *Their Sisters' Keepers*; Odem, *Delinquent Daughters*; Ruth Alexander, *"Girl Problem"*; and Knupfer, *Reform and Resistance*.

31. See Butler, *Gendered Justice*; Dodge, *Whores and Thieves*; and Gross, *Colored Amazons*.

32. For additional background on the development and significance of women's reformatory and custodial institutions, see Rafter, *Partial Justice*.

33. See Holt, "Marking," and Earl Lewis, "To Turn on a Pivot," for important discussions regarding how racial identity and formation were shaped by black people's varied

responses to the state. Michel Foucault's work is also useful in addressing how families and communities outside of state institutions became socialized to accept certain ideas about what constituted illegal behavior and criminality. See Foucault, *Discipline and Punish* and *History of Sexuality*. Works such as Painter, *Narrative of Hosea Hudson*; Kelley, *Race Rebels*; Hunter, *To 'Joy My Freedom*; and SenGupta, "Elites, Subalterns, and American Identities," demonstrate that black people resisted, as well as coexisted with, state control.

34. Jno W. Wright, "Afro-American Women—They, Not White Women, Really Need Protection," *New York Age*, December 13, 1906.

35. Paul, "Group of Virginia Negroes," 31–33.

36. See letter from Moore to Dunbar, January 23, 1898, in Metcalf, "Letters of Paul and Alice Dunbar," 393.

37. Elsa Barkley Brown, "Imaging Lynching," 108.

38. See, for example, Kelley, "'We Are Not What We Seem'"; Wolcott, *Remaking Respectability*, 93–130; and Phillips, *AlabamaNorth*.

39. Elsa Barkley Brown, "Imaging Lynching," 108.

40. Inmate #2507, Verified History, August 12, 1917, BH.

41. Ibid.

42. Inmate #2507, Information of Patient's Mother, September 16, 1917, BH.

43. Inmate #2507, Verified History, August 12, 1917, BH. The file notes: "It seems possible that she may be living with a consort."

44. Mitchell, *Righteous Propagation*, 9–10.

45. Inmate #2507, letter from Inmate's Mother to Superintendent, June 22, 1920, BH.

CHAPTER ONE

1. Quoted anonymously in Joint Committee to Study the Employment of Colored Women in New York City and Brooklyn, *New Day*, 12–13.

2. Inmate #2490, Verified Statement, July 9, 1917, BH.

3. Inmate #3507, History Blank, August 27, 1923, BH.

4. Inmate #3499, History Blank, August 21, 1923, BH.

5. Inmate #3499, letter from Dorothy Carpenter, City Mission Society, to Amos T. Baker, July 25, 1924, BH.

6. This term takes off from the title of Christine Stansell's study of white women: *City of Women*.

7. James Weldon Johnson, *Black Manhattan*, 3–26; Scheiner, *Negro Mecca*, 1–6; Harris, *In the Shadow of Slavery*; Foote, *Black and White Manhattan*; Berlin and Harris, *Slavery in New York*.

8. Scheiner, *Negro Mecca*, 4, 6.

9. Painter, *Exodusters*; Mitchell, *Righteous Propagation*.

10. Ida B. Wells, "Pleading for Her Race," *Brooklyn Eagle*, December 11, 1894.

11. Ida B. Wells, *Southern Horrors: Lynch Law in All Its Phases* (1892), in Wells, *Southern Horrors*, 70, 72.

12. Wells, *Southern Horrors*, 68.

13. Scheiner, *Negro Mecca*, 8.

14. "20,000 Southern Negroes Planning to Come North," *Brooklyn Eagle*, March 17, 1901.

15. Scheiner, *Negro Mecca*, 8–9. Immigration from the Caribbean also contributed to

the city's growing black population; at least 28,000 people arrived from the West Indies between 1900 and 1920.

16. See Henri, *Black Migration*; Painter, *Standing at Armageddon*; Trotter, *Great Migration*; Clark-Lewis, *Living In, Living Out*, 9–66; Jones, *Labor of Love*, 110–95; Hunter, *To 'Joy My Freedom*, 232–38; Griffin, *"Who Set You Flowin'?,"* 13–47; Grossman, *Land of Hope*, 13–119; Earl Lewis, *In Their Own Interests*; Marks, *Farewell*, 19–48; Phillips, *AlabamaNorth*; Mitchell, *Righteous Propagation*; and Hahn, *Nation Under Our Feet*.

17. Paul, "Group of Virginia Negroes," 33–34.

18. Inmate #3486, letter from Inmate's Aunt to Superintendent Baker, October 21, 1924, BH.

19. Locke, "Community Life of a Harlem Group of Negroes," 8.

20. Both quotes from Scheiner, *Negro Mecca*, 116.

21. Washington, *Up from Slavery*, 107, 106–7.

22. Washington, "Industrial Education for the Negro," 13–14.

23. Gaines, *Uplifting the Race*, 179–208, esp. 180–84.

24. Paul Laurence Dunbar, "Negroes of the Tenderloin," *New York Sun*, September 4, 1897.

25. "Wealthy Negro Citizens," *New York Times*, July 14, 1895. Also see Osofsky, *Harlem*, 5–6.

26. Haynes, "Conditions among Negroes in the Cities," 111.

27. Ovington, *Walls Came Tumbling Down*, 21. Also see Wilder, *Covenant with Color*, 113–18.

28. Paul Laurence Dunbar, "Negroes of the Tenderloin," *New York Sun*, September 4, 1897.

29. Ibid.

30. Joint Committee to Study the Employment of Colored Women in New York City and Brooklyn, *New Day*, 13.

31. Inmate #2490, Information Concerning Patient, Laboratory of Social Hygiene, August 9, 1917, BH.

32. Joint Committee to Study the Employment of Colored Women in New York City and Brooklyn, *New Day*, 13.

33. Du Bois, *Philadelphia Negro*.

34. Du Bois, *Black North*, 5.

35. Ibid. Also see Tera W. Hunter's discussion of Du Bois's analysis of black Philadelphia in "'Brotherly Love.'"

36. Osofsky, *Harlem*, 4.

37. Miller, "Surplus Negro Women," 523.

38. U.S. Bureau of the Census, *Negro Population*, 150. The figures in 1900 were 46,618 black men and 52,614 black women, while the figures in 1910 were 64,034 black men and 70,157 black women.

39. See Carby, "Policing the Black Woman's Body," esp. 741.

40. Du Bois, *Some Notes*, 3.

41. "For the Benefit of the Colored Race," *Standard Union*, ca. 1911, Item #494, HNCF.

42. Du Bois, *Black North*, 5.

43. Matthews, "Some of the Dangers," 64, 68.

44. For the meanings of this term, see Meyerowitz, *Women Adrift*.

45. Eleanor Alexander, *Lyrics of Sunshine and Shadow*, 52–54, 59; Hull, *Color, Sex, and Poetry*, 34–35. For more information on Moore's background, see the biographical

entry for Mrs. Alice Dunbar Nelson in *The National Cyclopedia of the Colored Race*, ed. Clement Richardson (Montgomery, AL: National Publishing Co., 1919), 489; and Gaines, *Uplifting the Race*, 209–33. Straight College is now Dillard University.

46. Eleanor Alexander, *Lyrics of Sunshine and Shadow*, 61.

47. Ibid., 44, 66–73. The photograph attached to Moore's published book attracted the attention of poet Paul Laurence Dunbar. Their two-year courtship was conducted mostly through correspondence. Also see Gaines, *Uplifting the Race*, 210.

48. Eleanor Alexander, *Lyrics of Sunshine and Shadow*, 44; Gaines, *Uplifting the Race*, 211.

49. Hull, *Color, Sex, and Poetry*, 40–41; letter from Moore to Dunbar, July 6, 1895, in Metcalf, "Letters of Paul and Alice Dunbar," 57.

50. Letter from Moore to Dunbar, December 18, 1897, in Metcalf, "Letters of Paul and Alice Dunbar," 296. A year later, Moore was still unable to retrieve the watch.

51. Hull, *Color, Sex, and Poetry*, 41; Metcalf, "Letters of Paul and Alice Dunbar."

52. Letter from Moore to Dunbar, July 6, 1895, in Metcalf, "Letters of Paul and Alice Dunbar," 2, 57. For a reference to Moore's teacher certification, see letter from Dunbar to Moore, March 26, 1897, 133–35, in ibid.

53. Letter from Moore to Dunbar, June 19, 1897, in Metcalf, "Letters of Paul and Alice Dunbar," 164.

54. Inmate #2490, Statement of Girl, July 9, 1917, BH.

55. Du Bois, "Negroes of Farmville, Virginia," 194.

56. Ibid.

57. Inmate #2490, Statement of Girl, July 9, 1917, BH.

58. Du Bois, "Negroes of Farmville, Virginia," 179.

59. Ibid., 178.

60. Fannie Barrier Williams, "Northern Negro's Autobiography," 12. Stephanie Shaw notes that during the Jim Crow era some black families prevented their daughters from taking domestic work because "one eminent source of danger was white males, who might not only victimize these daughters, but against whom black families had no recourse" (Shaw, *What a Woman Ought to Be*, 24).

61. Inmate #2490, Staff Meeting, Laboratory of Social Hygiene, August 26, 1917, BH.

62. Inmate #2490, Verified History, July 9, 1917, BH. Payne also had three miscarriages.

63. Hunter, "'Brotherly Love,'" 145.

64. Inmate #3489, Summary Report of Application for Parole, ca. 1928, BH.

65. Anderson, *This Was Harlem*, 35.

66. Letter from Dunbar to Moore, March 7, 1897, in Metcalf, "Letters of Paul and Alice Dunbar," 122.

67. Letter from Moore to Dunbar, February 1, 1898, in Metcalf, "Letters of Paul and Alice Dunbar," 415.

68. Inmate #2490, Statement of Girl, July 9, 1917, BH.

69. Inmate #2490, Verified History, July 9, 1917; and Staff Meeting, Laboratory of Social Hygiene, August 26, 1917, BH.

70. Inmate #2490, Verified History, July 9, 1917, BH.

71. See Eleanor Alexander, *Lyrics of Sunshine and Shadow*, 1–12; and Hull, *Color, Sex, and Poetry*, 46–47.

72. See Metcalf's commentary in "Letters of Paul and Alice Dunbar," 243; and Eleanor Alexander, *Lyrics of Sunshine and Shadow*, 130–45.

73. Letter from Moore to Dunbar, December 18, 1897, in Metcalf, "Letters of Paul and Alice Dunbar," 296. After the incident, Dunbar wrote apologetically: "I might have told you before but I was ashamed even half-drunk as I was of my own bestiality. . . . I will give you a whole life of devotion to wipe out that one night's madness" (letter from Dunbar to Moore, November 22, 1897, in ibid., 251).

74. See Eleanor Alexander, *Lyrics of Sunshine and Shadow*, 165–70.

75. U.S. Bureau of the Census, *Statistics of Women at Work*, 34. "Indian" and "Mongolian" (Asian) were included in this category. Also see Katzman, *Seven Days a Week*, 80–85.

76. Peiss, *Cheap Amusements*, 12.

77. Wilder, *Covenant with Color*, 44.

78. Harris, "Slavery, Emancipation, and Class Formation." Also see Harris, *In the Shadow of Slavery*.

79. "The Dusky Race: Condition of the Colored Population of New-York," *New York Times*, March 2, 1869.

80. "Wealthy Negro Citizens," *New York Times*, July 4, 1895.

81. Fannie Barrier Williams, "Our Women Bread Winners," *New York Age*, October 6, 1904, Item #551, HNCF.

82. Inmate #2504, Statement of Girl, August 8, 1917, BH.

83. U.S. Bureau of the Census, *Statistics of Women at Work*, 9–10, 12. Among young and presumably single immigrant white women, the proportion who were employed was high—56 percent of those aged sixteen to twenty and 42 percent of those aged twenty-one to twenty-four—but fell sharply thereafter; only 20 percent of those aged twenty-five to thirty-four were employed. Also see Katzman, *Seven Days a Week*, 81–84.

84. Fannie Barrier Williams, "Our Women Bread Winners," *New York Age*, October 6, 1904, Item #551, HNCF. Also see "Immigration Evils," *New York Age*, May 16, 1891.

85. "The Negro in New York," *New York Sun*, February 10, 1901, Item #507, HNCF. Marcy Sacks notes that "black servants . . . had been a mark of stature in nineteenth-century New York, harkening back to the city's slave era. But by the last decade of the century, the white elite's custom of using black servants had given way to the practice of employing white foreigners or Asians to work in their homes" (Sacks, "'To Be a Man and Not a Lackey,'" 47).

86. Bureau of Social Hygiene, *Housing Conditions*, 59.

87. Fannie Barrier Williams, "Our Women Bread Winners," *New York Age*, October 6, 1904, Item #551, HNCF.

88. Inmate #2507, Mental Examination, Attitude, September 26, 1917, BH.

89. Inmate #3333, History Blank, December 26, 1922, BH.

90. Inmate #4501, Catholic Protective Society, Parole Report, October 1928, BH.

91. Joint Committee to Study the Employment of Colored Women in New York City and Brooklyn, *New Day*, 13.

92. "Negress Besieged House," *New York Times*, August 15, 1901.

93. Inmate #4498, letter to Inmate from Her Sister (confiscated), February 5, [ca. 1926], BH.

94. Inmate #760, ca. April 30, 1912, vol. 3 (1911–12), PM. I use pseudonyms for inmates' names but retain their original case numbers.

95. Inmate #814, ca. December 18, 1911, vol. 3 (1911–12), PM.

96. Inmate #4118, letter from Inmate to Superintendent Leo Palmer, December 4, 1927, BH.

97. Inmate #2490, Verified History, July 9, 1917, BH.

98. *Twenty-Four Hundred Negro Families in Harlem: An Interpretation of the Living Conditions of Small Wage Earners*, New York Urban League (May 1927), 24, 23, SCH. One hundred and three women were employed in miscellaneous occupations such as stenography, dressmaking, and hairdressing.

99. "Gimbel Discharges All Colored Help," *New York Age*, February 6, 1913.

100. Paul, "Group of Virginia Negroes," 28–29.

101. Inmate #3724, letter from Dorothy Carpenter, City Mission Society, to Superintendent Amos Baker, February 10, 1925, BH.

102. Inmate #4079, letter from Elizabeth Kjaer, City Mission Society, to Superintendent Amos Baker, July 16, 1926, and September 4, 1926, BH.

103. Riis, *How the Other Half Lives*, 115.

104. Federation of Churches and Christian Organizations in New York City, Eighth Annual Report, January 1904, 16.

105. "Negro Colonies Affect Realty," *New York Sun*, January 21, 1912, Item #507, HNCF.

106. Inmate #2490, Verified History, July 9, 1917, BH.

107. *Twenty-Four Hundred Negro Families in Harlem: An Interpretation of the Living Conditions of Small Wage Earners*, New York Urban League (May 1927), 8, 11, 13, SCH.

108. "Housing Conditions among Negroes in Harlem, New York City," *Bulletin of the National League on Urban Conditions among Negroes* 4, no. 2 (January 1915): 9.

109. Inmate #2473, Home Conditions, July 21, 1917, BH.

110. Inmate #3483, letter from Amy Prevost to Superintendent Amos Baker, January 15, 1923, BH.

111. Inmate #3720, letter from Amy Prevost to Superintendent Amos Baker, October 8, 1925, BH.

112. Bureau of Social Hygiene, *Housing Conditions*, 57.

113. Ogburn, "Richmond Negro in New York City," 50.

114. Inmate #2480, Statement of Girl, June 23, 1917, BH.

115. Inmate #2504, Statement of Girl, August 8, 1917, BH.

116. Clyde, "Negro in New York City," 29.

117. Bureau of Social Hygiene, *Housing Conditions*, 61.

118. Pleck, "Two-Parent Household," 21–23.

119. Blascoer, *Colored School Children*, 78.

120. Inmate #2507, Home Condition, September 16, 1917, BH.

121. Osofsky, *Harlem*, 138–41.

122. Du Bois, *Philadelphia Negro*, 194. Lawrence Veiller said that in immigrant households "the lodger evil . . . led to the breaking up of homes and families, to the downfall and subsequent degraded career of young women to grave immoralities" (*Housing Reform*, 35).

123. Inmate #635, ca. August 1911, vol. 3 (1911–12), PM.

124. Inmate #1330, ca. February 1928, vol. 11 (1927–28), PM.

125. Inmate #2493, Staff Meeting, September 8, 1917, BH.

126. Inmate #2493, Verified History, July 12, 1917, BH.

127. Interview with Mabel Hampton by Joan Nestle, *Feminary* 10, no. 2, MHSC; Inmate #3696, BH. I have revealed this inmate's name in accordance with the Freedom of Information Act of 1966, 5 USC Sec. 552, Part I, Subchapter II.

128. Du Bois, *Black North*, 11–12.

129. Samuel J. Battle, February 1960, 15, Oral History Research Office, Rare Book and Manuscript Library, Columbia University, New York, NY.

130. Paul, "Group of Virginia Negroes," 31–33.

131. See Gellman and Quigley, *Jim Crow New York*; Harris, *In the Shadow of Slavery*; Scheiner, *Negro Mecca*, 170–220; and Wilder, *Covenant with Color*.

132. *1895 N.Y. Laws Ch. 1042*.

133. Ibid. My interpretation of the law was esp. influenced by Scheiner, *Negro Mecca*, 191–92.

134. "A Misdirected Effort," *New York Times*, June 18, 1895.

135. "Comedy in Color," *New York Herald*, June 17, 1895; "A Misdirected Effort," *New York Times*, June 18, 1895; "Colored Folk and Their Rights," *New York Tribune*, June 10, 1895; "Hotel Men Are Worried," *New York Times*, June 19, 1895; "Seeking to Gain Profit," *New York Times*, June 21, 1895; "Malby's Law Denounced," *New York Times*, August 14, 1895.

136. "A Misdirected Effort," *New York Times*, June 18, 1895.

137. Riis, *How the Other Half Lives*, 117. For a critical view of how Riis approached his subjects, see Yochelson and Czitrom, *Rediscovering Jacob Riis*.

138. Ogburn, "Richmond Negro in New York City"; Johnstone, "Negro in New York"; Hopper, "Northern Negro Group"; Paul, "Group of Virginia Negroes"; Locke, "Community Life of a Harlem Group of Negroes"; Clyde, "Negro in New York City."

139. David Levering Lewis, *W. E. B. Du Bois*, 190. Du Bois addresses this specifically in *Dusk of Dawn*, 58–59.

140. Hopper, "Northern Negro Group," 2.

141. Ibid., 24.

142. "Her Views on the Malby Law," *New York Times*, June 22, 1895.

143. "More Slavery at the South: A Negro Nurse," *Independent* 62 (January 25, 1912): 196–200, reprinted in *Plain Folk: The Life Stories of Undistinguished Americans*, ed. David M. Katzman and William M. Tuttle Jr. (Urbana: University of Illinois Press, 1982), 182.

144. "The Urban Negro Population," *Courier-Journal*, August 1900, Item #456, HNCF. See also Sacks, "'To Be a Man and Not a Lackey,'" 45.

145. Sacks, "'To Show Who Was in Charge,'" 800.

146. Blascoer, *Colored School Children*, 23.

147. McAdoo, *Guarding a Great City*, 98.

148. "Three Colored Women Get the Best of Two Officers," *Brooklyn Eagle*, May 12, 1896.

149. Inmate #2496, Statement of Girl, July 20, 1917, BH.

150. "Notorious Stool Pigeon for Police Engaged in Trapping Decent, Hard-Working Girls," *New York Age*, July 5, 1924; also see *New York Age*, July 12 and 19, 1924.

151. Blascoer, *Colored School Children*, 23.

152. Ibid., 24.

153. "20,000 Negroes Live in Harlem," *New York Age*, May 11, 1911.

154. "Many Arrests for Loitering," *New York Age*, August 10, 1911.

155. "Housing Conditions among Negroes in Harlem, New York City," *Bulletin of the National League on Urban Conditions among Negroes* 4, no. 2 (January 1915): 25.

156. Ibid.

157. Du Bois, *Some Notes*, 3.

CHAPTER TWO

1. May Enoch (colored), In the Matter of the Inquest into the Death of Robert J. Thorpe, Before Hon. Jacob E. Bausch, Coroner, and a Jury, August 22, 1900, Case #32015, Box 608, DAP.

2. "Mob Rule in New York. Negroes Shot Down. Police Charge Crowds" (unidentified newspaper clipping, ca. August 16, 1900), Item #456, HNCF. On the Draft Riots, see Jane E. Dabel, *Respectable Woman*, 109–28; Peterson, "Contesting Space"; Harris, *In the Shadow of Slavery*, 280–88; and Bernstein, *New York City Draft Riots*.

3. Marilynn Johnson, *Street Justice*, 57–69, highlights black women's encounters with the police. Most scholars have addressed this incident through the lens of rising ethnic and racial tensions and interracial violence at the turn of the century in the urban North. See, for example, James Weldon Johnson, *Black Manhattan*, 126–30; Ottley and Weatherby, *Negro in New York*, 166–68; Scheiner, *Negro Mecca*, 121–29; Osofsky, *Harlem*, 46–52; and Luker, *Social Gospel in Black and White*, 179–80.

4. Weisenfeld, *African American Women and Christian Activism*; Sacks, *Before Harlem*, 39–71; Val Marie Johnson, "Defining Social Evil," 319–61.

5. For working-class communities' response to police brutality in the urban South, see Hunter, *To 'Joy My Freedom*.

6. For more on police brutality in New York, see Marilynn Johnson, *Street Justice*.

7. Gaines, *Uplifting the Race*, 1–5, esp. 2.

8. Elsa Barkley Brown, "Imaging Lynching," 108.

9. "Negro Pastor Defies Police to Answer," *New York Times*, August 27, 1900.

10. Bederman, *Manliness and Civilization*, 1–44, esp. 16–31.

11. Mitchell, *Righteous Propagation*, 51–75, esp. 57–58.

12. Affidavit of Benjamin McCoy, September 7, 1900, CPL, *Story of the Riot*, 25.

13. "A Disgrace to the Police" (editorial), *New York Times*, August 17, 1900.

14. Weisenfeld, *African American Women and Christian Activism*, 69–74; Sacks, *Before Harlem*; Val Marie Johnson, "Defining Social Evil," 319–61.

15. "Housing Conditions among Negroes in Harlem, New York City," *Bulletin of the National Urban League on Urban Conditions among Negroes* 4, no. 2 (January 1915): 25.

16. Griffin, "Black Feminists and Du Bois," 35. Also see Griffin, "'Ironies of the Saint,'" 215–19.

17. Welter, "Cult of True Womanhood." Although Welter located the origins of this notion of middle-class white womanhood in the Northeast, the ideology became hegemonic. Pascoe, *Relations of Rescue*, shows that it was influential across the continent. Rural, poor, and working-class white women, as well as black women, were unable to live up to these standards.

18. See, for example, Jacqueline Dowd Hall, "Mind That Burns in Each Body," 335. See also Feimster, *Southern Horrors*.

19. Higginbotham, "African-American Women's History," esp. 256–58 and 262–66.

20. Griffin, "Black Feminists and Du Bois," 35; see also Griffin, "'Ironies of the Saint,'" 218–19. Barbara Omolade (*Rising Song*, 13) argues that

> protecting black women was the most significant measure of black manhood and the central aspect of black male patriarchy. Black men felt outrage and shame at their frequent inability to protect black women, not merely from the whippings and hard work, but also from the master/lover's touch. During and after slavery, black men spoke out angrily against the harsh treatment of black women, many

vowing never again to allow black women to be sexually abused and economically exploited. Their methods often became rigidly patriarchal; however, they did in many instances keep black women from becoming the open prey of the white man.

21. Statement of Edward Smith, October 22, 1900, Case #32015, *People v. Arthur Harris*, County of New York, Box 608, DAP. This warning did not identify the assailant as a white man.

22. Griffin, "Black Feminists and Du Bois," 35.

23. Weisenfeld, *African American Women and Christian Activism*, 70.

24. On the politics of respectability, see Higginbotham, *Righteous Discontent*, 185–229.

25. Ross, "'Not the Sort that Would Sit on the Doorstep,'" 39. Also see Brown and Kimball, "Mapping the Terrain of Black Richmond."

26. May Enoch (colored), In the Matter of the Inquest into the Death of Robert J. Thorpe, Before Hon. Jacob E. Bausch, Coroner, and a Jury, August 22, 1900, Case #32015, Box 608, DAP.

27. Val Marie Johnson, "Defining Social Evil," 319–59; Marilynn Johnson, *Street Justice*, 57; Weisenfeld, *African American Women and Christian Activism*, 63. See account of Edward Round (night watchman for the American Theatre), In the Matter of the Inquest into the Death of Robert J. Thorpe, August 22, 1900, Case #32015, Box 608, DAP.

28. For information about Harris and Enoch's living arrangement, see Osofsky, *Harlem*, 46–47. On the Tenderloin, see Gilfoyle, *City of Eros*, 203–10, esp. 209–10; and Anderson, *This Was Harlem*, 13; quotation from Scheiner, *Negro Mecca*, 114.

29. Marilynn Johnson, *Street Justice*, 57.

30. Matthews, "Negroes of New York."

31. "Two Women Chase and Capture a Sneak Thief," *New York Journal*, July 23, 1900, Reel 26, DAS.

32. "Tenderloin Robberies as Told by Moss Agents," *Brooklyn Eagle*, August 9, 1899.

33. "Binning Arrests Three in the Tenderloin, but All Are Exonerated," *The World*, June 20, 1900, Reel 26, DAS.

34. Statement of Arthur Harris, Fifth Police Precinct Station House, Washington, DC, August 19, 1900, Case #32015, Box 608, DAP. Also see Osofsky, *Harlem*, 46.

35. "Harris is Caught; Pleads Self-Defense," *The World*, August 27, 1900.

36. Information about May Enoch's background from Statement of Arthur Harris, Fifth Police Precinct Station House, Washington, DC, August 19, 1900, Case #32015, Box 608, DAP; also see Osofsky, *Harlem*, 47.

37. Quoted in Marilynn Johnson, *Street Justice*, 41–42; also see Gilfoyle, *City of Eros*, 203.

38. Marilynn Johnson, *Street Justice*, 42. See also the 1894 Lexow Committee Investigation, in Chin, *New York City Police Corruption Investigation Commissions*, vol. 1.

39. Marilynn Johnson, *Street Justice*, 42–45.

40. Ibid., 102.

41. "With Magistrate Pool," *New York Times*, August 31, 1898.

42. Ibid.

43. "Price, Pool, and Tenderloin," *New York Times*, September 1, 1898.

44. Ryan, *Women in Public*, 58–94, esp. 70–74.

45. Testimony of Mrs. James Lockett, In the Matter of the Investigation of the Conduct of the Police Force during the "Negro" Riot (Before Committee on Rules and Disci-

pline), September 19, 1900, p. 124, New York City of the Mayor Robert Van Wyck Administration, Departmental Correspondence, Received 1898–1901, Roll 4, NYCMA. Lockett was arrested along with her husband during the riot.

46. "The Race Prejudice Persists," *Brooklyn Eagle*, August 16, 1900, Item #456, HNCF.

47. "The Urban Negro Population," *Courier-Journal*, n.d. [August 1900], Item #456, HNCF, which repeats the conclusions of an article in the *New York Evening Post*.

48. "The Negro Riot—A Warning," *Brooklyn Citizen*, August 16, 1900, Item #456, HNCF. For a discussion of how negative stereotypes were reflected in early-twentieth-century entertainment, see Sacks, "'To Be a Man and Not a Lackey,'" 44–45.

49. For more on Marshall's Hotel, see Fronc, "Horns of the Dilemma."

50. Letter from Moore to Dunbar, February 8, 1898, in Metcalf, "Letters of Paul and Alice Dunbar," 433. In their letters, Moore and Dunbar often referred to each other as husband and wife before they eloped on March 6, 1898. Kevin Gaines addresses this correspondence and Dunbar's article in *Uplifting the Race*, 181–82.

51. Paul Laurence Dunbar, "The Negroes of the Tenderloin," *New York Sun*, September 4, 1897. Dunbar also expressed these sentiments in his 1902 novel, *Sport of the Gods* (New York: New American Library, 1999). For an extended discussion of how the book illuminated Dunbar's racial uplift perspective, see *Uplifting the Race*, 182, 184, 187–93.

52. Paul Laurence Dunbar, "The Negroes of the Tenderloin," *New York Sun*, September 4, 1897.

53. Matthews, "Negroes of New York."

54. On the political implications of black women's rape in the South during Reconstruction, see Hannah Rosen, "'Not That Sort of Women'"; Hannah Rosen, *Terror in the Heart of Freedom*; and Cardyn, "Sexualized Racism."

55. Discussing the 1991 confirmation hearings for Supreme Court justice Clarence Thomas, who protested that Anita Hill's charges of sexual harassment represented a televised "lynching," Elsa Barkley Brown ("Imaging Lynching," 102) asks: "I wonder why it is that people don't remember the lynching of Black women and the brutality of that experience. Why it is that the other experiences of violence that have so permeated the history of Black women in the United States—the rape, the sexual and other forms of physical abuse as employees in white homes, the contemporary domestic and public sexual and other physical violence—are not as vividly and importantly retained in our memory." Darlene Clark Hine has observed that many black women migrated as a result of the sexual abuse they experienced from black and white men. See her "Black Migration" and "Rape and the Inner Lives of Black Women."

56. "Charges against Policemen—A Detective on Trial for an Illegal Arrest—Complaints by Colored Women against Patrolmen," *New York Times*, March 25, 1879. Significantly, the *Times* revealed that all of the complaints were referred to the Committee on Rules and Discipline for investigation. I am indebted to Marilynn Johnson for sharing her early research about black women and police brutality.

57. Marilynn Johnson, *Street Justice*, 22.

58. Cooper, *Voice from the South*, 91.

59. Schechter, *Ida B. Wells-Barnett*, 43; Wells, *Crusade for Justice*, 18–20.

60. Harper, "Woman's Political Future," 245.

61. See Deborah Gray White, *Too Heavy a Load*, 21–55; and Shaw, "Black Club Women."

62. See, for instance, Dale, "'Social Equality'"; Mack, "Law, Society, Identity"; and Goings and Page, "African Americans versus the Memphis Street Railway Company."

63. Welke, "When All the Women Were White." Also see Giddings, *Ida*, 40–68, esp. 54–56, 60–68; and Higginbotham, "African-American Women's History," 258–66.

64. Inmate #575, ca. October 15, 1906, vol. 1 (1905–08), PM; B0053 Registers of Female Inmates Received, 1893–1933, AU. I use pseudonyms for inmates' names but retain their original case numbers.

65. Inmate #744, ca. June 22, 1910, vol. 2 (1909–10), PM.

66. Inmate #4498, Preliminary Investigation, H8804, Blanche S. Beardsley, ca. March 1926, Probation Bureau City Magistrates Court, BH.

67. Marilynn Johnson (*Street Justice*, 308 n. 12) argues that, like other daily newspapers, the

> *Times* covered only those brutality cases it considered most sensational or newsworthy. There were no doubt many routine cases that were not publicized, and certain types of incidents may have been omitted altogether. As an elite Republican paper, the *Times* was eager to chronicle the abuses of a Tammany-controlled police department. . . . Similarly, abuses against women, children, the sick or the elderly, and other vulnerable individuals received special attention because of their dramatic value in vilifying the police. It is thus likely that brutality complaints brought by poor immigrants and ordinary working men and women were underrepresented in the *Times'* pages.

68. *New York Times*, March 25, 1879. These women's predicaments with authority over their respectability and place within the public sphere have ample precedents during both the imposition and the overturning of segregation. Respectability came into play in Montgomery, Alabama, in 1955, when black people were deciding which case of bus driver harassment to press. Unmarried mothers had been rejected as plaintiffs for test cases; Rosa Parks, who was married and an NAACP member, was considered a perfect central character. See Sitkoff, *Struggle for Black Equality*, 39.

69. "Not Quite Free Yet," *New York Times*, February 26, 1888.

70. "Policeman Accused by a Colored Woman," *New York Times*, November 22, 1894.

71. "A Policeman's Brutality: A Colored Woman Insulted and Beaten and No Help Given Her," *New York Times*, December 26, 1886, 5.

72. Ibid.

73. Ibid.

74. Statement of Herbert Small, In the Matter of the Inquest into the Death of Robert J. Thorpe, August 22, 1900, Case #32015, Box 608, DAP.

75. Account of Edward Rounds, In the Matter of the Inquest into the Death of Robert J. Thorpe, August 22, 1900, Case #32015, Box 608, DAP.

76. "Race Riot in New York City: Ten Thousand White People Spread Terror in the Tenderloin District," *New York Age*, August 23, 1900, Item #457, HNCF.

77. "Foresaw Brother's End," *The World (Evening)*, August 16, 1900.

78. *New York Times*, August 14, 1900, 12. For more on the lack of attention paid to May Enoch's role in the riot, see Weisenfeld, *African American Women and Christian Activism*, 73.

79. See weather report, *New York Evening Post*, August 11, 1900; and "Hottest August 11 Recorded—Cooler Weather Promised," *New York Herald*, August 12, 1900. The *Herald* reported that twenty-six persons died from the effects of the heat and that forty-six suffered from heat prostration. See also "Hottest Day of the Year," *New York Times*, August 12, 1900.

80. Statement of Arthur Harris, August 19, 1900, Fifth Precinct Station-House, Washington, DC, Case #32015, Box 608, DAP.

81. Statement of Edward Smith, October 22, 1900, *People v. Arthur Harris*, County of New York, Case #32015, Box 608, DAP.

82. Statement of Arthur Harris, August 19, 1900, Fifth Precinct Station-House, Washington, DC, Case #32015, Box 608, DAP. The events leading to the death of policeman Robert Thorpe can be found in the *People v. Arthur Harris* inquest and indictment papers. Also see Marilynn Johnson, *Street Justice*, 57–58; Weisenfeld, *African American Women and Christian Activism*, 69–70; Val Marie Johnson, "Defining Social Evil," 319–59; Sacks, *Before Harlem*, 39–40; and Osofsky, *Harlem*, 46–47.

83. "Negroes Wound a Policeman," *New York Times*, August 13, 1900; "Thorpe Dies of Wounds," *New York Times*, August 14, 1900.

84. From Roosevelt Hospital to Coroner's Office, Borough of Manhattan, New York, Statement and Particulars of the Death of Robert J. Thorpe, August 13, 1900, Case #32015, Box 608, DAP; "Thorpe's Fiancée May Die of Broken Heart," *The World*, August 19, 1900.

85. Osofsky, "Race Riot," esp. 19–22; Shapiro, *White Violence*, 93–95; Sacks, *Before Harlem*, 40; Weisenfeld, *African American Women and Christian Activism*, 69–71.

86. "Race Riot in New York City: Ten Thousand White People Spread Terror in the Tenderloin District," *New York Age*, August 23, 1900, Item #457, HNCF.

87. "Quiet After Rioting," *New York Evening Post*, August 16, 1900. See also Affidavit of Josephine Bullock, September 10, 1900, CPL, *Story of the Riot*, 55.

88. The *Southwestern Christian Advocate*, a Methodist journal, argued that "the occurrence tends to confirm us in the opinion that we have so long held, that the North is being more rapidly Southernized in its feeling toward the Negro than is the South being influenced by what has always been understood to be the feeling of the North toward him" (*Southwestern Christian Advocate*, August 23, 1900, Item #457, HNCF).

89. "Rector Accuses Police," *New York Times*, August 20, 1900.

90. "New York's Race Riot," *New York Evening Telegram*, August 16, 1900, Item #456, HNCF. Other reports also noted the similarities between northern and southern violence.

91. At least twelve southern newspaper editors wrote to the New York *World* about their reaction to the riot. See "Southern Editors Read a Lesson to New York on Our Race Riots," *The World*, August 17, 1900.

92. "New York vs. New Orleans," *New York Sun*, August 16, 1900, Item #456, HNCF.

93. Marilynn Johnson, *Street Justice*, 57–113.

94. In the Matter of the Investigation of the Conduct of the Police Force during the "Negro" Riot (Before Committee on Rules and Discipline), September 19, 1900, New York City of the Mayor Robert Van Wyck Administration, Departmental Correspondence, Received 1898–1901, Roll 4, NYCMA.

95. Affidavit of Paul Leitenberger and Alfred E. Borman (white), September 13, 1900, CPL, *Story of the Riot*, 47.

96. Affidavit of Thomas Hughes (white), September 30, 1900, CPL, *Story of the Riot*, 45.

97. "Quieter on West Side," *New York Tribune*, August 17, 1900, Item #456, HNCF.

98. Affidavit of Albert Saunders, September 5, 1900, CPL, *Story of the Riot*, 25.

99. Affidavit of Mrs. Kate Jackson, August 31, 1900, CPL, *Story of the Riot*, 33–34; Osofsky, "Race Riot," 21.

100. Affidavit of Headly Johnson, September 8, 1900, CPL, *Story of the Riot*, 24. Also see *Mail Express*, August 16, 1900, Item #456, HNCF; and *New York Tribune*, August 17, 1900.

101. "Race Riot on West Side," *New York Times*, August 16, 1900.

102. Affidavit of William Hamer, August 31, 1900, CPL, *Story of the Riot*, 30; Affidavit of Mrs. Annie Hamer, September 6, 1900, ibid., 30–31.

103. Affidavit of William Hamer, August 31, 1900, CPL, *Story of the Riot*, 30.

104. "Negroes Attacked in New York," *Independent*, August 16, 1900; "Westside Race Riot—Mob Attacks Negroes for Policeman's Death," *New York Tribune*, August 16, 1900; "The Race Riots in New York," *Outlook*, August 25, 1900; "Race Riot on West Side," *New York Times*, August 16, 1900.

105. Affidavit of Belle Johnson, September 5, 1900, CPL, *Story of the Riot*, 13.

106. Affidavit of Walter Gregory, September 6, 1900, CPL, *Story of the Riot*, 52.

107. Affidavit of John Wolf, October 11, 1900, CPL, *Story of the Riot*, 67.

108. Affidavit of John Hains, August 28, 1900, CPL, *Story of the Riot*, 50–51; Affidavit of Mrs. Louise Francis, August 28, 1900, ibid., 54.

109. Affidavit of Thomas Hughes (white), September 30, 1900, CPL, *Story of the Riot*, 45.

110. My thinking about the complexity of the black working-class and labor history has been influenced by the work of Nell Irvin Painter, especially *Narrative of Hosea Hudson* and *Sojourner Truth*; Hunter, *To 'Joy My Freedom*, 120–24; Hunter, "'Brotherly Love'"; Kelley, *Race Rebels*; Kelley, "'We Are Not What We Seem'"; Elsa Barkley Brown, "Negotiating and Transforming the Public Sphere"; and Trotter, *Black Milwaukee*. Also see Harrison, *Peaceable Kingdom*; Ross, "'Not the Sort that Would Sit on the Doorstep'"; and Bailey, "'Will the Real Bill Banks Please Stand Up?'"

111. "West Side Riots," *New York Tribune*, August 17, 1900; "Negro Pastor Defies Police to Answer," *New York Times*, August 27, 1900. Marilynn Johnson (*Street Justice*, 64–65) asks:

> Why did middle-class blacks suddenly rally in support of the victims of police brutality? For decades, police had harassed and beaten African-American suspects with little or no vocal protest from black elites. Since most of the victims were poor and without political influence, black leaders had generally been unwilling to risk their reputations in defending such individuals. The riot, however, presented a different scenario in which police violence was more blatant and widely dispersed. Although the majority of victims were working-class—longshoremen, bellhops, janitors, etc.—they also included a few elite or educated individuals. . . . Complaints by such respectable persons lent credibility to the claims of others and showed that no one with dark skin was immune from attack. Moreover, the riot itself was one manifestation of the increasing segregation and discrimination that characterized black life in New York around the turn of the century, changes that acutely affected middle-class blacks. As racial boundaries solidified, these "respectable" black citizens increasingly felt the impact of white racism in their daily lives.

112. "Negro Pastor Defies Police to Answer," *New York Times*, August 27, 1900.

113. *New York Tribune*, August 16, 1900.

114. "Negro Pastor Defies Police to Answer," *New York Times*, August 27, 1900.

115. CPL, *Story of the Riot*, 5.

116. In another section of his statement, Moss argued that "those colored people who have illicit dealings with the police—keepers of gambling, disorderly, and badger houses—seeing the signs of coming trouble, closed their places and kept off the streets" (CPL, *Story of the Riot*, 2).

117. See Wolcott, *Remaking Respectability*, 4–6.

118. Affidavit of John Hains, August 28, 1900, CPL, *Story of the Riot*, 50.

119. Osofsky, "Race Riot," 21.

120. Affidavit of Charles Bennett (who signed his name with an X), August 31, 1900, CPL, *Story of the Riot*, 28. Also see testimony of Charles Bennett, In the Matter of the Investigation of the Conduct of the Police Force during the "Negro" Riot (Before Committee on Rules and Discipline), September 19, 1900, p. 80, New York City of the Mayor Robert Van Wyck Administration, Departmental Correspondence, Received 1898–1901, Roll 4, NYCMA.

121. Affidavit of Stephen Small (who signed his name with an X), September 11, 1900, CPL, *Story of the Riot*, 7.

122. Affidavit of William L. Hall, September 1, 1900, CPL, *Story of the Riot*, 35.

123. Affidavit of George L. Meyers, August 26, 1900, CPL, *Story of the Riot*, 64.

124. Testimony of James Joseph Lockett, In the Matter of the Investigation of the Conduct of the Police Force during the "Negro" Riot (Before Committee on Rules and Discipline), September 19, 1900, p. 122, New York City of the Mayor Robert Van Wyck Administration, Departmental Correspondence, Received 1898–1901, Roll 4, NYCMA.

125. Affidavit of Maria Williams (who signed her name with an X) and Carrie Wells, September 4, 1900, CPL, *Story of the Riot*, 38.

126. My interpretation was influenced by Weisenfeld's argument that "the larger narrative constructed by the CPL, the newspapers, and other commentators on the riot placed women in a secondary role, "marking their presence or absence in relation to men and to the public sphere." She notes that "almost all of the women who testified for *Story of the Riot* appear in relation to a man who is the primary victim of assault, and, most often, these women are out on the streets accompanied by their husbands. . . . Thus, just as part of the masculinist agenda of the league entailed claiming the right of African American men to control 'their' public space, it also intended to restrict women to the private realm." See Weisenfeld, *African American Women and Christian Activism*, 73. Also see Carby, "Policing the Black Woman's Body," esp. 741.

127. Affidavit of Maria Williams (who signed her name with an X) and Carrie Wells, September 4, 1900, CPL, *Story of the Riot*, 38. Wells and Williams noted that "Mr. and Mrs. Miller . . . know of us; Mrs. McGurk . . . , Mrs. Kloze . . . all can . . . vouch for our character."

128. Affidavit of Mrs. Rosa Lewis, September 13, 1900, CPL, *Story of the Riot*, 37.

129. Affidavit of Mrs. Lucinda Thomson (who signed her name with an X), September 24, 1900, CPL, *Story of the Riot*, 20. In this statement she mentions her daughter.

130. Affidavit of Lucy A. Jones, August 28, 1900, CPL, *Story of the Riot*, 54.

131. Affidavit of Mrs. Irene Wells, August 31, 1900, CPL, *Story of the Riot*, 39.

132. Statement of Harry Reed, August 22, 1900, CPL, *Story of the Riot*, 74.

133. Statements of Richard A. Taylor, September 6, 1900, and Mrs. Margaret Taylor, September 7, 1900, CPL, *Story of the Riot*, 56–58. Also see "Negro Pastor Defies Police to Answer," *New York Times*, August 27, 1900.

134. Affidavit of John Wolf, October 11, 1900, CPL, *Story of the Riot*, 66–67.

135. Affidavit of William Elliot, August 24, 1900, CPL, *Story of the Riot*, 72–73.

136. Affidavit of Stephen Small (who signed his name with an X), September 11, 1900, CPL, *Story of the Riot*, 6.

137. Affidavit of Mrs. Rosa Lewis, September 13, 1900, CPL, *Story of the Riot*, 37.

138. Affidavit of Mrs. Kate Jackson, August 31, 1900, CPL, *Story of the Riot*, 34.

139. Affidavit of Mrs. Elizabeth Mitchell, August 31, 1900, CPL, *Story of the Riot*, 33.

140. Editorial, *New York Age*, August 23, 1900, Item #457, HNCF.

141. Affidavit of Nicholas J. Sherman, August 24, 1900, CPL, *Story of the Riot*, 77–78.

142. Testimony of James J. Lockett, In the Matter of the Investigation of the Conduct of the Police Force during the "Negro" Riot (Before Committee on Rules and Discipline), September 19, 1900, p. 126, New York City of the Mayor Robert Van Wyck Administration, Departmental Correspondence, Received 1898–1901, Roll 4, NYCMA.

143. Affidavit of Mrs. Elizabeth Brown, September 20, 1900, CPL, *Story of the Riot*, 21. Brown noted that in the hospital at Bellevue her brother was "beaten and maltreated by the attendants" and had a "gash in his head about three inches long, and similar cuts on his wrist and two on his leg." Also see "Insane from Race Riot Blow," *New York Times*, August 20, 1900.

144. "Negroes Buying Arms and Cartridges For To-Night's Anticipated Troubles," *The World (Evening)*, August 16, 1900.

145. "The Tammany Democratic Mob Sentiment," *New York Age*, September 13, 1900, Item #457, HNCF.

146. "Police in Control in Riotous District," *New York Times*, August 17, 1900.

147. Affidavit of Alfred Bradshaw (who signed his name with an X), September 4, 1900, CPL, *Story of the Riot*, 43.

148. Affidavit of Headly Johnson, September 8, 1900, CPL, *Story of the Riot*, 24; "Police in Control in Riotous District," *New York Times*, August 17, 1900.

149. Testimony of Lavinia Lockett, In the Matter of the Investigation of the Conduct of the Police Force during the "Negro" Riot (Before Committee on Rules and Discipline), September 19, 1900, p. 125, New York City of the Mayor Robert Van Wyck Administration, Departmental Correspondence, Received 1898–1901, Roll 4, NYCMA.

150. "Police Use Clubs Freely," *New York Tribune*, August 17, 1900. Also see testimony of Inspector Walter Thompson, In the Matter of the Investigation of the Conduct of the Police Force during the "Negro" Riot (Before Committee on Rules and Discipline), September 26, 1900, p. 248, New York City of the Mayor Robert Van Wyck Administration, Departmental Correspondence, Received 1898–1901, Roll 4, NYCMA.

151. "Negroes Buying Arms and Cartridges for To-Night's Anticipated Troubles," *The World (Evening)*, August 16, 1900.

152. "Police in Control in Riotous District," *New York Times*, August 17, 1900.

153. CPL, *Story of the Riot*, 2.

154. "More Rioting Feared," *New York Evening Sun*, August 16, 1900, Item #456, HNCF.

155. "Police in Control in Riotous District," *New York Times*, August 17, 1900.

156. "Negro Pastor Defies Police to Answer," *New York Times*, August 27, 1900.

157. Ibid.

158. For information regarding Brooks, see *The National Cyclopedia of the Colored Race*, ed. Clement Richardson (Montgomery, AL: National Publishing Company, 1919), 223.

159. "Negro Pastor Defies Police to Answer," *New York Times*, August 27, 1900.

160. "Avenging Mobs Hunt Negroes in New York Streets (Terrorized Negroes Dragged Bodily from Broadway Cars)," *New York Herald*, August 16, 1900. One white woman, Mary Wilkinson, was reportedly fined for "waving a bread knife in West Thirty-ninth street" ("Wednesday's Rioters Dealt With," *New York Sun*, August 17, 1900).

161. Weisenfeld, *African American Women and Christian Activism*, 73.

162. CPL, *Story of the Riot*, 1.

163. Mitchell, *Righteous Propagation*, 57. Deborah Gray White ("Cost of Club Work,"

257) argues that the fact that "some men found shelter in the acceptance of the promiscuous black woman stereotype and that some cautioned black women not to extend their influence beyond the home should come as no surprise, for around the turn of the century it was easier to do battle with black women than with white racists."

164. "Negro Pastor Defies Police to Answer," *New York Times*, August 27, 1900. Also see Marilynn Johnson, *Street Justice*, 66.

165. "Negro Pastor Defies Police to Answer," *New York Times*, August 27, 1900.

166. Ibid. See also Bederman, *Manliness and Civilization*.

167. "Condemns the Police," *New York Times*, August 20, 1900.

168. See "Rector Accuses Police," "Colored Pastor's Demand," and "Feelings at Mount Olivet," *New York Times*, August 20, 1920.

169. CPL, *Story of the Riot*, 3. CPL officers included Rev. W. H. Brooks, D.D. (president), T. S. P. Miller, M.D. (vice president), Rev. H. P. Miller (secretary), and James E. Garner (treasurer). See "Colored Pastor's Demand," *New York Times*, August 20, 1900.

170. See Brooks's speech in "Negroes' Public Protest," *New York Times*, September 13, 1900.

171. CPL, *Story of the Riot*, 4.

172. "Negroes' Public Protest," *New York Times*, September 13, 1900. Lyons was a member of the National Association of Colored Women, and her statement was reminiscent of several of Ida B. Wells's arguments in *Southern Horrors*. Also see "Negroes Denounce Action of Police," *New York Press*, September 13, 1900, Item #457, HNCF, where Lyons was quoted as saying, "Are you ready to come out and say that every time a man of African blood is insulted you are insulted? . . . I want every respectable Afro-American here to get a permit to carry a revolver. It doesn't follow that you are to pull it out. To be caught unprepared once is no disgrace but don't be caught again." Shapiro also notes Lyons's Carnegie Hall speech in *White Violence*, 485 n. 3.

173. Peterson, "Contesting Space," 67.

174. For background on the significance of women in public space, see Ryan, *Women in Public*; and Walkowitz, *City of Dreadful Delight*, 41–80.

175. Higginbotham, *Righteous Discontent*, 204. For more on how black women's presence in the street was viewed negatively, see Brown and Kimball, "Mapping the Terrain of Black Richmond," 98–99.

176. Val Marie Johnson ("Defining Social Evil," 354, 319–59) also addresses this issue: "As individuals and as a couple Arthur Harris and May Enoch were a highly risky focus for protest by African-American men or women because they were not legally married and Thorpe was arresting May for prostitution—points that were broadcast repeatedly by whites during the conflict. Both illegitimate unions and commercial sex were particularly problematic specters for African-Americans." Michele Mitchell (*Righteous Propagation*, 202) notes that "marriage was perceived as both a personal act and as an institution with ramifications for the entire Afro-American collective."

177. Statement of Arthur Harris, August 19, 1900, Fifth Precinct Station-House, Washington, DC, Case #32015, Box 608, DAP. This statement was also published, in several forms, in various New York newspapers.

178. Schechter, "All the Intensity of My Nature," 66.

179. Ibid., 52.

180. "Fatally Cut by a Negro," *The Morning Telegraph*, August 13, 1900, Reel 26, DAS. Deborah Gray White argues, "No matter how much they needed protection, black woman would seldom be able to insist on it, for in doing so they implicitly challenged black men

to risk the lynch mob, judicial retribution, or psychological belittlement" (White, "Cost of Club Work," 257).

181. Deborah Gray White discusses the conflict that occurred between black men and women over the issue of black women's protection as well as black women's activism in *Too Heavy a Load*, 56–86.

182. "Mob of Thousands 'Looking for Trouble,'" *The World*, August 17, 1900.

183. "Pool Lets Streetwalkers Go," *New York Sun*, August 30, 1898.

184. "With Magistrate Pool," *New York Times*, August 31, 1898.

185. "Pool and the Police," *New York Times*, September 3, 1898. Many police officers understood Pool's high regard for legitimate evidence and his intent to lessen police brutality, yet in one case, Officer Rosenberg chose to ignore these prior warnings. Rosenberg came into Pool's court after arresting a black woman and argued that "she has been arrested many times before." Pushing the officer for more credible evidence, Judge Pool responded, "I don't believe you. . . . She is entitled to considerate and decent treatment, even if she is black." He emphasized Rosenberg's ethnicity (the paper described the officer as "very swarthy") when he said, "You're just as black as your prisoner, your heart is just as black." Rosenberg responded by ignoring the moral implications of Pool's statement, instead focusing on race, emphasizing and defending his status as a white man, and reinforcing his connection to the white judge: "I am just as white a man as you are, just exactly as white, sir." In the end, Judge Pool dismissed him from the court—and presumably dismissed the unidentified black woman as well. See Roediger, *Wages of Whiteness*; and Jacobsen, *Whiteness of a Different Color*.

186. Monday, August 29, 1898, Seventh District, Magistrate Court Docket Books, Office of the Mayor, New York City of the Mayor Robert Van Wyck Administration, Departmental Correspondence, Received 1898–1901, Roll 2, NYCMA.

187. "Magistrate Pool Summoned," *New York Times*, September 2, 1898. Also see "With Magistrate Pool," *New York Times*, August 31, 1898; and "Pool and the Police," *New York Times*, September 3, 1898.

188. "He Still Runs His Court," *New York Sun*, August 31, 1898.

189. Ibid.

190. "Magistrate Pool Summoned," *New York Times*, September 2, 1898. Also see "With Magistrate Pool," *New York Times*, August 31, 1898; and "Pool and the Police," *New York Times*, September 3, 1898. Fellow officers testified on Owens's behalf, arguing that "the Harris woman had been fined $5 about three weeks before for loitering on the streets and the Carroll woman had at one time been arrested for fighting" and that "the house in which the colored woman lived was one of the worst in the precinct and that he had made eight arrests there." Officers testified that Owens had been with the force since January 7, 1896, and, "according to [his] captain . . . [he had] an excellent record" ("He Still Runs His Court," *New York Sun*, August 31, 1898).

191. "He Still Runs His Court," *New York Sun*, August 31, 1898. Also see "With Magistrate Pool," *New York Times*, August 31, 1898; and "Pool and the Police," *New York Times*, September 3, 1898.

192. "Price, Pool and Tenderloin," *New York Times*, September 1, 1898. For more on New York police corruption during this period, see the 1894 Lexow Committee Investigation in Chin, *New York City Police Corruption Investigation Commissions*, vol. 1.

193. Osofsky, "Race Riot," 24.

194. Ibid.

195. Ottley, *New World A-Coming*, 26.

196. "Housing Conditions among Negroes in Harlem, New York City," *Bulletin of the National Urban League on Urban Conditions among Negroes* 4, no. 2 (January 1915): 25.

CHAPTER THREE

1. Du Bois, *Black North*, 5.
2. Gordon, "Black and White Visions of Welfare."
3. See Gaines, *Uplifting the Race*; Shaw, *What a Woman Ought to Be*; Higginbotham, *Righteous Discontent*; and Wolcott, *Remaking Respectability*.
4. Matthews, "Colored Race."
5. Wilson, *Segregated Scholars*, 90, 93–94.
6. On white reformers' interest in and work with black urban communities, see Lasch-Quinn, *Black Neighbors*, 9–46, esp. 17–19.
7. Matthews, "Redemption of Our City (Colored)," 57; Fitzpatrick, *Endless Crusade*.
8. Hunter, *To 'Joy My Freedom*, 168–86.
9. Higginbotham, *Righteous Discontent*, 211–21, esp. 211.
10. Kellor, *Out of Work*.
11. Layten, "Northern Phase of a Southern Problem," 317. Although these women were characterized as migrants from rural Virginia, Maryland, and the Carolinas, many had participated in intraregional migrations, including periods of residence in southern cities, before they reached the North. See Johnson and Campbell, *Black Migration*, 63; and Marks, *Farewell*, 33.
12. Miller, "Surplus Negro Women," 526–27.
13. Matthews, "Some of the Dangers," 62–69; Matthews, "Colored Race"; Kellor, "Associations."
14. Cash, "Victoria Earle Matthews," in *Notable Black American Women*, 737; Cash, "Victoria Earle Matthews," in *Black Women in America*. Also see Kramer, "Uplifting Our 'Downtrodden Sisterhood.'"
15. Cash, "Victoria Earle Matthews," in *Notable Black American Women*, 737; Cash, "Radicals and Realists," 9.
16. Hallie Q. Brown, *Homespun Heroines*, 209–10.
17. Ibid., 210; Rayford W. Logan, "Victoria Earle Matthews," *Dictionary of American Negro Biography* (New York: W. W. Norton, 1982), 130–31.
18. Richings, *Evidences of Progress*, 31.
19. *Woman's Era* 1, no. 9 (December 1894): 5.
20. Penn, *Afro-American Press*, 375–76; [Matthews], *Aunt Lindy*.
21. Richings, *Evidences of Progress*, 30. Matthews also wrote short stories that were published in *Waverly* magazine, *New York Weekly*, the *Family Story Paper*, and other journals. See Carby, *Reconstructing Womanhood*; and Tate, *Domestic Allegories*.
22. Victoria Earle Matthews, "The Awakening of the Afro-American Woman," an address delivered at the Annual Convention of the Society of Christian Endeavor, San Francisco, July 11, 1897 (New York: Published by the author, 1897), 8, James Weldon Johnson Memorial Collection of Negro Arts and Letters, Yale University, Beinecke Rare Book and Manuscript Library, New Haven, CT.
23. Matthews, "Redemption of Our City (Colored)," 57.
24. Matthews, "Colored Race."
25. "Brooklyn Literary Union: Victoria Earle Lectures on Stoic Philosophy to a Large

Audience," *Brooklyn Eagle*, February 4, 1891. Deborah Gray White addresses the conflict between black men and women in *Too Heavy a Load*, 56–68. Ida B. Wells struggled to deal with this issue before and during her antilynching crusade; see Schechter, *Ida B. Wells-Barnett*, 14–18.

26. "Novel Reading Demoralized," *New York Age*, May 9, 1891. Also see Val Marie Johnson, "Defining Social Evil," 373 n. 84.

27. Matthews, "Novel Reading Defended."

28. See Matthews, "Value of Race Literature," and Thornbrough, *T. Thomas Fortune*, 126.

29. See Schechter, *Ida B. Wells-Barnett*, 145–46; Thomas Holt, "Lonely Warrior," 49–50; and Giddings, *Ida*, 451–53. On Washington's sabotage of black critics, see Harlan, "Booker T. Washington," 4–6, 13–14.

30. See Deborah Gray White, *Too Heavy a Load*, 36–40.

31. Wells, *Crusade for Justice*, 78–80.

32. *Woman's Era* 2, no. 5 (August 1895): 5.

33. The corresponding secretary of the Woman's Loyal Union identified its members as "professional women, doctors, school-teachers, literary women, writers of poetry and prose, tradeswomen, artists, home-makers and housekeepers" (ibid.).

34. "Afro American Women: Organized to Suppress the Lynching of Colored Men," *Brooklyn Eagle*, March 19, 1893. The Woman's Loyal Union attempted to organize southern clubs as well; see *Woman's Era* 1, no. 4 (July 1894): 4.

35. *Brooklyn Eagle*, March 19, 1893.

36. *Woman's Era* 1, no. 5 (August 1894): 10. Among the male speakers at one event were Professor Scarborough of Wilberforce, T. T. Fortune, Dr. W. B. Derrick, and Bishop Turner.

37. Hallie Q. Brown, *Homespun Heroines*, 210; Cash, "Victoria Earle Matthews," in *Notable Black American Women*, 737. In 1895, the Woman's Loyal Union became a part of the National Federation of Afro-American Women (NFAAW); Matthews served as chair of the Executive Board as well as New York correspondent for the Boston-based journal the *Woman's Era*. One year later, the NFAAW and the National Colored Women's League of Washington were formed. Black clubwoman Hallie Q. Brown noted that club work allowed black women to band together for their protection as well as for the welfare of the race. A key player in this development, Matthews became the NACW's national organizer from 1897 to 1899.

38. *Woman's Era* 3, no. 5 (January 1897): 2. Also see Deborah Gray White, *Too Heavy a Load*, 24; and Shaw, "Black Club Women." Shaw's argument is particularly keen on addressing the long history of black self-help and community activism rather than what seemed to many scholars a specific response to the rise of Jim Crow.

39. Washington, Wood, and Williams, *New Negro for a New Century*, 382–83.

40. Hunton, "Negro Womanhood Defended."

41. Frances Keyser, Obituary, *New York Age*, March 14, 1907.

42. Matthews, "Colored Race." Also see the 1895 and 1896 reports of the Woman's Loyal Union of New York and Brooklyn that highlight Matthews's investigations through surveys and eyewitness accounts. See *A History of the Club Movement: Among the Colored Women of the United States* (Washington, DC: National Association of Colored Women's Clubs, Inc., 1902 [1978]), 14, 66, Reel 1. See also Wilson, *Segregated Scholars*, 93–94.

43. Matthews, "Some of the Dangers," 68; Wilson, *Segregated Scholars*, 93–95.

44. Osofsky, *Harlem*, 56–57; Cash, "Womanhood and Protest, 162.

45. Certificate of Incorporation of The White Rose Mission and Industrial Association, August 24, 1899, WRC.

46. Mrs. Lydia Hiller, "Needs of Colored Girls," letter to the editor, *Commercial Advertiser*, February 13, 1899, Item #493, HNCF.

47. "Home for Colored Girls," *New York Tribune*, January 17, 1902.

48. Seventy-fifth Annual Report, New York City Mission and Tract Society, Woman's Branch (February 1898), 23, in Guichard Parris Collection, Box 30, Rare Book and Manuscript Library, Columbia University, New York, NY.

49. Seventy-sixth Annual Report, New York City Mission and Tract Society, Woman's Branch (February 1899), 35, in Guichard Parris Collection, Box 30, Rare Book and Manuscript Library, Columbia University, New York, NY. The report says that a similar institution is needed for young black men "which shall be . . . a kind of Pratt Institute, or a Tuskegee School in New York City."

50. Ibid.

51. Matthews, "Colored Race."

52. Matthews, "Redemption of Our City (Colored)," 58.

53. Letter from Victoria Earle Matthews to Booker T. Washington, January 8, 1898, in Harlan, *Booker T. Washington Papers*, 361–62.

54. Annual Report for the White Rose Working Girls' Home for the Year Ending December 31, 1907, WRC; Lassalle Best, "History of the White Rose Mission and Industrial Association," 3, Writer's Program, Reel 3, SCH. For instance, on one evening in 1907, the Society decided that a twelve-year-old "runaway boy" found in New York's Pennsylvania station at 8 P.M., who was "hungry with no place to stay," should be referred to the White Rose Home until his parents in Philadelphia could be notified. See Second Annual Report of the Traveler's Aid Society (Committee) for the Year Ending May 1, 1907, 17, NYPL.

55. Mary Kendall Hyde, "White Rose Home—Its Work and Need," n.d., MG 565, WRC.

56. Matthews, "Some of the Dangers," 62.

57. Letter from Victoria Earle Matthews to Booker T. Washington, January 8, 1898, in Harlan, *Booker T. Washington Papers*, 362.

58. Letter from Victoria Earle Matthews to Booker T. Washington, January 12, 1898, in Harlan, *Booker T. Washington Papers*, 364.

59. Lassalle Best, "History of the White Rose Mission and Industrial Association," 1, Writer's Program, Reel 3, SCH.

60. Letter from Victoria Earle Matthews to Booker T. Washington, January 8, 1898, in Harlan, *Booker T. Washington Papers*, 362.

61. See Annual Report for the Year Ending December 31, 1912 (cover), White Rose Industrial Association, WRC.

62. Frances R. Keyser, "Victoria Earle Matthews," in Hallie Q. Brown, *Homespun Heroines*, 212. Matthews, Moore, and Dunbar were all proponents of racial uplift and well known in the literary world since the leading black newspaper publicized their books. See "Books Make the Best Presents," *New York Age*, January 5, 1900.

63. Lassalle Best, "History of the White Rose Mission and Industrial Association," 2, Writer's Program, Reel 3, SCH.

64. Frances R. Keyser, "Victoria Earle Matthews," in Hallie Q. Brown, *Homespun Heroines*, 212

65. Ibid.

66. Quoted in Kramer, "Uplifting Our 'Downtrodden Sisterhood,'" 249.

67. Thornbrough, *T. Thomas Fortune*, 126. Also see Kramer, "Uplifting Our 'Downtrodden Sisterhood,'" 255.

68. Frances R. Keyser, "Victoria Earle Matthews," in Hallie Q. Brown, *Homespun Heroines*, 212.

69. Letter from Moore to Dunbar, March 1, 1898, in Metcalf, "Letters of Paul and Alice Dunbar," 489. Also see the discussion of Moore's racial uplift work in Hull, *Color, Sex, and Poetry*, 41–42; and Kramer, "Uplifting Our 'Downtrodden Sisterhood,'" 249–50.

70. Letter from Moore to Dunbar, February 8, 1898, in Metcalf, "Letters of Paul and Alice Dunbar," 433.

71. Letter from Moore to Dunbar, January 23, 1898, in Metcalf, "Letters of Paul and Alice Dunbar," 393.

72. Ibid.

73. Letter from Moore to Dunbar, January 12, 1898, in Metcalf, "Letters of Paul and Alice Dunbar," 359–60.

74. Ibid.

75. Letter from Moore to Dunbar, February 16, 1898, in Metcalf, "Letters of Paul and Alice Dunbar," 447–48.

76. Annual Report for the Year Ending December 31, 1911, White Rose Industrial Association, 4–7, WRC.

77. Higginbotham, *Righteous Discontent*, 204–5, 212, 216–21; Carby, "Policing the Black Woman's Body."

78. Peiss, "'Charity Girls.'"

79. Matthews, "Colored Race."

80. Inmate #3501, History Blank, August 21, 1923, BH.

81. Inmate #3494, History Blank, August 13, 1923, BH.

82. Inmate #3489, History Blank, August 1, 1923, BH.

83. Inmate #3502, History Blank, August 22, 1923, BH.

84. Inmate #3377, Preliminary Investigation, Anna Doyle, ca. May 1922, Probation Bureau, City Magistrates' Courts, BH.

85. "Race Is Dancing Itself to Death," *New York Age*, January 8, 1914.

86. "Dancing in the Shadow," *New York Age*, June 3, 1909.

87. "Race Is Dancing Itself to Death," *New York Age*, January 8, 1914.

88. On black leaders' conviction that appropriate demeanor was crucial to winning equality, see Shane White, "'It Was a Proud Day.'" In particular, during the celebration of emancipation in antebellum New York, *Freedom's Journal*, a leading black newspaper, criticized black Brooklynites for the "imposing spectacle" they caused and contended that "nothing serves more to keep us in our present degraded condition, than these foolish exhibitions of ourselves" (46). For turn-of-the-century reform efforts regarding decorum, see Mitchell, *Righteous Propagation*, chaps. 3 and 4.

89. Inmate #2496, Mental Examination, September 7, 1917, BH.

90. Walls, "Delinquent Negro Girl," 33.

91. Odem, *Delinquent Daughters*; Ruth Alexander, *"Girl Problem."*

92. "White Rose Mission Settlement," *New York Age*, July 6, 1905.

93. Ibid.

94. *New York Age*, July 20, 1905.

95. Lassalle Best, "History of the White Rose Mission and Industrial Association," 2, Writer's Program, Reel 3, SCH.

96. Letter from Mary White Ovington to W. E. B. Du Bois, May 20, 1906, in Aptheker, *Correspondence of W. E. B. Du Bois*, 119. See also Val Marie Johnson, "Defining Social Evil," chap. 4, esp. 391–96.

97. Matthews, "Protecting Colored Girls."

98. Lassalle Best, "History of the White Rose Mission and Industrial Association," 2, Writer's Program, Reel 3, SCH.

99. Constitution of the White Rose Mission and Industrial Association, Article III, Section 2, ca. 1915, WRC.

100. See Weisenfeld, *African American Women and Christian Activism*, 117–19. For more information on Nannie Helen Burroughs, see also Wolcott, "Bible, Bath, and Broom," and Higginbotham, *Righteous Discontent*, esp. 211–21.

101. *New York Age*, July 16, 1914, 1, 7; Weisenfeld, *African American Women and Christian Activism*, 117–19.

102. *New York Age*, July 16, 1914, 1, 7; Weisenfeld, *African American Women and Christian Activism*, 117–19.

103. Matthews, "Protecting Colored Girls."

104. Excerpt from "The National Urban League," address by Eugene Kinckle Jones, executive secretary of the National Urban League, at Urban League Annual Conference, Cleveland, Ohio, December 4, 1924, Guichard Parris Collection, Series IV: National League Administrative Files, Box 53, Rare Book and Manuscript Library, Columbia University, New York, NY.

105. Matthews, "Protecting Colored Girls."

106. "New York's Colored People," *Federation* 2 (June 1902): 34.

107. Letter from Frances A. Kellor to W. E. B. Du Bois, May 16, 1905; and letter from Victoria Earle Matthews to Dr. Du Bois, May 16, 1905, Du Bois Papers, Reel 2, W. E. B. Du Bois and University of Massachusetts at Amherst Library. See also David Levering Lewis, *W. E. B. Du Bois*, 346–47.

108. Fitzpatrick, *Endless Crusade*, 139; Salem, *To Better Our World*, 66–67. See also Lasch-Quinn, *Black Neighbors*, 12, 17.

109. O'Connell, "Frances Kellor," 394; Freedman, *Their Sisters' Keepers*, 109–42; Fitzpatrick, *Endless Crusade*, 92–165; Lasch-Quinn, *Black Neighbors*, 9–46.

110. Kellor, "Associations," 698.

111. Maxwell, "Frances Kellor"; Fitzpatrick, *Endless Crusade*, 17–18.

112. Kellor, *Experimental Sociology*, 2.

113. Kellor, "Criminal Anthropology"; Lombroso and Ferrero, *Female Offender*. See also Freedman, *Their Sisters' Keepers*, 111; and Fitzpatrick, *Endless Crusade*, 58–64.

114. Kellor, "Criminal Negro," January 1901, 60.

115. Kellor's southern investigations included Mississippi, Louisiana, Alabama, Georgia, Florida, South Carolina, North Carolina, and Virginia.

116. Kellor, "Criminal Negro," February 1901, 190. Also see ibid., January–May 1901; and Kellor, *Experimental Sociology*, 171. Also see Carby, "Policing the Black Woman's Body," 740–41.

117. Kellor, "Criminal Negro," March 1901, 312.

118. Ibid.

119. Ibid., 312–13.

120. Ibid. Her critique encompassed a eugenicist component; when discussing immigrant and poor white women, she noted that "children coming from conditions similar to those [of] negroes [have] an equal percentage of immorality, so that racial tendencies alone, cannot explain it" (313).

121. Fitzpatrick, *Endless Crusade*, 130–39, esp. 131.

122. Ibid., 139. Also see Kellor, *Out of Work*, 77–103.

123. Kellor, "Evils of the Intelligence Office Systems," 377.

124. Third Annual Report of the New York State Reformatory for Women at Bedford Hills, 1904, 40, NYSL.

125. Kellor, "Evils of the Intelligence Office Systems," 380.

126. Kellor, "Assisted Emigration from the South," 12–13.

127. Mary White Ovington, "The Colored Woman in Domestic Service in New York City," *Bulletin of the Inter-Municipal Committee on Household Research* 1 (May 1905): 11, NYPL.

128. Kellor, "Southern Colored Girls in the North: The Problems of their Protection," 584.

129. Kellor, "Problem of the Negro Girl," 8; Kellor, "Southern Colored Girls in the North," 7; Kellor, "Opportunities for Southern Negro Women," 471.

130. Victoria Earle Matthews, "The Awakening of the Afro-American Woman," an address delivered at the Annual Convention of the Society of Christian Endeavor, San Francisco, July 11, 1897 (New York: Published by the author, 1897), 8, James Weldon Johnson Memorial Collection of Negro Arts and Letters, Yale University, Beinecke Rare Book and Manuscript Library, New Haven, CT.

131. Kellor, *Experimental Sociology*, 171.

132. Kellor, "Agencies for the Prevention of Crime," 205.

133. Hine, "Black Migration to the Urban Midwest," 244–45.

134. Kellor, *Experimental Sociology*, 171. Also see Kellor, "Some Old Needs of the New South."

135. Kellor, "Agencies for the Prevention of Crime," 205.

136. "Conditions in the North: Problems Affecting the Negro Race Is Freely Discussed," *New York Age*, January 27, 1910.

137. Ovington, *Half a Man*, 153–54, 148.

138. Ibid., 162.

139. Lasch-Quinn, *Black Neighbors*, 41. The National Urban League later attempted to broaden employment opportunities.

140. Annual Report for the National League for the Protection of Colored Women, New York, November 1910, 3, NYPL.

141. Kellor, "Assisted Emigration from the South," 13.

142. Frances A. Kellor, "To Help Negro Women," *Boston Traveler*, May 31, 1905, Item #554, HNCF.

143. Kellor, *Out of Work*, 83.

144. Ibid., 97.

145. T.J.J., Review of *Out of Work*, 181.

146. *Bulletin of the Inter-Municipal Committee on Household Research* 1 (November 1904): 2–3, NYPL.

147. Mary W. Ovington was also on the program. See *Bulletin of the Inter-Municipal Committee on Household Research* 1 (May 1905): 3, NYPL. See also letter from Frances Kellor to W. E. B. Du Bois, May 13, 1905, Du Bois Papers, Reel 2, W. E. B. Du Bois and University of Massachusetts at Amherst Library.

148. *New York Age*, March 7, 1907, 4; Rhodes, "Protection of Girls' Travel," 115; *New York Age*, January 27, 1910, 1; Annual Report of the National League for the Protection of Colored Women, New York, November 1910, 3–4, NYPL.

149. Osofsky, *Harlem*, 57–58.

CHAPTER FOUR

1. Doty, *Society's Misfits*, 9.
2. The emphasis on defining middle-class white women as chaste is addressed in Cott, "Passionlessness."
3. Welter, "Cult of True Womanhood," 152. While Welter focused on the behavior and activities of middle-class white New Englanders, her ideas were applied to women across racial and class lines. In Doty's case, she and other administrators focused on the tenets to respectable femininity in response to Doty's interactions with unfeminine criminals and chose to ignore the fact that as a lawyer/activist she failed to live up to those same tenets.
4. Carby, *Reconstructing Womanhood*, 25.
5. Higginbotham, "African-American Women's History," 256–58; Higginbotham, *Righteous Discontent*, 189–90.
6. Carby, *Reconstructing Womanhood*, 25. Kathleen Brown discusses how distinctions between female indentured servants and enslaved women were constructed in *Good Wives*, 107–36.
7. Rafter, "Hard Times," 243. See also Gross, *Colored Amazons*, 116–18.
8. Kellor, "Criminal Sociology," 517.
9. For quotation, see Rafter, "Hard Times," 243. See also Freedman, *Their Sisters' Keepers*.
10. My structural and administrative understanding of the New York State Prison for Women at Auburn has been influenced by Rafter, "Hard Times," esp. 248; Rafter, *Partial Justice*; and David W. Lewis, "Female Criminal."
11. For an important discussion of these two powerful stereotypes, see Deborah Gray White, *Ar'n't I a Woman?*, 27–61.
12. See Gross, *Colored Amazons*, 87–100.
13. Lombroso and Ferrero, *Criminal Woman*, 286–87.
14. Lombroso and Ferrero, *Female Offender*. In *Creating Born Criminals*, 113–14, Nicole Hahn Rafter notes that Moriz Benedickt published the first book on criminal anthropology in 1881.
15. Cole, *Suspect Identities*, 23.
16. Lombroso and Ferrero, *Female Offender*, 112–13. In Nicole Hahn Rafter and Mary Gibson's translation of the Italian text, they note that although Lombroso uses the "Red Indian and Negro beauties" as examples of female criminality, "there is no indication that . . . [the] woman had broken the law[.] Lombroso uses her photograph to demonstrate the supposedly savage, masculine appearance of black women, traits he then uses to illustrate his theory that criminals are atavisms." See Lombroso and Ferrero, *Criminal Woman*, 149.
17. For more information on Alphonse Bertillion and the Bertillion system, see Cole, *Suspect Identities*, 32–59.
18. Quoted in ibid., 57.
19. Doty, *Society's Misfits*, 30.
20. Cole, *Suspect Identities*, 57. See also Gross, *Colored Amazons*, 133–38.
21. Inmate #1419, April 9, 1929, vol. 12 (1928–29), PM; Physician's Report, March 8, 1929, Box 2, PF.
22. Inmate #1419, School Report, March 8, 1929, Box 2, PF.
23. Inmate #1419, Shop and Laundry Attendant, March 8, 1929, Box 2, PF.
24. Inmate #1419, Physician's Report, March 8, 1929, Box 2, PF.

25. Rafter, "Hard Times," 239.

26. Annual Report of the Superintendent of State Prisons of the State of New York, 1893, 136–37, State Prison for Women, NYSL. In the end, there were 104 inmates, as one woman was transferred to an insane asylum and another was given a special commutation. Transferred inmates arrived from Kings, Onondaga, Albany, New York (via Sing Sing Prison), Monroe, and Erie counties. .

27. Prison Visitor Report, November 30, 1902, Prison Visitor Reports 1902, Women's Prison Association Collection, NYPL; also see Annual Report of the Women's Prison Association, 1902, 29–30, Women's Prison Association Collection, NYPL.

28. Rafter, "Hard Times," 239.

29. Ibid., 245.

30. Prison Visitor Reports 1902, Women's Prison Association Collection, NYPL.

31. *New York Times*, December 8, 1895. Also see Minor, *Slavery of Prostitution*, 223; and Doty, *Society's Misfits*, 9.

32. State of New York, No. 58, In Assembly, Annual Report of the Superintendent of State Prisons of the State of New York, Third Annual Report, September 30, 1895, 158, 164, State Prison for Women, NYSL. The report notes that there were thirty-nine "foreigners," but two black women came from the West Indies.

33. U.S. Bureau of the Census, *Negro Population*, 51; Annual Report of the Superintendent of State Prisons for the Year Ending September 30, 1910, 334, State Prison for Women, NYSL.

34. Robert, "Care of Women in State Prisons," 94. The report notes that there were thirty-three "foreigners," but one black woman came from Jamaica.

35. Annual Report of the Superintendent of State Prisons of the State of New York for the Year Ending September 30, 1911, 249, 254, 253, State Prison for Women, NYSL.

36. Consider, for instance, that New York's black population in 1930 was 3.3 percent, but black women accounted for more than 20 percent of Auburn's population in 1931. See U.S. Bureau of the Census, *Negroes in the United States*, 15, and Annual Report of the Prison Officials for State Prison for Women, Auburn, NY, for the fiscal year ending June 30, 1931, 175, 179, NYSL. The report noted that there were 45 "Negroes," 27 "Foreign Born," and 51 "Whites" out of 123 inmates.

37. See Rafter, *Partial Justice*; Dodge, *Whores and Thieves*; Butler; *Gendered Justice*; and Gross, *Colored Amazons*.

38. See Annual Report of the Superintendent of State Prisons of the State of New York, Third Annual Report, September 30, 1895, 143, State Prison for Women, NYSL.

39. Annual Reports of the Superintendent of State Prisons of the State of New York, 1893, 1894, State Prison for Women, NYSL; Rafter, "Hard Times," 242.

40. Annual Report of the Women's Prison Association, 1900, 8, Women's Prison Association Collection, NYPL.

41. Annual Report of the Women's Prison Association, 1903, 113, Women's Prison Association Collection, NYPL; Rafter, "Hard Times," 241–43.

42. Doty, *Society's Misfits*, 94.

43. Rafter, "Hard Times," 240–41.

44. Annual Report of the Women's Prison Association, 1908, 52, 53, Women's Prison Association Collection, NYPL.

45. "Girls Have a Rough Time in Secret Prison Inquiry," *New York Tribune*, November 15, 1913. Doty's alias, Maggie Martin, was never recorded in Auburn's Bertillion ledger.

46. Madeleine Doty, Appendix B, "Report on the Auburn Women's Prison to the New York Commission on Prison Reform," Moreland Report, Commission on Prison Reform Preliminary Report, No. 16 (1914), 24, NYSL.

47. Doty, *Society's Misfits*, 47–48.

48. Inmate #648, ca. October 1908, vol. 1 (1905–08), PM.

49. Inmate #649, October 1908, vol. 1 (1905–08), PM. This inmate was punished in December 1908 with thirty additional days; see vol. 3 (1911–12), PM.

50. Inmate #841, ca. September 1912, vol. 3 (1911–12), PM.

51. "Find Auburn Clean Outside, That's All," *New York Tribune*, November 16, 1913; "Reveal More Evils of Auburn Prison," *New York Times*, November 16, 1913.

52. Annual Report of the Superintendent of State Prisons for the Year Ending September 30, 1913, 116, 227, State Prison for Women, NYSL.

53. "Girls Have a Rough Time in Secret Prison Inquiry," *New York Tribune*, November 15, 1913; also see "Women 'Convicts' Test Auburn Prison," *New York Times*, November 15, 1913; and "Women Investigators, Five Days in Prison, Declare the System Is Intolerable," *New York Herald*, November 15, 1913.

54. Doty, *Society's Misfits*, 19.

55. Ibid., 31.

56. Ibid.

57. See Frances Alice Kellor, "Psychological and Environmental Study of Women Criminals I," *American Journal of Sociology* 5, no. 4 (January 1900): 527–43. Also see Fitzpatrick, *Endless Crusade*, 62–65; Lasch-Quinn, *Black Neighbors*, 17; and Freedman, *Their Sisters' Keepers*, 109–15.

58. Doty, *Society's Misfits*, 41–42, 45, 44.

59. Inmate #881, April 22, 1914, vol. 4 (1912–17), PM; Doty, *Society's Misfits*, 48.

60. Doty, *Society's Misfits*, 58. She explained: "I no longer cared whether I made a success of my prison investigation or not. I had one consuming desire—to get out" (60). See "Women 'Convicts' Test Auburn Prison," *New York Times*, November 15, 1913.

61. Inmate #881, FIF; Inmate #881, April 22, 1914, vol. 4 (1912–17), PM.

62. See Gross, *Colored Amazons*, 72–100. Gross notes that badger theft "demonstrated a more volatile combination of financial, social, and emotional motivating factors" (73).

63. Ibid.; Inmate #881, FIF; Inmate #881, April 22, 1914, vol. 4 (1912–17), PM.

64. Meyerowitz, *Women Adrift*, 24–25.

65. Doty, *Society's Misfits*, 46. Doty noted: "All night I heard Minerva sighing and groaning. She had confessed to the morphine habit." In another instance she noted Jones's physical pain and long-neglected health problems (59–60).

66. "To go to Miss Madaline Z. Doty, 121 Washington Place, New York City," Inmate #881, April 22, 1914, vol. 4 (1912–17), PM. See other black inmates in Doty's charge: #724 (March 9, 1914), #916 (March 2, 1914); white inmate #778 (November 30, 1915), FIF.

67. Doty, *Society's Misfits*, 46.

68. See "End of Torture of Women at Auburn, Riley Orders," *New York Tribune*, December 1, 1913; "Orders Reforms in Women's Prison," *New York Times*, December 1, 1913.

69. Doty, *Society's Misfits*, 46.

70. Ibid., 52.

71. At the end of her experiment, as an inspector for the Prison Commission on Reform, Doty made four general recommendations: improve the prisoners' diet; reevaluate the 1½ cent a day wage for labor, with special attention to women's need to learn domes-

tic skills as well as a trade; provide more exercise for prisoners within and outside of the institution as an emotional outlet; and normalize prison life so that "the convict [would] not come back into a strange, uninviting world after a term of imprisonment, without having some sense of being a responsible citizen." See Doty, Moreland Report, Commission on Prison Reform Preliminary Report, No. 16 (1914), 25, NYSL.

72. Inmates #763 and #764, FIF. I have revealed the inmates' names in accordance with the Freedom of Information Act of 1966, 5 USC Sec. 552, Part I, Subchapter II.

73. See U.S. Bureau of the Census, *Negro Population*, 101, Table: Negro Population of Urban Communities: 1910 and 1900.

74. Inmates #764 and #763, FIF. The Bertillion ledger indicates that Harriet was born in Hackensack, New Jersey, while Helen was born in Poughkeepsie. Harriet Smith also told the parole board that she was born in Hackensack. See Inmate #764, May 23, 1911, vol. 3 (1911–12), PM.

75. "Colored Women's Horrible Crime," *Poughkeepsie Daily Eagle*, February 13, 1909.

76. The sisters' mother seems to have come from New Jersey. Although the mother is referred to as Mrs. Smith, there is no evidence of a husband or father in the records at the time of the offense and trial. See Inmates #763 and #764, FIF.

77. "Manslaughter Verdict against Harriet Smith, but in the Second Degree," *Poughkeepsie News-Press*, November 16, 1909.

78. *Poughkeepsie Evening Star*, November 15, 1909.

79. *Poughkeepsie Daily Eagle*, November 16, 1909.

80. Ibid., February 13, 1909, 6; *Poughkeepsie News-Press*, November 16, 1909.

81. *Poughkeepsie News-Press*, November 16, 1909.

82. "Manslaughter Verdict against Harriet Smith, but in the Second Degree," *Poughkeepsie News-Press*, November 16, 1909.

83. Ibid., 3.

84. "Smith Sisters Sent to Prison," *Poughkeepsie News-Press*, November 17, 1909.

85. *Poughkeepsie News-Press*, November 16, 1909.

86. *Poughkeepsie Daily Eagle*, November 17, 1909.

87. Ibid.

88. *Poughkeepsie News-Press*, November 17, 1909.

89. *Poughkeepsie Daily Eagle*, November 17, 1909.

90. Inmates #764 and #763, May 23, 1911, vol. 3 (1911–12), PM.

91. Inmate #764, May 23, 1911, vol. 3 (1911–12), PM.

92. Higginbotham, *Righteous Discontent*; Gaines, *Uplifting the Race*.

93. An important analysis of working-class respectability and religion can be found in Higginbotham, "Rethinking Vernacular Culture."

94. See Gross, *Colored Amazons*; Rafter, *Partial Justice*; and Dodge, *Whores and Thieves*. For a contemporary account, see Watterson, *Women in Prison*.

95. On the structural problems that working-class and poor families faced, see Neckerman, "Emergence of 'Underclass' Family Patterns."

96. U.S. Bureau of the Census, *Negro Population*, 265, 264, 263.

97. Du Bois, *Philadelphia Negro*, 67.

98. See Hunter, "'Brotherly Love,'" 130–31.

99. Osofsky, *Harlem*, 4.

100. Walls, "Delinquent Negro Girl," 32.

101. Inmate #717, August 21, 1911, vol. 3 (1911–12), PM. See another example in Gross, *Colored Amazons*, 90–93.

Notes to Pages 136-42

102. Inmate #3247, Verified History, June 21, 1922, BH. While this case is from Bedford, these problems were typical of those experienced by women who ended up at Auburn.

103. Inmate #4498, letter from Inmate to Her Sister, ca. February 5, 1926, BH.

104. Inmate #964, FIF; Inmate #964, vol. 4 (1912–17), PM.

105. "Husband in Way, So Infuriated Wife Attempts to Shoot Him with Pistol," *New York Amsterdam News*, December 23, 1925.

106. Inmate #1513, May 31, 1930, vol. 13 (1929–30), PM.

107. Inmate #1513, Physician's Report, March 12, 1930, and District Attorney Report, ca. 1929, Box 2, PF.

108. Inmate #1513, May 31, 1930, vol. 13 (1929–30), PM.

109. "Wife Held for Fatal Stabbing," *New York Amsterdam News*, October 14, 1925; Inmate #1353, FIF.

110. "2 to 8 Years for Killing Husband," *New York Amsterdam News*, November 18, 1925.

111. Inmate #1145, letter from Inmate's former employer to Parole Board, n.d., Box 1, PF.

112. "Common Law Wife Stabs Man to Death in 122nd St.," *New York Amsterdam News*, March 24, 1926.

113. Inmate #1469, September 26, 1929, page "A" "B," vol. 13 (1929–30), PM.

114. Gordon, *Heroes of Their Own Lives*; Gross, "Exploring Crime and Violence."

115. Brenzel, *Daughters of the State*.

116. San Gupta [SenGupta], "Black and 'Dangerous'?," 106.

117. Inmate #1337, letter from District Attorney Richmond County, Albert Fach, to Honorable E. S. Jennings, Agent and Warden, Auburn Prison, June 2, 1927, Box 2, PF.

118. Inmate #1337, Prisoner's Preliminary Statement, Auburn Prison, August 27, 1917, Box 2, PF.

119. Inmate #1337, letter from District Attorney Richmond County, Albert Fach, to Honorable E. S. Jennings, Agent and Warden, Auburn Prison, June 2, 1927, Box 2, PF.

120. Inmate #1337, Prisoner's Preliminary Statement, Auburn Prison, August 27, 1917, Box 2, PF.

121. Inmate #1337, Physician of the Prison, Statement of the Prison Physician Relative to the Application for Parole, September 23, 1927, Box 2, PF.

122. Inmate #1337, November 28, 1927, 37, vol. 11 (1927–28), PM.

123. Inmate #1337, letter from Lora Wagner (Inmate's mother's employer) to Warden Jennings, September 1, 1927, Box 2, PF.

124. Inmate #1337, letter from the Employer of Inmate's Mother to Parole Board, September 1927, Box 2, PF.

125. Inmate #1337, November 28, 1927, vol. 11 (1927–28), PM.

126. Inmate #1337, Statement of the Prison Physician, September 23, 1927, Box 2, PF.

127. Inmate #1245, Inmate's Statement, ca. 1925, Box 1, PF.

128. Inmate #1245, February 16, 1926, vol. 9 (1925–26), PM.

129. Inmate #1245, letter from Inmate's Husband to the Parole Board, January 6, 1926, Box 2, PF.

130. Inmate #608, ca. September 1910, vol. 2 (1909–10), PM.

131. Inmate #733, ca. June 1910, vol. 2 (1909–10), PM.

132. Inmate #1123, letter from Ernest K. Coulter of the New York Society for the Prevention of Cruelty to Children to Superintendent Charles F. Rattigan, August 24, 1922, Box 2, PF.

133. Rafter, *Partial Justice*, 107–15; Gross, *Colored Amazons*, 77–81; Dodge, *Whores and Thieves*, 89–96.

134. Inmate #964, vol. 4 (1912–17), PM.

135. Inmate #940, vol. 4 (1912–17), PM.

136. Inmate #853, ca. December 12, 1912, vol. 4 (1912–17), PM.

137. See Chad Heap's study on slumming in New York and Chicago, *Slumming*, 120.

138. Gross, *Colored Amazons*, 72–84.

139. McAdoo, *Guarding a Great City*, 99.

140. "Women Gave Him 'Come Hither' Sign," *New York Amsterdam News*, Inmate #1444, ca. 1927, Box 2, PF.

141. "Woman Gave Him 'Come Hither' Sign," *New York Amsterdam News*, February 7, 1923. See Gross, *Colored Amazons*, 72–73. Similarly, in the earlier case of Philipbor, he was "strongly apposed [*sic*] to having his name appear in connection with the matter" ("Colored Women Arrested," *Brooklyn Eagle*, June 4, 1900).

142. "Colored Women Arrested," *Brooklyn Eagle*, June 4, 1900.

143. Inmate #1283, District Attorney Report, ca. 1923, Box 1, PF.

144. See "Negro Highway Woman," *New York Evening Sun*, August 18, 1904; and "Accuses Woman of Highway Robbery," *The World*, August 19, 1904, Reel 33, DAS.

145. "Highwaywoman Arrested," *The World*, August 18, 1904, Roll 33, DAS.

146. For a discussion of treating, see Peiss, "'Charity Girls'"; and Clement, *Love for Sale*, 144–76, 212–39.

147. Inmate #871, ca. August 4, 1913, vol. 4 (1912–17), PM.

148. "18 and 19-Year-Old Girl Gets Five Years," *New York Amsterdam News*, December 20, 1922; "In the Courts," *New York Amsterdam News*, January 31, 1923. Also see Inmate #1263, FIF.

149. "Police Say Woman Confessed Thefts," *New York Amsterdam News*, May 27, 1925. See also Gross, *Colored Amazons*, 40–43.

150. Inmate #1328, letter from Inmate's husband to the Parole Board (first letter), n.d., Box 2, PF. Pitts's case is unusual; only fifty women were committed both to Bedford and to Auburn.

151. Inmate #2504, Statement of Girl, August, 8, 1917, BH.

152. Inmate #1328, Box 2, PF.

153. Inmate #2504, Verified History, August 8, 1917; and Staff Meeting, October 13, 1917, BH.

154. Inmate #2504, Verified History, August 8, 1917, BH.

155. Abelson, *When Ladies Go A-Thieving*, 4.

156. Ibid., 12, 8–9.

157. Inmate #1297, letter from Inmate's friend to Bohn, July 7, 1928, Box 1, PF.

158. "Manhattan Woman Faces Death Penalty," *New York Times*, November 26, 1931.

159. Appellant's Brief, People of the State of New York against Ruth Brown, New York Court of Appeals, Cases and Briefs, vol. 44 (March 14–March 31, 1931), 31, NYSL.

160. Ibid., 14, 20. The account in the *Amsterdam News* emphasized the criminal behavior of the speakeasy's owner rather than the actions of Ruth Brown, John Dawson, and Theodore Ryan. See "John Dawson Burns as Gang at Sam Harris' Celebrates," *New York Amsterdam News*, June 15, 1932, Reel 40, #587, TNCF.

161. Appellant's Brief, People of the State of New York against Ruth Brown, New York Court of Appeals, Cases and Briefs, 14, 20, NYSL.

162. "Manhattan Woman Faces Death Penalty," *New York Times*, November 26, 1931.

163. *New York Amsterdam News*, June 15, 1932, Reel 40, #587, TNCF.

Notes to Pages 149–56

309

164. Direct Examination (Ruth Brown) by Miss Scheuer, The People of the State of New York against Ruth Brown, New York Court of Appeals, 351, NYSL. For more of Brown's testimony, see ibid., 350–62.

165. Inmate #1636, FIF; "Opening Address by Miss Scheuer on Behalf of Defendant Ruth Brown," The People of the State of New York against Ruth Brown and John Dawson, New York Court of Appeals, 29, NYSL. I have used the inmate's name under the Freedom of Information Act of 1966, 5 USC Sec. 552, Part I, Subchapter II.

166. Summation of Charles Hickey, Court of Appeals, 434, NYSL.

167. Ibid., 436.

168. *New York Times*, June 7, 1932. Also see State of New York, *Public Papers of Franklin D. Roosevelt, Forty-Eighth Governor of the State of New York*, 1932 (Albany: J. B. Lyon Company, 1939), 430. Roosevelt's papers noted that "at the time the Court of Appeals affirmed the judgment of conviction in this case, Judge Lehman dissented and voted for reversal on the ground that there was not evidence of premeditation and deliberation."

169. On the end of the reformatory movement, see Rafter, *Partial Justice*, 177–91.

CHAPTER FIVE

1. Inmate #2811, Verified History, September 2, 1919, BH.

2. Ibid.

3. Viola Justin, "Negro Officer Uplifts Race," *Salvation Tribune*, August 19, 1911, TNCF.

4. "Woman's Loyal Union Give Reception," *New York Age*, March 25, 1909.

5. Viola Justin, "Negro Officer Uplifts Race," *Salvation Tribune*, August 19, 1911, TNCF. For a reference to Victoria Earle Matthews's perspective, see "Negroes of New York."

6. Viola Justin, "Negro Officer Uplifts Race," *Salvation Tribune*, August 19, 1911, TNCF.

7. Ibid.; James, *Holding Aloft*, 174–75.

8. For an engaged discussion of the NLPCW and later National Urban League committee members, see Weiss, *National Urban League*, 48–57.

9. Layten, "Northern Phase of a Southern Problem," 315–16.

10. A folder noting the name, office, and salary of employees of the National League on Urban Conditions Among Negroes, ca. 1911, shows that Campbell was defined as a probation secretary with an annual salary of $65. See Folder-Receipts, National League on Urban Conditions Among Negroes, Box 5, LHWC.

11. Viola Justin, "Negro Officer Uplifts Race," *Salvation Tribune*, August 19, 1911, TNCF.

12. Ibid.

13. Meeting of the Executive Board of the National League on Urban Conditions Among Negroes, February 7, 1912 (National League for the Protection of Colored Women reports between October 1, 1911, and February 1, 1912), in Folder-Minutes, National League on Urban Conditions Among Negroes, Box 5, LHWC.

14. Walton asked Haynes to "arrange for this" and added, "The reason of course you will not mention to [the replacement] or Miss Campbell" (letter from Elizabeth Walton to George E. Haynes, August 6, 1911, Box 3, GHC). Haynes's reply acknowledges that he "followed the suggestions of . . . [the] letter of August 6th" (letter from George Haynes to

Elizabeth Walton, August 14, 1911, Box 3, GHC). I am indebted to Francille Wilson for sharing her research on the Haynes Collection.

15. Ibid.

16. Nancy J. Weiss (*National Urban League*, 29) notes: "Although the Urban League itself actually came into being in 1911 with the consolidation of the three organizations, it has always claimed the year of its birth as 1910, when the Committee on Urban Conditions was formed."

17. For background, see Parris and Brooks, *Blacks in the City*; and Weiss, *National Urban League*.

18. *New York Age*, January 18, 1912, TNCF.

19. Ibid., March 28, 1912, TNCF.

20. The Annual Report of the National League for the Protection of Colored Women, 1910–11, NULP, reported that a study of the institutional facilities for the care of delinquent colored girls found that "the accommodations for delinquent colored girls in New York City . . . are so inadequate that many convicted girls . . . have been turned back to their old surroundings" (24).

21. Minutes of the Committee for the Protection of Women, January 6, 1913, Committee for Protection of Colored Women, 1913–14, Series 11, Box 1, NULP.

22. Walls, "Delinquent Negro Girl," 29.

23. Ibid.

24. Minutes of the Committee for the Protection of Women, January 6, 1913, Committee for Protection of Colored Women, 1913–14, Series 11, Box 1, NULP.

25. Walton's written notation on Campbell's 1912 typewritten committee report underscores the position the executive board member had taken the previous year, that work at the docks was more important than work with the courts. See Report of the National League for the Protection of Colored Women, September 1912, Box 4, GHC.

26. Elizabeth Walton to Wood, December 20, 1912, 1175 Box 55, National Urban League, Correspondence, LHWC.

27. Walton to Wood, January 1, 1913, 1175 Box 55, National Urban League, Correspondence, LHWC.

28. Walton to Wood, March 13, 1913, 1175 Box 55, National Urban League, Correspondence, LHWC.

29. Walton to Wood, May 20, 1913, 1175 Box 55, National Urban League, Correspondence, LHWC.

30. Letter from Eugene Kinckle Jones to Mr. L. Hollingsworth Wood, May 20, 1913, National Urban League, Correspondence, 1175 Box 55, LHWC.

31. Letter from Eugene Kinckle Jones to George Haynes, May 20, 1913, National Urban League, Correspondence, 1175 Box 55, LHWC. Jones sent a copy of Haynes's letter to Wood explaining his assessment of Campbell's behavior: "I am sending it to you with as much additional vehemence as paper and ink can transmit. I feel that this is a matter which is one of discipline, and demands a precedent which will give us momentum for further office efficiency" (letter from Jones to Wood, May 20, 1913, National Urban League, Correspondence, 1175 Box 55, LHWC).

32. See Holt, "Lonely Warrior"; and Schechter, *Ida B. Wells-Barnett*.

33. Ovington, *Walls Came Tumbling Down*, 106. Ovington's description also referred to Boston's radical activist Monroe Trotter.

34. Fannie Barrier Williams, "Northern Negro's Autobiography," 7.

35. Ovington, *Walls Came Tumbling Down*, 124.

Notes to Pages 165–68

36. For another perspective on a similar dilemma, see Carlton-LaNey, "Career of Birdye Henrietta Haynes."

37. Minutes of a Special Meeting of the Executive Board of the National League on Urban Conditions Among Negroes, Inc., June 11, 1913, Minutes of the Executive Board, June–December 1913 Folder, Series 11, Box 1, NULP.

38. "Protest against Removal," *New York Age*, June 12, 1913.

39. *New York Age*, April 22, 1915. See "Appeal for Negro Magdalens," *New York City Evening Globe*, April 16, 1917, Reel 500, TNCF.

40. Painter, *Narrative of Hosea Hudson*, 20.

41. Walton to Wood, May 20, 1913, National Urban League, Correspondence, 1175 Box 55, LHWC.

42. Letter from Eugene Kinckle Jones to George Haynes, May 20, 1913, National Urban League, Correspondence, 1175 Box 55, LHWC.

43. Minutes of a Special Meeting of the Executive Board of National League on Urban Conditions Among Negroes, Inc., June 11, 1913, Minutes of the Executive Board, June–December 1913 Folder, Series 11, Box 1, NULP.

44. For background on Campbell's early life and participation in the African Blood Brotherhood, see James, *Holding Aloft*, 173–77. Carole Boyce Davis calls for a scholarly biography of Grace Campbell in *Left of Karl Marx*, 243 n. 24.

45. "Home Reorganized," *New York Age*, July 25, 1913.

46. See Viola Justin, "Negro Officer Uplifts Race," *Salvation Tribune*, August 19, 1911, TNCF.

47. Inmate #663, ca. March 10, 1915, vol. 4 (1912–17), PM.

48. Inmate #885, ca. April 1915, vol. 4 (1912–17), PM.

49. Inmate #791, ca. June 26, 1915, vol. 4 (1912–17), PM.

50. *New York Age*, March 1, 1917.

51. Campbell, "Tragedy of the Colored Girl in Court."

52. "Manhattan Y.W.C.A.," *New York Age*, December 21, 1918.

53. Higginbotham, *Righteous Discontent*, 185–229.

54. Inmate #2503, Grace Campbell, Information Concerning the Patient, September 15, 1917; and Inmate #2507, Probation Report from Grace P. Campbell, Empire Friendly Shelter, Inc., to Alice Smith, Probation Officer, 9th District Magistrates Court, August 2, 1917, BH.

55. Thelma Berlack, "Grace Campbell First in Harlem to Tackle Problem of Unmarried Mother," *New York Amsterdam News*, February 2, 1929.

56. W. E. B. Du Bois, "Close Ranks," *Crisis* 16 (July 1918): 111; and "Returning Soldiers," *Crisis* 18 (May 1919): 13–14.

57. Kornweibel, *"Seeing Red,"* 20. Kornweibel notes that "Chandler Owen and A. Philip Randolph coined the term 'New Crowd Negroes' to describe the new generation of militants" that "were genuine supporters of social and economic revolution but rejected communist affiliation."

58. P-138, Negro Activities, June 17, 1921, Reel 918, Federal Bureau of Investigation, Investigative Case Files of the Bureau, 1908–22, National Archives, University of Maryland at College Park.

59. Foner, *American Socialism*, 309. See also Turner and Turner, *Richard B. Moore*; and Hill, "Racial and Radical."

60. "The Klan Forces Us to Protect Ourselves," *Crusader* (November 1921).

61. James, *Holding Aloft*, 174.

62. Report of J. C. Tucker, May 25, 1920 (Special Report), Friend of Negro Freedom, Reel 672, and Report made by P-136, May 27, 1920, "In Re: Negro Activities," Reel 672, M1085-RG 65, Federal Bureau of Investigation, Investigative Case Files of the Bureau, 1908–22, National Archives, University of Maryland at College Park.

63. Campbell, "Tragedy of the Colored Girl in Court."

64. "District Attorney Probes Shooting," *New York Amsterdam News*, December 16, 1925.

65. Quinn, "Revisiting Anna Moscowitz Kross's Critique," 686, 669–76.

66. "First Woman Magistrate Judges Fallen Sisters," *New York Times Magazine*, November 9, 1919.

67. "Mrs. Jean H. Norris Appointed to Bench," *New York Times*, October 28, 1919.

68. Quinn, "Revisiting Anna Moscowitz Kross's Critique," 678.

69. "Honor Woman Magistrate," *New York Times*, November 16, 1919. This statement was made by New York City mayor Hylan, who appointed Norris to the bench.

70. "'Judge' Norris Sits First Day on Bench," *New York Times*, November 4, 1919.

71. "Mrs. Norris Ousted as Unfit for Bench; Guilty on 5 Charges," *New York Times*, June 26, 1931.

72. "'Judge' Norris Sits First Day on Bench," *New York Times*, November 4, 1919.

73. Ibid.

74. "N.Y. Woman Magistrate Is Making Record," *New York Age*, July 26, 1924.

75. Ibid.

76. "Woman Magistrate Advises Supervision of Harlem's Dance Halls and Cabarets," *New York Age*, April 11, 1925, 3.

77. SenGupta, *From Slavery to Poverty*, 173. For a succinct explanation of the development of the Women's Prison Association and the Isaac Hopper Home, see SenGupta, *From Slavery to Poverty*, 170–203.

78. Ovington, *Walls Came Tumbling Down*, 10.

79. Ibid., 11.

80. Ibid., 14.

81. See SenGupta, *From Slavery to Poverty*, 172, 170–203. Also see Roediger, *Wages of Whiteness*, 133–63.

82. Peretti, *Nightclub City*, 129.

83. *New York Age*, April 11, 1925.

84. Ibid.

85. Norris, "Methods of Dealing with Women Offenders," 34.

86. Ibid., 39.

87. Inmate #3696, Admission Record, July 9, 1924, BH. I have revealed the inmate's name in accordance with the Freedom of Information Act of 1966, 5 USC Sec. 552, Part I, Subchapter II. See Chapter 7 for an extended discussion of Mabel Hampton's arrest.

88. Interview with Mabel Hampton by Joan Nestle, ca. 1981, MHSC; Joan Nestle, "'I Lift My Eyes to the Hill': The Life of Mabel Hampton as Told by a White Woman," in Nestle, *Fragile Union*, 34.

89. Mitgang, *Man Who Rode the Tiger*, 191–92.

90. "Mrs. Jean Norris Appointed to Bench," *New York Times*, October 28, 1919; "'Judge' Norris Sits First Day on Bench," *New York Times*, November 4, 1919; "First Woman Magistrate Judges Fallen Sisters," *New York Times Magazine*, November 9, 1919.

91. "Woman Magistrate Defends Vice Squad," *New York Times*, February 18, 1920.

92. Diner, *Erin's Daughters*, 106, 114–19.

93. Ibid. "Opinion in the Matter of Jean H. Norris," Supreme Court, Appellate Division, First Judicial Department, in Chin, *New York City Police Corruption Investigation Commissions*, 3:240.

94. "Police Vice Squad Indorsed by Women," *New York Times*, February 20, 1920.

95. "Removal of Judge Norris Is Demanded by Seabury," *New York Times*, May 29, 1931.

96. For a detailed account of Norris in the context of the Seabury investigation, see Peretti, *Nightclub City*, 123–45, esp. 127–31.

97. "Mrs. Norris Ousted as Unfit for Bench; Guilty on 5 Charges," *New York Times*, June 26, 1931; Peretti, *Nightclub City*, 128–29; Mitgang, *Man Who Rode the Tiger*, 192.

98. "Mrs. Norris Ousted as Unfit for Bench; Guilty on 5 Charges," *New York Times*, June 26, 1931.

99. "Opinion in the Matter of Jean H. Norris," Supreme Court, Appellate Division, First Judicial Department, in Chin, *New York City Police Corruption Investigation Commissions*, 3:240.

100. Mitgang, *Man Who Rode the Tiger*, 192; "Removal of Judge Norris Is Demanded by Seabury," *New York Times*, May 29, 1931.

101. "Opinion in the Matter of Jean H. Norris," Supreme Court, Appellate Division, First Judicial Department, in Chin, *New York City Police Corruption Investigation Commissions*, 3:245.

102. "Mrs. Norris Ousted as Unfit for Bench; Guilty on 5 Charges," *New York Times*, June 26, 1931, 1; "Order Removing Jean H. Norris from the Office of the City Magistrates of the City of New York" (June 25, 1931), in Chin, *New York City Police Corruption Investigation Commissions*, 3:245.

103. "The Case of Magistrate Norris," editorial, *New York Times*, June 26, 1931, 22.

104. "Mrs. Norris Ousted as Unfit for Bench; Guilty on 5 Charges," *New York Times*, June 26, 1931.

105. "Acuna Shifts Story of One 'Frame-Up,'" *New York Times*, January 9, 1931.

106. "77 Minor Girls Imprisoned Unlawfully by 7 Judges; Corrigan Acts to Free All," *New York Times*, January 9, 1931.

CHAPTER SIX

1. Inmate #3476, History Blank, July 10, 1923, BH.

2. Inmate #3476, letter from Rev. George Sims, Union Baptist Church, to Superintendent Amos T. Baker, October 2, 1923; and History Blank, July 10, 1923, BH.

3. Inmate #3476, History Blank, July 10, 1923, BH.

4. See Act of May 29, 1923, Ch. 868, § 1, 1923 N.Y. Laws 1687.

5. On reformers' efforts to safeguard young black women, see Higginbotham, *Righteous Discontent*; Parris and Brooks, *Blacks in the City*; Salem, *To Better Our World*; Weisenfeld, *African American Women and Christian Activism*; Gordon, "Black and White Visions of Welfare," 559, 578–580; and Christina Simmons, "African Americans and Sexual Victorianism," 4.

6. For a discussion of the relationship between the black working poor and New York State's welfare resources during the nineteenth century, see San Gupta [SenGupta], "Black and 'Dangerous'?"

7. Generally, scholars and public policy makers have placed women at the center of the problems in black families and communities. The classic view is Frazier, *Negro Family*. The major rebuttal to that perspective, as well as to the Moynihan report, is Gutman,

Black Family. See also Franklin, *Ensuring Inequality*; and Stevenson, "Black Family Structure." For a critical reevaluation of E. Franklin Frazier's assessment of the black family, see Scott, *Contempt and Pity*, 41–55.

8. Mary Odem's work on working-class parents and their daughters in Alameda and Los Angeles counties in California provides a significant exploration of these issues. In *Delinquent Daughters*, Odem argues that "rather than seeing the court system as a top-down model of class control, . . . we should conceive of it as a triangulated network of struggles and negotiations among working-class parents, their teenage daughters, and court officials" (158). See also Ruth Alexander, *"Girl Problem."*

9. For these years, records exist for seventy-five wayward minor cases. The fifteen black women's inmate numbers are 2486, 2503, 2682, 3365, 3367, 3374, 3387, 3476, 3708, 3711, 4028, 4035, 4059, 4107, and 4498, BH.

10. For discussions of social control, gender, and class in relation to young women and familial conflict that influenced my interpretation of these cases, see Ruth Alexander, *"Girl Problem,"* 12; Brenzel, *Daughters of the State*; Gordon, *Heroes of Their Own Lives*; Stansell, *City of Women*; Lunbeck, "'New Generation of Women'"; Sangster, "Incarcerating 'Bad Girls'"; and Sangster, "She Is Hostile to Our Ways."

11. The "wayward minor laws" include all of the iterations of the law that governed the conduct of young delinquent women, although the law was not referred to by this phrase until 1923.

12. New York City Consolidation Act of 1882, Ch. 410, 1882 N.Y. Laws 367. Also see Tappan, *Delinquent Girls in Court*, 44.

13. Act of May 13, 1886, Ch. 353, § 1, 1886 N.Y. Laws 559, 560 (expanding the covered conduct to other forms of delinquency in addition to prostitution, and applying the law to any woman over the age of twelve); Ruth Alexander, *"Girl Problem,"* 50.

14. Act of May 7, 1903, Ch. 436, § 1, 1903 N.Y. Laws, 1022 (utilizing the "in danger of becoming morally depraved" phrase and adding petit larceny as a basis for committal); Act of April 20, 1914, Ch. 445, § 1, 1914 N.Y. Laws, 1906 (modifying the list of institutions available for commitment); Act of April 21, 1920, Ch. 295, § 1, 1920 N.Y. Laws, 848, 849–50 (providing for parole and for the return to court of women deemed unfit for rehabilitation); Act of May 29, 1923, Ch. 868, § 1, 1923 N.Y. Laws 1687.

15. Act of April 8, 1925, Ch. 389, secs. 1–2, §§ 913-a to -d, 1925 N.Y. Laws 711, 711–12 (substituting the word "person" for "female"); Patrick J. Shelly, "Wayward Minors Put Under New Law's Guidance," *New York Times*, March 7, 1926, X19.

16. Act of April 20, 1914, Ch. 445, § 1, 1914 N.Y. Laws 1905, 1906. In the 1923 amendments, the legislature eliminated the names of specific private reformatories and provided for commitment in "any religious, charitable or other reformative institution authorized by law to receive commitments" (Act of May 29, 1923, Ch. 868, § 1, 1923 N.Y. Laws at 1687).

17. Act of April 21, 1920, Ch. 295, § 5, 1920 N.Y. Laws 848, 850.

18. Ruth Alexander argues: "While New York's incorrigible-girl and wayward-minor laws upheld the principle of filial obedience, they simultaneously affirmed the state's obligation to compensate for the ineptitude of working-class, immigrant, and African American parents by devising measures to restore young women to lives of morality and obedience" (*"Girl Problem,"* 52). Mary Odem states: "The juvenile court functioned as a place of moral instruction and discipline of working-class parents as well as their daughters. Parents were required to attend court hearings with their daughters, and there they frequently found themselves subject to the scrutiny of court officials" (*Delinquent Daughters*, 150).

19. Inmate #2503, letter from Helen Cobb, Superintendent of Bedford, to J. A. Armstrong, Justice of the Peace, August 17, 1917, BH.

20. Patrick J. Shelly, "Wayward Minors Put Under New Law's Guidance," *New York Times*, March 7, 1926.

21. Gaines, *Uplifting the Race*, 158–59.

22. Matthews, "Some of the Dangers," 158.

23. Kellor, *Experimental Sociology*, 33.

24. Ibid., 171.

25. Addams, "Social Control," 22.

26. Inmate #3476, History Blank, Statement of Girl, June 29, 1917, BH: "Father has always worked steadily" as a bricklayer "and for many years mother has done janitress and laundry work so that the family income has been more than sufficient"; Statement of Girl, August 8, 1917, BH: she "had a very good home with [her foster parents] and . . . never wanted anything she did not get." Also see Inmate #4107, Church Mission of Help Summary for Bedford Files, June 7, 1926, BH: the home in which she lived is described as "excellent," "clean," and "comfortable."

27. On the connections between black neighborhoods and vice, see D'Emilio and Freedman, *Intimate Matters*, 199; Gaines, *Uplifting the Race*, 158; and Mumford, *Interzones*, 19–35. See also Brown and Kimball, "Mapping the Terrain of Black Richmond," which addresses how blacks dealt with issues of morality, respectability, and urban space.

28. Inmate #2503, Statement of Girl, August 8, 1917, BH.

29. See Inmate #2486, Statement of Girl, June 29, 1917; and Home Conditions: Information of Mother, July 25, 1917, BH.

30. Inmate #2486, Statement of Girl, June 29, 1917, BH.

31. Addams, "Social Control," 22.

32. Inmate #3708, History Blank, July 19, 1924, BH.

33. Inmate #3711, Statement of Girl, August 2, 1924, BH.

34. See Inmate #2486, Staff Meeting, August 11, 1917, BH.

35. Tappan, *Delinquent Girls in Court*, 151.

36. Waterman, *Prostitution and Its Repression*, 40.

37. Gillin, *Criminology and Penology*, 807.

38. See Carrietta V. Owens, "Investigation of Colored Women at Night Court. From June 8th to August 8th 1914," Folder–Women's Court–Negro Cases, Box 63, COF.

39. Fernald, Hayes, and Dawley, *Study of Women Delinquents*, 169.

40. See Carrietta V. Owens, "Investigation of Colored Women at Night Court. From June 8th to August 8th 1914," Folder–Women's Court–Negro Cases, Box 63, COF.

41. Ruth Alexander notes that interracial, lesbian relationships between inmates were a particularly significant form of inmate subculture (*"Girl Problem,"* 96). Estelle Freedman ("Prison Lesbian," 400) comments: "Assigning the male aggressor role to Black women and preserving a semblance of femininity for their white partners racialized the sexual pathology of inversion." Regina Kunzel ("Situating Sex," 253, 261–62) outlines various investigators' explanations "for the attraction of white girls to black girls." Margaret Otis ("Perversion Not Commonly Noted," 113–14) provides excerpts written by reform school girls involved in same-sex, interracial relationships.

42. Carrietta V. Owens, "Investigation of Colored Women at Night Court. From June 8th to August 8th 1914," Folder–Women's Court–Negro Cases, Box 63, COF.

43. "Sojourner Truth's Work Marching On," *The Survey*, December 13, 1913.

44. Inmate #2466, Information Concerning the Patient, June 6, 1917, BH.

45. "Conference of Social Workers: Two Important Sessions Held Monday at United Charities Building," *New York Age*, December 7, 1911.

46. See Inmate #2486, Verified History, July 1917; and Inmate #3705, History Blank, July 18, 1924, BH.

47. "The Sojourner Truth House and Its Work: Splendid Accomplishment of Organization for Care of Wayward Girls," *New York Age*, September 28, 1916.

48. See "The Problem of a Shelter for Colored Girls" (n.d.), Box 10, COF.

49. Ibid.

50. "The Sisterhood of Woman," *New York Age*, June 12, 1913.

51. Mrs. Edwin F. Horne, "The Problem of the Negro Girl," *New York Amsterdam News*, January 31, 1923.

52. For information regarding how this problem persisted well into the 1930s and 1940s, see Tappan, *Delinquent Girls in Court*, 152.

53. Inmate #2486, Verified History, July 1917, BH.

54. Inmate #2486, Statement of Girl, June 29, 1917, BH.

55. For more on "white slavery," see Ruth Rosen, *Lost Sisterhood*, 112–35. References to black women in white slavery were uncommon, but the campaigns against white slavery affected black communities. See Mumford, *Interzones*, 14–18. Moreover, black reformers sometimes used the language of anti–white slavery campaigns to stress the need for young black women's protection. For specific language regarding the "black side of white slavery," see Layten, "Northern Phase of a Southern Problem," 315, 324.

56. Inmate #2486, Information of Mother, July 25, 1917, BH.

57. Inmate #2486, Verified History, July 25, 1917, BH.

58. Ibid.

59. Inmate #2486, Information of Mother, July 25, 1917, BH.

60. Inmate #2486, Information of Father, July 30, 1917; and Verified History, July 1917, BH.

61. Inmate #2480, Staff Meeting, August 3, 1917, BH.

62. See Freedman, *Their Sisters' Keepers*, 138; and Rafter, *Partial Justice*, 69–74.

63. Rafter, *Partial Justice*, 36.

64. Act of April 21, 1920, Ch. 295, § 5, 1920 N.Y. Laws 848, 850.

65. Inmate #2503, letter from Inmate's Mother to Superintendent Helen Cobb, October 28, 1918, BH.

66. See Minutes of Committee for Protection of Colored Women, January 6, 1913, Series 11, Box 1, NULP.

67. Odem, *Delinquent Daughters*, 159; Lunbeck, *Psychiatric Persuasion*, 82–83.

68. Inmate #3365, letter from Inmate to Superintendent Amos T. Baker, January 5, 1925, BH.

69. The following inmates were committed for some or all of these reasons: 2486, 2503, 2682, 3365, 3374, 3387, 3476, 3708, 4028, and 4107.

70. Inmate #3365, History Blank, February 8, 1923, BH.

71. Inmate #3365, Recommendation for Parole, August 7, 1923, BH.

72. Inmate #3365, History Blank, February 8, 1923, BH.

73. Inmate #3365, Admission Record, February 1, 1923, BH.

74. Inmate #3365, Recommendation for Parole, August 7, 1923, BH.

75. Inmate #3374, History Blank, February 13, 1923, BH.

76. Inmate #3374, Preliminary Investigation of Probation Officer Anna Doyle, February 7, 1923, BH.

77. Ibid.

78. Odem, *Delinquent Daughters*, 179.

79. Inmate #4107, Summary Report on Application for Parole, January 7, 1930, BH.

80. Inmate #4107, Church Mission of Help Summary, June 7, 1926, BH.

81. Inmate #4107, History Blank, June 5, 1926, BH.

82. Inmate #4107, Preliminary Investigation of Probation Officer A. C. Susth, n.d., BH.

83. Inmate #4107, Church Mission of Help Summary, June 7, 1926, BH.

84. Inmate #4107, Preliminary Investigation of Probation Officer, BH.

85. Inmate #3711, Commitment Papers, July 24, 1924, BH.

86. See Odem, *Delinquent Daughters*, 46; D'Emilio and Freedman, *Intimate Matters*, 97; Gutman, *Black Family*, 63–75; and Drake and Cayton, *Black Metropolis*, 590. For a lucid contextualization of the "cultural acceptance" theory, see Kunzel, "White Neurosis," 304.

87. Inmate #3367, letter from Amy M. Prevost to Superintendent Amos T. Baker, October 3, 1925, BH.

88. Inmate #3367, History Blank, February 6, 1923, BH.

89. Inmate #3367, letter from Amy M. Prevost to Superintendent Amos T. Baker, October 3, 1925, BH.

90. Inmate #3367, Recommendation for Parole, April 12, 1927, BH.

91. Inmate #3367, letter from Amy M. Prevost to Superintendent Amos T. Baker, October 3, 1925, BH.

92. On working-class and poor black parents' use of public institutions for child care, see San Gupta [SenGupta], "Black and 'Dangerous'?," 99–131.

93. Inmate #3367, History Blank, February 6, 1923, BH.

94. Inmate #3711, History Blank, August 2, 1924, BH.

95. Evelyn Brooks Higginbotham ("Rethinking Vernacular Culture," 171) argues that the "storefront Baptist, Pentecostal, and Holiness churches along with a variety of urban sects and cults . . . were doubtless more effective than middle-class reformers in policing the black woman's body and demanding conformity to strict guidelines of gender roles and sexual conduct."

96. Inmate #3711, History Blank, August 2, 1924; and letter from Amy M. Prevost to Superintendent Amos T. Baker, January 9, 1925, BH.

97. Act of April 8, 1925, Ch. 389, secs. 1–2, §§ 913-a to -d, 1925 N.Y. Laws 711, 711–12. Also see Odem and Schlossman, "Guardians of Virtue," 186–94, which concludes that "boys were far less likely than girls to have their lives scrutinized or disrupted for status and moral offenses."

98. Inmate #3711, History Blank, August 2, 1924, BH.

99. Inmate #3711, letter from Amy M. Prevost to Superintendent Amos T. Baker, January 28, 1926, BH.

100. Inmate #4059, History Blank, April 8, 1926, BH.

101. Inmate #4059, Recommendation for Parole, December 7, 1926, BH.

102. Inmate #4059, letter from Agent to Reformatory Worker, October 13, 1926, BH.

103. Inmate #4059, History Blank, April 8, 1926, BH.

104. Inmate #2486, Staff Meeting, August 11, 1917, BH.

105. Inmate #3476, letter from Inmate's Father to Superintendent Amos T. Baker, March 17, 1924, BH.

106. Inmate #4028, Admission Record, February 5, 1926, BH.

107. Inmate #4028, History Blank, February 16, 1926, BH.

108. Inmate #4028, letter from Inmate's Mother to Superintendent Amos T. Baker, June 20, 1926, BH.

109. Inmate #4028, letter from Elizabeth Kjaer, Social Worker, City Mission Society, to Amos T. Baker, Superintendent, October 7, 1926, BH.

110. Inmate #4028, letter from Inmate's Mother to Amos T. Baker, Superintendent, June 20, 1926, BH.

111. Inmate #2682, Verified History, n.d., BH.

112. Inmate #2682, letter from Inmate's Mother to Superintendent Helen Cobb, July 20, 1919; and letter from Superintendent Helen Cobb to Inmate's Mother, July 24, 1919, BH.

113. Inmate #2682, letter from Inmate's Mother to Superintendent Helen Cobb, January 18, 1920, BH.

114. Inmate #2682, letter from Superintendent Helen Cobb to Inmate's Mother, January 19, 1920, BH. Parker's mother wrote yet another letter on March 20, 1920, requesting her daughter's release, but Parker was not released until July 20, 1920.

115. Inmate #3367, letter from Inmate's Mother to Bedford Superintendent, March 21, 1927, BH.

116. See Ruth Alexander, "Girl Problem," 106; and Odem, Delinquent Daughters, 188.

117. Inmate #2503, letter from Superintendent Helen Cobb to J. A. Armstrong, Justice of the Peace, June 14, 1919, BH.

118. Letter from Amy M. Prevost to Amos T. Baker, September 26, 1925, BH.

119. Inmate #3387, letter from Inmate's Aunt to Amy M. Prevost, March 2, 1924, BH.

CHAPTER SEVEN

1. James Weldon Johnson, Black Manhattan, 160–61.

2. Anderson, This Was Harlem, 139.

3. James Weldon Johnson, Black Manhattan, 160–61. Regarding the practice of slumming, see Mumford, Interzones, 133–56; and Heap, Slumming.

4. Brandt, No Magic Bullet; Clement, Love for Sale, esp. chap. 4.

5. Freedman, Their Sisters' Keepers, 109–42; Odem, Delinquent Daughters, 1–7, 95–127; Ruth Alexander, "Girl Problem," 1–7, 33–66.

6. Meyerowitz, "Sexual Geography"; Clement, Love for Sale, 212–39.

7. For black women's testimony about the post–World War II era, see Danielle L. McGuire, "'It Was Like All of Us Had Been Raped.'" I thank Nancy Hewitt for encouraging me to think about these connections. For another case from the 1866 Memphis Riot, see Hannah Rosen, Terror in the Heart of Freedom, 61–83, esp. 75–83.

8. Higginbotham ("African-American Women's History," 262) writes that the "metalanguage of race signifies . . . the imbrications of race within the representation of sexuality."

9. My thinking about working-class women's sexuality has been influenced by Peiss, "'Charity Girls'"; Peiss, Cheap Amusements; and Stansell, City of Women.

10. Examples of black women expressing same-sex desire are found in Hansen, "'No Kisses Is Like Youres'"; Griffin, Beloved Sisters; and Kennedy and Davis, Boots of Leather. See also Gross, Colored Amazons, 84–87.

11. Hammonds, "Black (W)holes," 138.

12. Higginbotham, Righteous Discontent, 185–229. Elsa Barkley Brown ("Imaging Lynching," 108) has pointed out that "the struggle to present Black women and the Black community as 'respectable' eventually led to repression within the community."

13. Hine, "Rape and the Inner Lives of Black Women." See also Carby, "Policing the Black Woman's Body"; and Guy-Sheftall, *Daughters of Sorrow*. For scholarly work that explores black women's responses to negative stereotypes, see Hine, "Rape and the Inner Lives of Black Women"; Salem, *To Better Our World*; Higginbotham, *Righteous Discontent*; Deborah Gray White, *Too Heavy a Load*; Mitchell, *Righteous Propagation*; and Gaines, *Uplifting the Race*. See also Gross, *Colored Amazons*, 72–100.

14. Hammonds, "Toward a Genealogy of Black Female Sexuality," 175. Hazel Carby ("'It Jus Be's Dat Way Sometime,'" 332) addresses the heroine in Harlem Renaissance literary texts: "The duty of the black heroine toward the black community was made coterminous with her desire as a woman, a desire which was expressed as a dedication to uplift the race. This displacement from female desire to female duty enabled the negotiation of racist constructions of black female sexuality but denied sensuality, and in this denial lies the class character of its cultural politics." See also Mitchell, "Silences Broken," esp. 440.

15. On black women's sexuality in relation to the blues, see Carby, "'It Jus Be's Dat Way Sometime,'" 330–41. Angela Davis (*Blues Legacies*, 40) argues that "the blues women openly challenged the gender politics implicit in traditional cultural representations of marriage and heterosexual love relationships." See also Ducille, "Blue Notes"; and Spillers, "Interstices," 74.

16. All women who entered Bedford were asked who told them about sex, when and at what age they had their first sexual encounter, and whether that encounter was consensual. Finally, they were asked whether they practiced prostitution and, if they did, at what age they entered the trade as well as how much money they earned.

17. Inmate #3724, Admission Record, August 1924; and Recommendation for Parole, March 10, 1925, BH.

18. Hammonds, "Toward a Genealogy of Black Female Sexuality," 176.

19. Inmate #3706, History Blank, July 8, 1924, BH.

20. Regina Kunzel ("Pulp Fictions," 1468–69) argues that "case records often reveal as much, if not more, about those conducting the interview as they do about those interviewed." Timothy Gilfoyle ("Prostitutes in History," 139–40) discusses the difficult questions that historians of sexuality must pose regarding their evidence.

21. State of New York, State Board of Charities, *Report of the Special Committee*, 7.

22. See Inmate #2475, Conduct Record, October–December 1918; and Inmate #4044, Conduct Record, June 13, 1926, BH.

23. Otis, "Perversion Not Commonly Noted," 113.

24. Morgan, "'Some Could Suckle over Their Shoulder'"; Deborah Gray White, *Ar'n't I a Woman*, 29–34. Also see Higginbotham, "African-American Women's History," 27–61.

25. According to Jennifer Morgan ("Some Could Suckle over Their Shoulder," 170), white male travelers "grappled with the character of the female African body—a body both desirable and repulsive, available and untouchable, productive and reproductive, beautiful and black." See also Kathleen Brown, *Good Wives*, 107–36; and Walter Johnson, *Soul by Soul*, 135–61.

26. Gilman, "Black Bodies," 209.

27. Deborah Gray White, *Ar'n't I a Woman*, 30.

28. Higginbotham, "African-American Women's History," 263.

29. "Experiences of the Race Problem," 46.

30. Inmate #3533, History Blank, October 24, 1923; and Inmate #3521, History Blank, September 20, 1923, BH.

31. Inmate #3333, History Blank, December 26, 1922; and Inmate #3728, Admission Record, August 19, 1924, BH.

32. Inmate #3699, Admission Record, July 10, 1924; and Inmate #3502, History Blank, August 22, 1923, BH.

33. Inmate #4477, Escape Description Record, July 19, 1928, BH.

34. Inmate #3696, History Blank, July 10, 1924; Recommendation for Parole, ca. January 1925; and History Blank, July 10, 1924, BH. I have revealed this inmate's name and case file in accordance with the Freedom of Information Act of 1966, 5 USC Sec. 552, Part I, Subchapter II.

35. Inmate #3696, History Blank, July 10, 1924, BH.

36. Nestle, "Lesbians and Prostitutes," 169.

37. After returning from Europe, Hampton's employer was apparently so "indignant at the idea of her apartment having been used for purposes of prostitution that she refused to appear" in court to vouch for Hampton's character. Although Hampton had been in "faithful service" for at least two years, her employer disregarded friends' advice and chose not to support Hampton. See Inmate #3696, letter from Amy M. Prevost to Dr. Amos T. Baker, November 13, 1924, BH.

38. Spingarn, *Laws Relating to Sex Morality*, 32–33; see also Vagrants, Crim P. 887, Subdivisions 1–4, esp. 4e, "permitting premises to be used for a purpose forbidden thereby is valid where testimony is sufficient to show that such use was with the guilty knowledge of defendant" (33).

39. Joan Nestle, "'I Lift My Eyes to the Hill': The Life of Mabel Hampton as Told by a White Woman," in Nestle, *Fragile Union*, 34.

40. Inmate #3696, Recommendation for Parole, January 13, 1925, BH.

41. Inmate #3474, History Blank, July 1923, BH.

42. Inmate #3489, History Blank, August 1, 1923; and Preliminary Investigation, ca. June 1923, BH.

43. Ogburn, "Richmond Negro in New York City," 60–61.

44. Inmate #3535, History Blank, October 18, 1923, BH.

45. Inmate #2480, Statement of Girl, June 23, 1917, BH.

46. Inmate #4501, letter from Inmate to Friend, January 19, 1928, BH.

47. Inmate #3377, History Blank, February 16, 1923, BH.

48. Inmate #3377, letter from Minister to Bedford Reformatory, August 13, 1923, BH.

49. Inmate #4058, letter of Inmate's Mother to Superintendent Baker, April 26, 1926, BH.

50. "Silk and Lights Blamed for Harlem Girls' Delinquency," *Baltimore Afro-American*, May 19, 1928, Reel 31, TNCF.

51. Inmate #2505, Mental Examination, Attitude Toward Offense, September 18, 1917, BH.

52. "Race Is Dancing Itself to Death," *New York Age*, January 8, 1914. See also Hunter, "'Sexual Pantomimes'"; Hunter, *To 'Joy My Freedom*, 168–86; and Kelley, "'We Are Not What We Seem,'" 75–112, esp. 84–86.

53. See Higginbotham, *Righteous Discontent*, 194–204; Gaines, *Uplifting the Race*, 152–78; and Mitchell, *Righteous Propagation*, 76–140.

54. Inmates #3696, 3389, 4058, 2796, BH.

55. Inmate #3501, History Blank, August 21, 1923, BH.

56. Mitchell, *Righteous Propagation*, chaps. 3 and 4.

57. Inmate #4028, History Blank, ca. February 1926, BH.

58. Inmate #3722, History Blank, August 26, 1924, BH.

59. Inmate #3721, History Blank, October 10, 1924, BH.

60. Inmate #2760, History Blank, ca. December 7, 1925; Inmate #3699, History Blank, July 19, 1924, BH.

61. Inmate #2504, Statement of Girl, August 8, 1917, BH.

62. Inmate #3705, History Blank, July 18, 1924; and Inmate #4498, History Blank, ca. March 30, 1926, BH.

63. Clement, *Love for Sale*, 18–25.

64. Inmates 3535, 3538, 4092, 3376, 3475, 4137, 4042, 3694, BH.

65. Inmate #4137, History Blank, ca. July 7, 1926, BH.

66. See Peiss, *Cheap Amusements*, 108–14; and Clement, *Love for Sale*, 45–75.

67. Inmate #2505, Statement of Girl, August 2, 1917, BH.

68. Inmate #2504, Statement of Girl, August 8, 1917, BH.

69. Inmates #3367, 3386, 2505, BH.

70. Inmate #2480, Statement of Girl, June 23, 1917, BH.

71. Inmate #3718, BH. Also see Inmates #3533, 3474, 4498, BH.

72. Nestle, "Excerpts from the Oral History of Mabel Hampton," 930; see also Nestle, *Fragile Union*, 32.

73. Excerpt from tape-recorded oral history interviews with Mabel Hampton, an African American lesbian, by Joan Nestle, MH-2, Box 3, MHSC.

74. Inmate #4501, Summary Report on Application for Parole, ca. 1928, BH.

75. Inmate #2480, Statement of Girl, June 23, 1917, BH.

76. Inmate #4078, History Blank, ca. May 1, 1926, BH.

77. Inmate #3706, History Blank, July 18, 1924, BH.

78. See McLaurin, *Celia*, 104–22.

79. Inmate #3494, Recommendation for Parole, ca. 1924, BH. For background on black prostitution, see Mumford, *Interzones*, 93–117.

80. Carrietta V. Owens, "Investigation of Colored Women at Night Court. From June 8th to August 8th 1914," Folder–Women's Court–Negro Cases, Box 63, p. 7, COF.

81. Inmate #3497, History Blank, August 13, 1923, BH.

82. Inmate #3706, History Blank, July 18, 1924, BH.

83. Carrietta V. Owens, "Investigation of Colored Women at Night Court. From June 8th to August 8th 1914," Folder—Women's Court—Negro Cases, Box 63, p. 7, COF. For background on reformers' argument about the relationship between women's low wages and prostitution, see Freedman, *Their Sisters' Keepers*, 114, 123–24.

84. Inmate #2497, Verified History, July 26, 1917, BH.

85. Inmate #3365, History Blank, February 8, 1923, BH.

86. Inmate #4063, History Blank, ca. April 23, 1926, BH.

87. Inmate #3376, History Blank, February 13, 1923, BH.

88. Inmate #2480, Information Concerning the Patient, June 23, 1917, BH.

89. Meyerowitz, "Sexual Geography," 307. The young women who revealed their engagement in sexual pleasure disregarded the pronouncements of black leaders, who regarded sex as foremost a reproductive measure. Mitchell (*Righteous Propagation*, 90) notes, "For both black reformers and compilers of home manuals, appropriation of mainstream texts was a ready means through which a mass audience of black women and men might be persuaded that sex was not merely for pleasure."

90. Mumford, "Homosex Changes," 400, 402–5.

91. For analyses of the song, see Angela Davis, *Blues Legacies*, 39–40; and Carby,

322

"'It Jus Be's Dat Way Sometime,'" 337. In reference to particular parties, see Mumford, "Homosex Changes," 404.

92. Higginbotham, "Rethinking Vernacular Culture." In his discussion of Chicago minister Clarence Cobbs, Wallace D. Best argues that the black working class seemed more accepting of gay black men than the black middle class; see Best, *Passionately Human*, 188–89.

93. Garber, "Spectacle in Color." See also "Dr. A. C. Powell Scores Pulpit Evils," *New York Age*, November 16, 1929, 1; "Dr. Powell's Crusade against Abnormal Vice Is Approved," *New York Age*, November 23, 1929; and "Corruption in the Pulpit," *New York Amsterdam News*, December 11, 1929, 20. George Chauncey also discusses this issue in *Gay New York*, 254–57.

94. Nestle, *Fragile Union*, 36. David Levering Lewis (*When Harlem Was in Vogue*, 107–8) notes that "for a quarter, you would see all kinds of people making the party scene; formally dressed society folks from downtown, policemen, painters, carpenters, mechanics, truckmen in their workingmen's clothes, gamblers, lesbians, and entertainers of all kinds." He stresses that "rent parties were a function . . . of economics, whatever their overlay of camaraderie, sex, and music." See also Hazzard-Gordon, *Jookin'*, 94–116.

95. Mabel Hampton interview by Joan Nestle, May 21, 1981, Hampton tape, 10, MHSC.

96. Ibid., 11.

97. Mabel Hampton interview by Joan Nestle, *LFL Coming Out Stories*, June 21, 1981, 8, Box 3, MHSC. Another version of this interview is in Nestle, *Fragile Union*, 36.

98. See Chauncey, *Gay New York*, 244–57; and Best, *Passionately Human*, 188–89.

99. Higginbotham, "Rethinking Vernacular Culture," 171.

100. Mabel Hampton interview by Joan Nestle, May 21, 1981, Hampton tape, 9, MHSC. The statements quoted in the text came in response to Nestle's questions "How would you describe the twenties? Was it a good period to be gay?"

101. Mabel Hampton interview by Joan Nestle, *LFL Coming Out Stories*, June 21, 1981, 9, Box 3, MHSC.

102. In "Black (W)holes," Evelynn Hammonds argues that "rather than assuming that black female sexualities are structured along an axis of normal and perverse paralleling that of white women we might find that for black women a different geometry operates" (139). I thank Doreen Drury for her critical questions regarding this issue. See also Nestle, "Lesbians and Prostitutes," 169.

103. Dietzler, *Detention Houses*, 27. See also Brandt, *No Magic Bullet*, 52–121; and Clement, *Love for Sale*, 114–43.

104. Spaulding, *Experimental Study*, 271–72.

105. Inmate #3715, Recommendation for Parole, ca. 1925, BH. This inmate was considered for parole from February until August 1925 but was not released because of her venereal disease.

106. See Brenzel, *Daughters of the State*.

107. Katharine Bement Davis, "A Plan for the Conversion of the Laboratory of Social Hygiene at Bedford Hills in to a State Clearing House . . . ," Bureau of Social Hygiene General Material 1911–16, Box 6, Record Group 2, Rockefeller Boards, Rockefeller Archive Center, Tarrytown, NY.

108. New York State Reformatory for Women at Bedford Hills, *Annual Report of the New York State Reformatory for Women at Bedford for the Year Ending September 30, 1901* (Albany: J. B. Lyon, 1902), 7, NYSL. Almost twenty-four years later, Bedford still

assessed its mission as rehabilitating young women who, administrators believed, were "unfit to make the fight alone" or whose lives were "wrecked by chance misfortune." See New York State, *Salient Facts about the New York State Reformatory for Women, Bedford Hills* (Bedford Hills: The Reformatory, 1926), 3, NYSL. For background regarding the trajectory of women's prison reform from private benevolence to state control, see Sen-Gupta, *From Slavery to Poverty*, 170–203.

109. See, for example, Inmate #2507, letter from Inmate to Superintendent Cobb, March 1, 1920, BH.

110. New York State Reformatory for Women at Bedford, *Annual Report of the New York State Reformatory for Women at Bedford for the Year Ending September 30, 1901* (Albany: J. B. Lyon, 1902), 17–18, NYSL. Expectant mothers and inmates who had children no older than two years were also housed in a separate cottage. See Barrows, "Reformatory Treatment of Women," 156.

111. Inmate #4092, History Blank, ca. May 1926, BH.

112. See Inmate #3715, letter from Inmate to Superintendent Baker (Harriman Cottage), August 7, 1925, BH. According to a State Commission of Prisons report, Harriman Cottage was designated for "more unruly colored girls" (State of New York, State Commission of Prisons, *Thirty-First Annual Report* [Albany: The Commission, 1925], 172, NYSL).

113. Freedman, *Their Sisters' Keepers*, 138–39.

114. Chute, "Probation and Suspended Sentence," 559.

115. State of New York, *New York State Reformatory for Women at Bedford, Sixth Annual Report of the New York State Reformatory for Women at Bedford* (Albany: J. B. Lyon, 1906), 17, NYSL. According to Davis, administrators noticed the change in the type of inmate committed to Bedford in 1905.

116. Freedman, *Their Sisters' Keepers*, 138–39.

117. State of New York, State Commission of Prisons, *Twentieth Annual Report of the State Commission of Prisons* (Albany: The Commission, 1914), 116–19, NYSL; State of New York, State Board of Charities, *Report of the Special Committee*, 3–29.

118. State of New York, State Commission of Prisons, *Twentieth Annual Report of the State Commission of Prisons* (Albany: The Commission, 1914), 117, NYSL.

119. For the administrators' reference to harmful intimacy, see State of New York, State Board of Charities, *Report of the Special Committee*, 7.

120. "Miss Davis Stands by Bedford Home," *New York Herald*, December 24, 1914, 8.

121. State of New York, State Board of Charities, *Report of the Special Committee*, 26–27.

122. Ibid., 26.

123. State of New York, State Board of Charities, *Annual Report for the Year 1915* (Albany: J. B. Lyon, 1915), 96, NYSL. Although the Board of Managers responded to critics, the report did not specify who had opposed its decision.

124. Ibid.

125. State of New York, New York State Reformatory for Women at Bedford, *Seventeenth Annual Report of the New York State Reformatory for Women at Bedford Hills, N.Y.* (Albany: J. B. Lyon, 1918), 8, NYSL.

126. Ibid., 8, 16.

127. State of New York, State Commission of Prisons, *Thirty-first Annual Report of the State Commission of Prisons* (Albany: The Commission, 1925), 172, NYSL.

128. See, for example, Inmate #4044, Conduct Record, June 13, 1926, BH. One white inmate was cited in this record as having aided a black inmate who "passed a note from

one of the Gibbons girls," who were black, to a white inmate during an institutional base-ball game.

129. Freedman, "Prison Lesbian," 400–401.

130. Freedman notes that "at the same time, assigning the male aggressor role to Black women and preserving a semblance of femininity for their white partners racialized the sexual pathology of inversion. In this interpretation, white women were not really lesbians, for they were attracted to men, for whom Black women temporarily substituted. Thus the prison literature racialized both lesbianism and butch/femme roles, implicitly blaming Black women for aggression and, indeed, homosexuality, by associating them with a male role" (ibid.). See also Knupfer, "'To Become Good, Self-Supporting Women,'" 437–41; and Sarah Potter, "'Undesirable Relations.'"

131. Otis, "Perversion Not Commonly Noted," 113–14.

132. Ibid., 113.

133. Kunzel, "Situating Sex," 262.

134. Otis, "Perversion Not Commonly Noted," 114.

135. Spaulding, "Emotional Episodes," 305. As Hazel V. Carby argues in her study of black female writers' response to ideologies of white and black womanhood, "The figurations of black women existed in an antithetical relationship with the values embodied in the cult of true womanhood, an absence of the qualities of piety and purity being a crucial signifier. Black womanhood was polarized against white womanhood in the structure of the metaphoric system of female sexuality, particularly through the association of black women with overt sexuality and taboo sexual practices" (*Reconstructing Womanhood*, 32).

136. Moreno, *Who Shall Survive?*, 229; see also Lunbeck, *Psychiatric Persuasion*, 295–96.

137. Kunzel, "Situating Sex," 262.

138. Otis, "Perversion Not Commonly Noted," 114.

139. Moreno noted that black women were "the subject adored and rarely the wooer. . . . While overtly she responds with affection, she almost invariably ridicules the courtship" (*Who Shall Survive?*, 230).

140. Ruth Alexander, *"Girl Problem,"* 92; Rafter, *Creating Born Criminals*, 181–82. White working-class women's arrest and imprisonment for sexual delinquency departed from the traditional script of the virtuous white woman needing protection from the black male rapist, yet administrators' concerns and responses to interracial same-sex romantic relationships showed how they were influenced still by society's long-standing anxieties about white female and black male unions, even to the point of perceiving black women as men. See Freedman, "Prison Lesbian," 399–400; and Kunzel, "Situating Sex," 261–62. For more on the protection of white women from black men, see Jacquelyn Dowd Hall's cogent analysis of the rape-lynch narrative in her "'Mind that Burns in Each Body.'"

141. State of New York, State Board of Charities, *Report of the Special Committee*, 18.

142. Ibid.

143. Spaulding, *Experimental Study*, 329.

144. Somerville, "Scientific Racism," 260. Somerville poses the cogent question: "Did the girls' intimacy trouble the authorities because it was homosexual or because it was interracial?" (261). Also see Duggan, *Sapphic Slashers*.

145. State of New York, State Board of Charities, *Report of the Special Committee*, 18. Committee investigators asked Taft, "Do you think the relations between the white girls and the colored girls may be continued after the white girls leave the institution so that they may take up with living in colored neighborhoods?"

146. Ibid., 17–18.

147. See Duggan, *Sapphic Slashers*.

148. Spaulding, *Experimental Study*, 270, 272, 273.

149. Ibid., 306–8.

150. State of New York, State Board of Charities, *Report of the Special Committee*, 8. See also Sarah Potter, "'Undesirable Relations,'" 400.

151. Kunzel, "Situating Sex," 253–70, esp. 253–56.

152. Spaulding, "Emotional Episodes," 305.

153. Inmate #2466, Conduct Report, May 12 and October 27, 1919, BH. See conduct infractions such as "writing notes" and "receiving a note" in Inmate #2496, Conduct Report, May 9 and July 23, 1918, BH.

154. Spaulding, "Problem of a Psychopathic Hospital," 818. Another study contradicted Spaulding's assessment, noting that white women were not attracted to especially dark black women but to those with a lighter hue. This study was nevertheless laden with racist stereotyping. It rejected the premise held by "some administrators of women's prisons" who "think . . . white women associate masculine strength and virility with dark color," noting instead that "usually it is not the very dark negro women who are sought after for such liaisons, but the lighter colored ones; and those who are most personable, the cleanest and the best groomed" (Fishman, *Sex in Prison*, 28).

155. Inmate #2503, letter from Superintendent Helen Cobb to Department of Child Welfare, Westchester County, May 28, 1918; Information Concerning Patient, August 8, 1917; Staff Meeting, September 29, 1917; and letter from Superintendent Helen Cobb to Inmate's Mother, October 29, 1918, BH.

156. Hammonds, "Black (W)holes," 139. Also see Gross, *Colored Amazons*, 84–97.

157. Inmate #2503, letter from Church Mission of Help to Bedford, June 9, 1921, and letter from Church Mission of Help to Superintendent Baker, ca. June 1921, BH.

158. Inmate #4092, Family History, ca. 1926, BH.

159. Nestle, "Lesbians and Prostitutes," 169. Billie Holiday noted the prevalence of same-sex relations when she was an inmate in the Federal Women's Reformatory at Alderson, Virginia; see Holiday, *Lady Sings the Blues*, 132.

160. Nestle, *Fragile Union*, 34–35.

161. Inmate #3696, letter from Amy M. Prevost to Dr. Amos T. Baker, November 13, 1924, BH.

162. Nestle, *Fragile Union*, 34. For more of Hampton's observations regarding 1920s Harlem, see Faderman, *Odd Girls*, 76.

163. Nestle, *Fragile Union*, 40–41, 43.

164. Inmate #4501, Parole Report, March 1–2, 1929, BH.

165. Inmate #4501, Parole Report, ca. February 27, 1929, BH.

166. See Kunzel, "Situating Sex."

167. Inmate #2380, Conduct Report and Confiscated Letter, n.d., BH.

168. See Ruth Alexander, *"Girl Problem,"* 96–97.

169. Mabel Hampton interview by Joan Nestle, May 21, 1981, Hampton tape, 9, MHSC.

CHAPTER EIGHT

1. Probation, in contrast, was an alternative to incarceration granted during court sentencing. See Gillin, *Criminology and Penology*, 679, 807–8.

2. Rothman, *Conscience and Convenience*, 193, 194; Pisciotta, *Benevolent Repression*, 5; Ruth Alexander, *"Girl Problem,"* 124.

3. Address to Parole Prisoners, Released at the September 14, 1908, meeting, Superintendent Cornelius Collins, vol. 1 (1905–08), PM.

4. Rafter, "Hard Times," 238; Ruth Alexander, *"Girl Problem,"* 122–48.

5. Address to Parole Prisoners, September 14, 1908, vol. 1 (1905–08), PM.

6. Inmate #3743, Conditional Discharge, Form G-232, April 14, 1925; Synopsis of Rules and Regulations, ca. 1924; and Inmate #4041, Conditional Charge, Rules and Regulations, ca. 1926, BH.

7. Specific guidelines are located in case files: "Unless other arrangements are made with you, you are expected to return to the Institution, to be held in trust for you, a certain percentage of your wages each month, as follows. For the 1st and 2nd months—⅔ of your wages, For the 3rd and 4th months—½ of your wages, For the 5th and following months—¼ of your wages."

8. September 14, 1908, vol. 1 (1905–08), PM.

9. Ruth Alexander, *"Girl Problem,"* 45–46.

10. Brenzel, *Daughters of the State*, 138–44. Freedman (*Their Sisters' Keepers*, 92–95) explains that housewives claimed to welcome inmates "right into the family" and to "treat them like daughters, with the hope that the former criminals would marry and establish their own domiciles." See also Ruth Alexander, *"Girl Problem,"* 134–35; and Lekkerkerker, *Reformatories for Women*, 539–66.

11. Deutsch, *Women and the City*, 55–77, esp. 71–75.

12. Inmate #3696, letter from Inmate to Superintendent Amos Baker, ca. July 1926, BH.

13. See Tera Hunter's discussion of how white employers sought to control black women's leisure in *To 'Joy My Freedom*, 168–86.

14. Freedman, *Their Sisters' Keepers*, 93–95.

15. Inmate #3475, Parole Sheet, February 28, 1923, BH.

16. Inmate #3533, letter from Dorothy Carpenter, City Mission Society, to Superintendent Amos Baker, February 10, 1925, BH.

17. Inmate #663, Registers of Female Inmates Received, 1893–1933; and Minutes of the Board of Parole, vol. 4 (1912–17), AU.

18. Annual Report of the New York State Reformatory for Women at Bedford Hills, 1903, 41, NYSL.

19. Rothman, *Conscience and Convenience*, 159–60.

20. Inmate #3332, letter from Employer to Superintendent Amos Baker, ca. October 1923, BH.

21. On white women's desire to avoid domestic work, see Katzman, *Seven Days a Week*, 29–31; and Kessler-Harris, *Out to Work*, 127–41. On black women's job options in cities, see Giddings, *When and Where I Enter*, 142–52; and Jones, *Labor of Love*, 110–95. Tera Hunter discusses black women's agency in the domestic service labor market in *To 'Joy My Freedom*, 28–29. See also Harley, "For the Good of the Family and Race."

22. Inmate #3511, letter from Amy Prevost to Superintendent Amos Baker, June 25, 1924, BH.

23. Inmate #3521, letter from Inmate to Superintendent Amos Baker, April 14, 1924, BH.

24. Inmate #3521, letter from Superintendent Amos Baker to Dorothy Carpenter, City Mission Society, April 16, 1924, BH.

25. In *Out to Work*, Alice Kessler-Harris notes that white women "sacrificed higher wages for the relative satisfactions of working with compatriots or of doing respected work." She also contends that "sexual divisions in the job market tended to restrict vocational ambition, bunched together women of like ethnic and racial groups and limited some jobs to women of particular racial and ethnic backgrounds" (141).

26. Inmate #3743, Conditional Discharge, Form G-232, April 14, 1925, BH.

27. Inmate #3533, letter from Dorothy Carpenter, City Mission Society, to Superintendent Amos Baker, February 20, 1925, BH.

28. Inmate #3346, letter from Inmate to Superintendent Amos Baker, January 12, 1925, BH.

29. Inmate #3521, letter from Inmate to Superintendent Amos Baker, May 1, 1924; and letter from Superintendent Baker to Inmate, May 2, 1924, BH.

30. Inmate #1128, Police Report, March 4, 1925, Box 1, PF.

31. Inmate #1128, letter from Inmate to Superintendent James Long, October 25, 1925, Box 1, PF.

32. Inmate #1128, letter from Inmate to Superintendent James Long, November 23, 1925, Box 1, PF.

33. Inmate #1128, letter from Inmate to Superintendent James Long, October 25, 1925, Box 1, PF.

34. Inmate #1128, letter from Superintendent James Long to Captain Stanley Shepherd, Salvation Army, December 2, 1925, Box 1, PF.

35. Inmate #3377, letter from Inmate to Superintendent Amos Baker, January 9, 1924, BH.

36. Inmate #3389, Parole Report, March 16, 1924, BH.

37. Fernald, Hayes, and Dawley, *Study of Women Delinquents*, 171, found that black women often served their institutional sentences without probation because of "meager facilities for supervising colored girls" and "several of the private institutions in the city refuse to take colored women." I argue that the behavior of probation officers mirrored that of parole officers.

38. Inmate #3494, letter from Inmate's Fiancé to Superintendent Amos Baker, April 24, 1924, BH.

39. Inmate #3458, letter from Inmate to Superintendent Leo Palmer, December 4, 1927, BH. This inmate's fiancé had already written to Superintendent Palmer requesting the Parole Board's decision after he had been investigated by a parole officer; see letter from Inmate's Fiancé to Superintendent Leo Palmer, November 28, 1927, BH.

40. Inmate #3346, letter from Church Mission of Help Worker to Superintendent Amos Baker, July 12, 1923, BH.

41. Inmate #2504, letter from Inmate's Husband to Superintendent Helen Cobb, January 1, 1919, BH.

42. Inmate #2504, letter from Inmate's Husband to Parole Officer, ca. April 1919, BH.

43. Inmate #2504, letter from Parole Officer to Superintendent Helen Cobb, April 28, 1919, BH.

44. Inmate #2504, letter from Superintendent Cobb to Inmate's Husband, n.d., BH.

45. Inmate #2504, letter from Inmate's Husband to Superintendent Helen Cobb, May 4, 1919, BH. For black veterans' responses to the situation in postwar America, see Barbeau and Henri, *Unknown Soldiers*, 175–89; and David Levering Lewis, *When Harlem Was in Vogue*, 3–24.

46. Inmate #2504, letter from Department of Treasury, Bureau of War Risk Insur-

ance, to Superintendent, Reformatory for Women, Bedford Hills, May 15, August 9, October 7, October 23, 1919, BH.

47. Inmate #4137, letter from Inmate's Attorney to Superintendent Amos Baker, July 3, 1926; letter from Superintendent Amos Baker to Inmate's Attorney, July 6, 1926; and Parole Sheet, September 1, 1926, BH.

48. In *Delinquent Daughters*, Mary Odem cogently argues that working-class families used the state to regulate the behavior of female relatives by taking them to court; however, Bedford and Auburn parole records reveal a continuing interaction between the state and families after imprisonment. Ruth Alexander (*"Girl Problem,"* 47–52, 103–22) examines working-class families' use of the state after imprisonment, but she does not specifically address the implications for black families as distinct from white native-born and immigrant families. See also Hicks, "'In Danger of Becoming Morally Depraved.'"

49. Inmate #4087, letter from Inmate's Brother to Amy Prevost, New York State Reformatory Worker, Church Mission of Help, June 20, 1927, BH.

50. Inmate #2778, letter from Inmate's Sister to Superintendent Christian, n.d., BH.

51. Inmate #3504, letter from Inmate's Mother to Elizabeth Kjaer, City Mission Society, December 8, 1925, BH.

52. Inmate #2496, letter from Inmate's Father to Superintendent Helen Cobb, January 9, 1918, and letter from Inmate's Aunt to Superintendent Helen Cobb, January 15, 1918, BH.

53. Inmate #2486, letter from Inmate's Mother to Superintendent Helen Cobb, August 12, 1918, August 13, 1918, BH.

54. Inmate #2486, letter from Jones's Mother to Social Worker, April 21, 1920, BH.

55. On black immigrants and American citizenship, see Watkins-Owens, *Blood Relations*, 82–85.

56. Inmate #3705, letter from Inmate's Father to Superintendent Amos Baker, August 18, 1924, BH.

57. Inmate #3705, letter from Inmate's Father to Superintendent Amos Baker, March 21, 1925, BH.

58. Inmate #2778, letter from Inmate's Father to Superintendent Amos Baker, April 2, 1925, BH.

59. After Elliot's father contacted immigration officials, they wrote Bedford for more information concerning the case. See Inmate #2778, letter from Inspector in Charge, Law Division of U.S. Department of Labor Immigration, Service Officer of Commissioner of Immigration, Ellis Island, New York Harbor, to Superintendent Amos Baker, July 9, 1925, BH.

60. Inmate #3696, letter from Inmate's Aunt to Superintendent Amos Baker, June 12, 1925, BH. I have revealed this inmate's name in accordance with the Freedom of Information Act of 1966, 5 USC Sec. 552, Part I, Subchapter II.

61. Inmate #3696, letter from Inmate to Superintendent Amos Baker, n.d., BH. The last major conflict between Mabel and her aunt centered on Mabel's unauthorized trips from New Jersey to New York City. In a letter to Mabel's parole officer, her aunt revealed that "Monday about 10 am [Mabel] notified me she was leaving my home to-day. She did not say where she was going she became furious because my daughter told you that she went back and forth to Ny and that she had left" her job. See letter from Inmate's Aunt to Amy Prevost, Church Mission of Help, June 9, 1926, BH.

62. Inmate #3711, letter from Inmate to Superintendent Amos Baker, July 10, 1925, BH.

63. Robin D. G. Kelley (*Race Rebels*, 39) argues that "to understand the significance of internal conflicts among African Americans, we need to examine how communities are constructed and sustained rather than begin with the presumption that a tight-knit, harmonious black community has always existed . . . across time and space." Also see Kelley, "'We Are Not What We Seem'"; Higginbotham, "African-American Women's History," 270–74; and Wolcott, "Culture of the Informal Economy."

64. On white native-born and immigrant working-class families' uses of the state, see Gordon, *Heroes of Their Own Lives*; Ruth Alexander, *"Girl Problem,"* 103–22; and Odem, *Delinquent Daughters*, 38–62, 157–84.

CHAPTER NINE

1. Inmate #1443, March 1, 1932, vol. 14 (1930–33), PM. Moore's first name is not given in these records.

2. Hazel Carby ("Policing the Black Woman's Body," 739–40) calls this response to black female migration a "moral panic": "a series of responses, from institutions and from individuals, that identify the behavior of . . . migrating women as a social and political problem . . . that had to be rectified in order to restore a moral social order."

3. Ibid. Also see Weisenfeld, *African American Women and Christian Activism*, 77–79.

4. Carby, "Policing the Black Woman's Body," 739–40. See also Morton, *Disfigured Images*; Higginbotham, "African-American Women's History"; and Hammonds, "Toward a Genealogy of Black Female Sexuality."

5. Painter, "Soul Murder and Slavery," 18.

6. Ibid., 15.

7. Ibid., 16.

8. Inmate #1443, March 1, 1932, vol. 14 (1930–33), PM.

9. On working-class families' relationship with the state, see Brenzel, *Daughters of the State*; Odem, *Delinquent Daughters*; and Ruth Alexander, *"Girl Problem."*

10. There is no standard comment about southern parole in either the institutions' annual reports or the other types of prison literature. The bulk of the information is contained in administrators' correspondence with parole officers, inmates, and black families associated with Auburn and Bedford between 1905 and 1935. I have also used the transcripts of the parole board commissions (1905–35) at the New York State Prison for Women at Auburn.

11. See Inmates #2798, 2811, 3486, BH.

12. On the racial assumptions of the 1924 Johnson-Reed Act, which restricted immigration, see Jacobsen, *Whiteness of a Different Color*, 82–90.

13. Osofsky, *Harlem*, 128. Osofsky notes that in 1930, "less than 25 percent of New York City's [black] . . . population was born in New York State. There were more [blacks] . . . in the city in 1930 than the combined Negro populations of Birmingham, Memphis, and St. Louis."

14. Inmate #3504, letter from Baker to Dorothy Carpenter, City Mission Society, July 11, 1924, BH.

15. Inmate #1614, ca. March 15, 1933, vol. 14 (1930–33), PM.

16. Inmate #3504, letter from Baker to Dorothy Carpenter, City Mission Society, July 11, 1924, BH.

17. Inmate #3721, letter from Superintendent Amos Baker to Amy Prevost, Octo-

Notes to Pages 252–57

ber 12, 1925, BH. Although their numbers were relatively small, white women from the South consistently received parole in New York State rather than in the South.

18. Spaulding, *Experimental Study*, 307.

19. Inmate #3381, letter from Medical Superintendent, Matteawan Hospital, to Superintendent Amos Baker, September 13, 1923, BH.

20. For more on administrators' linkage of rural life and rehabilitation, see Brenzel, *Daughters of the State*, 138–44; Freedman, *Their Sisters' Keepers*, 92–95; and Ruth Alexander, *"Girl Problem,"* 134–35.

21. Inmate #1545, March 1, 1932, vol. 14 (1930–33), PM. Investigations that uncovered questionable social and economic circumstances of particular areas of the South usually failed to deter officials.

22. Auburn Inmate #962 was deported in 1920 to Hungary, along with her husband, after she was charged with recruiting girls for prostitution. Inmate #1332 (1925) was deported to Germany after being charged with grand larceny and was also suspected of being a German spy (see FIF). At Bedford, black and white immigrant women were deported for violating the Immigration Act of February 5, 1917; reasons given were that the inmate had "been found practicing prostitution subsequent to her entry into the United States" or "was a person likely to become a public charge at the time of her entry" (U.S. Department of Labor, Warrant—Arrest of Alien, Assistant Secretary of Labor; see cases #2766 [Trinidad], #3320 [Russia], #4062 [Sweden], and #4072 [Poland], BH).

23. Auburn's School Report, which discusses the curriculum used for women as well as men, states: "As a very large number of the men attending school are foreigners, it is necessary . . . to spend more than half the time in conversation drills, which help the men not only understand English but also to insure habits of enunciation and pronunciation" (Inmate #1128, School Report, September 19, 1923, Box 1, PF).

24. Inmate #1416, ca. May 1928 and December 1, 1928, vol. 11 (1927–28), PM.

25. Inmate #4500, letter from Amy Prevost to Superintendent Leo Palmer, January 23, 1928, BH.

26. Inmate #4500, letter from Superintendent Leo Palmer to Amy Prevost, January 24, 1928, BH.

27. Inmate #4499, letter from Harry M. Hirsch, Superintendent State and Alien Poor, State of New York—Department of Charities, to Amy Prevost, February 10, 1928, BH.

28. Southern penal reform first addressed prison labor conditions and the special needs of juvenile male offenders (black and white); only later did it attend to the needs of young white women. See Zimmerman, "Penal Reform Movement."

29. Polansky, "'I Certainly Hope.'"

30. Tera Hunter's study of Atlanta (*To 'Joy My Freedom*, 45–46, 145–67, 189) has informed my discussion of the problems in southern cities; also see Hickey, *Hope and Danger*.

31. Inmate #3346, letter from Superintendent Amos Baker to State Board of Charities, July 30, 1923; and letter from Postmaster, H. J. Slaughter, to Superintendent Amos Baker, August 2, 1923, BH.

32. "Race Women Prisoners Clean Streets of New Orleans; Ball and Chain about Ankles," *Chicago Defender*, November 4, 1911; "Pathetic Appeal from Jefferson Prisoners: Negro Women in Local County Bastile Make Complaint to State Prison Inspector Dr. Oates Will Investigate," *The Voice of the People*, September 11, 1914, TNCF. Also see "Female Prisoners" in Curtin, *Black Prisoners*, 113–29; and Gregory, "Persistence and Irony."

33. Report of Ways and Means Committee, Virginia Federation of Colored Women's Clubs, 1912–13, 2, State Library of Virginia; Winona Hall, "Janie Porter Barrett"; Aery, "Helping Wayward Girls"; "Open Home for Wayward Girls," *Norfolk Journal and Guide*, July 31, 1915, HNCF; "Industrial Home School Opens for Wayward Girls," *Pennsylvania Post*, August 20, 1915, HNCF; "Dedicate New Building at Negro Girls' School," *Richmond Times-Dispatch*, May 23, 1916, HNCF.

34. See Dietzler, *Detention Houses*. According to the General Appropriation Act of March 26, 1918, under specific provisions, the home for "wayward, incorrigible or vicious colored girls" between twelve and thirty who were committed for misdemeanors or committed by judges or justices of the commonwealth would receive its first $10,000 for "necessary improvement, support, clothing and furnishings." See letter from C. Lee Moore, Auditor Public Accounts, to Honorable J. T. Mastin, Secretary, State Board of Charities and Corrections, June 4, 1918, Box 32, Virginia Industrial School for Colored Girls Folder, Executive Papers of Westmoreland Davis, Library of Virginia.

35. See Chapter 75 of the Acts of Assembly (Approved February 21, 1920), "an ACT to provide for the conveyance by the Industrial Home School for Wayward Colored Girls of its property, real and personal to the Commonwealth of Virginia; that the Commonwealth will assume control, operation and management of the same," in *Acts and Joint Resolutions of the General Assembly of the State of Virginia*, 63, Library of Virginia. For a South Carolina case in which the state legislature refused to provide funding for a black female reformatory, see Joan Marie Johnson, "Colors of Social Welfare in the New South."

36. See Annual Reports of the Industrial Home School for Colored Girls, especially for 1923, 1924, 1925, Janie Porter Barrett School for Girls Collection, Library of Virginia. For praise of the institution, see Daniel, *Women Builders*, 53–78.

37. Inmate #3721, letter from Associated Charities to Superintendent Amos Baker, October 19, 1925; and Inmate #4477, letter from Louise McMaster (General Secretary), Family Services of Richmond, to Superintendent Leo Palmer, December 27, 1928, BH.

38. For more on the temptations of black leisure in southern cities, see W. E. B. Du Bois, "The Problem of Amusements," in Du Bois, *On Sociology*, 226–37; Hunter, *To 'Joy My Freedom*, 145–86; and Brown and Kimball, "Mapping the Terrain of Black Richmond," 97–105.

39. Inmate #3748, letter from Miss Mina Padgett, Lynchburg Associated Charities, to Miss Elizabeth E. J. Kjaer, City Mission Society, December 1, 1925, BH. See also Polansky, "'I Certainly Hope,'" 138–59.

40. Sixth Annual Report of the Industrial Home School for Colored Girls (1921), 23, Janie Porter Barrett School for Girls Collection, Library of Virginia.

41. I have been unable to find any documentation regarding monetary payments made by northern to southern institutions.

42. Inmate #4499, letter from Amy Prevost to Superintendent Leo Palmer, January 23, 1928, BH.

43. Inmate #4499, letter from Inmate in Harriman Cottage to Amy Prevost, September 6, 1928, BH.

44. Inmate #4499, letter from Inmate's Mother to Superintendent Leo Palmer, August 9, 1928, BH.

45. Inmate #4499, letter from North Carolina County Welfare Worker to Amy Prevost, May 31, 1928, BH. Also see Painter, "'Social Equality,'" 54–55; Hunter, *To 'Joy My Freedom*, 107–8; and Litwack, *Trouble in Mind*, 203–4.

46. Inmate #4499, letter from Inmate to Superintendent Leo Palmer, October 2, 1929, BH.

47. Inmate #4498, letter from Superintendent Leo Palmer to Inmate, March 8, 1927, BH.

48. Inmate #3486, letter from Inmate to Superintendent Baker, May 31, 1924, BH.

49. Inmate #3486, letter from Superintendent Amos Baker to Inmate, April 17, 1924, BH.

50. Inmate #3486, letter from Baker to Inmate, September 13, 1924, BH.

51. Inmate #3486, letter from Baker to Inmate, February 8, 1926, BH.

52. On problems in southern cities, see Hunter, *To 'Joy My Freedom*, 45–46, 145–67, 189. On social welfare in southern cities, see Neverdon-Morton, *Afro-American Women*; and Rabinowitz, *Race Relations*.

53. Elsa Barkley Brown, "To Catch a Vision of Freedom," 68–69; Hunter, "'Brotherly Love,'" 138–40.

54. Inmate #4498, letter from Inmate to Superintendent Baker, December 31, 1926, BH.

55. Inmate #4498, letter from Superintendent Baker to Inmate, January 5, 1927, BH. This inmate was called into court as a material witness for another case, and when she did not provide an adequate home address, the judge had her sent to Bedford under a wayward minor statute. For a middle-class perspective on black families' attention to women and domestic labor, see Shaw, *What a Woman Ought to Be*, 1, 14.

56. Inmate #1141, letter from Inmate to Superintendent, December 20, 1926, Box 1, PF. She was finally discharged February 8, 1927.

57. Inmate #4087, letter from Inmate to Mrs. Fisk in Gibbons Cottage, January 20, 1927, BH.

58. Inmate #4087, Classification Summary, Church Mission of Help, January 18, 1932; letter from Mary Kevin, Assistant Secretary, Church Mission of Help, to Miss Amy Prevost, November 17, 1928; Admission Record, ca. May 4, 1926; and Psychometric Examination, January 8, 1932, BH.

59. Inmate #534, 1907, vol. 1 (1905–08), PM. Simms was released in New York with the provision that her sister was approved by the parole board.

60. Inmate #3374, letter from Inmate to Superintendent Amos Baker, June 12, 1925; and letter from Inmate's Aunt to Superintendent Amos Baker, May 29, 1925, BH.

61. Inmate #3374, letter from Inmate's Aunt to Superintendent Baker, September 7, 1925, BH.

62. Ibid.

63. Inmate #3374, letter from Inmate's Aunt to Superintendent Amos Baker, April 4, 1926, BH.

64. Inmate #3374, letter from (District Visitor) Atlanta Family Welfare Society to Amy Prevost, October 14, 1925, BH.

65. Inmate #3374, letter from Inmate's Aunt to Superintendent Amos Baker, November 10, 1926, BH. Before she could be sent back to New York, Smith ran away. Her aunt found her three months later, sick in an alley. Smith was sent back to New York, where she died of cancer the following year. For a discussion of working-class blacks and respectability in a southern city, see Brown and Kimball, "Mapping the Terrain of Black Richmond."

66. Inmate #3497, letter from Amy Prevost to Superintendent Amos Baker, February 21, 1924, BH.

67. Inmate #3497, letter from Worker with Colored Children, Division of Child Care, City of Charleston, Department of Health and Welfare, to Amy Prevost, July 22 and August 7, 1925, BH.

68. Inmate #3497, Newspaper article in file, November 10, 1926, BH.

1. Harriet Jones, quoted in John Langston Gwaltney, *Drylongso: A Self Portrait of Black America* (New York: Vintage Books, 1980), xix. Gwaltney interviewed people in cities across the northeastern United States.

2. Ibid., 10.

3. Inmate #3365, letter from Inmate to Superintendent Amos Baker, January 1, 1925, BH.

4. Patrick J. Shelly, "Wayward Minors Put Under New Law's Guidance," *New York Times*, March 7, 1926.

5. Inmate #3365, Conduct Reports, September 26 and 28, 1923, BH.

6. Inmate #3365, History Blank, February 8, 1923, BH.

7. Nina Bernstein, "Ward of the State: The Gap in Ella Fitzgerald's Life," *New York Times*, June 23, 1996.

8. Inmate #3521, letter from Inmate to Superintendent Amos T. Baker, May 1, 1924, BH.

bibliography

MANUSCRIPT AND MICROFILM COLLECTIONS

Columbia University, Rare Book and Manuscript Library, New York, New York
  Guichard Parris Collection
  L. Hollingsworth Wood Collection
Fisk University, Special Collections, Nashville, Tennessee
  George Haynes Collection
Hampton University, Hampton, Virginia
  Hampton University News Clippings File (microfilm, Alexandria, Va.:
    Chadwyck-Healey, 1988)
Haverford College, Quaker and Special Collections, Haverford, Pennsylvania
  L. Hollingsworth Wood Collection
Lesbian Herstory Archives, Brooklyn, New York
  Mabel Hampton Special Collection
Library of Congress, Manuscripts Division, Washington, DC
  National Urban League Papers
Library of Virginia, Archives and Manuscripts, Richmond, Virginia
  Janie Porter Barrett School for Girls Collection
  Annual Reports of the Industrial Home School for Colored Girls
  Executive Papers of Westmoreland Davis
National Archives, University of Maryland at College Park
  FBI File—Grace P. Campbell and African Blood Brotherhood
New York City Municipal Archives, Records, and Information Services,
    New York, New York
  District Attorney Indictment Papers, New York County, Court of General Sessions
  District Attorney Scrapbooks, New York County (microfilm)
New York Public Library, Rare Books and Manuscripts Division, Astor, Lenox, and
    Tilden Foundations, New York, New York
  Committee of Fourteen Collection
  Women's Prison Association Collection
New York State Archives, State Education Department, Albany, New York
  Auburn Correctional Facility, Records of the Department of Correctional Services,
    Division of Parole
  Auburn Prison Female Inmate Case Files, 1920–30
  Female Inmate Identification File, 1909–33
  Inmate Record Cards, [ca. 1921–33]
  Minutes of Meetings of Board of Parole, 1905–52
  Registers of Female Inmates Received, 1893–1933
  Bedford Hills Correctional Facility, Records of the Department of
    Correctional Services
  Inmate Case Files, ca. 1915–30, 1955–65

New York State Library, Cultural Education Center, Albany, New York
  Annual Reports for the Prison for Women, 1893–1933
  Annual Reports of the New York State Reformatory for Women at Bedford Hills,
    1897–1933
  Annual Reports of the Superintendent of State Prisons of the State of New York
  New York Court of Appeals, 1931
Rockefeller Archive Center, Tarrytown, New York
  Bureau of Social Hygiene (microfilm)
  Rockefeller Boards
Schomburg Center for Research in Black Culture, Manuscripts, Archives, and
    Rare Books Division, New York Public Library, New York, New York
  White Rose Mission and Industrial Association Collection
Tuskegee Institute News Clippings File (microfilm, Tuskegee: The Institute,
    [1896–1966]; Sanford, N.C.: Microfilming Corporation of America, 1976)
W. E. B. Du Bois Library, Special Collections and University Archives
  The Papers of W. E. B. Du Bois, 1803–1965 (microfilm)
Yale University, Beinecke Rare Book and Manuscript Library, New Haven, Connecticut
  James Weldon Johnson Memorial Collection of Negro Arts and Letters

NEWSPAPERS AND PERIODICALS

Arena

Brooklyn Eagle

Chicago Defender

Colored American
  Magazine

Crisis

Crusader

Evening Sun

Federation

Independent

New York Age

New York Amsterdam
  News

New York City Evening
  Globe

New York Evening Post

New York Herald

New York Sun

New York Times

New York Tribune

Poughkeepsie Daily Eagle

Poughkeepsie Evening Star

Poughkeepsie News-Press

Southern Workman

Voice of the Negro

The Woman's Era

The World

PRIMARY SOURCES

Addams, Jane. "Social Control." *Crisis* 1 (June 1911): 22–23.

Aery, William Anthony. "Helping Wayward Girls: Virginia's Pioneer Work." *Southern Workman* (November 1915): 598–604.

Aptheker, Herbert, ed. *Correspondence of W. E. B. Du Bois*, vol. 1, *Selections, 1877–1934*. Amherst: University of Massachusetts Press, 1973.

Baker, Ray Stannard. *Following the Color Line: American Negro Citizenship in the Progressive Era*. New York: Doubleday, 1908. Reprint, New York: Harper & Row, 1964.

Barrows, Isabel. "Reformatory Treatment of Women in the United States." In *Penal and Reformatory Institutions*, edited by Charles Richmond Henderson, 129–67. New York: Charities Publication Committee, 1910.

Blascoer, Frances. *Colored School Children in New York*. 1915. Reprint, New York: Negro Universities Press, 1970.

Brown, Hallie Q., comp. and ed. *Homespun Heroines and Other Women of Distinction*. Xenia, OH: Aldine Publishing Co., 1926. Reprint, Freeport, NY: Books for Libraries Press, 1988.

Bureau of Social Hygiene. *Housing Conditions of Employed Women in the Borough of Manhattan*. New York: Bureau of Social Hygiene, 1922.

Campbell, Grace P. "Tragedy of the Colored Girl in Court." *New York Age*, April 25, 1925.

———. "Women Offenders and the Day Court." *New York Age*, April 18, 1925.

Chin, Gabriel J., ed. *New York City Police Corruption Investigation Commissions, 1894–1994*. Vols. 1 and 3. New York: William S. Hein & Co., Inc., 1997.

Chute, Charles L. "Probation and Suspended Sentence." *Journal of Criminal Law and Criminology* 12 (February 1922): 558–65.

Citizen's Protective League. *Story of the Riot*. New York: Citizen's Protective League, 1900. Reprint, New York: Arno Press and The New York Times, 1969.

Clyde, John P. "The Negro in New York City." M.A. thesis, Columbia University, 1899.

Cooper, Anna Julia. *A Voice from the South*. Xenia, OH: Aldine, 1892. Reprint, New York: Oxford University Press, 1988.

Daniel, Sadie Iola. *Women Builders*. Washington, DC: Associated Publishers, 1931.

Davis, Katharine Bement. "Crime and Its Cure." *Survey*, February 18, 1911, 851–54.

Dietzler, Mary Macey. *Detention Houses and Reformatories as Protective Social Agencies in the Campaign of the United States against Venereal Diseases*. Washington, DC: U.S. Government Printing Office, 1922.

Doty, Madeleine Z. Appendix B, "Report on the Auburn Women's Prison to the New York Commission on Prison Reform," Moreland Report, Commission on Prison Reform, Preliminary Report, No. 16. 1914.

———. *Society's Misfits*. New York: Century Co., 1916.

Drake, St. Clair, and Horace R. Cayton. *Black Metropolis: A Study of Negro Life in a Northern City*. New York: Harcourt, Brace, & World, 1945. Reprint, Chicago: University of Chicago Press, 1993.

Du Bois, W. E. B. *The Black North in 1901: A Social Study*. New York Times, November 1901. Reprint, New York: Arno Press and The New York Times, 1969.

———. *Dusk of Dawn: An Essay Toward an Autobiography of a Race Concept*. 1940. Reprint, New Brunswick, NJ: Transaction Publishers, 1984.

———. *The Negro American Family*. Atlanta University Publications, no. 13. Atlanta: Atlanta University Press, 1908.

———. "The Negroes of Farmville, Virginia." *Bulletin of the Department of Labor*, no. 14 (January 1898). Abridged version reprinted in *W. E. B. Du Bois: On Sociology and the Black Community*, edited with an introduction by Dan S. Green and Edwin D. Driver, 165–95. Chicago: University of Chicago Press, 1978.

———. *On Sociology and the Black Community*. Edited by Dan S. Green and Edwin D. Driver. Chicago: University of Chicago Press, 1978. Reprint, Chicago: Midway, 1987.

———. *The Philadelphia Negro: A Social Study*. Philadelphia: University of Pennsylvania Press, 1899. Reprinted with an introduction by Elijah Anderson, 1996.

———. *Some Notes on the Negroes in New York City, Compiled from the Reports of the U.S. Census and Other Sources*. Atlanta: Atlanta University Press, 1903.

"Experiences of the Race Problem: By a Southern White Woman." *Independent* 56 (March 17, 1904): 590–94.

Federation of Churches and Christian Organizations in New York City. Eighth Annual Report. January 1904.

Fernald, Mabel Ruth, Mary Holmes Stevens Hayes, and Almena Dawley, with Beardsley Rawl. *A Study of Women Delinquents in New York State*. New York: Century Co., 1920.

Fishman, Joshua F. *Sex in Prison: Revealing Sex Conditions in American Prisons*. New York: National Library Press, 1934.

337

Frazier, E. Franklin. *The Negro Family in the United States*. Chicago: University of Chicago Press, 1939.

Gillin, John Lewis. *Criminology and Penology*. New York: Century Co., 1926.

Harlan, Louis, ed. *The Booker T. Washington Papers*. Vol. 1. Urbana: University of Illinois Press, 1975.

Harper, Frances Ellen Watkins. "Woman's Political Future." 1893. Reprinted in *Black Women in Nineteenth-Century American Life*, edited by Bert James Loewenberg and Ruth Bogin, 244–47. University Park: Pennsylvania State University Press, 1976.

Haynes, George Edmund. "Conditions among Negroes in the Cities." *Annals of the American Academy of Political and Social Science* 49, no. 1 (July 1913): 105–19.

A History of the Club Movement: Among the Colored Women of the United States. Washington, DC: National Association of Colored Women's Clubs, Inc., 1902 [1978].

Holiday, Billie, with William Dufty. *Lady Sings the Blues*. New York: Lancer Books, 1969.

Hopper, Ernest Jasper. "A Northern Negro Group." M.A. thesis, Columbia University, 1912.

Hunton, Mrs. Addie. "Negro Womanhood Defended." *Voice of the Negro* 1 (July 1904): 280–81.

J., T. J. Review of *Out of Work*, by Frances Kellor. *Southern Workman* (March 1905): 181.

Johnson, James Weldon. *Black Manhattan*. New York: Knopf, 1930. Reprint, New York: Da Capo Press, 1991.

Johnstone, Robert Zachariah. "The Negro in New York, His Social Attainments and Prospects." M.A. thesis, Columbia University, 1911.

Joint Committee to Study the Employment of Colored Women in New York City and Brooklyn. *A New Day for the Colored Woman Worker: A Study of Colored Women in Industry in New York City*, investigators Jessie Clark and Gertrude E. McDougald. New York: C. P. Young, printers, 1919.

Justesen, Benjamin R., ed. *In His Own Words: The Writings, Speeches, and Letters of George Henry White*. Lincoln, NE: iUniverse, Inc., 2004.

Kellor, Frances A. "Agencies for the Prevention of Crime." *Southern Workman* 32 (April 1903): 203–7.

———. "Assisted Emigration from the South: The Women." *Charities* 15 (October 1905): 11–14.

———. "Associations for Protection of Colored Women." *Colored American Magazine* 9 (December 1905): 695–99.

———. "Criminal Anthropology in Its Relation to Criminal Jurisprudence." *American Journal of Sociology* 4 (January 1899): 515–27.

———. "The Criminal Negro." *Arena* 25 (January 1901): 59–68; (February 1901): 190–97; (March 1901): 308–16; (April 1901): 419–28; (May 1901): 510–20.

———. "Criminal Sociology: II. Criminality among Women." *Arena* (May 1900): 516–24.

———. "The Evils of the Intelligence Office Systems." *Southern Workman* (July 1904): 377–80.

———. *Experimental Sociology: Descriptive and Analytical*. New York: Macmillan Company, 1901.

———. "Opportunities for Southern Negro Women in Northern Cities." *Voice of the Negro* 1 (July 1905): 470–73.

———. *Out of Work: A Study of Employment Agencies: Their Treatment of the*

Unemployed, and Their Influence Upon Homes and Business. New York: G. P. Putnam's Sons, 1904.

———. "The Problem of the Negro Girl from the South." *New York Times*, March 19, 1905.

———. "Some Old Needs of the New South: Changes Which May Lead to a Diminishing of Crime." *Charities* 10 (May 2, 1903): 439–40.

———. "Southern Colored Girls in the North." *Bulletin of the Inter-Municipal Committee on Household Research* 1 (May 1905): 5–9.

———. "Southern Colored Girls in the North: The Problems of their Protection." *Charities* 13 (March 18, 1905): 584–85.

———. "To Help Negro Women." *Boston Traveler*, May 31, 1905.

Layten, S. W. "A Northern Phase of a Southern Problem." *A.M.E. Church Review* (March 1910): 315–25.

Lekkerkerker, Eugenia C. *Reformatories for Women in the United States.* The Hague: J. B. Wolters, 1931.

Locke, Benjamin. "The Community Life of a Harlem Group of Negroes." M.A. thesis, Columbia University, 1913.

Lombroso, Cesare, and Guglielmo Ferrero. *Criminal Woman, the Prostitute, and the Normal Woman.* Translated by Nicole Hahn Rafter and Mary Gibson. 1895. Reprint, Durham, NC: Duke University Press, 2004.

———. *The Female Offender.* New York: D. Appleton and Co., 1895.

Matthews, Victoria Earle. "The Colored Race, North and South: Boys Compelled to Work in Chain Gangs at the South: Girls Sold to Houses of Ill-Fame at the North." *Witness* (1899), Item #493, Hampton University News Clippings File, Hampton University, Hampton, Virginia.

———. "The Negroes of New York." *New York Sun*, September 14, 1897.

———. "Protecting Colored Girls." *New York Tribune*, March 30, 1905.

———. "Some of the Dangers Confronting Southern Girls in the North." *Proceedings of the Hampton Negro Conference* 2 (July 1898): 62–69.

———. "The Value of Race Literature: An Address (1895)." Reprinted in *The Massachusetts Review* 27 (Summer 1986): 170–85.

[Matthews], Victoria Earle. *Aunt Lindy. A Story Founded on Real Life.* New York: J. J. Little, 1893.

———. "Novel Reading Defended." *New York Age*, May 23, 1891.

Matthews, Virginia [*sic*]. "The Redemption of Our City (Colored)." *Federation* 2 (July 1902): 57–58.

McAdoo, William. *Guarding a Great City.* New York: Harper & Brothers, 1906.

Miller, Kelly. "Surplus Negro Women." *Southern Workman* 34 (October 1905): 522–28.

Minor, Maude. *The Slavery of Prostitution: A Plea for Emancipation.* New York: Macmillan Company, 1916.

Moreno, J. L. *Who Shall Survive? A New Approach to the Problems of Human Interrelations.* Washington, DC: Nervous and Mental Disease Publishing, Co., 1934.

National League for the Protection of Colored Women. Annual Report. November 1910.

Norris, Jean. "Methods of Dealing with Women Offenders." *New York University Law Review* 3 (March 1926): 31–39.

Ogburn, William Fielding. "The Richmond Negro in New York City: His Social Mind as Seen in His Pleasures." Master's thesis, Columbia University, 1909.

Otis, Margaret. "A Perversion Not Commonly Noted." *Journal of Abnormal Psychology* 3, no. 2 (June–July 1913): 113–16.

Ovington, Mary White. "The Colored Woman in Domestic Service in New York City." *Bulletin of the Inter-Municipal Committee on Household Research* 1, no. 7 (May 1905): 9–12.

———. *Half a Man: The Status of the Negro in New York City.* New York: Longmans, Green, and Co., 1911. Reprint, New York: Negro Universities Press, 1969.

———. *The Walls Came Tumbling Down.* New York: Harcourt, Brace and Company, 1947.

Paul, Seymour. "A Group of Virginia Negroes in New York City." Master's thesis, Columbia University, 1912.

Penn, I. Garland. *The Afro-American Press and Its Editors.* Springfield, MA: Willey and Co., 1891. Reprint, Salem, NH: Ayer Co., 1988.

Potter, Frank Hunter. "A Reformatory Which Reforms." *Outlook* (February 5, 1910): 303–7.

Rhodes, E. M. "The Protection of Girls' Travel: A National Movement." *Colored American Magazine* 13 (August 1907): 113–19.

Richardson, Clement, ed. *The National Cyclopedia of the Colored Race.* Montgomery, AL: National Publishing Company, 1919.

Richings, G. F. *Evidences of Progress among Colored People.* Philadelphia: Geo. S. Ferguson Co., 1896.

Riis, Jacob A. *How the Other Half Lives: Studies among the Tenements of New York.* 1890. Reprint, New York: Penguin Books, 1997.

Robert, Jeanne. "Care of Women in State Prisons." *Review of Reviews* 44 (July 1911): 76–84. Reprinted in *Prison Reform*, compiled by Corinne Bacon, 91–101. New York: AMS Press, 1974.

Spaulding, Edith. "Emotional Episodes among Psychopathic Delinquent Women." *Journal of Nervous and Mental Disease* 54, no. 4 (October 1921): 298–323.

———. *An Experimental Study of Psychopathic Delinquent Women.* New York: Rand, McNally, 1923. Reprint, Glen Ridge, NJ: Patterson Smith, 1969.

———. "The Problem of a Psychopathic Hospital Connected with a Reformatory Institution." *Medical Record* 99, no. 20 (May 14, 1921): 815–21.

Spingarn, Arthur B. *Laws Relating to Sex Morality in New York City.* New York: Century Co., 1915. Revised by W. Bruce Cobb in 1926.

State of New York, State Board of Charities. *Report of the Special Committee Consisting of Commissioners Kevin, Smith, and Mulry, Appointed to Investigate Charges Made against the New York State Reformatory for Women at Bedford Hills, New York.* Albany: J. B. Lyon, 1915.

U.S. Bureau of the Census. *Negroes in the United States, 1920–1932.* New York: Greenwood Press, 1935.

———. *Negro Population in the United States, 1790–1915.* Washington, DC: U.S. Government Printing Office, 1918. Reprint, New York: Arno Press and The New York Times, 1968.

———. *Statistics of Women at Work.* Washington, DC: U.S. Government Printing Office, 1907.

Veiller, Lawrence. *Housing Reform: A Handbook for Practical Use in American Cities.* New York: Charities Publication Committee, 1911.

Walls, Ellie Alma. "The Delinquent Negro Girl in New York, Her Need of Institutional Care." M.A. thesis, Columbia University, 1912.

Washington, Booker T. "Industrial Education for the Negro." In *The Negro Problem: A Series of Articles by Representative American Negroes of To-Day*, edited by Booker T. Washington, W. E. B. Du Bois, Paul Laurence Dunbar et al. New York: James Pratt & Co., 1903.

———. *Up from Slavery.* 1901. Reprint, New York: Dover Publications Inc., 1995.

Washington, Booker T., Norman Barton Wood, and Fannie Barrier Williams. *A New Negro for a New Century.* Chicago: American Publishing House, 1900. Reprint, New York: Arno Press and The New York Times, 1969.

Waterman, Willoughby Cyrus. *Prostitution and Its Repression in New York City, 1900–1931.* New York: Columbia University Studies in History, Economics, and Public Law, 1932.

Wells, Ida B. *Crusade for Justice: The Autobiography of Ida B. Wells.* Edited by Alfreda M. Duster. Chicago: University of Chicago Press, 1970.

———. *Southern Horrors and Other Writings: The Antilynching Campaign of Ida B. Wells, 1892–1900.* Edited by Jacqueline Jones Royster. Boston: Bedford Books, 1997.

Williams, Fannie Barrier. "A Northern Negro's Autobiography." *Independent* 57 (July 14, 1904): 91–96. Reprinted in *The New Woman of Color: The Collected Writings of Fannie Barrier Williams, 1893–1918*, edited by Mary Jo Deegan, 5–13. Dekalb: Northern Illinois University Press, 2002.

SECONDARY SOURCES

Abelson, Elaine S. *When Ladies Go A-Thieving: Middle-Class Shoplifters in the Victorian Department Store.* New York: Oxford University Press, 1989.

Alexander, Eleanor. *Lyrics of Sunshine and Shadow: The Courtship and Marriage of Paul Laurence Dunbar and Alice Ruth Moore.* New York: Plume, 2001.

Alexander, Elizabeth. "'We Must Be about Our Father's Business': Anna Julia Cooper and the In-Corporation of the Nineteenth-Century African-American Woman Intellectual." *Signs* 20 (Winter 1995): 336–56.

Alexander, Leslie M. *African or American? Black Identity and Political Activism in New York City, 1784–1861.* Urbana: University of Illinois Press, 2008.

Alexander, Ruth. *The "Girl Problem": Female Sexual Delinquency in New York, 1890–1930.* Ithaca, NY: Cornell University Press, 1995.

Anderson, Jervis. *This Was Harlem: A Cultural Portrait, 1900–1950.* New York: Farrar, Straus, and Giroux, 1982.

Bailey, Peter. "'Will the Real Bill Banks Please Stand Up?' Towards a Role Analysis of Mid-Victorian Working-Class Respectability." *Journal of Social History* 7 (Spring 1979): 336–53.

Barbeau, Arthur E., and Florette Henri. *The Unknown Soldiers: African-American Troops in World War I.* Philadelphia, PA: Temple University Press, 1974. Reprint, New York: Da Capo Press, 1996.

Bederman, Gail. *Manliness and Civilization: A Cultural History of Gender and Race in the United States, 1880–1917.* Chicago: University of Chicago Press, 1995.

Berlin, Ira, and Leslie Harris, eds. *Slavery in New York.* New York: New Press, 2005.

Bernstein, Iver. *The New York City Draft Riots: Their Significance for American Society and Politics in the Age of Civil War.* New York: Oxford University Press, 1990.

Best, Wallace D. *Passionately Human, No Less Divine: Religion and Culture in Black Chicago.* Princeton, NJ: Princeton University Press, 2005.

Biondi, Martha. *To Stand and Fight: The Struggle for Civil Rights in Postwar New York City*. Cambridge, MA: Harvard University Press, 2003.

Blight, David. *Race and Reunion: The Civil War in American Memory*. Cambridge, MA: Belknap Press of Harvard University Press, 2001.

Brandt, Allan M. *No Magic Bullet: A Social History of Venereal Disease in the United States since 1880*. New York: Oxford University Press, 1985.

Brenzel, Barbara. *Daughters of the State: A Social Portrait of the First Reform School for Girls in North America, 1856–1905*. Cambridge, MA: MIT Press, 1983.

Brown, Elsa Barkley. "Imaging Lynching: African American Women, Communities of Struggle, and Collective Memory." In *African American Women Speak Out on Anita Hill–Clarence Thomas*, edited by Geneva Smitherman, 100–24. Detroit, MI: Wayne State University Press, 1995.

———. "Negotiating and Transforming the Public Sphere: African American Political Life in the Transition from Slavery to Freedom." *Public Culture* 7 (Fall 1994): 107–46.

———. "To Catch a Vision of Freedom: Reconstructing Southern Black Women's Political History, 1865–1880." In *African American Women and the Vote, 1837–1965*, edited by Ann D. Gordon with Bettye Collier-Thomas, John Bracey, Arlene Voski Arakian, and Joyce Arrech Berkmen, 66–99. Amherst: University of Massachusetts Press, 1997.

———. "'What Has Happened Here': The Politics of Difference in Women's History and Feminist Politics." In *"We Specialize in the Wholly Impossible": A Reader in Black Women's History*, edited by Darlene Clark Hine, Wilma King, and Linda Reed, 39–54. Brooklyn, NY: Carlson Publishing, 1995.

Brown, Elsa Barkley, and Greg D. Kimball. "Mapping the Terrain of Black Richmond." In *The New African American Urban History*, edited by Kenneth W. Goings and Raymond A. Mohl, 66–115. London: Sage Publications, 1996.

Brown, Kathleen. *Good Wives, Nasty Wenches, and Anxious Patriarchs: Gender, Race, and Power in Colonial Virginia*. Chapel Hill: University of North Carolina Press, 1996.

Butler, Anne M. *Gendered Justice in the American West: Women Prisoners in Men's Penitentiaries*. Urbana: University of Illinois Press, 1997.

———. "Still in Chains: Black Women in Western Prison, 1865–1910." In *"We Specialize in the Wholly Impossible": A Reader in Black Women's History*, edited by Darlene Clark Hine, Wilma King, and Linda Reed, 321–34. Brooklyn, NY: Carlson Publishing, 1995.

Bynum, Victoria E. *Unruly Women: The Politics of Social and Sexual Control in the Old South*. Chapel Hill: University of North Carolina Press, 1992.

Carby, Hazel V. "'It Jus Be's Dat Way Sometime': The Sexual Politics of Black Women's Blues." In *Unequal Sisters: A Multicultural Reader in U.S. Women's History*, 2d ed., edited by Ellen Carole DuBois and Vicki L. Ruiz, 330–41. New York: Routledge, 1994.

———. "Policing the Black Woman's Body in an Urban Context." *Critical Inquiry* 18 (Summer 1992): 738–55.

———. *Reconstructing Womanhood: The Emergence of the Afro-American Woman Novelist*. New York: Oxford University Press, 1987.

Cardyn, Lisa. "Sexualized Racism/Gendered Violence: Outraging the Body Politic in the Reconstruction South." *Michigan Law Review* 100 (February 2002): 675–867.

342

Carlton-LaNey, Iris. "The Career of Birdye Henrietta Haynes, a Pioneer Settlement House Worker." *Social Service Review* 68 (June 1994): 254–73.

Carter, Julian. "Normality, Whiteness, Authorship: Evolutionary Sexology and the Primitive Pervert." In *Science and Homosexualities*, edited by Vernon A. Rosario, 155–76. New York: Routledge, 1997.

Cash, Floris Barnett. "Radicals and Realists: African American Women and the Settlement House Spirit in New York City." *Afro-Americans in New York Life* 15 (Fall 1991): 7–17.

———. "Victoria Earle Matthews." In *Black Women in America*, 2d ed., vol. 2, edited by Darlene Clark Hine et al., 335–37. New York: Oxford University Press, 2005.

———. "Victoria Earle Matthews." In *Notable Black American Women*, edited by Jessie Carney Smith, 736–39. Detroit: Gale Research Inc., 1992.

———. "Womanhood and Protest: The Club Movement among Black Women, 1892–1922." Ph.D. diss., State University of New York at Stony Brook, 1986.

Chauncey, George, Jr. "From Sexual Inversion to Homosexuality: Medicine and the Changing Conceptualization of Female Deviance." In *History of Women in the United States*, edited by Nancy F. Cott, 324–56. Paris: K. G. Saur, 1993.

———. *Gay New York: Gender, Urban Culture, and the Making of the Gay Male World, 1890–1940*. New York: Basic Books, 1994.

Clark-Lewis, Elizabeth. *Living In, Living Out: African American Domestics and the Great Migration*. New York: Kodansha International, 1996.

Clement, Elizabeth Alice. *Love for Sale: Courting, Treating, and Prostitution in New York City, 1900–1945*. Chapel Hill: University of North Carolina Press, 2006.

Cole, Simon A. *Suspect Identities: A History of Fingerprinting and Criminal Identification*. Cambridge, MA: Harvard University Press, 2001.

Cott, Nancy F. "Passionlessness: An Interpretation of Victorian Sexual Ideology, 1790–1850." *Signs* 4 (Winter 1978): 219–33.

Curtin, Mary Ellen. *Black Prisoners and Their World, Alabama, 1865–1900*. Charlottesville: University Press of Virginia, 2000.

———. "'The Human World' of Black Women in Alabama Prisons, 1870–1900." In *Hidden Histories of Women in the New South*, edited by Virginia Bernhard, Betty Brandon, Elizabeth Fox-Genovese, Theda Purdue, and Elizabeth Hayes Turner, 11–30. Columbia: University of Missouri Press, 1994.

Dabel, Jane E. *A Respectable Woman: The Public Roles of African American Women in Nineteenth-Century New York*. New York: New York University Press, 2008.

Dale, Elizabeth. "'Social Equality Does Not Exist among Themselves, nor among Us': Baylies vs. Curry and Civil Rights in Chicago, 1888." *American Historical Review* 102 (April 1997): 311–39.

Davis, Angela. *Blues Legacies and Black Feminism: Gertrude "Ma" Rainey, Bessie Smith and Billie Holiday*. New York: Vintage Books, 1998.

Davis, Carole Boyce. *Left of Karl Marx: The Political Life of Black Communist Claudia Jones*. Durham, NC: Duke University Press, 2008.

D'Emilio, John, and Estelle B. Freedman. *Intimate Matters: A History of Sexuality in America*. New York: Perennial Library, 1988.

Deutsch, Sarah. *Women and the City: Gender, Space, and Power in Boston, 1870–1940*. New York: Oxford University Press, 2000.

Diner, Hasia R. *Erin's Daughters in America: Irish Immigrant Women in the Nineteenth Century*. Baltimore, MD: Johns Hopkins University Press, 1983.

Dodge, L. Mara. *Whores and Thieves of the Worst Kind: A Study of Women, Crime, and Prisons, 1835–2000.* Dekalb: Northern Illinois University Press, 2006.

Ducille, Ann. "Blue Notes on Black Sexuality: Sex and the Texts of Jessie Fauset and Nella Larsen." *Journal of the History of Sexuality* 3, no. 3 (1993): 418–44.

Duggan, Lisa. *Sapphic Slashers: Sex, Violence, and American Modernity.* Durham, NC: Duke University Press, 2000.

Faderman, Lillian. *Odd Girls and Twilight Lovers: A History of Lesbian Life in Twentieth-Century America.* New York: Columbia University Press, 1991.

Feimster, Crystal N. *Southern Horrors: Women and the Politics of Rape and Lynching.* Cambridge, MA: Harvard University Press, 2009.

Fitzpatrick, Ellen. *Endless Crusade: Women Social Scientists and Progressive Reform.* New York: Oxford University Press, 1990.

Foner, Philip S. *American Socialism and Black Americans: From the Age of Jackson to World War II.* Westport, CT: Greenwood Press, 1977.

Foote, Thelma Wills. *Black and White Manhattan: The History of Racial Formation in Colonial New York City.* Oxford: Oxford University Press, 2004.

Foucault, Michel. *Discipline and Punish: The Birth of the Prison.* Translated by Alan Sheridan. New York: Vintage Books, 1979.

———. *History of Sexuality.* Translated by Robert Hurley. New York: Vintage Books, 1978.

Franklin, Donna L. *Ensuring Inequality: The Structural Transformation of the African-American Family.* New York: Oxford University Press, 1995.

Freedman, Estelle. "The Prison Lesbian: Race, Class, and the Construction of the Aggressive Female Homosexual, 1915–1965." *Feminist Studies* 22 (Summer 1996): 397–423.

———. *Their Sisters' Keepers: Women's Prison Reform in America, 1830–1930.* Ann Arbor: University of Michigan Press, 1981.

Fronc, Jennifer. "The Horns of the Dilemma: Race Mixing and the Enforcement of Jim Crow in New York City." *Journal of Urban History* 33 (November 2006): 3–25.

Gaines, Kevin K. *Uplifting the Race: Black Leadership, Politics, and Culture in the Twentieth Century.* Chapel Hill: University of North Carolina Press, 1996.

Garber, Eric. "A Spectacle in Color: The Lesbian and Gay Subculture of Jazz Age Harlem." In *Hidden from History: Reclaiming the Gay and Lesbian Past*, edited by Martin Baumal Duberman, Martha Vicinus, and George Chauncey Jr., 318–31. New York: New American Library, 1989.

Gellman, David N., and David Quigley, eds. *Jim Crow New York: A Documentary History of Race and Citizenship, 1777–1877.* New York: New York University Press, 2003.

Giddings, Paula J. *Ida: A Sword among Lions: Ida B. Wells and the Campaign against Lynching.* New York: Amistad, 2008.

———. *When and Where I Enter: The Impact of Black Women on Race and Sex in America.* New York: Bantam Books, 1984.

Gilfoyle, Timothy J. *City of Eros: New York City, Prostitution, and the Commercialization of Sex, 1790–1920.* New York: W. W. Norton, 1992.

———. "Prostitutes in History: From Parables of Pornography to Metaphors of Modernity." *American Historical Review* 104 (February 1999): 117–41.

Gilman, Sander L. "Black Bodies, White Bodies: Toward an Iconography of Female Sexuality in Late Nineteenth-Century Art, Medicine, and Literature." *Critical Inquiry* 12, no. 1 (Autumn 1985): 204–22.

Goings, Kenneth W., and Brian D. Page. "African Americans versus the Memphis Street Railway Company: Or, How to Win the Battle but Lose the War, 1890–1920." *Journal of Urban History* 30 (January 2004): 131–51.

Gordon, Linda. "Black and White Visions of Welfare: Women's Welfare Activism, 1890–1945." *Journal of American History* 78 (September 1991): 559–90.

———. *Heroes of Their Own Lives: The Politics and History of Family Violence.* New York: Penguin Books, 1988.

Gordon, Linda, and Paul O'Keefe. "Incest as a Form of Family Violence: Evidence from Historical Case Records." *Journal of Marriage and the Family* 46 (February 1984): 27–34.

Gregory, Jane. "Persistence and Irony in the Incarceration of Women in the Texas Penitentiary, 1907–1910." MA thesis, Rice University, 1994.

Griffin, Farah Jasmine, ed. *Beloved Sisters and Loving Friends: Letters from Rebecca Primus of Royal Oak, Maryland, and Addie Brown of Hartford, Connecticut, 1854–1868.* New York: Knopf, 1999.

———. "Black Feminists and Du Bois: Respectability, Protection, and Beyond." *Annals of the American Academy of Political Science* 568 (March 2000): 28–40.

———. "'Ironies of the Saint': Malcolm X, Black Women, and the Price of Protection." In *Sisters in the Struggle: African American Women in the Civil Rights–Black Power Movement*, edited by Bettye Collier-Thomas and V. P. Franklin, 214–29. New York: New York University Press, 2001.

———. "Who Set You Flowin'?" *The African-American Migration Narrative.* New York: Oxford University Press, 1995.

Gross, Kali N. *Colored Amazons: Crime, Violence, and Black Women in the City of Brotherly Love.* Durham, NC: Duke University Press, 2006.

———. "Examining the Politics of Respectability in African American Studies." *University of Pennsylvania Almanac* 43 (April 1, 1997): 15–16.

———. "Exploring Crime and Violence in Early-Twentieth-Century Black Women's History." In *Contesting the Archives: Finding Women in the Sources*, edited by Nupur Chaudhuri, Sherry Katz, and Mary Elizabeth Perry, 56–73. Urbana: University of Illinois Press, 2010.

Grossman, James R. *Land of Hope: Chicago, Black Southerners, and the Great Migration.* Chicago: University of Chicago Press, 1989.

Gutman, Herbert G. *The Black Family in Slavery and Freedom, 1750–1925.* New York: Vintage Books, 1976.

Guy-Shefthall, Beverly. *Daughters of Sorrow: Attitudes Toward Black Women, 1880–1920.* Brooklyn, NY: Carlson Publishing, 1990.

Hahn, Steven. *A Nation Under Our Feet: Black Political Struggles in the Rural South from Slavery to the Great Migration.* Cambridge, MA: Harvard University Press, 2003.

Hall, Jacqueline Dowd. "The Mind that Burns in Each Body: Women, Rape and Sexual Violence." In *Powers of Desire: The Politics of Sexuality*, edited by Ann Snitow, Christine Stansell, and Sharon Thompson, 328–49. New York: Monthly Review Press, 1983.

Hall, Winona. "Janie Porter Barrett, Her Life and Contributions to Social Welfare in Virginia." M.A. thesis, Howard University, 1954.

Hammonds, Evelynn M. "Black (W)holes and the Geometry of Black Female Sexuality." *differences: A Journal of Feminist Cultural Studies* 6, nos. 2–3 (Summer 1994): 126–45.

———. "Toward a Genealogy of Black Female Sexuality: The Problematic of Silence." In *Feminist Genealogies, Colonial Legacies, Democratic Futures*, edited by M. Jacqui Alexander and Chandra Talpade Mohanty, 170–82. New York: Routledge, 1995.

Hansen, Karen V. "'No Kisses Is Like Youres': An Erotic Friendship between Two African-American Women during the Mid-Nineteenth Century." *Gender & History* 7 (August 1995): 153–82.

Harlan, Louis. "Booker T. Washington and the Politics of Accommodation." In *Black Leaders of the Twentieth Century*, edited by John Hope Franklin and August Meier, 1–18. Urbana: University of Illinois Press, 1982.

Harley, Sharon. "For the Good of the Family and Race: Gender, Work, and Domestic Roles in the Black Community, 1880–1930." In *Black Women in America: Social Science Perspectives*, edited by Micheline R. Malson, Elisabeth Mudimbe-Boyi, Jean F. O'Barr, and Mary Wyer, 159–72. Chicago: University of Chicago Press, 1988.

———. "When Your Work Is Not Who You Are: The Development of a Working-Class Consciousness among Afro-American Women." In *"We Specialize in the Wholly Impossible": A Reader in Black Women's History*, edited by Darlene Clark Hine, Wilma King, and Linda Reed, 25–37. Brooklyn, NY: Carlson Publishing, 1995.

Harris, Leslie M. *In the Shadow of Slavery: African Americans in New York City, 1626–1863*. Chicago: University of Chicago Press, 2003.

———. "Slavery, Emancipation, and Class Formation in Colonial and Early National New York City." *Journal of Urban History* 30 (March 2004): 349–50.

Harrison, Brian. *Peaceable Kingdom: Stability and Change in Modern Britain*. Oxford: Clarendon Press, 1982.

Hazzard-Gordon, Katrina. *Jookin': The Rise of Social Dance Formations in African-American Culture*. Philadelphia: Temple University Press, 1990.

Heap, Chad. *Slumming: Sexual and Racial Encounters in American Nightlife, 1885–1940*. Chicago: University of Chicago Press, 2009.

Henri, Florette. *Black Migration: Movement North, 1900–1920*. New York: Doubleday, 1975.

Hickey, Georgina. *Hope and Danger in the New South City: Working-Class Women and Urban Development in Atlanta, 1890–1940*. Athens: University of Georgia Press, 2003.

Hicks, Cheryl D. "'In Danger of Becoming Morally Depraved': Single, Black Women, Working-Class Black Families, and New York State's Wayward Minor Laws, 1917–1928." *University of Pennsylvania Law Review* 151, no. 6 (June 2003): 2093–2121.

Higginbotham, Evelyn Brooks. "African-American Women's History and the Metalanguage of Race." *Signs* 17 (Winter 1992): 251–74.

———. "Rethinking Vernacular Culture: Black Religion and Race Records in the 1920s and 1930s." In *The House That Race Built: Black Americans, U.S. Terrain*, edited by Wahneema Lubiano, 157–77. New York: Pantheon Books, 1997.

———. *Righteous Discontent: The Women's Movement in the Black Baptist Church, 1880–1920*. Cambridge, MA: Harvard University Press, 1993.

Hill, Robert A. "Racial and Radical: Cyril V. Briggs, *The Crusader*, and the African Blood Brotherhood, 1919–1922." Introduction to *The Crusader*, edited by Robert A. Hill. New York: Garland Publishing, 1987.

Hine, Darlene Clark. "Black Migration to the Urban Midwest: The Gender Dimension, 1915–1945." In *The New African American History*, edited by Kenneth W. Goings and Raymond A. Mohl, 240–65. London: Sage Publications, 1996.

———. "Rape and the Inner Lives of Black Women in the Middle West: Thoughts on the Culture of Dissemblance." In *Hine Sight: Black Women and the Reconstruction of American History*, 37–48. Brooklyn, NY: Carlson Publishing, 1994.

Holt, Thomas C. "The Lonely Warrior: Ida B. Wells-Barnett and the Struggle for Black Leadership." In *Black Leaders of the Twentieth Century*, edited by John Hope Franklin and August Meier, 39–61. Urbana: University of Illinois Press, 1982.

———. "Marking: Race, Race-making and the Writing of History." *American Historical Review* 100 (February 1995): 1–20.

Hoy, Suellen. "Caring for Chicago's Women and Girls: The Sisters of Good Shepherd, 1859–1911." *Journal of Urban History* 23 (March 1997): 260–94.

Hull, Gloria T. *Color, Sex, and Poetry: Three Women Writers of the Harlem Renaissance*. Bloomington: Indiana University Press, 1987.

Hunter, Tera W. "The 'Brotherly Love' for Which This City Is Proverbial Should Extend to All: The Everyday Lives of Working-Class Women in Philadelphia and Atlanta in the 1890s." In *W. E. B. Du Bois, Race, and the City: The Philadelphia Negro and Its Legacy*, edited by Michael B. Katz and Thomas J. Sugrue, 127–51. Philadelphia: University of Pennsylvania Press, 1998.

———. "'Sexual Pantomimes,' the Blues Aesthetic, and Black Women in the South." In *Music and the Racial Imagination*, edited by Ronald Radano and Philip V. Bohlman, 145–64. Chicago: University of Chicago Press, 2000.

———. *To 'Joy My Freedom: Southern Black Women's Lives and Labors after the Civil War*. Cambridge, MA: Harvard University Press, 1997.

Jacobsen, Matthew. *Whiteness of a Different Color: European Immigrants and the Alchemy of Race*. Cambridge, MA: Harvard University Press, 1998.

James, Winston. *Holding Aloft the Banner of Ethiopia: Caribbean Radicalism in Early Twentieth-Century America*. London: Verso, 1998.

Johnson, Daniel, and Rex Campbell. *Black Migration in America: A Social Demographic History*. Durham, NC: Duke University Press, 1981.

Johnson, Joan Marie. "The Colors of Social Welfare in the New South: Black and White Clubwomen in South Carolina, 1900–1930." In *Before the New Deal: Social Welfare in the South*, edited by Elna Green, 160–80. Athens: University of Georgia Press, 1999.

Johnson, Marilynn. *Street Justice: A History of Police Violence in New York City*. Boston: Beacon Press, 2003.

Johnson, Val Marie. "Defining Social Evil: Moral Citizenship and Governance in New York City, 1890–1920." Ph.D. diss., New School University, 2002.

Johnson, Walter. *Soul by Soul: Life Inside the Antebellum Slave Market*. Cambridge, MA: Harvard University Press, 1999.

Jones, Jacqueline. *Labor of Love, Labor of Sorrow: Black Women, Work, and the Family from Slavery to the Present*. New York: Vintage Books, 1985.

Katzman, David. *Seven Days a Week: Women and Domestic Service in Industrializing America*. Urbana: University of Illinois Press, 1978.

Kelley, Robin D. G. *Race Rebels: Culture, Politics, and the Black Working Class*. New York: Free Press, 1994.

———. "'We Are Not What We Seem': Rethinking Black Working-Class Opposition in the Jim Crow South." *Journal of American History* 80 (June 1993): 75–112.

Kennedy, Elizabeth Lapovsky, and Madeline D. Davis. *Boots of Leather, Slippers of Gold: The History of a Lesbian Community*. New York: Routledge, 1993.

Kessler-Harris, Alice. *Out to Work: A History of Wage-Earning Women in the United States*. Oxford: Oxford University Press, 1982.

Knupfer, Anne Meis. *Reform and Resistance: Gender, Delinquency, and America's First Juvenile Court*. New York: Routledge, 2001.

———. "'To Become Good, Self-Supporting Women': The State Industrial School for Delinquent Girls at Geneva, Illinois, 1900–1935." *Journal of the History of Sexuality* 9 (October 2000): 420–46.

Kornweibel, Theodore, Jr. *"Seeing Red": Federal Campaigns against Black Militancy, 1919–1925*. Bloomington: Indiana University Press, 1998.

Kramer, Steve. "Uplifting Our 'Downtrodden Sisterhood': Victoria Earle Matthews and New York City's White Rose Mission, 1897–1907." *Journal of African American History* 91 (Summer 2006): 243–66.

Kunzel, Regina G. "Pulp Fictions and Problem Girls: Reading and Rewriting Single Pregnancy in the Postwar United States." *American Historical Review* 100 (December 1995): 1465–87.

———. "Situating Sex: Prison Sexual Culture in the Mid-Twentieth-Century United States." *GLQ: Journal of Lesbian and Gay Studies* 8 (May 2002): 253–70.

———. "White Neurosis, Black Pathology: Constructing Out-of-Wedlock Pregnancy in the Wartime and Postwar United States." In *Not June Cleaver: Women and Gender in Postwar America, 1945–1960*, edited by Joanne Jay Meyerowitz, 304–33. Philadelphia: Temple University Press, 1994.

Lasch-Quinn, Elisabeth. *Black Neighbors: Race and the Limits of Reform in the American Settlement House Movement, 1890–1945*. Chapel Hill: University of North Carolina Press, 1993.

Lemke-Santangelo, Gretchen. *Abiding Courage: African American Migrant Women and the East Bay Community*. Chapel Hill: University of North Carolina Press, 1996.

Levenstein, Lisa. *A Movement without Marches: African American Women and the Politics of Poverty in Postwar Philadelphia*. Chapel Hill: University of North Carolina Press, 2009.

Lewis, David Levering. *W. E. B. Du Bois: Biography of a Race, 1868–1919*. New York: Henry Holt and Co., 1993.

———. *When Harlem Was in Vogue*. New York: Knopf, 1981. Reprint, New York: Oxford University Press, 1989.

Lewis, David W. "The Female Criminal and the Prisons of New York, 1825–1845." *New York History* 42 (July 1961): 215–36.

Lewis, Earl. "Afro-American Adaptive Strategies: The Visiting Habits of Kith and Kin among Black Norfolkians during the First Great Migration." *Journal of Family History* 12 (January 1987): 407–20.

———. *In Their Own Interests: Race, Class, and Power in Twentieth-Century Norfolk, Virginia*. Berkeley: University of California Press, 1991.

———. "To Turn on a Pivot: Writing African American into a History of Overlapping Diasporas." *American Historical Review* (June 1995): 765–87.

Litwack, Leon. *Trouble in Mind: Black Southerners in the Age of Jim Crow*. New York: Vintage Books, 1999.

Logan, Rayford W. *The Negro in American Life and Thought: The Nadir, 1877–1901*. New York: Dial Press, 1954.

Lowell, Josephine Shaw. "House of Refuge for Women." In *Women in Prison, 1834–1928*, edited by David Rothman and Shelia Rothman, 16–20. New York: Garland, 1987.

Luker, Ralph. *The Social Gospel in Black and White: American Racial Reform, 1885–1912*. Chapel Hill: University of North Carolina Press, 1991.

Lunbeck, Elizabeth. "'A New Generation of Women': Progressive Psychiatrists and the Hypersexual Female." *Feminist Studies* 13 (Fall 1987): 513–43.

———. *The Psychiatric Persuasion: Knowledge, Gender, and Power in Modern America*. Princeton, NJ: Princeton University Press, 1994.

Mack, Kenneth W. "Law, Society, Identity, and the Making of the Jim Crow South: Travel and Segregation on Tennessee Railroads, 1875–1900." *Law & Social Inquiry* 24 (Spring 1999): 377–409.

Malone, Jacqui. *Steppin' on the Blues: The Visible Rhythms of African American Dance*. Urbana: University of Illinois Press, 1996.

Mancini, Matthew. *One Dies, Get Another: Convict Leasing in the American South, 1866–1928*. Columbia: University of South Carolina Press, 1996.

Manz, William H. "Desegregation in New York: The Jamaica School War, 1895–1900." *New York State Bar Journal* 76 (May 2004): 10–18.

Marks, Carole. *Farewell—We're Good and Gone: The Great Black Migration*. Bloomington: Indiana University Press, 1989.

Maxwell, William Joseph. "Frances Kellor in the Progressive Era: A Case Study in the Professionalization of Reform." Ph.D. diss., Teacher's College, Columbia University, 1968.

McGuire, Danielle L. "'It Was Like All of Us Had Been Raped': Sexual Violence, Community Mobilization, and the African American Freedom Struggle." *Journal of American History* 91 (December 2004): 906–31.

McLaurin, Melton A. *Celia, A Slave*. New York: Bard, 1991.

Metcalf, Eugene Wesley, Jr. "The Letters of Paul and Alice Dunbar: A Private History." Ph.D. dissertation, University of California, Irvine, 1973.

Meyerowitz, Joanne. "Sexual Geography and Gender Economy: The Furnished-Room Districts of Chicago, 1890–1930." In *Unequal Sisters: A Multi-Cultural Reader in U.S. Women's History*, 3rd. ed., edited by Vicki L. Ruiz and Ellen Carol DuBois, 307–23. New York: Routledge, 2000.

———. *Women Adrift: Independent Wage Earners in Chicago, 1880–1930*. Chicago: University of Chicago Press, 1988.

Mitchell, Michele. *Righteous Propagation: African Americans and the Politics of Racial Destiny after Reconstruction*. Chapel Hill: University of North Carolina Press, 2004.

———. "Silences Broken, Silences Kept: Gender and Sexuality in African-American History." *Gender & History* 11, no. 3 (November 1999): 397–408.

Mitgang, Herbert. *The Man Who Rode the Tiger: The Life and Times of Judge Samuel Seaberry*. 1963. Reprint, New York: Fordham University Press, 1996.

Morgan, Jennifer L. "'Some Could Suckle over Their Shoulder': Male Travelers, Female Bodies, and the Gendering of Racial Ideology, 1500–1770." *William and Mary Quarterly*, 3rd ser., 54 (January 1997): 167–92.

Morton, Patricia. *Disfigured Images: The Historical Assault on Afro-American Women*. Westport, CT: Greenwood Press, 1991.

Mumford, Kevin J. "Homosex Changes: Race, Cultural Geography, and the Emergence of the Gay." *American Quarterly* 48 (September 1996): 395–414.

———. *Interzones: Black/White Districts in Chicago and New York in the Early Twentieth Century*. New York: Columbia University Press, 1997.

Nadasen, Premilla. *Welfare Warriors: The Movement for Welfare Rights in the United States*. New York: Routledge, 2005.

Naison, Mark. *Communists in Harlem during the Great Depression*. Urbana: University of Illinois Press, 1983.

Neckerman, Kathryn M. "The Emergence of 'Underclass' Family Patterns, 1900–1940." In *The "Underclass" Debate: Views from History*, edited by Michael B. Katz, 194–219. Princeton, NJ: Princeton University Press, 1993.

Nestle, Joan. "Excerpts from the Oral History of Mabel Hampton." *Signs* 18, no. 4 (Summer 1993): 925–35.

———. *A Fragile Union: New and Selected Writings*. San Francisco, CA: Cleis Press, 1998.

———. "Lesbians and Prostitutes: An Historical Sisterhood." In Joan Nestle, *A Restricted Country*, 157–77. New York: Firebrand Books, 1987.

Neverdon-Morton, Cynthia. *Afro-American Women of the South and the Advancement of the Race, 1895–1925*. Knoxville: University of Tennessee Press, 1989.

O'Connell, Lucille. "Frances Kellor." In *Notable American Women*, vol. 4, *The Modern Period*, 393–94. Cambridge, MA: Harvard University Press, 1980.

Odem, Mary. *Delinquent Daughters: Protecting and Policing Adolescent Female Sexuality in the United States, 1885–1920*. Chapel Hill: University of North Carolina Press, 1995.

Odem, Mary, and Steven Schlossman. "Guardians of Virtue: The Juvenile Court and Female Delinquency in Early 20th Century Los Angeles." *Crime and Delinquency* 37 (April 1991): 186–203.

Omolade, Barbara. *The Rising Song of African American Women*. New York: Routledge, 1994.

Orleck, Annelise. *Storming Caesar's Palace: How Black Mothers Fought Their Own War on Poverty*. Boston: Beacon Press, 2005.

Oshinsky, David. *"Worse than Slavery": Parchman Farm and the Ordeal of Jim Crow Justice*. New York: Free Press, 1996.

Osofsky, Gilbert. *Harlem: The Making of a Ghetto*. 2d ed. New York: Harper & Row, 1971.

———. "Race Riot, 1900: A Study of Ethnic Violence." *Journal of Negro Education* 32 (Winter 1963): 16–24.

Ottley, Roi. *New World A-Coming: Inside Black America*. Cleveland, OH: World Publishing Company, 1943.

Ottley, Roi, and William Weatherby, eds. *The Negro in New York: An Informal Social History*. New York: Oceana Publications Inc., 1967.

Painter, Nell Irvin. *Exodusters: Black Migration to Kansas after Reconstruction*. New York: W. W. Norton, 1976.

———. *The Narrative of Hosea Hudson: The Life and Times of a Black Radical*. New York: W. W. Norton, 1994.

———. "'Social Equality' and 'Rape' in the Fin-de-Siecle South." Chap. 4 in *Southern History across the Color Line*. Chapel Hill: University of North Carolina Press, 2002.

———. *Sojourner Truth: A Life, a Symbol*. New York: W. W. Norton, 1996.

———. "Soul Murder and Slavery: Toward a Fully Loaded Cost Accounting." Chap. 1 in *Southern History across the Color Line*. Chapel Hill: University of North Carolina Press, 2002.

———. *Standing at Armageddon: The United States, 1877–1919*. New York: W. W. Norton, 1987.

Parris, Guichard, and Lester Brooks. *Blacks in the City: History of the National Urban League*. Boston: Little, Brown and Company, 1971.

Pascoe, Peggy. *Relations of Rescue: The Search for Female Moral Authority in the American West, 1874–1939*. New York: Oxford University Press, 1990.

Peiss, Kathy. "'Charity Girls' and City Pleasures: Historical Notes on Working-Class Sexuality, 1880–1920." In *Passion and Power: Sexuality in History*, edited by Kathy Peiss and Christina Simmons with Robert A. Padgug, 57–69. Philadelphia, PA: Temple University Press, 1989.

———. *Cheap Amusements: Working Women and Leisure in Turn-of-the-Century New York*. Philadelphia, PA: Temple University Press, 1986.

Peretti, Burton W. *Nightclub City: Politics and Amusement in Manhattan*. Philadelphia: University of Pennsylvania Press, 2007.

Peterson, Carla L. "Contesting Space in Antebellum New York: Black Community, City Neighborhoods, and the Draft Riots of 1863." In *"We Shall Independent Be": African American Place Making and the Struggle to Claim Space in the United States*, edited by Angel David Nieves and Leslie M. Alexander, 47–69. Boulder: University Press of Colorado, 2008.

Phillips, Kimberley L. *AlabamaNorth: African American Migrants, Community, and Working-Class Activism in Cleveland, 1915–1945*. Urbana: University of Illinois Press, 1999.

Pisciotta, Alexander. *Benevolent Repression: Social Control and the American Reformatory-Prison Movement*. New York: New York University Press, 1994.

Pleck, Elizabeth. "Two-Parent Household: Black Family Structure in Late-Nineteenth-Century Boston." *Journal of Social History* 6 (Fall 1972): 3–31.

Polansky, Lee S. "'I Certainly Hope That You Will Be Able to Train Her': Reformers and the Georgia Training School for Girls." In *Before the New Deal: Social Welfare in the South*, edited by Elna Green, 128–59. Athens: University of Georgia Press, 1999.

Potter, Sarah. "'Undesirable Relations': Same-Sex Relationships and the Meaning of Sexual Desire at a Women's Reformatory during the Progressive Era." *Feminist Studies* 30 (Summer 2004): 394–415.

Quinn, Mae C. "Revisiting Anna Moscowitz Kross's Critique of New York City's Women's Court: The Continued Problem of Solving the 'Problem' of Prostitution with Specialized Criminal Courts." *Fordham Urban Law Journal* 33 (2006): 665–726.

Rabinowitz, Howard. *Race Relations in the Urban South, 1865–1890*. Urbana: University of Illinois Press, 1980.

Rainwater, Lee, and William L. Yancey. *The Moynihan Report and the Politics of Controversy, Including the Text of Daniel Patrick Moynihan's The Negro Family: The Case for National Action*. Cambridge, MA: MIT Press, 1967.

Rafter, Nicole Hahn. *Creating Born Criminals*. Urbana: University of Illinois Press, 1997.

———. "Hard Times: Custodial Prisons for Women and the Example of the New York State for Women at Auburn, 1893–1933." In *Judge, Lawyer, Victim, Thief: Women, Gender Roles, and Criminal Justice*, edited by Nicole Hahn Rafter and Elizabeth A. Stanko, 237–60. Boston: Northeastern University Press, 1982.

———. *Partial Justice: Women, Prisons, and Social Control*. New Brunswick, NJ: Transaction Publishers, 1990.

Roediger, David. *The Wages of Whiteness: Race and the Making of the American Working Class*. New York: Verso, 1991.

Rosen, Hannah. "'Not That Sort of Women': Race, Gender and Sexual Violence during the Memphis Riot of 1866." In *Sex, Love, Race: Crossing Boundaries in North American History*, edited by Martha Hodes, 267–93. New York: New York University Press, 1999.

———. *Terror in the Heart of Freedom: Citizenship, Sexual Violence, and the Meaning of Race in the Postemancipation South*. Chapel Hill: University of North Carolina Press, 2009.

Rosen, Ruth. *The Lost Sisterhood: Prostitution in America, 1900–1918*. Baltimore, MD: Johns Hopkins University Press, 1982.

Rosenzweig, Roy. *Eight Hours for What We Will: Workers and Leisure in an Industrial City, 1870–1920*. New York: Cambridge University Press, 1983.

Ross, Ellen. "'Not the Sort that Would Sit on the Doorstep': Respectability in Pre–World War I London Neighborhoods." *International Labor and Working-Class History* 27 (Spring 1985): 39–59.

Rothman, David. *Conscience and Convenience: The Asylum and Its Alternatives in Progressive America*. Boston: Little, Brown and Company, 1980.

Ryan, Mary P. *Women in Public: Between Banners and Ballots, 1825–1880*. Baltimore, MD: Johns Hopkins University Press, 1990.

Sacks, Marcy Sarah. *Before Harlem: The Black Experience in New York City Before World War I*. Philadelphia: University of Pennsylvania Press, 2006.

———. "'To Be a Man and Not a Lackey': Black Men, Work, and the Construction of Manhood in Gilded Age New York City." *American Studies* 45 (Spring 2004): 39–63.

———. "'To Show Who Was in Charge': Police Repression of New York City's Black Population at the Turn of the Twentieth Century." *Journal of Urban History* 31 (September 2005): 799–819.

Salem, Dorothy. *To Better Our World: Black Women in Organized Reform, 1890–1920*. Brooklyn, NY: Carlson Publishing, 1990.

Sangster, Joan. "Incarcerating 'Bad Girls': The Regulation of Sexuality Through the Female Refuges Act in Ontario, 1920–1945." *Journal of the History of Sexuality* 7 (October 1996): 239–75.

———. "She Is Hostile to Our Ways: First Nations Girls Sentenced to the Ontario Training School for Girls, 1933–1960." *Law and History Review* 20 (Spring 2002): 59–96.

Schechter, Patricia. "All the Intensity of My Nature: Ida B. Wells, Anger, and Politics." *Radical History Review* 70 (Winter 1998): 49–77.

———. *Ida B. Wells-Barnett and American Reform, 1880–1930*. Chapel Hill: University of North Carolina Press, 2001.

Scheiner, Seth M. *Negro Mecca: A History of the Negro in New York City, 1865–1920*. New York: New York University Press, 1967.

Schlossman, Steven L., and Stephanie Wallach. "The Crime of Precocious Sexuality: Female Juvenile Delinquency in the Progressive Era." *Harvard Educational Review* 48 (February 1978): 65–95.

Scott, Daryl Michael. *Contempt and Pity: Social Policy and the Image of the Damaged Black Psyche, 1880–1996*. Chapel Hill: University of North Carolina Press, 1997.

San Gupta [SenGupta], Gunja. "Black and 'Dangerous'? African American Working Poor Perspectives on Juvenile Reform and Welfare in Victorian New York, 1840–1890." *Journal of Negro History* 86 (Spring 2001): 99–131.

SenGupta, Gunja. "Elites, Subalterns, and American Identities: A Case Study of African-American Benevolence." *American Historical Review* 109 (October 2004): 1104–39.

Bibliography

———. *From Slavery to Poverty: The Racial Origins of Welfare in New York, 1840–1918*. New York: New York University Press, 2009.

Shapiro, Herbert. *White Violence and Black Response: From Reconstruction to Montgomery*. Amherst: University of Massachusetts Press, 1988.

Shaw, Stephanie J. "Black Club Women and the Creation of the National Association of Colored Women." *Journal of Women's History* 3 (Fall 1991): 10–25.

———. *What a Woman Ought to Be and to Do: Black Professional Women Workers during the Jim Crow Era*. Chicago: University of Chicago Press, 1996.

Simmons, Christina. "African Americans and Sexual Victorianism in the Social Hygiene Movement, 1910–1940." *Journal of the History of Sexuality* 4 (July 1993): 51–75.

Sitkoff, Harvard. *The Struggle for Black Equality, 1954–1992*. Rev. ed. New York: Hill and Wang, 1993.

Somerville, Siobhan. "Scientific Racism and the Emergence of the Homosexual Body." *Journal of the History of Sexuality* 5 (October 1994): 243–66.

Spillers, Hortense J. "Interstices: A Small Drama of Words." In *Pleasure and Danger: Exploring Female Sexuality*, edited by Carole S. Vance, 73–100. Boston: Routledge and Kegan Paul, 1984.

Stansell, Christine. *City of Women: Sex and Class in New York, 1789–1860*. Urbana: University of Illinois Press, 1987.

Stevenson, Brenda. "Black Family Structure in Colonial and Antebellum Virginia: Amending the Revisionist Perspective." In *The Decline in Marriage among African Americans*, edited by M. Belinda Tucker and Claudia Mitchell-Kernan, 27–56. New York: Russell Sage Foundation, 1995.

Strange, Carolyn. *Toronto's Girl Problem: The Perils and Pleasures of the City*. Toronto: University of Toronto Press, 1995.

Tappan, Paul W. *Delinquent Girls in Court: A Study of the Wayward Minor Court of New York*. New York: Columbia University Press, 1947. Reprint, Glen Ridge, NJ: Patterson Smith, 1969.

———. *Juvenile Delinquency*. New York: McGraw-Hill, 1949.

Tate, Claudia. *Domestic Allegories of Political Desire: The Black Heroine's Text at the Turn of the Century*. New York: Oxford University Press, 1992.

Thornbrough, Lou. *T. Thomas Fortune: Militant Journalist*. Chicago: University of Chicago Press, 1972.

Trotter, Joe William. *Black Milwaukee: The Making of an Industrial Proletariat, 1915–1945*. Urbana: University of Illinois Press, 1985.

———, ed. *The Great Migration in Historical Perspective: New Dimensions of Race, Class, and Gender*. Bloomington: Indiana University Press, 1991.

Turner, W. Burghardt, and Joyce Moore Turner. *Richard B. Moore, Caribbean Militant in Harlem: Collected Writings, 1920–1972*. Bloomington: Indiana University Press, 1988.

Walkowitz, Judith R. *City of Dreadful Delight: Narratives of Sexual Danger in Late-Victorian London*. Chicago: University of Chicago Press, 1992.

Watkins-Owens, Irma. *Blood Relations: Caribbean Immigrants and the Harlem Community, 1900–1930*. Bloomington: Indiana University Press, 1996.

Watterson, Kathryn. *Women in Prison: Inside the Concrete Womb*. Rev. ed. Boston: Northeastern University Press, 1996.

Weisenfeld, Judith. *African American Women and Christian Activism: New York's Black YWCA, 1905–1945*. Cambridge, MA: Harvard University Press, 1997.

353

Weiss, Nancy J. *The National Urban League, 1910–1940.* New York: Oxford University Press, 1974.

Welke, Barbara. "When All the Women Were White, and All the Blacks Were Men: Gender, Class, Race, and the Road to Plessy, 1855–1914." *Law and History Review* 13 (Autumn 1995): 261–316.

Welter, Barbara. "The Cult of True Womanhood, 1820–1860." *American Quarterly* 18 (Summer 1966): 151–74.

White, Deborah Gray. *Ar'n't I a Woman? Female Slaves in the Plantation South.* Rev. ed. New York: W. W. Norton, 1999.

———. "The Cost of Club Work, the Price of Black Feminism." In *Visible Women: New Essays on American Activism,* edited by Nancy A. Hewitt and Suzanne Lebsock, 247–69. Urbana: University of Illinois Press, 1993.

———. *Too Heavy a Load: Black Women in Defense of Themselves, 1894–1994.* New York: W. W. Norton, 1999.

White, Shane. "'It Was a Proud Day': African Americans, Festivals, and Parades in the North, 1741–1834." In *The New African American Urban History,* edited by Kenneth W. Goings and Raymond A. Mohl, 45–51. Thousand Oaks, CA: Sage, 1996.

Wilder, Craig Steven. *A Covenant with Color: Race and Social Power in Brooklyn.* New York: Columbia University Press, 2000.

———. *In the Company of Black Men: The African Influence on African American Culture in New York City.* New York: New York University Press, 2001.

Williams, Rhonda Y. *The Politics of Public Housing: Black Women's Struggles against Urban Inequality.* New York: Oxford University Press, 2004.

Wilson, Francille Rusan. *The Segregated Scholars: Black Social Scientists and the Creation of Black Labor Studies, 1890–1950.* Charlottesville: University of Virginia Press, 2006.

Wolcott, Victoria W. "Bible, Bath, and Broom: Nannie Helen Burroughs's National Training School and African-American Racial Uplift." *Journal of Women's History* 9 (Spring 1997): 88–110.

———. "The Culture of the Informal Economy: Numbers Runners in Inter-War Detroit." *Radical History Review* 69 (Fall 1997): 47–75.

———. *Remaking Respectability: African American Women in Interwar Detroit.* Chapel Hill: University of North Carolina Press, 2001.

Yochelson, Bonnie, and Daniel Czitrom. *Rediscovering Jacob Riis: Exposure Journalism and Photography in Turn-of-the-Century New York.* New York: New Press, 2007.

Zimmerman, Jane. "The Penal Reform Movement in the South during the Progressive Era, 1890–1917." *Journal of Southern History* 17 (November 1951): 470–92.

index

7, 32–34, 37; and white reformers, 9; racial discrimination of North, 11; and citizenship, 26, 32; freedom as motivation of, 27, 60; and Harlem, 27, 256–57, 276; incarceration rates of, 48

273; and respectability, 12, 158; moral behavior defined by, 15; interracial interactions within, 48; and arrest rates for blacks, 48–49; and sexuality of working-class black women, 206. *See also* Female felons; Parole in New York; Parole in South; Police officers; Probation

Crouch, Odessa, 143–44
Crusader, 172
Cuyler, P. L., 83

Darwin, Charles, 128
Davis, Ellie, 199
Davis, Katharine Bement, 113, 116, 222, 223, 224, 241
Dawson, John, 155, 157, 309 (n. 160)
Diedling, Rudolph, 224
Dillard, Annie, 197–99
Diner, Hasia R., 178
Disfranchisement, in South, 254
Dixon, Hazel, 24–25
Dodge, Grace, 101
Domestic abuse: black women's vulnerability to, 16, 52; and black southern women migrants, 35, 36–37, 255; and assaults by women, 141, 144–45, 255; and manslaughter charges against women, 145–46
Domesticity: and working-class black women, 3; and white women's protection, 57; and female felons, 129, 130, 136, 141, 154–55, 157; ideals of, 161; and parole in New York, 240, 247, 274, 327 (n. 10)
Domestic Relations Court, 174
Domestic service: and black southern women migrants, 24, 114, 116, 274; demand for black women in, 30, 39, 41, 94, 116, 118, 142, 241, 274, 285 (n. 85); as relic of slavery, 34–35, 38; and sexual harassment, 35, 216, 284 (n. 60); and poverty, 36, 37; working conditions of, 40, 52, 115, 121, 149, 160, 240, 263; white elite reformers' promotion of, 93; black middle-class reformers' promotion of, 94; in brothels, 94, 115, 119; and White Rose Mission, 102; and employment agencies, 115–16; and prop-

erty crimes, 152, 153, 154; and parole in North, 238, 240–41, 242, 274; and parole in South, 261, 262, 263
Doty, Madeleine: investigation of female felons, 125–26, 128, 129–30, 132–36, 151, 305 (n. 45), 306 (n. 60), 306 (n. 65); and tenets of respectable femininity, 134, 304 (n. 3); recommendations of, 306–7 (n. 71)
Draft Riots of July 1863, 5, 25, 71, 83
Dreier, Mary, 115
Drew, Simon P. W., 26
Du Bois, W. E. B.: on working-class black women, 13, 52; study of Philadelphia blacks, 30, 46–47, 283 (n. 35), 287 (n. 139); on proportion of black women to black men, 30–31, 52, 91, 118; on male lodgers, 44; on Tenderloin race riot of 1900, 52; and Ovington, 109, 176; and Atlanta University Studies Conference, 111–12, 120; and Kellor, 120; on marriages, 141; and black women's criminality, 141–42; and World War I, 171
Dunbar, Paul Laurence: and black southern migrants, 28–29; and working-class blacks, 34, 46, 62; and Alice Ruth Moore, 36, 37, 284 (n. 47), 285 (n. 73), 290 (n. 50); on Tenderloin, 60, 62; and racial uplift, 62, 290 (n. 51), 300 (n. 62); and White Rose Mission, 102

Eddy, Frances, 113
Eddy, Mary, 113
Edmonds, Miranda, 200–201, 214
Education: and black southern women migrants, 2, 32–33; industrial education, 100, 102; and White Rose Mission, 100, 102–5, 109, 121; and female felons, 130; and New York State Prison for Women at Auburn, 132, 258, 331 (n. 23)
Elliot, Suzette, 249–50, 329 (n. 59)
Elliot, William, 77–78
Emancipation, 1, 254
Empire Friendly Shelter, 16, 169–71, 177
Empire State Federation of Women's Clubs, 31, 109–10, 169
Employment: and parole in New York, 239–42, 251, 274, 327 (n. 7), 327 (n. 10);

attempts after Tenderloin race riot of 1900, 79; Ida B. Wells's antilynching campaign, 83, 98, 299 (n. 25); and Campbell, 172; and parole in South, 255; of black women, 290 (n. 55). *See also* Antiblack violence

Lyons, Albro, 83

Lyons, Maritcha, 83, 85, 98, 296 (n. 172)

Malby, George, 45

Mason, Daisy, 196

Matthews, Victoria Earle: journalism of, 6, 95–96, 99; and racial uplift, 15, 63, 121, 162, 275, 300 (n. 62); and protection of black women, 15, 121, 158, 275; and black southern women migrants, 31–32, 95, 100, 275; and Alice Ruth Moore, 33; and race relations, 48; on degeneracy, 59; and respectability, 63, 98; and Ida B. Wells's antilynching campaign, 83; and social-scientific investigations, 92, 119, 299 (n. 42); as black southern migrant, 95; fiction of, 96, 97, 298 (n. 21), 300 (n. 62); racial background of, 96, 108; on racial progress, 96, 113; and working-class black women, 96–97, 106, 185; and Booker T. Washington, 98, 100–101, 102, 103; and women's organizations, 99, 299 (n. 37); financial support of, 100, 101, 108–9, 110; death of, 109; lack of recognition of work, 111–12; and legacy of slavery, 117; and Du Bois, 120; and arrests of black women, 160; and Campbell, 162, 172. *See also* White Rose Mission

Matthews, William, 33, 95

McAdoo, William, 49, 150

McCoy, Benjamin, 56

McDonald, Mary, 150–51

Meyerowitz, Joanne, 135

Meyers, George L., 75

Middle-class black women: and morality, 2, 36, 37; objectives and accomplishments of, 3; and racial uplift, 6; and respectability, 9, 68, 83–84, 140; and police brutality, 67–68; protection of, 83; reform efforts of, 98

Miller, Kelly, 30

Mimms, Constance, 195, 272, 274

Mitchell, Charles A., 78, 295 (n. 143)

Mitchell, Michele, 8, 15, 82, 281 (n. 20), 296 (n. 176), 322 (n. 89)

Moore, Alice Ruth: as activist, 12; education of, 32–33; and socioeconomic status, 32–34, 37; as successful southern migrant, 33–34; and domestic abuse, 36, 37, 285 (n. 73); and Dunbar, 36, 37, 284 (n. 47), 285 (n. 73), 290 (n. 50); on Tenderloin, 62; and White Rose Mission, 102–5; and racial uplift, 300 (n. 62)

Moore, Fred R., 175

Moore, Lynette, 202, 229–30

Moore, Patricia, 33

Moore (parole board commissioner), 253, 254

Morality: and black southern women migrants, 7, 8, 31–32, 90, 100, 116–17, 156, 159, 160, 254, 256, 268, 269, 330 (n. 2); and working-class black women, 8, 14, 15, 17–18, 32, 35–36, 82, 99, 106, 140, 186, 206, 209, 217–18, 272; and black middle-class reformers, 8–9, 99, 107, 121, 273; and legacy of slavery, 12, 15, 93, 113–14; and working-class blacks, 17, 28, 34, 73, 89, 183, 185, 194–95, 203; and excess in population of black women, 30; and black families, 32, 36, 138, 187–88, 202, 214, 247, 249, 251–52, 263, 264–68, 273; and employment reform, 92; and white elite reformers, 93, 117–18, 121, 186; of Matthews, 97; Kellor on, 113–17; and race relations, 119; and black women's physical strength, 126; and female felons, 126–27, 138, 140, 141, 151, 157; and Norris, 178, 179; and wayward minor laws, 183, 184, 194, 196, 315 (n. 14), 315 (n. 18); and unmarried single mothers, 196–200; and working-class white women, 205, 325 (n. 140); and premarital sex, 208, 215, 216, 218–19; and leisure activities, 212, 213; and same-sex relationships, 220; and parole in South, 257–58, 262, 263, 268, 269

Morchauser (judge), 137–38

Moreno, J. L., 325 (n. 139)

363

107–9, 111, 158, 164, 165–69, 174–76, 203; and race riots, 14, 171; and Malby law, 45–46; and working-class black women, 51; and Tenderloin race riot of 1900, 52, 70–72, 88; and black southern migrants, 63; and white immigrants, 71, 101; and social reform, 93; Kellor on, 119; and domestic tensions, 142; in South, 160; and same-sex relationships, 190, 208–9, 224, 225–32, 232, 316 (n. 41), 324–25 (n. 128), 325 (n. 130), 325 (nn. 144–45), 326 (n. 154). *See also* Antiblack violence

Race riots, 7, 171, 172. *See also* Draft Riots of July 1863; Tenderloin race riot of 1900

Racial advancement: and emancipation, 1; and respectability, 2, 54, 214; Matthews on, 63, 96, 185; and black middle-class reformers, 93, 273; and self-help, 94, 100

Racial identity, 281–82 (n. 33)

Racial justice, 13, 89

Racial progress: and black families, 8; and working-class blacks, 29; and black women's behavior, 58, 89; and respectability, 90; Matthews on, 96, 113; and black middle-class reformers, 99

Racial uplift: and black middle-class reformers, 3, 8–9, 29, 74, 93, 105–6, 108, 140, 272–73; and middle-class black women, 6; everyday work of, 11–12; and Matthews, 15, 63, 121, 162, 275, 300 (n. 62); and respectability, 54; and Dunbar, 62, 290 (n. 51), 300 (n. 62); and black women, 65; and class relations, 74; and W. H. Brooks, 81; and working-class blacks, 103–7, 272; and Campbell, 160–61, 162, 170

Racism: and criminal justice system, 11, 16, 17, 158, 160–61, 162, 166, 180, 188–93, 203, 252, 273; politics of respectability reinforcing, 58; Dunbar on, 63; prevalence of, 120; proper behavior as counter to, 170; and parole in New York, 242, 243–44, 251

Rafter, Nicole Hahn, 126, 127–28, 304 (n. 14), 304 (n. 16)

Rainey, Gertrude Ma, 219

Randall Island, 4

Randolph, A. Philip, 312 (n. 57)

Rape: and slavery, 57, 64, 96, 114, 126, 209, 255, 288–89 (n. 20), 290 (n. 55); and Bedford prison records, 208, 232; and working-class black women, 216, 217

Reconstruction era, 1, 6, 23, 26, 47

Reed, Harry, 77

Reform movements. *See* Black elite reformers; Black middle-class reformers; Prison reform; Progressive Era; White elite reformers

Respectability: Cooper on, 2; of working-class black women, 2, 3, 8, 14, 16, 55, 75–78, 83–84, 99, 136, 139–40, 156, 157, 272; politics of, 9–10, 54, 58, 67, 82, 85, 120, 137, 139–40, 170, 207, 319 (n. 12); and black middle-class reformers, 9–10, 98, 99, 105, 107, 120, 301 (n. 88); and working-class blacks, 10, 12, 13, 14, 16, 17, 19, 29, 53–54, 73–80, 89, 183, 187, 195, 203, 256, 273, 275, 281 (n. 27), 316 (n. 26); and black families, 10, 16, 24, 137, 140, 214, 248, 250, 265, 266–67, 268, 273; and citizenship rights, 12, 54, 56, 58, 73, 89, 275; and criminal justice system, 12, 158; and black communities, 18, 54, 63, 73, 187, 199, 203, 214; and parole in South, 18, 265, 266–67, 268; and black southern migrants, 28; living conditions conflated with, 42; and public sphere, 55, 291 (n. 68); whites' testimony for black women, 67–68; W. H. Brooks on, 81; and legacy of slavery, 93; and femininity, 127, 134, 304 (n. 3); and female felons, 129, 130, 136–41, 151, 154–55, 156; and leisure activities, 213

Rice, Frank, 151

Riis, Jacob, 42, 46

Riverdale Colored Orphanage, 24

Roberts, Susie, 145–46

Robinson, Alexander, 79

Roosevelt, Franklin D., 156, 310 (n. 168)

Ross, Ellen, 58

Ross, Mary, 86

Rounds, Edward, 68

Ryan, Mary, 61

Ryan, Theodore, 155, 309 (n. 160)

74; and black middle-class reformers,
99. *See also* Class relationships
Sojourner Truth Home, 190, 191, 195
Somerville, Siobhan, 226, 325 (n. 144)
South: reaction to Tenderloin race riot of
1900 in, 71, 292 (n. 91); convict lease
system of, 92, 254, 260; penal system
of, 113–14; paternalistic society of, 119,
254, 255; race relations in, 160; social
welfare programs of, 260. *See also* Black
southern migrants; Black southern
women migrants; Parole in South
Southern Workman, 117, 119–20
Spaulding, Edith, 226–29, 326 (n. 154)
Spencer, Mamie, 129–30, 137, 141
Standard Union, 31
Stansell, Christine, 282 (n. 6)
State: black families use of resources of to
regulate female kin, 3, 10–11, 17, 18, 147,
181, 183, 186–89, 192, 193–96, 200, 202,
238, 248, 251–52, 272, 273–74, 275,
314–15 (n. 7), 329 (n. 48); working-class
blacks' relationship with, 3, 53–54, 55,
56, 201–2, 275–76; and working-class
black women's defense of civil rights,
15, 54; and Malby law, 45–46; and protection from antiblack violence, 89;
support for white elite reformers, 92;
view of improper parenting, 185, 186,
196, 200, 202, 203, 273, 315 (n. 18); reforming role of, 273. *See also* New York
State Prison for Women at Auburn;
New York State Reformatory for
Women at Bedford; State rehabilitative
programs
State Board of Charities, 224, 226, 258–59
State Charities Aid Association, 199
State Charities Law, 224
State Commission of Prisons, 224
State rehabilitative programs: and New
York State Reformatory for Women
at Bedford, 5, 157, 193–94, 202, 222–
23, 226, 232, 239, 252, 274, 323–24
(n. 108); and working-class black
women, 10, 165–66, 175, 177, 188–89,
190, 191–93, 202, 273; black families'
use of, 183; and parole in South, 260,
268, 269
Stewart, Daisy, 142–43

Stone, Helen, 130
Stone, Mary, 109
Streets, Vincent, 80
Striker, Bessie, 66, 68
The Survey, 190

Taft, Julia Jessie, 226
Taylor, Margaret, 77
Taylor, Richard, 77
Tenderloin, 5, 59–62, 63, 68–69, 74
Tenderloin race riot of 1900: and blacks
moving to Harlem, 6, 25, 88; and
Enoch, 14, 15, 52, 53, 68, 81, 83, 88;
and police protection, 17, 56, 72–73,
78–79; and race relations, 52, 70–72,
88; meanings and consequences of,
54; W. H. Brooks on, 55, 81; and hot
weather, 69, 291 (n. 79); and Walters-
Healy fight, 70; arrest of blacks during,
71, 72, 79–80; and police treatment of
blacks, 71–73; and police brutality, 73,
74, 75–80, 275, 293 (n. 111); and black
communities, 73–80, 89–90; and intraracial class dynamics, 74; and police
corruption, 74, 77, 85–88, 293 (n. 116);
economic repercussions of, 77–78, 90;
psychological effects of, 78, 90; police
quelling post-riot incidents, 79–80; and
black women's protection, 88–89; and
public sphere, 294 (n. 126)
Thomas, Clarence, 290 (n. 55)
Thompkins, P. Butler, 82–83
Thompson, Lucinda, 77
Thorpe, Robert: and Tenderloin race riot
of 1900, 14, 53, 81, 88; Enoch's confrontation with, 54, 55, 66, 69, 81–82,
84, 88, 296 (n. 176); altercation with
Harris, 54, 69–70, 84, 88; assumptions
about Enoch, 58, 84; in Tenderloin, 68,
69; whites' reaction to death of, 70, 72;
Owens as partner of, 87
Thorpe, Samuel, 69
Tombs, 4, 161
Towns, Faith, 159–60, 163
Traveler's Aid Society, 163
True womanhood, 57, 126, 288 (n. 17), 325
(n. 135)
Tucker, Lucille, 150
Tulsa race riot of 1921, 172